Lecture Notes in Computer Science   9031

Commenced Publication in 1973
Founding and Former Series Editors:
Gerhard Goos, Juris Hartmanis, and Jan van Leeuwen

Advanced Research in Computing and Software Science

Subline of Lecture Notes in Computer Science

More information about this series at http://www.springer.com/series/7407

Björn Franke (Ed.)

Compiler Construction

24th International Conference, CC 2015
Held as Part of the European Joint Conferences
on Theory and Practice of Software, ETAPS 2015
London, UK, April 11–18, 2015
Proceedings

 Springer

Editor
Björn Franke
University of Edinburgh
Edinburgh
United Kingdom

ISSN 0302-9743   ISSN 1611-3349   (electronic)
Lecture Notes in Computer Science
ISBN 978-3-662-46662-9   ISBN 978-3-662-46663-6   (eBook)
DOI 10.1007/978-3-662-46663-6

Library of Congress Control Number: 2015933998

LNCS Sublibrary: SL1 – Theoretical Computer Science and General Issues

Springer Heidelberg New York Dordrecht London

Printed on acid-free paper

Springer-Verlag GmbH Berlin Heidelberg is part of Springer Science+Business Media
(www.springer.com)

Foreword

ETAPS 2015 was the 18th instance of the European Joint Conferences on Theory and Practice of Software. ETAPS is an annual federated conference that was established in 1998, and this year consisted of six constituting conferences (CC, ESOP, FASE, FoSSaCS, TACAS, and POST) including five invited speakers and two tutorial speakers. Prior to and after the main conference, numerous satellite workshops took place and attracted many researchers from all over the world.

ETAPS is a confederation of several conferences, each with its own Program Committee and its own Steering Committee (if any). The conferences cover various aspects of software systems, ranging from theoretical foundations to programming language developments, compiler advancements, analysis tools, formal approaches to software engineering, and security. Organizing these conferences into a coherent, highly synchronized conference program enables the participation in an exciting event, having the possibility to meet many researchers working in different directions in the field, and to easily attend talks at different conferences.

The six main conferences together received 544 submissions this year, 152 of which were accepted (including 10 tool demonstration papers), yielding an overall acceptance rate of 27.9%. I thank all authors for their interest in ETAPS, all reviewers for the peer-reviewing process, the PC members for their involvement, and in particular the PC Co-chairs for running this entire intensive process. Last but not least, my congratulations to all authors of the accepted papers!

ETAPS 2015 was greatly enriched by the invited talks by Daniel Licata (Wesleyan University, USA) and Catuscia Palamidessi (Inria Saclay and LIX, France), both unifying speakers, and the conference-specific invited speakers [CC] Keshav Pingali (University of Texas, USA), [FoSSaCS] Frank Pfenning (Carnegie Mellon University, USA), and [TACAS] Wang Yi (Uppsala University, Sweden). Invited tutorials were provided by Daniel Bernstein (Eindhoven University of Technology, the Netherlands and the University of Illinois at Chicago, USA), and Florent Kirchner (CEA, the Alternative Energies and Atomic Energy Commission, France). My sincere thanks to all these speakers for their inspiring talks!

ETAPS 2015 took place in the capital of England, the largest metropolitan area in the UK and the largest urban zone in the European Union by most measures. ETAPS 2015 was organized by the Queen Mary University of London in cooperation with the following associations and societies: ETAPS e.V., EATCS (European Association for Theoretical Computer Science), EAPLS (European Association for Programming Languages and Systems), and EASST (European Association of Software Science and Technology). It was supported by the following sponsors: Semmle, Winton, Facebook, Microsoft Research, and Springer-Verlag.

The organization team comprised:

- General Chairs: Pasquale Malacaria and Nikos Tzevelekos
- Workshops Chair: Paulo Oliva
- Publicity chairs: Michael Tautschnig and Greta Yorsh
- Members: Dino Distefano, Edmund Robinson, and Mehrnoosh Sadrzadeh

The overall planning for ETAPS is the responsibility of the Steering Committee. The ETAPS Steering Committee consists of an Executive Board (EB) and representatives of the individual ETAPS conferences, as well as representatives of EATCS, EAPLS, and EASST. The Executive Board comprises Gilles Barthe (satellite events, Madrid), Holger Hermanns (Saarbrücken), Joost-Pieter Katoen (Chair, Aachen and Twente), Gerald Lüttgen (Treasurer, Bamberg), and Tarmo Uustalu (publicity, Tallinn). Other members of the Steering Committee are: Christel Baier (Dresden), David Basin (Zurich), Giuseppe Castagna (Paris), Marsha Chechik (Toronto), Alexander Egyed (Linz), Riccardo Focardi (Venice), Björn Franke (Edinburgh), Jan Friso Groote (Eindhoven), Reiko Heckel (Leicester), Bart Jacobs (Nijmegen), Paul Klint (Amsterdam), Jens Knoop (Vienna), Christof Löding (Aachen), Ina Schäfer (Braunschweig), Pasquale Malacaria (London), Tiziana Margaria (Limerick), Andrew Myers (Boston), Catuscia Palamidessi (Paris), Frank Piessens (Leuven), Andrew Pitts (Cambridge), Jean-Francois Raskin (Brussels), Don Sannella (Edinburgh), Vladimiro Sassone (Southampton), Perdita Stevens (Edinburgh), Gabriele Taentzer (Marburg), Peter Thiemann (Freiburg), Cesare Tinelli (Iowa City), Luca Vigano (London), Jan Vitek (Boston), Igor Walukiewicz (Bordeaux), Andrzej Wąsowski (Copenhagen), and Lenore Zuck (Chicago).

I sincerely thank all ETAPS SC members for all their hard work to make the 18th edition of ETAPS a success. Moreover, thanks to all speakers, attendants, organizers of the satellite workshops, and to Springer for their support. Finally, many thanks to Pasquale and Nikos and their local organization team for all their efforts enabling ETAPS to take place in London!

January 2015   Joost-Pieter Katoen

Preface

This volume contains the papers presented at CC 2015: 24th International Conference on Compiler Construction held during April 10–17, 2015 in London.

There were 34 submissions. Each submission was reviewed by at least three Program Committee members. The committee decided to accept 11 papers. The program also included one invited talk.

CC brings together a unique blend of scientists and engineers working on processing programs in a general sense. The conference is the most targeted forum for the discussion of progress in analyzing, transforming, or executing input that describes how a system operates, including traditional compiler construction as a special case. This year's topics of interest included, but were not limited to: Compiler Engineering and Compiling Techniques, Compiler Analysis and Optimization, and Formal Techniques in Compilers.

We take this opportunity to thank our invited speaker, to congratulate the authors, and to thank them for submitting their fine work to the Compiler Construction conference. Many thanks to the Local Organization team and to the Steering Committee of ETAPS for making CC 2015 possible.

February 2015   Björn Franke

Organization

Program Committee

David August	Princeton University, USA
Lennart Beringer	Princeton University, USA
John Cavazos	University of Delaware, USA
Christophe Dubach	University of Edinburgh, UK
Heiko Falk	Ulm University, Germany
Björn Franke	University of Edinburgh, UK
Sabine Glesner	Technische Universität Berlin, Germany
David Gregg	Trinity College Dublin, Ireland
Sebastian Hack	Saarland University, Germany
Kevin Hammond	University of St. Andrews, UK
Andrew Kennedy	Microsoft Research Cambridge, UK
Tulika Mitra	National University of Singapore, Singapore
Matthieu Moy	Laboratoire Verimag, France
Alan Mycroft	Cambridge University, UK
Rodric Rabbah	IBM Thomas J. Watson Research Center, USA
John Regehr	University of Utah, USA
Ian Rogers	Google, USA
David Whalley	Florida State University, USA
Jingling Xue	University of New South Wales, Australia
Ayal Zaks	Intel Corporation, USA
Olivier Zendra	Inria Nancy, France

Additional Reviewers

Beard, Stephen	Oh, Taewook
Chisnall, David	Orchard, Dominic
Ghosh, Soumyadeep	Schlesinger, Sebastian
Grauer-Gray, Scott	Schneider, Sigurd
Jahier, Erwan	Streit, Kevin
Jones, Timothy	Sui, Yulei
Jähnig, Nils	Urma, Raoul-Gabriel
Klös, Verena	Vanderbruggen, Tristan
Kuperstein, Michael	White, Leo
Liu, Feng	Ye, Ding
Mikulcak, Marcus	

Contents

Invited Paper

Compiler Engineering and Compiling Techniques

Analysis and Optimisation

Formal Techniques

Invited Paper

A Graphical Model for Context-Free Grammar Parsing

Keshav Pingali[1] and Gianfranco Bilardi[2]

[1] The University of Texas, Austin,
Texas 78712, USA
pingali@cs.utexas.edu
[2] Università di Padova
35131 Padova, Italy
bilardi@dei.unipd.it

Abstract. In the compiler literature, parsing algorithms for context-free grammars are presented using string rewriting systems or abstract machines such as pushdown automata. Unfortunately, the resulting descriptions can be baroque, and even a basic understanding of some parsing algorithms, such as Earley's algorithm for general context-free grammars, can be elusive. In this paper, we present a graphical representation of context-free grammars called the Grammar Flow Graph (GFG) that permits parsing problems to be phrased as path problems in graphs; intuitively, the GFG plays the same role for context-free grammars that nondeterministic finite-state automata play for regular grammars. We show that the GFG permits an elementary treatment of Earley's algorithm that is much easier to understand than previous descriptions of this algorithm. In addition, look-ahead computation can be expressed as a simple inter-procedural dataflow analysis problem, providing an unexpected link between front-end and back-end technologies in compilers. These results suggest that the GFG can be a new foundation for the study of context-free grammars.

भज गोविन्दं भज गोविन्दं, गोविन्दं भज मूढ़मते।
संप्राप्ते सन्निहिते काले, न हि न हि रक्षति डुकृञ् करणे ॥१॥

Adore the Lord, adore the Lord, adore the Lord, you fool.
When death comes at its appointed time, the rules of grammar will not save you.

From ``Bhaja Govindam''
Adi Sankara (788 AD–820 AD)

1 Introduction

The development of elegant and practical parsing algorithms for context-free grammars is one of the major accomplishments of 20th century Computer Science. Two abstractions are used to present these algorithms: string rewriting systems and pushdown automata, but the resulting descriptions are unsatisfactory for several reasons.

- Even an elementary understanding of some grammar classes requires mastering a formidable number of complex concepts. For example, LR(k) parsing requires an understanding of rightmost derivations, right sentential forms, viable prefixes, handles, complete valid items, and conflicts, among other notions.

© Springer–Verlag Berlin Heidelberg 2015
B. Franke (Ed.): CC 2015, LNCS 9031, pp. 3–27, 2015.
DOI: 10.1007/978-3-662-46663-6_1

- Parsing algorithms for different grammar classes are presented using different abstractions; for example, LL grammars are presented using recursive-descent, while LR grammars are presented using shift-reduce parsers. This obscures connections between different grammar classes and parsing techniques.
- Although regular grammars are a proper subset of context-free grammars, parsing algorithms for regular grammars, which are presented using finite-state automata, appear to be entirely unrelated to parsing algorithms for context-free grammars.

In this paper, we present a novel approach to context-free grammar parsing that is based on a graphical representation of context-free grammars called the *Grammar Flow Graph*(GFG). *Intuitively, the GFG plays the same role for context-free grammars that the nondeterministic finite-state automaton (NFA) does for regular grammars*: parsing problems can be formulated as path problems in the GFG, and parsing algorithms become algorithms for solving these path problems. The GFG simplifies and unifies the presentation of parsing algorithms for different grammar classes; in addition, finite-state automata can be seen as an optimization of the GFG for the special case of regular grammars, providing a pleasing connection between regular and context-free grammars.

Section 2 introduces the GFG, and shows how the GFG for a given context-free grammar can be constructed in a straight-foward way. Membership of a string in the language generated by the grammar can be proved by finding what we call a *complete balanced GFG path* that generates this string. Since every regular grammar is also a context-free grammar, a regular grammar has both a GFG and an NFA representation. In Section 2.4, we establish a connection between these representations: we show that applying the continuation-passing style (CPS) optimization [1,2] to the GFG of a right-linear regular grammar produces an NFA that is similar to the NFA produced by the standard algorithm for converting a right-linear regular grammar to an NFA.

Earley's algorithm[3] for parsing general context-free grammars is one of the more complicated parsing algorithms in the literature [4]. The GFG reveals that this algorithm is a straightforward extension of the well-known "ε-closure" algorithm for simulating all the moves of an NFA (Section 3). The resulting description is much simpler than previous descriptions of this algorithm, which are based on dynamic programming, abstract interpretation, and Galois connections [3,5,6].

Look-ahead is usually presented in the context of particular parsing strategies such as SLL(1) parsing. In Section 4, we show that the GFG permits look-ahead computation to be formulated independently of the parsing strategy as a simple inter-procedural dataflow analysis problem, unifying algorithmic techniques for compiler front-ends and back-ends. The GFG also enables a simple description of parsers for LL and LR grammars and their sub-classes such as SLL, SLR and LALR grammars, although we do not discuss this in this paper.

Section 5 describes related work. Structurally, the GFG resembles the recursive transition network (RTN) [7], which is used in natural language processing and parsers like ANTLR [8], but there are crucial differences. In particular, the GFG is a single graph in which certain paths are of interest, not a collection of recursive state machines with an operational model like chart parsing for their interpretation. Although motivated by similar concerns, complete balanced paths are different from CFL-paths [9].

Proofs of the main theorems are given in the appendix.

2   Grammar Flow Graph (GFG) and Complete Balanced Paths

A context-free grammar Γ is a 4-tuple $<N, T, P, S>$ where N is a finite set of non-terminals, T is a finite set of terminals, $P \subseteq N \times (N \cup T)^*$ is the set of productions, and $S \in N$ is the start symbol. To simplify the development, we make the following standard assumptions about Γ throughout this paper.

- A1: S does not appear on the righthand side of any production.
- A2: Every non-terminal is used in a derivation of some string of terminals from S (no useless non-terminals [4]).

Any grammar Γ' can be transformed in time $O(|\Gamma'|)$ into an equivalent grammar Γ satisfying the above assumptions [10]. The running example in this paper is this grammar: $E \rightarrow int | (E + E) | E + E$. An equivalent grammar is shown in Figure 1, where the production $S \rightarrow E$ has been added to comply with A1.

2.1   Grammar Flow Graph (GFG)

Figure 1 shows the GFG for the expression grammar. Some edges are labeled explicitly with terminal symbols, and the others are implicitly labeled with ϵ. The GFG can be understood by analogy with inter-procedural control-flow graphs: each production is represented by a "procedure" whose control-flow graph represents the righthand side of that production, and a non-terminal A is represented by a pair of nodes $\bullet A$ and $A \bullet$, called the *start* and *end* nodes for A, that gather together the control-flow graphs for the productions of that non-terminal. An occurrence of a non-terminal in the righthand side of a production is treated as an invocation of that non-terminal.

The control-flow graph for a production $A \rightarrow u_1 u_2 .. u_r$ has $r + 1$ nodes. As in finite-state automata, node labels in a GFG do not play a role in parsing and can be chosen arbitrarily, but it is convenient to label these nodes $A \rightarrow \bullet u_1 u_2 .. u_r$ through $A \rightarrow u_1 u_2 .. u_r \bullet$; intuitively, the $\bullet$ indicates how far parsing has progressed through a production (these labels are related to *items* [4]). The first and last nodes in this sequence are called the *entry* and *exit* nodes for that production. If u_i is a terminal, there is a *scan edge* with that label from the *scan node* $A \rightarrow u_1 .. u_{i-1} \bullet u_i .. u_r$ to node $A \rightarrow u_1 .. u_i \bullet u_{i+1} .. u_r$, just as in finite-state automata. If u_i is a non-terminal, it is considered to be an "invocation" of that non-terminal, so there are *call* and *return* edges that connect nodes $A \rightarrow u_1 .. u_{i-1} \bullet u_i .. u_r$ to the *start* node of non-terminal u_i and its *end* node to $A \rightarrow u_1 .. u_i \bullet u_{i+1} .. u_r$.

Formally, the GFG for a grammar Γ is denoted by $GFG(\Gamma)$ and it is defined as shown in Definition 1. It is easy to construct the GFG for a grammar Γ in $O(|\Gamma|)$ time and space using Definition 1.

Definition 1. *If $\Gamma = <N, T, P, S>$ is a context-free grammar, $G = GFG(\Gamma)$ is the smallest directed graph $(V(\Gamma), E(\Gamma))$ that satisfies the following properties.*

$\diamond$ *For each non-terminal $A \in N$, $V(\Gamma)$ contains nodes labeled $\bullet A$ and $A \bullet$, called the* start *and* end *nodes respectively for A.*

$\diamond$ *For each production $A \rightarrow \epsilon$, $V(\Gamma)$ contains a node labeled $A \rightarrow \bullet$, and $E(\Gamma)$ contains edges $(\bullet A, A \rightarrow \bullet)$, and $(A \rightarrow \bullet, A \bullet)$.*

◇ *For each production* $A{\to}u_1u_2...u_r$
  - $V(\Gamma)$ *contains* $(r{+}1)$ *nodes labeled* $A{\to}{\bullet}u_1...u_r$, $A{\to}u_1{\bullet}...u_r$, ..., $A{\to}u_1...u_r{\bullet}$,
  - $E(\Gamma)$ *contains* entry *edge* $({\bullet}A, A{\to}{\bullet}u_1...u_r)$, *and* exit *edge* $(A{\to}u_1...u_r{\bullet}, A{\bullet})$,
  - *for each* $u_i \in T$, $E(\Gamma)$ *contains a* scan *edge*
    $(A{\to}u_1...u_{i-1}{\bullet}u_i..u_r, A{\to}u_1...u_i{\bullet}u_{i+1}..u_r)$ *labeled* u_i,
  - *for each* $u_i \in N$, $E(\Gamma)$ *contains a* call *edge* $(A{\to}u_1...u_{i-1}{\bullet}u_i...u_r, {\bullet}u_i)$ *and a* return *edge* $(u_i{\bullet}, A{\to}u_1...u_i{\bullet}u_{i+1}...u_r)$.
    Node $A{\to}u_1...u_{i-1}{\bullet}u_i...u_r$ *is a* call *node, and* matches *the* return *node*
    $A{\to}u_1...u_i{\bullet}u_{i+1}...u_r$.
◇ *Edges other than scan edges are labeled with* ϵ.

When the grammar is obvious from the context, a GFG will be denoted by $G{=}(V, E)$. Note that *start* and *end* nodes are the only nodes that can have a fan-out greater than one. This fact will be important when we interpret the GFG as a nondeterministic automaton in Section 2.3.

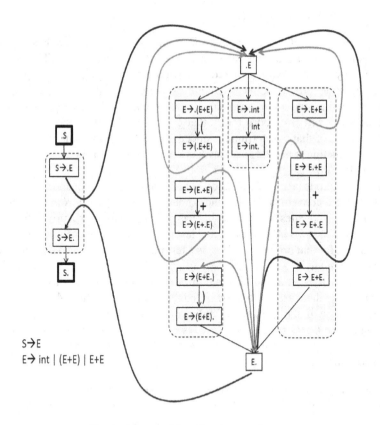

Fig. 1. Grammar Flow Graph example

Table 1. Classification of GFG nodes: a node can belong to several categories. ($A, B \in N$, $t \in T$, and $\alpha, \gamma \in (T + N)^*$)

Node type	Description
start	Node labeled $\bullet A$
end	Node labeled $A \bullet$
call	Node labeled $A \to \alpha \bullet B \gamma$
return	Node labeled $A \to \alpha B \bullet \gamma$
entry	Node labeled $A \to \bullet \alpha$
exit	Node labeled $A \to \alpha \bullet$
scan	Node labeled $A \to \alpha \bullet t \gamma$

2.2 Balanced Paths

The following definition is standard.

Definition 2. *A path in a GFG $G=(V, E)$ is a non-empty sequence of nodes $v_0, \ldots, v_l$, such that $(v_0, v_1), (v_1, v_2), \ldots, (v_{l-1}, v_l)$ are all edges in E.*

In a given GFG, the notation $v_1 \leadsto v_2$ denotes the edge from v_1 to v_2, and the notation $v_1 \leadsto^* v_n$ denotes a path from v_1 to v_n; the symbol "$\to$" is reserved for productions and derivations. If $Q_1 : v_1 \leadsto^* v_m$ and $Q_2 : v_m \leadsto^* v_r$ are paths in a GFG, the notation $Q_1 + Q_2$ denotes the concatenation of paths Q_1 and Q_2. In this spirit, we denote string concatenation by $+$ as well. It is convenient to define the following terms to talk about certain paths of interest in the GFG.

Definition 3. *A* complete path *in a GFG is a path whose first node is $\bullet S$ and whose last node is $S \bullet$.*

A path is said to generate *the word w resulting from the concatenation of the labels on its sequence of edges. By convention, $w = \epsilon$ for a path with a single node.*

The GFG can be viewed as a nondeterministic *finite-state* automaton (NFA) whose start state is $\bullet S$, whose accepting state is $S \bullet$, and which makes nondeterministic choices at *start* and *end* nodes that have a fan-out more than one. Each complete GFG path generates a word in the regular language recognized by this NFA. In Figure 1, the path $Q: \bullet S \leadsto S \to \bullet E \leadsto \bullet E \leadsto E \to \bullet (E + E) \leadsto E \to (\bullet E + E) \leadsto \bullet E \leadsto E \to \bullet int \leadsto E \to int \bullet \leadsto E \bullet \leadsto S \to E \bullet \leadsto S \bullet$ generates the string "(int". However, this string is not generated by the context-free grammar from which this GFG was constructed.

To interpret the GFG as the representation of a context-free grammar, it is necessary to restrict the paths that can be followed by the automaton. Going back to the intuition that the GFG is similar to an inter-procedural call graph, we see that Q is not an *inter-procedurally valid path* [11]: at $E \bullet$, it is necessary to take the return edge to node $E \to (E \bullet + E)$ since the call of E that is being completed was made at node $E \to (\bullet E + E)$. In general, the automaton can make a free choice at *start* nodes just like an NFA, but at *end* nodes, the return edge to be taken is determined by the call that is being completed.

The paths the automaton is allowed to follow are called *complete balanced paths* in this paper. Intuitively, if we consider matching *call* and *return* nodes to be opening and closing parentheses respectively of a unique color, the parentheses on a complete balanced path must be properly nested [12]. In the formal definition below, if K is a sequence of nodes, we let v, K, w represent the sequence of nodes obtained by prepending node v and appending node w to K.

Definition 4. *Given a GFG for a grammar* $\Gamma = <N, T, P, S>$, *the set of* balanced *sequences of* call *and* return *nodes is the smallest set of sequences of* call *and* return *nodes that is closed under the following conditions.*

- *The empty sequence is balanced.*
- *The sequence* $(A \rightarrow \alpha \bullet B\gamma), K, (A \rightarrow \alpha B \bullet \gamma)$ *is balanced if* K *is a balanced sequence, and production* $(A \rightarrow \alpha B\gamma) \in P$.
- *The concatenation of two balanced sequences* $v_1...v_f$ *and* $y_1...y_s$ *is balanced if* $v_f \neq y_1$. *If* $v_f = y_1$, *the sequence* $v_1...v_f y_2...y_s$ *is balanced.*

This definition is essentially the same as the standard definition of balanced sequences of parentheses; the only difference is the case of $v_f = y_1$ in the last clause, which arises because a node of the form $A \rightarrow \alpha X \bullet Y\beta$ is both a $return$ node and a $call$ node.

Definition 5. *A GFG path* $v_0 \rightsquigarrow^* v_l$ *is said to be a* balanced path *if its subsequence of* call *and* return *nodes is balanced.*

Theorem 1. *If* $\Gamma = <N, T, P, S>$ *is a context-free grammar and* $w \in T^*$, *w is in the language generated by* Γ *iff it is generated by a complete balanced path in* $GFG(\Gamma)$.

Proof. This is a special case of Theorem 4 in the Appendix.

Therefore, the parsing problem for a context-free grammar Γ can be framed in GFG terms as follows: given a string w, determine if there are complete balanced paths in $GFG(\Gamma)$ that generate w (recognition), and if so, produce a representation of these paths (parsing). If the grammar is unambiguous, each string in the language is generated by exactly one such path.

The parsing techniques considered in this paper read the input string w from left to right one symbol at a time, and determine reachability along certain paths starting at $\bullet S$. These paths are always *prefixes* of complete balanced paths, and if a prefix u of w has been read up to that point, all these paths generate u. For the technical development, similar paths are needed even though they begin at nodes other than $\bullet S$. Intuitively, these *call-return* paths (*CR-paths* for short) are just segments of complete balanced paths; they may contain *unmatched* call and return nodes, but they do not have *mismatched* call and return nodes, so they can always be extended to complete balanced paths.

Definition 6. *Given a GFG, a* CR-sequence *is a sequence of* call *and* return *nodes that does not contain a subsequence* v_c, K, v_r *where* $v_c \in$ call, *K is balanced,* $v_r \in$ return, *and* v_c *and* v_r *are not matched.*

Definition 7. *A GFG path is said to be a* CR-path *if its subsequence of* call *and* return *nodes is a CR-sequence.*

Unless otherwise specified, the origin of a CR-path will be assumed to be $\bullet S$, the case that arises most frequently.

2.3 Nondeterministic GFG Automaton (NGA)

Figure 2 specifies a push down automaton (PDA), called the nondeterministic GFG automaton (NGA), that traverses complete balanced paths in a GFG under the control of the input string. To match *call*'s with *return*'s, it uses a stack of "return addresses" as is done in implementations of procedural languages. The configuration of the automaton is a three-tuple consisting of the GFG node where the automaton currently is (this is called the PC), a stack of *return* nodes, and the partially read input string. The symbol $\longmapsto$ denotes a state transition.

The NGA begins at $\bullet S$ with the empty stack. At a *call* node, it pushes the matching *return* node on the stack. At a *start* node, it chooses the production *nondeterministically*. At an *end* node, it pops a *return* node from the stack and continues the traversal from there. If the input string is in the language generated by the grammar, the automaton will reach $S\bullet$ with the empty stack (the *end* rule cannot fire at $S\bullet$ because the stack is empty). We will call this a *nondeterministic GFG automaton* or *NGA* for short. It is a special kind of pushdown automaton (PDA). It is not difficult to prove that the NGA accepts exactly those strings that can be generated by some complete balanced path in $GFG(\Gamma)$ whence, by Theorem 1, the NGA accepts the language of Γ. (Technically, acceptance is by final state [13], but it is easily shown that the final state $S\bullet$ can only be reached with an empty stack.)

The nondeterminism in the NGA is called *globally angelic* nondeterminism [14] because the nondeterministic transitions at *start* nodes have to ensure that the NGA ultimately reaches $S\bullet$ if the string is in the language generated by the grammar. The recognition algorithms described in this paper are concerned with deterministic implementations of the globally angelic nondeterminism in the NGA.

NGA configuration ($PC \times C \times K$), where:

Program counter $PC \in V(\Gamma)$ (a state of the finite control)
Partially-read input strings $C \in T^* \times T^*$
($C = (u, v)$, where prefix u of input string $w = uv$ has been read)
Stack of return nodes $K \in V_R(\Gamma)^*$, where $V_R(\Gamma)$ is the set of return nodes

Initial Configuration: $<\bullet S, [\,], \bullet w>$
Accepting configuration: $<S\bullet, [\,], w\bullet>$

Transition function:

$$\text{CALL } <A{\to}\alpha\bullet B\gamma, C, K> \longmapsto <\bullet B, C, (A{\to}\alpha B\bullet\gamma, K)>$$

$$\text{START } <\bullet B, C, K> \longmapsto <B{\to}\bullet\beta, C, K> \text{ (nondeterministic choice)}$$

$$\text{EXIT } <B{\to}\beta\bullet, C, K> \longmapsto <B\bullet, C, K>$$

$$\text{END } <B\bullet, C, (A{\to}\alpha B\bullet\gamma, K)> \longmapsto <A{\to}\alpha B\bullet\gamma, C, K>$$

$$\text{SCAN } <A{\to}\alpha\bullet t\gamma, u\bullet tv, K> \longmapsto <A{\to}\alpha t\bullet\gamma, ut\bullet v, K>$$

Fig. 2. Nondeterministic GFG Automaton (NGA)

2.4   Relationship between NFA and GFG for Regular Grammars

Every regular grammar is also a context-free grammar, so a regular grammar has two graphical representations, an NFA and a GFG. A natural question is whether there is a connection between these graphs. We show that applying the continuation-passing style (CPS) optimization [1,2] to the NGA of a context-free grammar that is a right-linear regular grammar[1] produces an NFA for that grammar.

For any context-free grammar, consider a production $A{\rightarrow}\alpha B$ in which the last symbol on the righthand side is a non-terminal. The canonical NGA in Figure 2 will push the return node $A{\rightarrow}\alpha B\bullet$ before invoking B, but after returning to this exit node, the NGA just transitions to $A\bullet$ and pops the return node for the invocation of A. Had a return address not been pushed when the call to B was made, the NGA would still recognize the input string correctly because when the invocation of B completes, the NGA would pop the return stack and transition directly to the return node for the invocation of A. This optimization is similar to the continuation-passing style (CPS) transformation, which is used in programming language implementations to convert tail-recursion to iteration.

To implement the CPS optimization in the context of the GFG, it is useful to introduce a new type of node called a *no-op* node, which represents a node at which the NGA does nothing other than to transition to the successor of that node. If a production for a non-terminal other than S ends with a non-terminal, the corresponding *call* is replaced with a no-op node; since the NGA will never come back to the corresponding *return* node, this node can be replaced with a no-op node as well. For a right-linear regular grammar, there are no *call* or *return* nodes in the optimized GFG. The resulting GFG is just an NFA, and it is a variation of the NFA that is produced by using the standard algorithms for producing an NFA from a right-linear regular grammar [13].

3   Parsing of General Context-Free Grammars

General context-free grammars can be parsed using an algorithm due to Earley [3]. Described using derivations, the algorithm is not very intuitive and seems unrelated to other parsing algorithms. For example, the monograph on parsing by Sippu and Soisalon-Soininen [10] omits it, Grune and Jacobs' book describes it as "top-down restricted breadth-first bottom-up parsing" [5], and the "Dragon book" [4] mentions it only in the bibliography as "a complex, general-purpose algorithm due to Earley that tabulates LR-items for each substring of the input." Cousot and Cousot use Galois connections between lattices to show that Earley's algorithm is an abstract interpretation of a refinement of the derivation semantics of context-free grammars [6].

In contrast to these complicated narratives, a remarkably simple interpretation of Earley's algorithm emerges when it is viewed in terms of the GFG: *Earley's algorithm is the context-free grammar analog of the well-known simulation algorithm for non-deterministic finite-state automata (NFA)* [4]. While the latter tracks reachability along prefixes of complete paths, the former tracks reachability along prefixes of complete *balanced* paths.

---

[1] A right-linear regular grammar is a regular grammar in which the righthand side of a production consists of a string of zero or more terminals followed by at most one non-terminal.

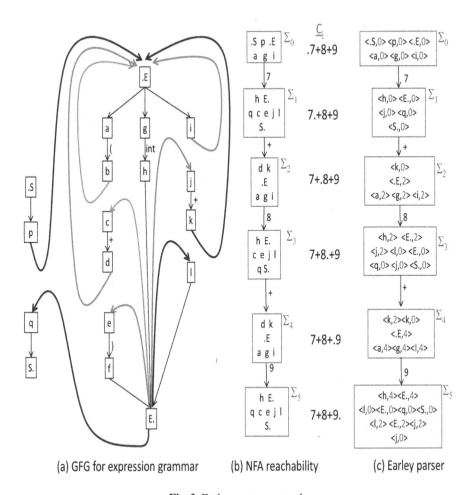

(a) GFG for expression grammar   (b) NFA reachability   (c) Earley parser

Fig. 3. Earley parser: example

3.1   NFA Simulation Algorithm

As a step towards Earley's algorithm, consider interpreting the GFG as an NFA (so non-deterministic choices are permitted at both *start* and *end* nodes). The NFA simulation on a given an input word $w[1..n]$ can be viewed as the construction of a sequence of node sets $\Sigma_0, ..., \Sigma_n$. Here, Σ_0 is the ϵ-closure of $\{\bullet S\}$. For $i = 1, \ldots, n$, set Σ_i is the ϵ-closure of the set of nodes reachable from nodes in Σ_{i-1} by scan edges labeled $w[i]$. The string w is in the language recognized by the NFA if and only if $S\bullet \in \Sigma_n$.

Figure 3(a) shows the GFG of Figure 1, but with simple node labels. Figure 3(b) illustrates the behavior of the NFA simulation algorithm for the input string "7+8+9". Each Σ_i is associated with a terminal string pair $C_i=u.v$, which indicates that prefix u of the input string $w = uv$ has been read up to that point.

(a) NFA Simulation of GFG

Sets of GFG nodes Σ: $\mathscr{P}(V(\Gamma))$
Partially-read input strings $C : T^* \times T^*$
Recognizer configurations $(\Sigma \times C)^+$
Acceptance: $S\bullet \in \Sigma_{|w|}$

$$\text{INIT} \quad \frac{}{(\bullet S \ \in \Sigma_0) \ \wedge \ (C^0 = \bullet w)} \qquad \text{CALL} \quad \frac{A{\to}\alpha\bullet B\gamma \in \Sigma_j}{\bullet B \in \Sigma_j} \qquad \text{START} \quad \frac{\bullet B \in \Sigma_j}{B{\to}\bullet\beta \in \Sigma_j}$$

$$\text{EXIT} \quad \frac{B{\to}\beta\bullet \in \Sigma_j}{B\bullet \in \Sigma_j} \qquad\qquad \text{END} \quad \frac{B\bullet \in \Sigma_j}{A{\to}\alpha B\bullet\gamma \in \Sigma_j}$$

$$\text{SCAN} \quad \frac{A{\to}\alpha\bullet t\gamma \in \Sigma_j \quad C^j = u\bullet tv}{(A{\to}\alpha t\bullet\gamma \in \Sigma_{j+1}) \wedge (C^{j+1} = ut\bullet v)}$$

(b) Earley recognizer

Non-negative integers: $\mathcal{N}$
Sets of tagged GFG nodes Σ: $\mathscr{P}(V(\Gamma) \times \mathcal{N})$
Partially-read input strings $C : T^* \times T^*$
Recognizer configurations $(\Sigma \times C)^+$
Acceptance: $<S\bullet, 0> \in \Sigma_{|w|}$

$$\text{INIT} \quad \frac{}{(<\bullet S, 0> \in \Sigma_0) \wedge (C^0 = \bullet w)} \qquad \text{CALL} \quad \frac{<A{\to}\alpha\bullet B\gamma, i> \in \Sigma_j}{<\bullet B, j> \in \Sigma_j}$$

$$\text{START} \quad \frac{<\bullet B, j> \in \Sigma_j}{<B{\to}\bullet\beta, j> \in \Sigma_j} \qquad \text{EXIT} \quad \frac{<B{\to}\beta\bullet, k> \in \Sigma_j}{<B\bullet, k> \in \Sigma_j}$$

$$\text{END} \quad \frac{<B\bullet, k> \in \Sigma_j \quad <A{\to}\alpha\bullet B\gamma, i> \in \Sigma_k}{<A{\to}\alpha B\bullet\gamma, i> \in \Sigma_j}$$

$$\text{SCAN} \quad \frac{<A{\to}\alpha\bullet t\gamma, i> \in \Sigma_j \quad C^j = u\bullet tv}{(<A{\to}\alpha t\bullet\gamma, i> \in \Sigma_{j+1}) \wedge (C^{j+1} = ut\bullet v)}$$

(c) Earley parser

Non-negative integers: $\mathcal{N}$
Program counter PC: $V(\Gamma) \times \mathcal{N}$
Stack of call nodes K: $V_R(\Gamma)^*$
Parser configurations: $(PC \times \mathcal{N} \times K)$
Acceptance: final configuration is $<<\bullet S, 0>, 0, [\,]>$

$$\text{INIT} \ <<S\bullet, 0>, |w|, [\,]>$$

$$\text{CALL}^{-1} \ <<\bullet B, j>, j, (<A{\to}\alpha\bullet B\gamma, i>, K)> \ \longmapsto \ <<A{\to}\alpha\bullet B\gamma, i>, j, K>$$

$$\text{START}^{-1} \ <<B{\to}\bullet\beta, j>, j, K> \ \longmapsto \ <<\bullet B, j>, j, K>$$

$$\text{EXIT}^{-1} \ <<B\bullet, k>, j, K> \ \longmapsto \ <<B{\to}\beta\bullet, k>, j, K>$$
$$\text{if } (<B{\to}\beta\bullet, k> \in \Sigma_j)(\text{non-determinism})$$

$$\text{END}^{-1} \ <<A{\to}\alpha B\bullet\gamma, i>, j, K> \ \longmapsto \ <<B\bullet, k>, j, (<A{\to}\alpha\bullet B\gamma, i>, K)>$$
$$\text{if } (<B\bullet, k> \in \Sigma_j \text{ and } <A{\to}\alpha\bullet B\gamma, i> \in \Sigma_k)(\text{non-determinism})$$

$$\text{SCAN}^{-1} \ <<A{\to}\alpha t\bullet\gamma, i>, (j+1), K> \ \longmapsto \ <<A{\to}\alpha\bullet t\gamma, i>, j, K>$$

Fig. 4. NFA, Earley recognizer, and Earley parser: input word is w

The behavior of this *NFA ε-closure algorithm* on a GFG is described concisely by the rules shown in Figure 4(a). Each rule is an inference rule or constraint; in some rules, the premises have multiple consequents. It is straightforward to use these rules to compute the smallest Σ-sets that satisfy all the constraints. The INIT rule enters $\cdot S$ into Σ_0. Each of the other rules is associated with traversing a GFG edge from the node in its assumption to the node in its consequence. Thus, the CALL, START, END, and EXIT rules compute the ε-closure of a Σ-set; notice that the END rule is applied to all outgoing edges from END nodes.

3.2 Earley's Algorithm

Like the NFA ε-closure algorithm, Earley's algorithm builds Σ sets, but it computes reachability only along CR-paths starting at $\cdot S$. Therefore, the main difference between the two algorithms is at *end* nodes: a CR-path that reaches an *end* node should be extended only to the *return* node corresponding to the last unmatched *call* node on that path.

One way to find this *call* node is to *tag* each *start* node with a unique ID (tag) when it is entered into a Σ-set, and propagate this tag through the nodes of productions for this non-terminal all the way to the *end* node. At the *end* node, this unique ID can be used to identify the Σ-set containing corresponding *start* node. The last unmatched *call* node on the path must be contained in that set as well, and from that node, the *return* node to which the path should be extended can easily be determined.

To implement the tag, it is simple to use the number of the Σ-set to which the *start* node is added, as shown in Figure 4(b). When the CALL rule enters a *start* node into a Σ set, the tag assigned to this node is the number of that Σ set. The END rule is the only rule that actually uses tags; all other rules propagate tags. If $<B\cdot, k> \in \Sigma_j$, then the matching *start* and *call* nodes are in Σ_k, so Σ_k is examined to determine which of the immediate predecessors of node $\cdot B$ occur in this set. These must be *call* nodes of the form $A\rightarrow\alpha\cdot B\gamma$, so the matching *return* nodes $A\rightarrow\alpha B\cdot\gamma$ are added to Σ_j with the tags of the corresponding *call* nodes. For a given grammar, this can easily be done in time constant with respect to the length of the input string. A string is in the language recognized by the GFG iff Σ_n contains $<S\cdot, 0>$. Figure 3(c) shows the Σ sets computed by the Earley algorithm for the input string "7+8+9".

We discuss a small detail in using the rules of Figures 4(a,b) to construct Σ-sets for a given GFG and input word. The existence of a unique smallest sequence of Σ-sets can be proved in many ways, such as by observing that the rules have the diamond property and are strongly normalizing [15]. A canonical order of rule application for the NFA rules is the following. We give a unique number to each GFG edge, and associate the index $\langle j, m \rangle$ with a rule instance that corresponds to traversing edge m and adding the destination node to Σ_j; the scheduler always pick the rule instance with the smallest index. This order completes the Σ sets in sequence, but many other orders are possible. The same order can be used for the rules in Figure 4(b) except that for the END rule, we use the number on the edge $(B\cdot, A \rightarrow \alpha B\cdot\gamma)$.

Correctness of the rules of Figure 4(b) follows from Theorem 2.

Theorem 2. *For a grammar $\Gamma=<N, T, P, S>$ and an input word $w, < S\cdot, 0 >\in \Sigma_{|w|}$ iff w is a word generated by grammar Γ.*

Proof. See Section A.2.

The proof of Theorem 2 shows the following result, which is useful as a characterization of the contents of Σ sets. Let $w[i..j]$ denote the substring of input w from position i to position j inclusive if $i \leq j$, and let it denote ϵ if $i > j$. It is shown that $<A \rightarrow \alpha \bullet \beta, i> \in \Sigma_j$ iff there is a CR-path $P : \bullet S \leadsto^* \bullet A \leadsto^* (A \rightarrow \alpha \bullet \beta)$ such that

1. $\bullet S \leadsto^* \bullet A$ generates $w[1..i]$, and
2. $\bullet A \leadsto^* (A \rightarrow \alpha \bullet \beta)$ is balanced and generates $w[(i+1)..j]$.

Like the NFA algorithm, Earley's algorithm determines reachability along certain paths but does not represent paths explicitly. Both algorithms permit such implicitly maintained paths to share "sub-paths": in Figure 3(c), $E\bullet$ in Σ_1 is reached by two CR-paths, Q_1: ($\bullet S \leadsto p \leadsto \bullet E \leadsto g \leadsto h \leadsto E\bullet$), and Q_2: ($\bullet S \leadsto p \leadsto \bullet E \leadsto i \leadsto \bullet E \leadsto g \leadsto h \leadsto E\bullet$), and they share the sub-path ($\bullet E \leadsto g \leadsto h \leadsto E\bullet$). This path sharing permits Earley's algorithm to run in $O(|w|^3)$ time for any grammar (improved to $O(|w|^3/log|w|)$ by Graham *et al* [16]), and $O(|w|^2)$ time for any unambiguous grammar, as we show in Theorem 3.

Theorem 3. *For a given GFG $G = (V, E)$ and input word w, Earley's algorithm requires $O(|w|^2)$ space and $O(|w|^3)$ time. If the grammar is unambiguous, the time complexity is reduced to $O(|w|^2)$.*

Proof. See Section A.2

Earley Parser. The rules in Figure 4(b) define a recognizer. To get a parser, we need a way to enumerate a representation of the parse tree, such as a complete, balanced GFG path, from the Σ sets; if the grammar is ambiguous, there may be multiple complete, balanced paths that generate the input word.

Figure 4(c) shows a state transition system that constructs such a path in reverse; if there are multiple paths that generate the string, one of these paths is reconstructed non-deterministically. The parser starts with the entry $<S\bullet, 0>$ in the last Σ set, and reconstructs in reverse the inference chain that produced it from the entry $<\bullet S, 0>$ in Σ_0; intuitively, it traverses the GFG in reverse from $S\bullet$ to $\bullet S$, using the Σ set entries to guide the traversal. Like the NGA, it maintains a stack, but it pushes the matching *call* node when it traverses a *return* node, and pops the stack at a *start* node to determine how to continue the traversal.

The state of the parser is a three-tuple: a Σ set entry, the number of that Σ set, and the stack. The parser begins at $<S\bullet, 0>$ in Σ_n and an empty stack. It terminates when it reaches $<\bullet S, 0>$ in Σ_0. The sequence of GFG nodes in the reverse path can be output during the execution of the transitions. It is easy to output other representations of parse trees if needed; for example, the parse tree can be produced in reverse post-order by outputting the terminal symbol or production name whenever a scan edge or exit node respectively is traversed in reverse by the parser.

To eliminate the need to look up Σ sets for the EXIT^{-1} and END^{-1} rules, the recognizer can save information relevant for the parser in a data structure associated with each Σ set. This data structure is a relation between the consequent and the premise(s) of each rule application; given a consequent, it returns the premise(s) that produced that consequent during recognition. If the grammar is ambiguous, there may be multiple premise(s) that produced a given consequent, and the data structure returns one of them non-deterministically. By enumerating these non-deterministic choices, it is possible to enumerate different parse trees for the given input string. Note that if the grammar is cyclic (that is, $A \xrightarrow{+} A$ for some non-terminal A), there may be an infinite number of parse trees for some strings.

3.3   Discussion

In Earley's paper, the *call* and *start* rules were combined into a single rule called *prediction*, and the *exit* and *end* rules were combined into a single rule called *completion* [3]. Aycock and Horspool pre-compute some of the contents of Σ-sets to improve the running time in practice [17].

Erasing tags from the rules in Figure 4(b) for the Earley recognizer produces the rules for the NFA ϵ-closure algorithm in Figure4(a). The only nontrivial erasure is for the *end* rule: k, the tag of the tuple $<B\bullet, k>$, becomes undefined when tags are deleted, so the antecedent $<A{\rightarrow}\alpha\bullet B\gamma, i> \in \Sigma_k$ for this rule is erased. Erasure of tags demonstrates lucidly the close and previously unknown connection between the NFA ϵ-closure algorithm and Earley's algorithm.

4   Preprocessing the GFG: Look-Ahead

Preprocessing the GFG is useful when many strings have to be parsed since the investment in preprocessing time and space is amortized over the parsing of multiple strings. *Look-ahead computation* is a form of preprocessing that permits pruning of the set of paths that need to be explored for a given input string.

Given a CR-path $Q: \bullet S \rightsquigarrow^* v$ which generates a string of terminals u, consider the set of all strings of k terminals that can be encountered along any CR extension of Q. When parsing a string $u\ell z$ with $\ell \in T^k$, extensions of path Q can be safely ignored if ℓ does not belong to this set. We call this set the *context-dependent look-ahead set* at v for path Q, which we will write as $CDL_k(Q)$ (in the literature on program optimization, Q is called the *calling context* for its last node v). LL(k) and LR(k) parsers use context-dependent look-ahead sets.

We note that for pruning paths, it is safe to use any superset of $CDL_k(Q)$: larger supersets may be easier to compute off-line, possibly at the price of less pruning on-line. In this spirit, a widely used superset is $FOLLOW_k(v)$, associated with GFG node v, which we call the *context-independent look-ahead set*. It is the union of the sets $CDL_k(Q)$, over all CR-paths $Q: \bullet S \rightsquigarrow^* v$. Context-independent look-ahead is used by SLL(k) and SLR(k) parsers. It has also been used to enhance Earley's algorithm. Look-ahead sets intermediate between $CDL_k(Q)$ and $FOLLOW_k(v)$ have also been exploited, for example in LALR(k) and LALL(k) parsers [10].

The presentation of look-ahead computations algorithms is simplified if, at every stage of parsing, there is always a string ℓ of k symbols that has not yet been read. This can be accomplished by (i) padding the input string w with k \$ symbols to form $w\$^k$, where $\$ \notin (T+N)$ and (ii) replacing $\Gamma=<N,T,P,S>$, with the *augmented grammar* $\Gamma'= <N'=N \cup \{S'\}, T'=T \cup \{\$\}, P'=P \cup \{S'{\to}S\$^k\}, S'>$.

Figure 5(a) shows an example using a stylized GFG, with node labels omitted for brevity. The set $FOLLOW_2(v)$ is shown in braces next to node v. If the word to be parsed is ybc, the parser can see that $yb \notin FOLLOW_2(v)$ for $v = S{\to}{\bullet}yLab$, so it can avoid exploration downstream of that node.

The influence of context is illustrated for node $v = L{\to}{\bullet}a$, in Figure 5(a). Since the *end* node $L{\bullet}$ is reached before two terminal symbols are encountered, it is necessary to look beyond node $L{\bullet}$, but the path relevant to look-ahead depends on the path that was taken to node ${\bullet}L$. If the path taken was $Q: {\bullet}S' \rightsquigarrow^* (S{\to}y{\bullet}Lab) \rightsquigarrow ({\bullet}L) \rightsquigarrow L{\to}{\bullet}a$, then relevant path for look-ahead is $L{\bullet} \rightsquigarrow (S{\to}yL{\bullet}ab) \rightsquigarrow^* S'{\bullet}$, so that $CDL_2(Q) = \{aa\}$. If the path taken was $R: {\bullet}S' \rightsquigarrow^* (S{\to}y{\bullet}Lbc) \rightsquigarrow ({\bullet}L) \rightsquigarrow L{\to}{\bullet}a$, then the relevant path for look-ahead is $(L{\bullet}) \rightsquigarrow (S{\to}yL{\bullet}bc) \rightsquigarrow^* S'{\bullet}$, and $CDL_2(R) = \{ab\}$.

We define these concepts formally next.

Definition 8. Context-dependent look-ahead: *If v is a node in the GFG of an augmented grammar $\Gamma'=<N',T',P',S'>$, the context-dependent look-ahead $CDL_k(Q)$ for a CR-path $Q: {\bullet}S' \rightsquigarrow^* v$ is the set of all k-prefixes of strings generated by paths $Q_s : v \rightsquigarrow^* S'{\bullet}$ where $Q + Q_s$ is a complete CR-path.*

Definition 9. Context-independent look-ahead: *If v is a node in the GFG for an augmented grammar $\Gamma'=<N',T',P',S'>$, $FOLLOW_k(v)$ is the set of all k-prefixes of strings generated by CR-paths $v \rightsquigarrow^* S'{\bullet}$.*

As customary, we let $FOLLOW_k(A)$ and $FOLLOW(A)$ respectively denote $FOLLOW_k(A{\bullet})$ and $FOLLOW_1(A{\bullet})$.

The rest of this section is devoted to the computation of look-ahead sets. It is convenient to introduce the function $s_1 +_k s_2$ of strings s_1 and s_2, which returns their concatenation truncated to k symbols. In Definition 10, this operation is lifted to sets of strings.

Definition 10. *Let T^* denote the set of strings of symbols from alphabet T.*

- *For $E \subseteq T^*$, $(E)_k$ is set of k-prefixes of strings in E.*
- *For $E, F \in T^*$, $E +_k F = (E + F)_k$.*

If $E=\{\epsilon,t,tu,abc\}$ and $F=\{\epsilon,x,xy,xya\}$, $(E)_2=\{\epsilon,t,tu,ab\}$ and $(F)_2=\{\epsilon,x,xy\}$. $E+_2F=(E+F)_2=\{\epsilon,x,xy,t,tx,tu,ab\}$. Lemma 1(a) says that concatenation followed by truncation is equivalent to "pre-truncation" followed by concatenation and truncation; this permits look-ahead computation algorithms to work with strings of length at most k throughout the computation rather than with strings of unbounded length truncated to k only at the end.

Lemma 1. *Function $+_k$ has the following properties.*

(a) $E +_k F = (E)_k +_k (F)_k$.
(b) $+_k$ is associative and distributes over set union.

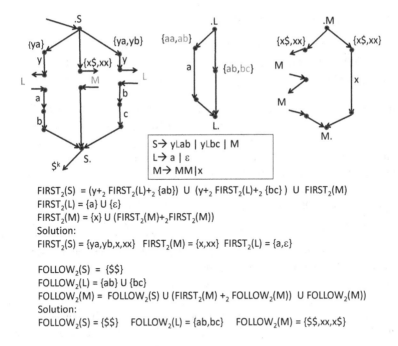

$S \rightarrow$ yLab | yLbc | M
$L \rightarrow$ a | ε
$M \rightarrow$ MM|x

$FIRST_2(S) = (y+_2 FIRST_2(L)+_2 \{ab\}) \cup (y+_2 FIRST_2(L)+_2 \{bc\}) \cup FIRST_2(M)$
$FIRST_2(L) = \{a\} \cup \{ε\}$
$FIRST_2(M) = \{x\} \cup (FIRST_2(M)+_2FIRST_2(M))$
Solution:
$FIRST_2(S) = \{ya,yb,x,xx\}$ $FIRST_2(M) = \{x,xx\}$ $FIRST_2(L) = \{a,ε\}$

$FOLLOW_2(S) = \{\$\$\}$
$FOLLOW_2(L) = \{ab\} \cup \{bc\}$
$FOLLOW_2(M) = FOLLOW_2(S) \cup (FIRST_2(M) +_2 FOLLOW_2(M)) \cup FOLLOW_2(M))$
Solution:
$FOLLOW_2(S) = \{\$\$\}$ $FOLLOW_2(L) = \{ab,bc\}$ $FOLLOW_2(M) = \{\$\$,xx,x\$\}$

(a) $FIRST_2$ and $FOLLOW_2$ computation

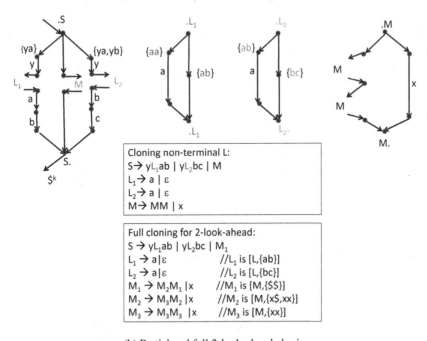

Cloning non-terminal L:
$S \rightarrow$ yL_1ab | yL_2bc | M
$L_1 \rightarrow$ a | ε
$L_2 \rightarrow$ a | ε
$M \rightarrow$ MM | x

Full cloning for 2-look-ahead:
$S \rightarrow$ yL_1ab | yL_2bc | M_1
$L_1 \rightarrow$ a|ε   //L_1 is [L,{ab}]
$L_2 \rightarrow$ a|ε   //L_2 is [L,{bc}]
$M_1 \rightarrow M_2M_1$ |x   //M_1 is [M,{\$\$}]
$M_2 \rightarrow M_3M_2$ |x   //M_2 is [M,{x\$,xx}]
$M_3 \rightarrow M_3M_3$ |x   //M_3 is [M,{xx}]

(b) Partial and full 2-look-ahead cloning

Fig. 5. Look-head computation example

4.1 Context-Independent Look-Ahead

$FOLLOW_k(v)$ can be computed by exploring CR-paths from v to $S'\bullet$. However, for the "bulk" problem of computing these sets for *many* GFG nodes, such as all *entry* nodes in a GFG, coordination of path explorations at different nodes can yield greater efficiency.

Although we do not use this approach directly, the GFG permits $FOLLOW_k$ computation to be viewed as an *inter-procedural backward dataflow analysis problem* [11]. Dataflow facts are possible $FOLLOW_k$ sets, which are the subsets of T^k, and which form a finite lattice under subset ordering (the empty set is the least element). For an edge e with label t, the dataflow transfer function $F_e(X)$ is $\{t\} +_k X$ (for ϵ edges, this reduces to the identity function as expected). For a path Q with edges labeled $t_1, ... t_n$, the composite transfer function is $(\{t_1\} +_k (\{t_2\} +_k ...(\{t_n\} +_k X)))$, which can be written as $(\{t_1\} +_k \{t_2\} +_k ...\{t_n\}) +_k X$ because $+_k$ is associative. If we denote the k-prefix of the terminal string generated by Q by $FIRST_k(Q)$, the composite transfer function for a path Q is $FIRST_k(Q) +_k X$. The confluence operator is set union. To ensure that dataflow information is propagated only along (reverse) CR-paths, it is necessary to find *inter-procedural summary functions* that permit look-ahead sets to be propagated directly from a *return* node to its matching *call* node. These summary functions are hard to compute for most dataflow problems but this is easy for $FOLLOW_k$ computation because the lattice L is finite, the transfer functions distribute over set union, and the $+_k$ operation is associative. For a non-terminal A, the summary function is $F_A(X) = FIRST_k(A) +_k X$, where $FIRST_k(A)$ is the set of k-prefixes of terminal strings generated by balanced paths from $\bullet A$ to $A\bullet$. The $FIRST_k$ relation can be computed efficiently as described in Section 4.1. This permits the use of the *functional approach* to inter-procedural dataflow analysis [11] to solve the $FOLLOW_k$ computation problem (the development below does not rely on any results from this framework).

$FIRST_k$ Computation. For $\Gamma=<N, T, P, S>$, $FIRST_k(A)$ for $A \in N$ is defined canonically as the set of k-prefixes of terminal strings derived from A [10]. This is equivalent to the following, as we show in Theorem 4.

Definition 11. *Given a grammar $\Gamma=<N, T, P, S>$, a positive integer k and $A \in N$, $FIRST_k(A)$ is the set of k-prefixes of terminal strings generated by balanced paths from $\bullet A$ to $A\bullet$.*

Following convention, we write $FIRST(A)$ to mean $FIRST_1(A)$.

Definition 12. *$FIRST_k$ is extended to a string $u_1 u_2...u_n \in (N \cup T)^*$ as follows.*

$$FIRST_k(\epsilon) = \{\epsilon\}$$
$$FIRST_k(t \in T) = \{t\}$$
$$FIRST_k(u_1 u_2...u_n) = FIRST_k(u_1) +_k ... +_k FIRST_k(u_n)$$

$FIRST_k$ sets for non-terminals can be computed as the least solution of a system of equations derived from the grammar.

Algorithm 1. *For $\Gamma=<N, T, P, S>$ and positive integer k, let $\mathcal{M}$ be the finite lattice whose elements are sets of terminal strings of length at most k, ordered by containment with the empty set being the least element. The $FIRST_k$ sets for the non-terminals are given by the least solution in $\mathcal{M}$ of this equational system:*

$$\forall A \in N \; FIRST_k(A) = \bigcup_{A \to \alpha} FIRST_k(\alpha)$$

Figure 5(a) shows an example.

$FOLLOW_k$ Computation

Algorithm 2. *Given an augmented grammar $\Gamma'=<N', T', P', S'>$ and positive integer k, let $\mathcal{L}$ be the lattice whose elements are sets of terminal strings of length k, ordered by containment with the empty set being the least element. The $FOLLOW_k$ sets for non-terminals other than S' are given by the least solution of this equational system:*

$$FOLLOW_k(S) = \{\$^k\}$$

$$\forall B \in N - \{S, S'\}.FOLLOW_k(B) = \bigcup_{A \to \alpha B \gamma} FIRST_k(\gamma) +_k FOLLOW_k(A)$$

Given $FOLLOW_k$ sets for non-terminals, $FOLLOW_k$ sets at all GFG nodes are computed by interpolation:
$FOLLOW_k(A \to \alpha \bullet \beta) = FIRST_k(\beta) +_k FOLLOW_k(A)$.

Figure 5(a) shows an example. M occurs in three places on the righthand sides of the grammar productions, so the righthand side of the equation for $FOLLOW_k(M)$ is the union of three sets: the first from $S \to M\bullet$, the second from $M \to M \bullet M$, and the third from $M \to MM\bullet$.

Using Context-Independent Look-Ahead in the Earley Parser. Some implementations of Earley's parser use a context-independent look-ahead of one symbol at *start* nodes and *end* nodes (this is called *prediction look-ahead* and *completion look-ahead* respectively) [3]. The practical benefit of using look-ahead in the Earley parser has been debated in the literature. The implementation of Graham *et al* does not use look-ahead [16]; other studies argue that some benefits accrue from using prediction look-ahead [5]. Prediction look-ahead is implemented by modifying the START rule in Figure 4(b):the production $B \to \beta$ is explored only if β might produce the empty string or a string that starts with the first look-ahead symbol. For this, the following formula is added to the antecedents of the START rule: $(\epsilon \in FIRST(\beta)) \vee (C^j = u.tv \wedge t \in FIRST(\beta))$.

Completion look-ahead requires adding the following check to the antecedents of the END rule in Figure 4(b):
$(C^j = u.tv) \wedge (t \in FIRST(\gamma) \vee (\epsilon \in FIRST(\gamma) \wedge t \in FOLLOW(A)))$.

4.2   Context-Dependent Look-Ahead

LL(k) and LR(k) parsers use context-dependent k-look-ahead. As one would expect, exploiting context enables a parser to rule out more paths than if it uses context-independent look-ahead. One way to implement context-dependent look-ahead for a grammar Γ is to reduce it to the problem of computing context-independent look-ahead for a related grammar Γ^c through an operation similar to *procedure cloning*.

In general, *cloning a non-terminal* A in a grammar Γ creates a new grammar in which (i) non-terminal A is replaced by some number of new non-terminals $A_1, A_2, ...A_c$ ($c \geq 2$) with the same productions as A, and (ii) all occurrences of A in the righthand sides of productions are replaced by some A_j ($1 \leq j \leq c$). Figure 5(b) shows the result of cloning non-terminal L in the grammar of Figure 5(a) into two new non-terminals L_1, L_2. Cloning obviously does not change the language recognized by the grammar.

The intuitive idea behind the use of cloning to implement context-dependent look-ahead is to create a cloned grammar that has a copy of each production in Γ for each context in which that production may be invoked, so as to "de-alias" look-ahead sets. In general, it is infeasible to clone a non-terminal for every one of its calling contexts, which can be infinitely many. Fortunately, contexts with the same look-ahead set can be represented by the same clone. Therefore, the number of necessary clones is bounded by the number of possible k-look-ahead sets for a node, which is $2^{|T|^k}$. Since this number grows rapidly with k, cloning is practical only for small values of k, but the principle is clear.

Algorithm 3. *Given an augmented grammar $\Gamma'=(N', T', P', S')$, and a positive integer k, $T_k(\Gamma')$ is following grammar:*

- *Nonterminals: $\{S'\} \cup \{[A, R] | A \in (N'-S'), R \subseteq T'^k\}$*
- *Terminals: T'*
- *Start symbol: S'*
- *Productions:*
   - *$S' \to \alpha$ where $S' \to \alpha \in \Gamma'$*
   - *all productions $[A, R] \to Y_1 Y_2...Y_m$ where for some $A \to X_1 X_2 X_3...X_m \in P'$*
     $Y_i = X_i$ if X_i is a terminal, and
     $Y_i = [X_i, FIRST_k(X_{i+1}...X_m) +_k R]$ otherwise.

Therefore, to convert the context-dependent look-ahead problem to the context-independent problem, cloning is performed as follows. For a given k, each non-terminal A in the original grammar is replaced by a set of non-terminals $[A, R]$ for every $R \subseteq T^k$ (intuitively, R will end up being the context-independent look-ahead at $[A, R]\bullet$ in the cloned grammar). The look-ahead R is then interpolated into each production of A to determine the new productions as shown in Algorithm 3.Figure 5(b) shows the result of full 2-look-ahead cloning of the grammar in Figure 5(a) after useless non-terminals have been removed.

5   Related Work

The connection between context-free grammars and procedure call/return in programming languages was made in the early 1960's when the first recursive-descent parsers were developed. The approach taken in this paper is to formulate parsing problems as path problems in the GFG, and the procedure call/return mechanism is used only to build intuition.

In 1970, Woods defined a generalization of finite-state automata called *recursive transition networks* (RTNs) [7]. Perlin defines an RTN as "..a forest of disconnected transition networks, each identified by a nonterminal label. All other labels are terminal labels. When, in traversing a transition network, a nonterminal label is encountered, control recursively passes to the beginning of the correspondingly labeled transition network. Should this labeled network be successfully traversed, on exit, control returns back to the labeled calling node" [18]. The RTN was the first graphical representation of context-free grammars, and all subsequent graphical representations including the GFG are variations on this theme. Notation similar to GFG *start* and *end* nodes was first introduced by Graham *et al* in their study of the Earley parser [16].

The RTN with this extension is used in the ANTLR system for LL(*) grammars [8].

The key difference between RTNs and GFGs is in the *interpretation* of the graphical representation. An interpretation based on a single locus of control that flows between productions is adequate for SLL(k)/LL(k)/LL(*) languages but inadequate for handling more general grammars for which multiple paths through the GFG must be followed, so some notion of multiple threads of control needs to be added to the basic interpretation of the RTN. For example, Perlin models LR grammars using a chart parsing strategy in which portions of the transition network are copied dynamically [18]. In contrast, the GFG is a *single* graph, and all parsing problems are formulated as path problems in this graph; there is no operational notion of a locus of control that is transferred between productions. In particular, the similarity between Earley's algorithm and the NFA simulation algorithm emerges only if parsing problems are framed as path problems in a single graph. We note that the importance of the distinction between the two viewpoints was highlighted by Sharir and Pnueli in their seminal work on inter-procedural dataflow analysis [11].

The logic programming community has explored the notion of "parsing as deduction" [19,20,21] in which the rules of the Earley recognizer in Figure 4(b) are considered to be inference rules derived from a grammar, and recognition is viewed as the construction of a proof that a given string is in the language generated by that grammar. The GFG shows that this proof construction can be interpreted as constructing complete balanced paths in a graphical representation of the grammar.

An important connection between inter-procedural dataflow analysis and reachability computation was made by Yannakakis [9], who introduced the notion of *CFL-paths*. Given a graph with labeled edges and a context-free grammar, CFL-paths are paths that generate strings recognized by the given context-free grammar. Therefore, the context-free grammar is external to the graph, whereas the GFG is a direct representation of a context-free grammar with labeled nodes (*start* and *end* nodes must be known) and labeled edges. If node labels are erased from a GFG and CFL-paths for the given grammar are computed, this set of paths will include all the complete balanced paths but in general, it will also include non-CR-paths that happen to generate strings in the language recognized by the context-free grammar.

6   Conclusions

In other work, we have shown that the GFG permits an elementary presentation of LL, SLL, LR, SLR, and LALR grammars in terms of GFG paths. These results and the results in this paper suggest that the GFG can be a new foundation for the study of context-free grammars.

Acknowledgments. We would like to thank Laura Kallmeyer for pointing us to the literature on parsing in the logic programming community, and Giorgio Satta and Lillian Lee for useful discussions about parsing.

References

1. Reynolds, J.C.: On the relation between direct and continuation semantics. In: Loeckx, I.J. (ed.) ICALP 1974. LNCS, vol. 14, pp. 141–156. Springer, Heidelberg (1974)
2. Sussman, G., Steele, G.: Scheme: An interpreter for extended lambda calculus. Technical Report AI Memo 349, AI Lab, M.I.T. (December 1975)
3. Earley, J.: An efficient context-free parsing algorithm. Commun. ACM 13(2), 94–102 (1970)
4. Aho, A., Lam, M., Sethi, R., Ullman, J.: Compilers: principles, techniques, and tools. Addison Wesley (2007)
5. Grune, D., Jacobs, C.: Parsing Techniques: A practical guide. Springer (2010)
6. Cousot, P., Cousot, R.: Parsing as abstract interpretation of grammar semantics. Theoret. Comput. Sci. 290, 531–544 (2003)
7. Woods, W.A.: Transition network grammars for natural language analysis. Commun. ACM 13(10) (October 1970)
8. Parr, T., Fisher, K.: LL(*): The foundation of the ANTLR parser generator. In: PLDI (2011)
9. Yannakakis, M.: Graph-theoretic methods in database theory. In: Principles of Database Systems (1990)
10. Sippu, S., Soisalon-Soininen, E.: Parsing theory. Springer (1988)
11. Sharir, M., Pnueli, A.: Two approaches to interprocedural dataflow analysis. In: Program Flow Analysis: Theory and Applications, pp. 189–234. Prentice-Hall (1981)
12. Cormen, T., Leiserson, C., Rivest, R., Stein, C. (eds.): Introduction to Algorithms. MIT Press (2001)
13. Hopcroft, J.E., Motwani, R., Ullman, J.D.: Introduction to Automata Theory, Languages, and Computation, 3rd edn. Addison-Wesley Longman Publishing Co., Inc., Boston (2006)
14. Clinger, W.D., Halpern, C.: Alternative semantics for mccarthy's amb. In: Brookes, S.D., Roscoe, A.W., Winskel, G. (eds.) Seminar on Concurrency. LNCS, vol. 197, pp. 467–478. Springer, Heidelberg (1985)
15. Terese: Term Rewriting Systems. Combridge University Press (2003)
16. Graham, S.L., Ruzzo, W.L., Harrison, M.: An improved context-free recognizer. ACM TOPLAS 2(3), 415–462 (1980)
17. Aycock, J., Horspool, N.: Practical Earley parsing. The Computer Journal 45(6), 620–630 (2002)
18. Perlin, M.: LR recursive transition networks for Earley and Tomita parsing. In: ACL 1991 (1991)
19. Pereira, F.C.N., Warren, D.: Parsing as deduction. In: 21st Annual Meeting of the Association for Computational Linguistics, pp. 137–144. MIT, Cambridge (1983)
20. Shieber, S.M., Schabes, Y., Pereira, F.C.N.: Principles and implementation of deductive parsing. Journal of Logic Programming 24(1 & 2), 3–36 (1995)
21. Sikkel, K.: Parsing Schemata. Texts in Theoretical Computer Science. Springer, Heidelberg (1997)

A   Appendix

A.1   Derivations, Parse Trees and GFG Paths

The following result connects complete balanced paths to parse trees.

Theorem 4. *Let* $\Gamma=<N,T,P,S>$ *be a context-free grammar and* $G = GFG(\Gamma)$ *the corresponding grammar flow graph. Let* $A \in N$. *There exists a balanced path from* $\bullet A$ *to* $A\bullet$ *with* n_{cr} *call-return pairs that generates a string* $w \in T^*$ *if and only if there exists a parse tree for* w *with* $n_{int} = n_{cr} + 1$ *internal nodes.*

Proof. We proceed by induction on n_{cr}. The base case, $n_{cr} = 0$, arises for a production $A \rightarrow u_1 u_2 \dots u_r$ where each u_j is a terminal. The GFG balanced path contains the sequence of nodes

$$\bullet A, A \rightarrow \bullet u_1 u_2 \dots u_r, \dots A \rightarrow u_1 u_2 \dots u_r \bullet, A \bullet$$

The corresponding parse tree has a root with label A and r children respectively labeled $u_1, u_2, \dots, u_r$ (from left to right), with $n_{int} = 1$ internal node. The string generated by the path and derived from the tree is $w = u_1 u_2 \dots u_r$.

Assume now inductively the stated property for paths with fewer than n_{cr} call-return pairs and trees with fewer than n_{int} internal nodes. Let Q be a path from $\bullet A$ to $A \bullet$ with n_{cr} call-return pairs. Let $A \rightarrow u_1 u_2 \dots u_r$ be the "top production" used by Q, *i.e.*, the second node on the path is $A \rightarrow \bullet u_1 u_2 \dots u_r$. If $u_j \in N$, then Q will contain a segment of the form

$$A \rightarrow u_1 \dots u_{j-1} \bullet u_j \dots u_r, Q_j, A \rightarrow u_1 \dots u_j \bullet u_{j+1} \dots u_r$$

where Q_j is a balanced path from $\bullet u_j$ to $u_j \bullet$, generating some word w_j. Let $\mathcal{T}_j$ be a parse tree for w_j with root labeled u_j, whose existence follows by the inductive hypothesis. If instead $u_j \in T$, then Q will contain the scan edge

$$(A \rightarrow u_1 \dots u_{j-1} \bullet u_j \dots u_r, A \rightarrow u_1 \dots u_j \bullet u_{j+1} \dots u_r)$$

generating the word $w_j = u_j$. Let $\mathcal{T}_j$ be a tree with a single node labeled $w_j = u_j$. The word generated by Q is $w = w_1 w_2 \dots w_r$. Clearly, the tree $\mathcal{T}$ with a root labeled A and r subtrees equal (from left to right) to $\mathcal{T}_1, \mathcal{T}_2, \dots, \mathcal{T}_r$ derives string w. Finally, it is simple to show that $\mathcal{T}$ has $n_{int} = n_{cr} + 1$ internal nodes.

The construction of a balanced path generating w from a tree deriving w follows the same structure.

A.2   Correctness and Complexity of Earley's Algorithm

The following result is an "inductive version" of Theorem 2, which asserts the correctness of the rules for the Earley parser.

Theorem 5. *Consider the execution of Earley's algorithm on input string* $w = a_1 a_2 \dots a_n$. *Let* z *be a GFG node and* i *and* j *be integers such that* $0 \le i \le j \le n$.

The following two properties are equivalent.

(A) The algorithm creates an entry $<z,i>$ in Σ_j.

(B) There is a CR-path $Q = (\bullet S)Q'z$ (represented as a sequence of GFG nodes beginning at $\bullet S$ and ending at z) that generates $a_1 a_2 \ldots a_j$ and whose prefix preceding the last unmatched call edge generates $a_1 a_2 \ldots a_i$.

Proof. Intuitively, the key fact is that each rule of Earley's algorithm (aside from initialization) uses an entry $<y,i'> \in \Sigma_{j'}$ and a GFG edge (y,z) to create an entry $<z,i> \in \Sigma_j$, where the dependence of i and j upon i' and j' depends on the type of edge (y,z). For a return edge, a suitable entry $<z',k> \in \Sigma_{i'}$ is also consulted. In essence, if a CR-path can be extended by an edge, then (and only then) the appropriate rule creates the entry for the extended path. The formal proof is an inductive formulation of this intuition and carries out a case analysis with respect to the type of edge that extends the path.

Part I. $B \Rightarrow A$ *(from CR-path to Earley entry).* The argument proceeds by induction on the length (number of edges) ℓ of path Q.
- Base cases ($\ell = 0, 1$).
The only path with no edges is $Q = (\bullet S)$, for which $i = j = 0$. The INIT rule produces the corresponding entry $<\bullet S, 0> \in \Sigma_0$. The paths with just one edge are also easily dealt with, as they are of the form $Q = (\bullet S)(S \rightarrow \bullet \sigma)$, that is, they contain one ENTRY edge.
- Inductive step (from $\ell - 1 \geq 1$ to ℓ).
Consider a CR-path $Q = (\bullet S)Ryz$ of length ℓ. It is straightforward to check that $Q' = (\bullet S)Ry$ is also a CR-path, of length $\ell - 1$. Hence, by the inductive hypothesis, an entry $<y,i'>$ is created by the algorithm in some $\Sigma_{j'}$, with Q' generating $a_1 a_2 \ldots a_{j'}$ and with the prefix of Q' preceding its last unmatched call edge generating $a_1 a_2 \ldots a_{i'}$.

Inspection of the rules for the Earley parser in Figure 4 reveals that, given $<y,i'> \in \Sigma_{j'}$ and given the presence edge (y,z) in the CR-path Q, an entry $<z,i> \in \Sigma_j$ is always created by the algorithm. It remains to show that i and j have, with respect to path Q, the relationship stated in property (B).
    - Frame number j. We observe that the string of terminals generated by Q is the same as the string generated by Q', except when (y,z) is a scan edge, in which case Q does generate $a_1 a_2 \ldots a_{j'+1}$. Correspondingly, the algorithm sets $j = j'$, except when (y,z) is a scan edge, in which case it sets $j = j' + 1$.
    - Tag i. We distinguish three cases, based on the type of edge.

    – When (y,z) is an *entry*, *scan*, or *exit* edge, Q has the same last unmatched call edge as Q'. Correspondingly, $i = i'$.
    – When (y,z) is a *call* edge, then (y,z) is the last unmatched call edge on Q. The algorithm correctly sets $i = j' = j$.
    – Finally, let (y,z) be a *return* edge, with $y = B\bullet$ and $z = A \rightarrow \alpha B\bullet\gamma$. Since Q is a CR-path, (y,z) must match the last unmatched call edge in Q', say, (z',y'), with $z' = A \rightarrow \alpha \bullet B\gamma$, and $y' = \bullet B$. We can then write $Q = (\bullet S)Q_1 z' y' Q_2 yz$ where Q_2 is balanced, whence Q and $(\bullet S)Q_1 z'$ have the same last unmatched call edge,

say (u, v). Let i' be such that the prefix of Q ending at z' generates $a_1 a_2 \ldots a_{i'}$ and let $k \le i'$ be such that the prefix of Q ending at u generates $a_1 a_2 \ldots a_k$. By the inductive hypothesis, corresponding to path $(\bullet S)Q_1 z'$, the algorithm will have created entry $<z' = A \to \alpha \bullet B\gamma, k> \in \Sigma_{i'}$. From entries $<y = B\bullet, i'> \in \Sigma_{j'}$ and $<z' = A \to \alpha \bullet B\gamma, k> \in \Sigma_{i'}$ as well as from return edge (y, z), the END rule of the algorithm, as written in Figure 4, creates $<z = A \to \alpha B \bullet \gamma, i = i'> \in \Sigma_j$.

Part II. $A \Rightarrow B$ (*from Earley entry to CR-path*). The argument proceeds by induction on the number q of rule applications executed by the algorithm when entry $<z, i>$ is first added to Σ_j. (Further "discoveries" that $<z, i> \in \Sigma_j$ are possible, but the entry is added only once.)

- Base case ($q = 1$). The only rule applicable at first is INIT, creating the entry $<\bullet S, 0> \in \Sigma_0$, whose corresponding path is clearly $Q = (\bullet S)$.
- Inductive step (from $q - 1 \ge 1$ to q). Let the q-th rule application of the algorithm be based on GFG edge (y, z) and on entry $<y, i'> \in \Sigma_{j'}$. Also let $<z, i> \in \Sigma_j$ be the entry created by the algorithm as a result of said rule application. By the inductive hypothesis, there is a CR-path $(\bullet S)Q' y$ generating $a_1 a_2 \ldots a_{j'}$ and with the prefix of Q' preceding its last unmatched call edge generating $a_1 a_2 \ldots a_{i'}$. To show that to entry $<z, i> \in \Sigma_j$ there corresponds a CR-path Q as in (B), we consider two cases, based on the type of edge (y, z).

- When (y, z) is an *entry*, *scan*, *exit* or *call* edge, we consider the path $Q = (\bullet S)Q' yz$. Arguments symmetric to those employed in Part I of the proof show that path the Q does satisfy property (B), with exactly the values i and j of the entry $<z, i> \in \Sigma_j$ produced by the algorithm.
- When (y, z) is a *return* edge, the identification of path Q requires more care. Let $y = B\bullet$ and $z = A \to \alpha B \bullet \gamma$. The END rule of Earley's algorithm creates entry $<z, i> \in \Sigma_j$ based on two previously created entries to each of which, by the inductive hypothesis, there corresponds a path, as discussed next.
  To entry $<y = B\bullet, k> \in \Sigma_j$, there correspond a CR-path of the form $Q' = (\bullet S)Q_1' x' y' Q_2 y$, with last unmatched call edge (x', y'), where $y' = \bullet B$ and Q_2 is balanced.
  To entry $<z' = A \to \alpha \bullet B\gamma, i> \in \Sigma_k$ there correspond a CR-path of the form $Q'' = (\bullet S)Q_1 z'$, where $z' = A \to \alpha \bullet B\gamma$.
  From the above two paths, as well as from return edge (y, z), we can form a third CR-path $Q = (\bullet S)Q_1 z' y' Q_2 yz$. We observe that is is legitimate to concatenate $(\bullet S)Q_1 z'$ with $y' Q_2 y$ via the call edge (z', y') since $y' Q_2 y$ is balanced. It is also legitimate to append return edge (y, z) to $(\bullet S)Q_1 z' y' Q_2 y$ (thus obtaining Q), since such edge does match (z', y'), the last unmatched call edge of said path.
  It is finally straightforward to check that the frame number j and the tag i are appropriate for Q.

Proof of Theorem 3. For a given GFG $G = (V, E)$ and input word w, Earley's algorithm requires $O(|w|^2)$ space and $O(|w|^3)$ time. If the grammar is unambiguous, the time complexity is reduced to $O(|w|^2)$.

Proof. – *Space complexity*: There are $|w| + 1$ Σ-sets, and each Σ-set can have at most $|V||w|$ elements since there are $|w| + 1$ possible tags. Therefore, the space complexity of the algorithm is $O(|w|^2)$.

- *Time complexity*: For the time complexity, we need to estimate the number of distinct rule instances that can be invoked and the time to execute each one (intuitively, the number of times each rule can "fire" and the cost of each firing).

  For the time to execute each rule instance, we note that the only non-trivial rule is the *end* rule: when $<B\bullet, k>$ is added to Σ_j, we must look up Σ_k to find entries of the form $<A{\rightarrow}\alpha\bullet B\gamma, i>$. To permit this search to be done in constant time per entry, we maintain a data structure with each Σ set, indexed by a non-terminal, which returns the list of such entries for that non-terminal. Therefore, all rule instances can be executed in constant time per instance.

  We now compute an upper bound on the number of distinct rule instances for each rule schema. The *init* rule schema has only one instance. The *start* rule schema has a two parameters: the particular *start* node in the GFG at which this rule schema is being applied and the tag j, and it can be applied for each outgoing edge of that *start* node, so the number of instances of this rule is $O(|V| * |V| * |w|)$; for a given GFG, this is $O(|w|)$.

  Similarly, the *end* rule schema has four parameters: the particular *end* node in the GFG, and the values of i, j, k; the relevant *return* node is determined by these parameters. Therefore, an upper bound on the number of instances of this schema is $O(|V||w|^3)$, which is $O(|w|^3)$ for a given GFG.

  A similar argument shows that the complexity of *call*, *exit* and *scan* rule schema instances is $O(|w|^2)$.

  Therefore the complexity of the overall algorithm is $O(|w|^3)$.

- *Unambiguous grammar*: As shown above, the cubic complexity of Earley's algorithm arises from the *end* rule. Consider the consequent of the *end* rule. The proof of Theorem 2 shows that $<A{\rightarrow}\alpha B\bullet\gamma, i> \in \Sigma_j$ iff $w[i..(j-1)]$ can be derived from αB. If the grammar is unambiguous, there can be only one such derivation; considering the antecedents of the *end* rule, this means that for a given return node $A{\rightarrow}\alpha B\bullet\gamma$ and given values of i and j, there can be exactly one k for which the antecedents of the *end* rule are true. Therefore, for an unambiguous grammar, the *end* rule schema can be instantiated at most $O(|w|^2)$ times for a given grammar. Since all other rules are bounded above similarly, we conclude that Earley's algorithm runs in time $O(|w|^2)$ for an unambiguous grammar.

A.3 Look-Ahead Computation

Proof of correctness of Algorithm 1:

Proof. The system of equations can be solved using Jacobi iteration, with $FIRST_k(A) = \{\}$ as the initial approximation for $A \in N$. If the sequence of approximate solutions for the system is $\mathcal{X}_0; \mathcal{X}_1; ...$, the set $\mathcal{X}_i[A]$ $(i \geq 1)$ contains k-prefixes of terminal strings generated by balanced paths from $\bullet A$ to $A\bullet$ in which the number of call-return pairs is at most $(i-1)$. Termination follows from monotonicity of set union and $+_k$, and finiteness of $\mathcal{M}$.

Proof of correctness of Algorithm 2:

Proof. The system of equations can be solved using Jacobi iteration. If the sequence of approximate solutions is $\mathcal{X}_0; \mathcal{X}_1; ...$, then $\mathcal{X}_i[B]$ $(i \geq 1)$ contains the k-prefixes of terminal strings generated by CR-paths from $B\bullet$ to $S'\bullet$ in which there are i or fewer unmatched *return* nodes.

Compiler Engineering
and Compiling Techniques

A Refactoring Library for Scala Compiler Extensions

Amanj Sherwany, Nosheen Zaza, and Nathaniel Nystrom

Università della Svizzera italiana (USI), Faculty of Informatics, Lugano, Switzerland
{amanj.sherwany,nosheen.zaza,nate.nystrom}@usi.ch

Abstract. Compiler plugins enable languages to be extended with new functionality by adding compiler passes that perform additional static checking, code generation, or code transformations. However, compiler plugins are often difficult to build. A plugin can perform arbitrary code transformations, easily allowing a developer to generate incorrect code. Moreover, the base compiler assumes many complex, sometimes undocumented invariants, requiring plugin developers to acquire intimate knowledge of the design and implementation of the compiler. To address these issues in the context of the Scala compiler plugin framework, we introduce Piuma. Piuma is a library that provides, first, an API to perform many common refactoring tasks needed by plugin writers, and, second, a DSL to eliminate much of the boilerplate code required for plugin development. We demonstrate the usefulness of our library by implementing five diverse compiler plugins. We show that, using Piuma, plugins require less code and are easier to understand than plugins developed using the base Scala compiler plugin API.

Keywords: Scala, compiler extensions, refactoring.

1 Introduction

To build complex applications more easily and efficiently, developers often use *domain-specific languages* (DSLs) [4, 22]. These special-purpose languages have abstractions tailored for specific problem domains. Often, DSLs are implemented on top of a general-purpose programming language like Scala [33], Ruby [15], Haskell [34], or Java [18]. This approach has the advantage that the DSL can reuse all the existing tools and infrastructure of the host language, such as IDEs, profilers, and debuggers. However, building a DSL on top of a general-purpose host language requires the host language to be easily extensible, allowing changes to both its semantics and syntax.

The Scala programming language [33] is a multi-paradigm language implemented on the Java virtual machine, that supporting both object-oriented and functional programming features. The language provides an expressive static type system and supports extending the syntax with new operators.

Moreover, like other recent languages including Java [18], C♯ [16, 21], and X10 [9], Scala provides an API to extend its compiler. Developers write *compiler plugins* to add new passes to the base Scala compiler. Compiler plugins are a useful tool in DSL development because they allow passes to, for instance, perform additional static analysis, to instrument code with additional dynamic checks, to perform optimizations, or to generate code for new language features.

© Springer-Verlag Berlin Heidelberg 2015
B. Franke (Ed.): CC 2015, LNCS 9031, pp. 31–48, 2015.
DOI: 10.1007/978-3-662-46663-6_2

Plugin developers can make nearly arbitrary changes to the base compiler, permitting implementation of complex language features, but unfortunately also permitting plugins to violate invariants assumed by the compiler. Breaking these often undocumented invariants may cause the compiler to generate incorrect Java bytecode or even to crash.

There are many ways to generate malformed bytecode using Scala compiler plugins. For example, a compiler plugin can add a "ghost" field to a class that can be seen by the Java VM when running the code, but not by the Scala compiler itself when importing the generated bytecode. This problem occurs because the Scala compiler embeds Scala-specific type information into the generated Java bytecode. If a plugin where to add a field but omit this extra information, another instance of the Scala compiler would not even see the field even though the field is present in the Java bytecode. This can result in other compilation units failing to compile correctly.

Since plugins add passes to the Scala compiler, running a plugin at the wrong point in the compilation can also allow bad code to be generated. For instance, a plugin could rename a field to have the same name as an existing field. If the plugin did this after the Scala type-checker runs, the error would not be detected and the bytecode would contain a duplicate field.

Based on an evaluation of several existing Scala compiler plugins, we developed Piuma, a refactoring library for the Scala compiler that enables easy implementation of correct compiler plugins. The library provides a set of refactoring methods commonly needed in compiler plugins. These methods are used, for instance, to safely rename definitions, to add new class, trait, or object members, and to extract expressions into methods. The library also provides a DSL for generating the boilerplate code necessary for writing Scala compiler plugins.

The rest of the paper is organized as follows: Section 2 introduces Piuma and motivates its usefulness. Section 3 covers the Piuma DSL. In Section 4, we demonstrate the design and usage of Piuma's refactoring libraries through code examples and use cases. We evaluate the library in Section 5 using a set of five case studies. Related work is discussed in Section 6. Finally, Section 7 concludes with a discussion of future work.

2   Overview

Scala offers a rich compiler API. However, because this API was designed primarily to implement the Scala compiler, merely exposing it to plugin developers does not provide the high-level abstractions for performing many of the common tasks in compiler plugins. For instance, a plugin might need to add a parameter to a method, to extract code into a method, or to rename a field. Performing these tasks with the Scala compiler plugin API requires the developer to implement complex AST transformations and to manage auxiliary data associated with the ASTs. Furthermore, exposing the entire compiler API permits programmers to perform potentially unsafe operations that can lead to exceptions during compilation, or worse, can generate malformed bytecode.

These shortcomings were the main motivation for Piuma, a refactoring framework for Scala compiler plugins. Piuma is composed of two components, a DSL that facilitates defining a compiler plugin without tedious boilerplate code, and a rich library of refactoring utilities. In the remainder of this section, we describe these two components and motivate their usefulness in more detail.

```scala
// define a new extension
class Example(val global: Global) extends Plugin {
  val components = List[PluginComponent](new Phase1(this))
}

// define a compilation phase
class Phase1(val plugin: Example) extends PluginComponent
  with Transform
  with TypingTransformers {

  val global: plugin.global.type = plugin.global
  override val runsRightAfter = Some("typer")
  val runsAfter = List[String]("typer")
  override val runsBefore = List[String]("patmat")
  val phaseName = "example"

  def newTransformer(unit: CompilationUnit) =
    new Phase1Transformer(unit)

  class Phase1Transformer(unit: CompilationUnit)
    extends TypingTransformer(unit) {

    override def transform(tree: Tree): Tree =
      super.transform(tree)
  }
}
```

Fig. 1. A simple Scala compiler extension

2.1 The Piuma DSL

The Scala compiler gives plugins access to nearly all features of the base Scala compiler, and gives them the flexibility to extend the semantics of the Scala language almost arbitrarily. Plugins can create and manipulate ASTs and symbols, extend the type system, and generate code. The design of the compiler follows the "cake pattern" [48], which allows both *datatype extension* by adding new ASTs, and *procedural extension* by adding more operations to existing AST nodes. However, this flexibility comes at the cost of ease-of-use and safety. Even simple extensions require a lot of complex boilerplate code. As an example, Fig. 1 shows the minimum setup required to create an extension with a single phase that does nothing more than traversing the AST.

To better understand how plugins are used and implemented, we performed a small survey of several publicly available Scala compiler plugins, including Avro [45], Scala-Dyno [3], Miniboxing [46], Uniqueness [19], and Continuations [35]. We found that none of these plugins added new types of AST nodes, while all added new functionality to existing AST node types. Based on this survey, we conclude that only procedural extension is needed for the majority of Scala compiler plugins. Adding AST node types is rarely necessary due to Scala's already flexible syntax.

```
// define a new extension
@plugin(Phase1)
class Example

// define a compilation phase
@treeTransformer("example")
class Phase1 {
  rightAfter("typer")
  before(List("patmat"))

  def transform(tree: Tree): Tree = super.transform(tree)
}
```

Fig. 2. Piuma DSL version of the simple compiler extension from Fig. 1

We have designed a macro-based DSL for implementing such extensions. Fig. 2 demonstrates how the same simple plugin as shown in Fig. 1 is implemented using this DSL. The DSL program defines a new plugin Example with a single phase Phase1. The phase performs a tree transformation, in this case the identity transformation. It runs immediately after the Scala typer and before the Scala compiler's pattern matcher phase. In Section 3 we describe this DSL in detail, using this example and others.

2.2   The Piuma Library

Suppose a developer is writing a plugin that performs partial evaluation [17, 23]. In the implementation, she creates specialized versions of a method, adding them into the class's companion object.[1] If the companion object does not exist, the plugin introduces one. This can be a tedious task, as shown in Fig. 3.

Every AST node in Scala has a Symbol attached to it, which includes type and other information about the node. The code first introduces a symbol for the companion object, called a "module" in the Scala compiler API. The code then initializes the symbol with its owner (its containing package or class), its type, and its parents (its supertypes). It then updates the owner of the method we want to insert into the module (code elided). It introduces a default constructor that calls the constructor of the new object's super-class, AnyRef, and appends the new constructor to the body of the module. Finally, it types the module tree. Failing to do any of these steps may lead to an exception during compilation, or worse, the compiler might silently generate malformed bytecode. With Piuma we can introduce a companion object in just a few lines of code, as shown in Fig. 4. The library ensures the object has a correct constructor and handles the symbol management for the new object and the method added to it, ensuring that other phases of the compiler can correctly access the object and method. In Section 4 we describe the design of the Piuma utilities.

---

[1] Scala, unlike Java, does not support static fields or methods. Instead, each class has a *companion object*, a singleton object with the same name as the class that contains the "static" members for the class.

```
// clazz: the symbol of the class for which we
//        want to create a companion object
// mthd:  a method we want to include in the object
val moduleName = clazz.name
val owner = clazz.owner
val moduleSymbol = clazz.newModule(moduleName.toTermName,
                              clazz.pos.focus, Flags.MODULE)
val moduleClassSymbol = moduleSymbol.moduleClass
moduleSymbol.owner = owner
moduleClassSymbol.owner = owner

val parents = List(Ident(definitions.AnyRefClass))
val moduleType = ClassInfoType(parents.map(_.symbol.tpe),
                          newScope, moduleClassSymbol)
moduleClassSymbol setInfo moduleType
moduleSymbol setInfoAndEnter moduleClassSymbol.tpe

// elided code: plugin writer needs to fix the owner
// of mthd and its children

val constSymbol =
  moduleClassSymbol.newClassConstructor(moduleSymbol.pos.focus)

constSymbol.setInfoAndEnter(MethodType(Nil, moduleSymbol.info)

val superCall = Select(Super(This(tpnme.EMPTY), tpnme.EMPTY),
                       nme.CONSTRUCTOR)
val rhs = Block(List(Apply(superCall, Nil)),
                Literal(Constant(())))
val constructor = DefDef(constSymbol, List(Nil), rhs)

localTyper.typed {
  ModuleDef(moduleSymbol, Template(parents, noSelfType,
                       List(cnstrct, mthd)))
}
```

Fig. 3. This listing shows how a new companion object with a single method is created for a class using the Scala compiler API

```
// clazz: the symbol of the class for which we
//        want to create a companion object
// mthd:  a method we want to include in the object
val module0 = clazz.mkCompanionObject
val module = module0.addMember(mthd)
```

Fig. 4. This listing shows how a new companion object with a single method is created for a class using the Piuma DSL

3   The Piuma DSL

The Piuma DSL extends Scala with features for defining compiler plugins and their components. In this section, we explain the design and use of this DSL in detail. We start by describing the general structure of a Scala compiler plugin and then describe the DSL constructs and the functionality they provide. Finally, we briefly describe how the DSL is implemented.

The Scala compiler consists of a sequence of compilation phases. Developers extend the compiler by creating plugins, composed of one or more phases inserted into this sequence. Compiler plugins are implemented by extending the `Plugin` class and providing a list of `PluginComponent`. Each of these components specifies a compiler phase and where it occurs in the compilation sequence. They also provide factory methods for creating the tree and symbol transformers that implement the phase.

The Piuma DSL extends Scala with four class annotations: `@plugin`, `@checker`, `@treeTransformer`, and `@infoTransformer`. The `@plugin` annotation generates boilerplate code for a compiler plugin itself. The other annotations generate boilerplate code for different `PluginComponent` implementations: `@checker` generates a type-checking component, `@treeTransformer` generates an AST-transforming component, and `@infoTransformer` generates a type-transforming component. Since the Scala compiler requires plugins and phases to be concrete classes, these annotations cannot appear on traits, abstract classes, or singleton objects. Annotated classes may still implement other traits. Fig. 5 shows the syntax of a compiler extension in the DSL.

The Piuma DSL is implemented using Scala's *annotation macros* [8]. For each annotation, macro expansion modifies the annotated class to extend a corresponding class from the Scala compiler API. It then mixes-in appropriate Piuma traits to facilitate access to the Piuma library.

3.1   The `@plugin` Annotation

The `@plugin` annotation is placed on a class that implements a compiler plugin. After macro expansion, the annotated class automatically extends the Scala class `Plugin`. The list of components provided by the plugin are specified as annotation arguments. Optionally, the class may provide a short description of its purpose, used when generating command-line usage information for the compiler.

3.2   Component Annotations

The three annotations `@checker`, `@treeTransformer`, and `@infoTransformer` are used to annotate classes that implement plugin components. Macro expansion generates boilerplate code in the annotated class for inserting the phase into the execution order. These annotations also specify the name of the phase using an annotation parameter.

In the body of a class annotated with one of the phase annotations, the programmer can optionally specify the class of the compiler plugin itself using the syntax `plugin` *PluginClass*. This introduces a field of the appropriate type into the class that refers to the plugin object. This field can be used to share information across the plugin's various compiler phases.

```scala
@plugin(MyChecker, MyTransformer, MyInfoTransformer)
class MyPlugin {
  describe("short_description")
  ...
}

@checker("my_checker")
class MyChecker {
  plugin MyPlugin // optional

  after(List("phase1", "phase2", ...))  // optional
  rightAfter("phase1")                  // optional
  before(List("phase1", "phase2", ...)) // optional

  def check(unit: CompilationUnit): Unit = ...
  ...
}

@treeTransformer("my_transformer")
class MyTransformer {
  plugin MyPlugin // optional

  after(List("phase1", "phase2", ...))  // optional
  rightAfter("phase1")                  // optional
  before(List("phase1", "phase2", ...)) // optional

  def transform(tree: Tree): Tree = ...
  ...
}

@infoTransformer("my_info_transformer")
class MyInfoTransformer {
  plugin MyPlugin // optional

  after(List("phase1", "phase2", ...))  // optional
  rightAfter("phase1")                  // optional
  before(List("phase1", "phase2", ...)) // optional

  def transform(tree: Tree): Tree = ...
  def transformInfo(sym: Symbol, tpe: Type): Type = ...
  ...
}
```

Fig. 5. Syntax of the Piuma DSL

@checker. This annotation is placed on classes that implement type-checking phases. A checker phase cannot perform AST transformations but can perform static analysis of a compilation unit. The class must implement a method with the signature: `check(CompilationUnit): Unit`. After macro expansion, the class extends the `PluginComponent` class from the Scala compiler API and implements a factory method for creating compiler phase objects that invoke the `check` method for each compilation unit.

@treeTransformer. The `@treeTransformer` annotation is placed on component classes that implement AST transformations. Annotated classes must implement a method with the signature: `transform(Tree): Tree`. After expansion, the class extends `PluginComponent with TypingTransform`. The expanded class creates a `TreeTransformer` that traverses the AST and invokes the provided `transform` method at each node.

@infoTransformer. The last annotation is `@infoTransformer`, which is placed on classes that transform types in the AST. The annotation is similar to `@treeTransformer`; however, classes must provide not only a `transform(Tree): Tree` method, but also a `transformInfo(Symbol, Type): Type` method. After expansion, an annotated class will extend `PluginComponent with InfoTransform`. A generated `InfoTransformer` class traverses the AST and invokes the provided `transform` and `transformInfo` methods for each node and symbol encountered.

4   The Piuma Library

Piuma offers a rich set of utilities for generating and refactoring Scala compiler ASTs. In general, these methods implement common refactoring and creation patterns when writing compiler plugins. They are implemented using the AST generators of the Scala compiler API, and Scala's quasiquotes, which are a notation that permits generating trees directly from code snippets [39]. We aimed to provide a library that is easy to use, yet flexible and expressive. Library users can use the Scala compiler API alongside library code if they need lower-level access to the compiler internals.

In this section, we discuss the design of the refactoring library and demonstrate its use through use cases and code examples. The library is divided into four main categories, as shown in Fig. 6. The reader can refer to Piuma's project page[2] for documentation and more examples.

4.1   Tree Extractors

Methods in the *tree extractor* category permit the selection of a sequence of ASTs to be placed in another, compatible class, object, trait, method or variable. Since Scala ASTs are immutable, extractor operations generate new ASTs and do not affect the original tree to which they are applied.

---

[2] `https://github.com/amanjpro/piuma`

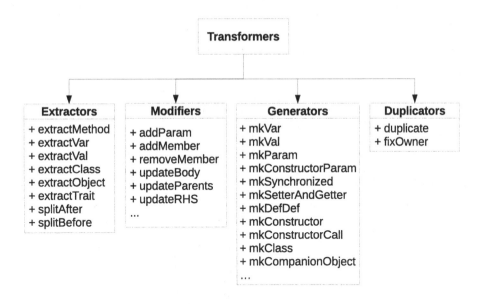

Fig. 6. The high-level design of Piuma's Library

Fig. 7(a) shows a code snippet that demonstrates a refactoring using a pair of tree extractor functions. Fig. 7(b) and (c) show the effect of applying the refactoring to a small method. The extractor function `splitAfter` scans the AST of the body of the original method `foo` in Fig. 7(b). When `splitAfter` finds the first occurrence of an AST node that satisfies a given predicate and returns the AST before and include the node and the AST after the node. In the example, the predicate matches a call to the `splitMe` method, specified using the Scala quasiquotes library [39]. Thus `splitAfter` returns the AST for the body of `foo` up to and including the call to `splitMe`, and another AST for the rest of the body.

It is possible to insert either or both of the ASTs returned by `splitAfter` into ASTs. In Fig. 7(c), `suffix` becomes the body of a new method `bar`. This is done by calling `extractMethod`, which takes a list of trees and a new method name as parameters. The new name must be unique in its scope, otherwise an exception is thrown.

The `extractMethod` operation handles free variables in the given method's body by adding parameters to the extracted method. That is, all free variables in `suffix` become parameters of `bar`. `extractMethod` also creates the AST of the new method and types it, and generates a call to the extracted method that can be substituted into the original method, as described in the next section. Piuma also creates a symbol for the new method, rebinding symbols of the extracted trees to their new owner, and placing them in the symbol table of the method owner. Without Piuma, the programmer would have to perform all these operations manually using the Scala compiler API.

```
// orig: the original method
// body: the body of orig

// Split body after the call to splitMe(),
val (prefix, suffix) = body.splitAfter((x:Tree) => x == q"splitMe()")

// Extract the code after the split into method bar
val (extracted, apply) = extractMethod(
    suffix,     // The body of the extracted method
    "bar"       // the name of the extracted method
    orig.symbol // the symbol of the original method
    ).get

// Replace the extracted code with a call to the new method
orig.updateRHS(Block(prefix, apply))
```

(a) Refactoring using Piuma tree extractor and tree modifier utilities

```
def foo(a: Int, b: String,
        c: Int): Int = {

  println(a)
  val d = c
  splitMe()
  println(d)
  a + b.size
}
```

```
def foo(a: Int, b: String,
        c: Int): Int = {
  println(a)
  val d = c
  splitMe()
  bar(a, b, d)
}
def bar(a: Int, b: Int,
        d: Int): Int = {
  println(d)
  a + b.size
}
```

(b) Before applying the refactoring in (a)   (c) After applying the refactoring in (a)

Fig. 7. A short example of refactoring with Piuma

Other useful Piuma extractors allow member extraction. It is possible, for instance, to extract an inner class and make it an outer class (using `extractClass`), to convert a local variable to a field (using `extractVar` or `extractVal`), or to move fields or methods across classes.

4.2 Tree Modifiers

Tree modifier utilities change AST nodes, for instance, adding or removing method parameters (`addParam` and `removeParam`, respectively), modifying a class or trait's body (`updateBody`, `addMember`, and `removeMember`) or its supertypes (`updateParents`). The `rename` method is used to change the name of a class, method, or variable. When a field is renamed, Piuma handles renaming its setters and getters as well. The tree modifiers also support updating method bodies (`updateRHS`). As an example, we can modify method `foo` from Fig. 7(b) to call the extracted method, as shown in Fig. 7(c). We do this with the call to `updateRHS`, as shown in Fig. 7(a).

```
// orig: the method to be specialized
// p:    the parameter we want to specialize
// v:    the value that we want to specialize p with
val specialized = orig.duplicate("new_name").removeParam(p, v)
```

Fig. 8. A simple example showing how a tree duplicator works

4.3 Tree Duplicators

Tree duplicators are mainly used to implement other Piuma functionalities, but can also be useful when writing plugins. For example, if a programmer needs to specialize a method, they can duplicate it first, then remove the specialized parameter from the duplicated tree, and substitute it with a value, as shown in Fig. 8.

Piuma's `duplicate` method differs from the compiler API's `duplicate` method in that it handles the creation of a new symbol for the new tree, and changes the binding of the node's children's symbols from their original owner to the duplicate.

The `fixOwner` method traverses an AST that has been duplicated and inserted into the AST at another location. It rebinds symbols in the traversed AST to change their owner (i.e., containing method, class, etc.) to the symbol at the new location in the AST.

4.4 Tree Generators

Piuma offers various AST generators that are simpler to use than the Scala compiler API tree generators. For instance, they handle setting the required flags that distinguish trees used to represent more than one syntactic construct (e.g., `var` and `val`, or class and trait trees). Symbol creation and binding is also handled for a generated AST, including all its descendant ASTs. Piuma generators facilitate other tasks that require multiple setup steps, such as surrounding the body of a method with a synchronization block, creating constructor parameters and constructor calls, and others.

5   Evaluation

To evaluate the design of Piuma, we performed a case study by reimplementing five Scala compiler plugins. In our selection, we considered plugins with varying purposes and which use a wide range of Scala compiler API functions. Below, we describe the original plugin and how Piuma is used to implement the plugin. We discuss the ease of implementation and compare the sizes of the Piuma version of the plugin with the original. All the plugins can be found at the Piuma project page. The five plugins and our results are summarized in Table 1. We used CLOC [10] to measure the number of lines in each plugin, ignoring comments and blank lines.

5.1   Memoization Plugin

This compiler plugin enables memoization of computations by introducing simple annotations in code. The design of this plugin is influenced by CEAL [20], a C-based

Table 1. Lines of code of the compiler plugin case studies

	Lines of code	
Plugin	Original	Piuma
Memoization	1190	410 (34.5%)
HPE	2007	1422 (70.9%)
Atomic	510	209 (41.0%)
ScalaDyno	209	169 (80.9%)
Avro	914	681 (74.5%)

language for self-adjusting computation [1]. Using the plugin, programmers annotate a variable to be *modifiable*, indicating that the variable may be modified throughout the program execution and that any computations that depend on the variable are to be recomputed incrementally when the variable is modified. A modifiable variable can be read or written like any other variable.

The plugin is implemented as a code transformation. When the plugin encounters a read of a modifiable variable in a given method, it extracts the continuation of the read within that method into a new method. The extracted statements are replaced with a call to a closure, which takes the parameters of the extracted method and the modifiable variable, and only calls the extracted method if it has not already been called for the same arguments. The original plugin has a single phase, and uses the Scala compiler API to perform mainly AST creation and transformation.[3]

We mostly relied on `splitAfter`, `extractMethod` and `addMember` methods from the Piuma library, in addition to Piuma DSL's annotations. The first two methods perform AST refactoring as described in Section 4. The methods take care of binding symbols of the transformed trees to their new owners, as well as rebinding the symbols of all their children AST nodes. This avoids errors when rebinding symbols manually. The `addMember` method is a tree generator that generates type-checked trees. Using Piuma, the source code is clearer and easier to understand, as the complexity of the above tasks is implemented in the library. We were able to reduce the size of the plugin from 1190 to 410 lines, a reduction of 65.6%.

5.2   Hybrid Partial Evaluation Plugin

Hybrid-partial evaluation (HPE) [40] borrows ideas from both online and offline partial evaluation. It performs offline-style specialization using an online approach without static binding-time analysis. We constructed a Scala plugin that implements HPE by allowing programmers to annotate variables that should be evaluated at compile time. The main transformation performed by the plugin is method specialization, which requires AST transformation and generation.[4]

We used `mkCompanionObject`, `duplicate`, and `removeParam` functions, and other AST transformation utilities, in addition to Piuma DSL's annotations. We were able to

---

[3] The original plugin was developed by the first author and can be found at
https://github.com/amanjpro/piuma/tree/kara/kara

[4] The original plugin was developed by the first author and can be found at
https://github.com/amanjpro/mina

reduce the code size from 2007 to 1422 (a reduction of 29.2%). Piuma's usefulness here comes from its ability to automatically change method symbol information after adding or removing parameters.

5.3   Atomic Scala Plugin

This plugin is a port of Java's atomic sets [47] implementation. It allows declaring atomic memory regions, to which object fields may be added. Fields in the same atomic set are protected by the same lock, and the compiler acquires this lock whenever one of the fields in the atomic set is used in a public method. The syntax of this plugin is expressed using Scala annotations, which are processed using the plugin to insert (possibly nested) synchronization blocks in public method bodies. The plugin is composed of six phases, one performs type-checking, another two process annotations and store global information to be shared with other phases, and the rest perform AST creation and transformation operations: adding fields to classes, changing constructor signatures and altering constructor calls accordingly, and surrounding method bodies with synchronization blocks.[5]

Various tree generators and modifiers were employed, as well as Piuma DSL's annotations. The code size was reduced from 510 to 209 lines (a 59.0% reduction), again making code clearer and more concise, due to hiding the boilerplate of creating trees and managing their symbols, as well as the symbols of their owners and child-ASTs.

5.4   ScalaDyno Plugin

ScalaDyno [3] simulates dynamic typing in Scala. It works by replacing any compilation errors encountered by the compiler with warnings, postponing type checking to run time. This was the smallest plugin we reimplemented, with only 209 lines of code. It mainly performs info-transformation. Still, we were able to reduce its size to 169 lines of code, a reduction of 19.14%, by applying Piuma's type-transformation functions and by using the Piuma DSL's annotations. The main source of code reduction was the DSL, which eliminated the boilerplate code for declaring the plugin and its phases.[6]

5.5   Avro Records Plugin

This compiler plugin is used to auto-generate Avro serializable classes [2] from case class definitions. Avro is a framework developed by Apache's Hadoop group for remote procedure calls and data serialization. The programmer mixes in the `AvroRecord` trait into their case classes; at compile time, the plugin automatically generates the necessary methods to make these classes Avro-serializable. The plugin mostly generates companion objects, adds methods and fields to classes. Other than using the Scala compiler

---

[5] The original plugin was developed by the second author and can be found at
`https://github.com/nosheenzaza/as`

[6] The source of the original plugin can be found at
`https://github.com/scaladyno/scaladyno-plugin`

API, it also employs Scala's TreeDSL [38], which aims to make the AST generation code simpler and more readable.[7]

This plugin was written for the Scala 2.8 compiler runtime. To use Piuma, we needed to port the plugin to Scala 2.11. We mostly relied on the tree generators mkVar, mkSetterAndGetter, and mkCompanionObject and on the tree modifiers addMember and updateRHS, as well as Piuma DSL's annotations. Even though the original plugin used a DSL that is more concise than Scala compiler API, we were still able to reduce the code size from 914 to 681 lines (a 25.49% reduction), again, mainly because symbol creation and binding was handled under the hood by Piuma rather than by the plugin code itself. Our line count results compare the Piuma version with the original Scala 2.8 version of the plugin.

5.6 Discussion

Piuma led to a reduction in code size for all benchmarks. The resulting code was more concise and easier to understand. The main advantage of using Piuma is its ability to hide the complexity of tree and symbol creation, binding, and tree typing. Symbol binding is especially tedious when refactoring already existing ASTs. The library also provides many functions to perform common AST refactoring tasks.

Applying Piuma's library functions can sometimes yield malformed trees. For example, classes in Scala, as in many other languages cannot contain a return statement, so attempting to add a block that contains a return statement causes a type-checking error. We rely on Scala's type checker to report such errors to the programmer, and we found it to be an adequate aid when we performed evaluation.

While reimplementing the plugins in Piuma, we noticed and took advantage of opportunities to extend the library to support commonly occurring refactoring patterns. Three of the case study plugins were originally implemented by the first two authors of this paper. The authors found that reimplementing the plugins using Piuma was far less time consuming and error-prone than writing the original implementation. While this observation is highly subjective, we feel it is worth mentioning.

6   Related Work

Language and compiler extensibility has been well studied for decades. This work includes macros [12, 41, 44], extensible compiler frameworks [13, 32], and language frameworks [25, 27].

Scala recently introduced a Lisp-like macro system [7]. Scala limits macro implementation to statically accessible modules. To make writing macros easier, Scala also provides quasiquotes [39], which Piuma uses also for AST generation and matching. Quasiquotes in Scala are not hygienic [26], nor are they statically type checked. A number of DSLs are already implemented using Yin-Yang [24], a macro-based framework for implementing DSLs, for instance, OptiML [43], a DSL for machine learning.

---

[7] The source of the original plugin can be found at
https://code.google.com/p/avro-scala-compiler-plugin/

Unlike compiler plugins, macros can fall short when it comes to modifying the static semantics of the programming language. Macros can only manipulate the ASTs on which they are explicitly invoked. This limitation makes implementing something like the partial evaluation plugin impossible with macros, as it needs to access and modify non-local ASTs.

Lightweight Modular Staging [36, 37] and the Scala-virtualized extension [30] are used to implement deep embedded DSLs. Users programmatically generate ASTs, taking advantage of Scala-virtualized's more expressive operator overloading features to support domain-specific syntax.

In Java, one can add type checkers using JavaCOP [29], the Checker framework [11], or the standard *annotation processor* mechanism found in Java 6 [5]. Java 8 type annotations, defined by JSR308 [14], are based on the Checker framework. All these approaches allow a developer to extend the type system with pluggable type checkers, but they do not allow any code transformation [6]. Piuma, on the other hand, permits code transformation, which is inherently more problematic than the restrictive compiler extensions that only perform static checking [31].

Scala has a refactoring library [42] which provides a set of refactoring utilities to be used within IDEs. The .NET compiler platform [16] also provides an API for code analysis and refactoring. Wrangler [28] is a refactoring framework for Erlang that integrates with Emacs and Eclipse. What makes our work different from these is that Piuma provides refactoring for the ASTs to be used in compiler plugins, while the others focus on source code refactoring for use in IDEs.

Extensible compiler frameworks such as JastAdd [13] and Polyglot [32] are used for implementing new languages on top of a base language compiler. Unlike compiler plugins, these frameworks are designed to allow arbitrary changes to the base language. Many of the issues that occur with compiler plugins occur also with these frameworks.

7   Conclusions and Future Work

Our evaluation shows Piuma's usefulness to plugin writers. All plugins became more concise and clearer. Plugins written in Piuma can concern themselves more with the plugin logic rather than with tedious details of AST transformations or symbol management.

The Scala compiler assumes many complex, undocumented invariants. While developing Piuma we discovered many of these invariants by trial-and-error, that is by inadvertently violating them and observing the compiler crash or generate incorrect bytecode. We are investigating ways to test plugins for correctness and ways to automatically re-establish invariants that do get broken.

Implementing a refactoring library inside a complex compiler such as Scala's enables not only compiler extensibility through plugins. The Piuma library could also be leveraged for implementing refactorings in an IDE, in optimization tools, or in other refactoring tools. We plan to extend the Piuma framework with more refactorings and implement additional static analyses to ensure that plugin writers have more assurance that the refactorings are being used correctly.

Acknowledgments. This work was supported by the Swiss National Science Foundation (project 200021-138091).

References

1. Acar, U.A.: Self-adjusting computation (an overview). In: Proceedings of the 2009 ACM SIG-PLAN Workshop on Partial Evaluation and Program Manipulation, PEPM 2009, pp. 1–6. ACM, New York (2009)
2. Apache Foundation: Apache Avro Records, `http://avro.apache.org/`
3. Bastin, C., Ureche, V., Odersky, M.: ScalaDyno: Making Name Resolution and Type Checking Fault-tolerant. In: Proceedings of the Fifth Annual Scala Workshop, SCALA 2014, pp. 1–5. ACM, New York (2014)
4. Bentley, J.: Programming pearls: little languages. Commun. ACM 29(8), 711–721 (1986)
5. Bloch, J.: JSR 175: A metadata facility for the Java programming langauges (2004), `http://jcp.org/en/jsr/detail?id=175`
6. Bracha, G.: Pluggable type systems. In: OOPSLA 2004 Workshop on Revival of Dynamic Languages (2004)
7. Burmako, E.: Scala Macros: Let Our Powers Combine! In: 4th Annual Workshop Scala 2013 (2013)
8. Burmako, E.: Macro annotations (2014), `http://docs.scala-lang.org/overviews/macros/annotations.html`
9. Charles, P., Grothoff, C., Saraswat, V., Donawa, C., Kielstra, A., Ebcioglu, K., von Praun, C., Sarkar, V.: X10: An object-oriented approach to non-uniform cluster computing. In: Proceedings of the 20th Annual ACM SIGPLAN Conference on Object-Oriented Programming, Systems, Languages, and Applications, OOPSLA 2005, pp. 519–538. ACM, New York (2005)
10. Danial, A.: Cloc, `http://cloc.sourceforge.net/`
11. Dietl, W., Dietzel, S., Ernst, M.D., Muslu, K., Schiller, T.W.: Building and Using Pluggable Type-Checkers. In: Software Enginnering in Practice Track, International Conference on Software Engineering (ICSE) (May 2011)
12. Dybvig, R., Hieb, R., Bruggeman, C.: Syntactic abstraction in Scheme. LISP and Symbolic Computation 5(4), 295–326 (1993)
13. Ekman, T., Hedin, G.: The JastAdd extensible Java compiler. In: Proceedings of the 22nd Annual ACM SIGPLAN Conference on Object-Oriented Programming Systems and Applications, OOPSLA 2007, pp. 1–18. ACM, New York (2007)
14. Ernst, M.: JSR 308: Annotations on Java Types (2004), `https://jcp.org/en/jsr/detail?id=308`
15. Flanagan, D., Matsumoto, Y.: The Ruby Programming Language, 1st edn. O'Reilly (2008)
16. Foundation, N.: NET compiler platform ("roslyn"), `https://github.com/dotnet/roslyn/` (2014)
17. Futamura, Y.: Partial evaluation of computation process–an approach to a compiler-compiler. Higher-Order and Symbolic Computation 12(4), 381–391 (1999)
18. Gosling, J., Joy, B., Steele, G., Bracha, G.: Java(TM) Language Specification, 3rd edn. (Java (Addison-Wesley)). Addison-Wesley Professional (2005)
19. Haller, P., Odersky, M.: Capabilities for uniqueness and borrowing. In: D'Hondt, T. (ed.) ECOOP 2010. LNCS, vol. 6183, pp. 354–378. Springer, Heidelberg (2010)
20. Hammer, M.A., Acar, U.A., Chen, Y.: CEAL: A C-based language for self-adjusting computation. In: Proceedings of the 30th ACM SIGPLAN Conference on Programming Language Design and Implementation, pp. 25–37 (2009)

21. Hejlsberg, A., Wiltamuth, S., Golde, P.: C# Language Specification. Addison-Wesley Longman Publishing Co., Inc.,, Boston (2003)
22. Hudak, P.: Modular domain specific languages and tools. In: The Fifth International Conference on Software Reuse (ICSR) (1998)
23. Jones, N.D., Gomard, C.K., Sestoft, P.: Partial Evaluation and Automatic Program Generation. Prentice-Hall, Inc., Upper Saddle River (1993)
24. Jovanovic, V., Nikolaev, V., Pham, N.D., Ureche, V., Stucki, S., Koch, C., Odersky, M.: Yin-Yang: Transparent Deep Embedding of DSLs. Technical report, EPFL (2013), http://infoscience.epfl.ch/record/185832
25. Klint, P., van der Storm, T., Vinju, J.: Rascal: A domain specific language for source code analysis and manipulation. In: Ninth IEEE International Working Conference on Source Code Analysis and Manipulation, SCAM 2009, pp. 168–177. IEEE (2009)
26. Kohlbecker, E., Friedman, D.P., Felleisen, M., Duba, B.: Hygienic macro expansion. In: Proceedings of the 1986 ACM Conference on LISP and Functional Programming, pp. 151–161. ACM (1986)
27. Konat, G.D.P., Vergu, V.A., Kats, L.C.L., Wachsmuth, G., Visser, E.: The Spoofax Name Binding Language. In: SPLASH, pp. 79–80. ACM (2012)
28. Li, H., Thompson, S., Orosz, G., et al.: Refactoring with Wrangler: Data and process refactorings, and integration with Eclipse. In: Proceedings of the Seventh ACM SIGPLAN Erlang Workshop (September 2008)
29. Markstrum, S., Marino, D., Esquivel, M., Millstein, T., Andreae, C., Noble, J.: JavaCOP: Declarative Pluggable Types for Java. ACM Trans. Program. Lang. Syst. 32(2), 4:1–4:37 (2010)
30. Moors, A., Rompf, T., Haller, P., Odersky, M.: Scala-virtualized. In: Proceedings of the ACM SIGPLAN 2012 Workshop on Partial Evaluation and Program Manipulation, PEPM 2012, pp. 117–120. ACM, New York (2012)
31. Nystrom, N.: Harmless Compiler Plugins. In: Proceedings of the 13th Workshop on Formal Techniques for Java-Like Programs, FTfJP 2011, pp. 4:1–4:6. ACM, New York (2011)
32. Nystrom, N., Clarkson, M.R., Myers, A.C.: Polyglot: An Extensible Compiler Framework for Java. In: Hedin, G. (ed.) CC 2003. LNCS, vol. 2622, pp. 138–152. Springer, Heidelberg (2003)
33. Odersky, M., et al.: The Scala programming language (2006-2013), http://www.scala-lang.org
34. Peyton Jones, S.L.: Haskell 98 language and libraries: the revised report. Cambridge University Press (2003), http://www.haskell.org/definition/haskell98-report.pdf
35. Rompf, T., Maier, I., Odersky, M.: Implementing first-class polymorphic delimited continuations by a type-directed selective cps-transform. ACM Sigplan Notices 44(9), 317–328 (2009)
36. Rompf, T., Odersky, M.: Lightweight modular staging: a pragmatic approach to runtime code generation and compiled DSLs. Commun. ACM 55(6), 121–130 (2012)
37. Rompf, T., Sujeeth, A.K., Amin, N., Brown, K.J., Jovanovic, V., Lee, H., Jonnalagedda, M., Olukotun, K., Odersky, M.: Optimizing data structures in high-level programs: New directions for extensible compilers based on staging. In: Giacobazzi, R., Cousot, R. (eds.) POPL, pp. 497–510. ACM (2013)
38. Scala Developers: TreeDSL, https://github.com/scala/scala/blob/2.11.x/src/compiler/scala/tools/nsc/ast/TreeDSL.scala
39. Shabalin, D., Burmako, E., Odersky, M.: Quasiquotes for Scala. Technical report, EPFL (2013), http://infoscience.epfl.ch/record/185242
40. Shali, A., Cook, W.R.: Hybrid Partial Evaluation. In: Proceedings of the 2011 ACM International Conference on Object Oriented Programming Systems Languages and Applications, OOPSLA 2011, pp. 375–390. ACM, New York (2011)

41. Steele, G.L., Gabriel, R.P.: The evolution of Lisp. In: The Second ACM SIGPLAN Conference on History of Programming Languages, HOPL-II, pp. 231–270. ACM, New York (1993)
42. Stocker, M., Sommerlad, P.: Scala Refactoring. Master's thesis, University of Applied Sciences Rapperswil (2010)
43. Sujeeth, A.K., Lee, H., Brown, K.J., Rompf, T., Chafi, H., Wu, M., Atreya, A.R., Odersky, M., Olukotun, K.: OptiML: An Implicitly Parallel Domain-Specific Language for Machine Learning. In: Getoor, L., Scheffer, T. (eds.) ICML, pp. 609–616. Omnipress (2011)
44. Tobin-Hochstadt, S., St-Amour, V., Culpepper, R., Flatt, M., Felleisen, M.: Languages As Libraries. In: Proceedings of the 32nd ACM SIGPLAN Conference on Programming Language Design and Implementation, PLDI 2011, pp. 132–141. ACM, New York (2011)
45. Tu, S., et al.: A Scala compiler plugin for Avro records (2011), http://code.google.com/p/avro-scala-compiler-plugin
46. Ureche, V., Talau, C., Odersky, M.: Miniboxing: improving the speed to code size tradeoff in parametric polymorphism translations. In: Proceedings of the 2013 ACM SIGPLAN International Conference on Object Oriented Programming Systems Languages & Applications, pp. 73–92. ACM (2013)
47. Vaziri, M., Tip, F., Dolby, J., Hammer, C., Vitek, J.: Type System for Data-Centric Synchronization. In: D'Hondt, T. (ed.) ECOOP 2010. LNCS, vol. 6183, pp. 304–328. Springer, Heidelberg (2010)
48. Zenger, M., Odersky, M.: Independently extensible solutions to the expression problem. In: 12th International Workshop on Foundations of Object-Oriented Languages (2005)

Feature-Specific Profiling

Vincent St-Amour, Leif Andersen, and Matthias Felleisen

PLT @ Northeastern University
{stamourv,leif,matthias}@ccs.neu.edu

Abstract. High-level languages come with significant readability and maintainability benefits. Their performance costs, however, are usually not predictable, at least not easily. Programmers may accidentally use high-level features in ways that compiler writers could not anticipate, and they may thus produce underperforming programs as a result.

This paper introduces *feature-specific profiling*, a profiling technique that reports performance costs in terms of linguistic constructs. With a feature-specific profiler, a programmer can identify specific instances of language features that are responsible for performance problems. After explaining the architecture of our feature-specific profiler, the paper presents the evidence in support of adding feature-specific profiling to the programmer's toolset.

1 Weighing Language Features

Many linguistic features,[1] come with difficult-to-predict performance costs. First, the cost of a specific use of a feature depends on its context. For instance, use of reflection may not observably impact the execution time of some programs but may have disastrous effects on others. Second, the cost of a feature also depends on its mode of use; a higher-order type coercion tends to be more expensive than a first-order coercion (see section 2).

When cost problems emerge, programmers often turn to performance tools such as profilers. A profiler reports costs, e.g., time or space costs, in terms of location, which helps programmers focus on frequently executed code. Traditional profilers, however, do little to help programmers find the cause of their performance woes or potential solutions. Worse, some performance issues may have a unique cause and yet affect multiple locations, spreading costs across large swaths of the program. Traditional profilers fail to produce actionable observations in such cases.

To address this problem, we propose *feature-specific profiling*, a technique that reports time spent in linguistic features. Where a traditional profiler may break down execution time across modules, functions, or lines, a feature-specific profiler assigns costs to instances of features—a specific type coercion, a particular software contract, or an individual pattern matching form—whose actual costs may be spread across multiple program locations.

---

[1] With "linguistic feature" we mean the constructs of a programming language itself, combinator-style DSLs as they are especially common in the Haskell world, or "macros" exported from libraries, such as in Racket or Rust.

© Springer-Verlag Berlin Heidelberg 2015
B. Franke (Ed.): CC 2015, LNCS 9031, pp. 49–68, 2015.
DOI: 10.1007/978-3-662-46663-6_3

Feature-specific profiling complements a conventional profiler's view of program performance. In many cases, this orthogonal view makes profiling information actionable. Because these profilers report costs in terms of specific features, they point programmers towards potential solutions, e.g., using a feature differently or avoiding it in a particular context.

In this paper, we

- introduce the idea of feature-specific profiling,
- explain the architecture of our prototype and its API for feature plug-ins,
- and present an evaluation of our prototype covering both the actionability of its results and the effort required to implement plug-ins.

The rest of this paper is organized as follows. In section 2 we describe the features that we chose to support in our prototype. In section 3 we outline the architecture of our framework and provide background on its instrumentation technique. In sections 4 and 5 we describe the implementation in detail. We present evaluation results in section 6, then explain the limitations of our architecture, relate to existing work, and conclude.

2   Feature Corpus

In principle, a feature-specific profiler should support all the features that a language offers or that the author of a library may create. This section presents the Racket (Flatt and PLT 2010) features that our prototype feature-specific profiler supports, which includes features from the standard library, and from three third-party libraries. The choice is partially dictated by the underlying technology; put differently, the chosen technology can deal with linguistic features whose dynamic extent obeys a stack-like behavior.

The list introduces each feature and outlines the information the profiler provides about each. We provide additional background for three features in particular—contracts, Marketplace processes (Garnock-Jones et al. 2014), and parser backtracking—which are key to the evaluation case studies presented in section 6.1.

We have identified the first four features below, as well as contracts and parser backtracking, as causes of performance issues in existing Racket programs. Marketplace processes hinder reasoning about performance while not being expensive themselves. The remaining constructs are considered expensive, and are often first on the chopping block when programmers optimize programs, but our tool does not discover a significant impact on performance in ordinary cases. A feature-specific profiler can thus dispel the myths surrounding these features by providing measurements.

Output. Our tool traces time programs spend in Racket's output subsystem back to individual console, file or network output function call sites.

Generic sequence dispatch. Racket's iteration forms can iterate over any sequence datatype, which includes built-in types such as lists and vectors as well as user-defined types. Operating generically requires dynamic dispatch and imposes a run-time cost. Our profiler reports which iteration forms spend significant time in dispatch and thus suggests which ones to replace with specialized iteration forms.

Type casts and assertions. Typed Racket, like other typed languages, provides type casts to help programmers get around the constraints of the type system. Like Java's casts, Typed Racket's casts are safe and involve runtime checks, which can have a negative impact on performance. Casts to higher-order types wrap values with proxies and are therefore especially expensive. Our tool reports time spent in each cast and assertion.

Shill security policies. The Shill scripting language (Moore et al. 2014) restricts how scripts can use system resources according to user-defined security policies. Shill enforces policies dynamically, which incurs overhead on every restricted operation. Because Shill is implemented as a Racket extension, it is an ideal test case for our feature-specific profiler. Our tool succeeds in reporting time spent enforcing each policy.

Pattern matching. Racket comes with an expressive pattern matching construct. Our profiler reports time spent in individual patterns matching forms, excluding time spent in form bodies.

Optional and keyword argument functions. Racket's functions support optional as well as keyword-based arguments. To this end, the compiler provides a special function-call protocol, distinct from, and less efficient than, the regular protocol. Our tool reports time spent on this protocol per function.

Method Dispatch. On top of its functional core, Racket supports class-based object-oriented programming. Method calls have a reputation for being more expensive than function calls. Our tool profiles the time spent performing method dispatch for each method call site, reporting the rare cases where dispatch imposes significant costs.

2.1   Contracts

Behavioral software contracts are a linguistic mechanism for expressing and dynamically enforcing specifications. They were introduced in Eiffel and have since spread to a number of platforms including Python, JavaScript, .NET and Racket.

When two components—e.g., modules or classes—agree to a contract, any value that flows from one component to the other must conform to the specification. If the value satisfies the specification, program execution continues normally. Otherwise, an exception is raised. Programmers can write contracts using the full power of the host language. Because contracts are checked dynamically, however, computationally intensive specifications can have a significant impact on program performance.

For specifications on objects (Strickland and Felleisen 2010), structures (Strickland et al. 2012) or closures (Findler and Felleisen 2002), the cost of checking contracts is non-local. The contract system defers checking until methods are called or fields are accessed, which happens after crossing the contract boundary. To predict how often a given contract is checked, programmers must understand where the contracted value may flow. Traditional profilers attribute costs to the location where contracts are checked, leaving it to programmers to trace those costs to specific contracts.

Figure 1 shows an excerpt from an HTTP client library. It provides `make-fetcher`, which accepts a user agent and returns a function that performs requests using that user agent. The HTTP client accepts only those requests for URLs that are on a whitelist, which it enforces with the underlined contract. The `driver` module creates a crawler that uses a fetching function from the `http-client` module. The crawler then calls this function to access web pages, triggering the contract each time. Because checking happens while executing crawler code, a traditional profiler attributes contract costs to `crawl`, but it is the contract between `http-client` and `driver` that is responsible.

```
                                                              driver.rkt

(require "http-client.rkt" "crawler.rkt")
(define fetch (make-fetcher "fetcher/1.0"))
(define crawl (make-crawler fetch))
... (crawl "etaps.org") ...


                                                          http-client.rkt

(provide (contract-out [make-fetcher (-> user-agent? (-> safe-url? html?))]))
(define (make-fetcher user-agent) (lambda (url) ...))
(define (safe-url? url) (member url whitelist))
```

Fig. 1. Contract for an HTTP client

Because of the difficulty of reasoning about the cost of contracts, performance-conscious programmers often avoid them. This, however, is not always possible. First, the Racket standard library uses contracts pervasively to preserve its internal invariants and provide helpful error messages. Second, many Racket programs combine untyped components written in Racket with components written in Typed Racket. To preserve the invariants of typed components, Typed Racket inserts contracts at typed-untyped boundaries (Tobin-Hochstadt and Felleisen 2006). Because these contracts are necessary for Typed Racket's safety and soundness, they cannot be avoided.

To provide programmers with an accurate view of the costs of contracts and their actual sources, our profiler provides several contract-related reports and visualizations.

2.2 Marketplace Processes

The Marketplace library allows programmers to express concurrent systems functionally as trees of sets of processes grouped within task-specific virtual machines (VMs)[2] that communicate via publish/subscribe. Marketplace is especially suitable for building network services; it has been used as the basis of an SSH server (see section 6.1.2) and a DNS server. While organizing processes in a hierarchy of VMs has clear software engineering benefits, deep VM nesting hinders reasoning about performance. Worse,

---

[2] These VMs are process containers running within a Racket OS-level process. The relationship with their more heavyweight cousins such as VirtualBox, or the JVM, is one of analogy only.

different processes often execute the same code, but because these processes do not map to threads, traditional profilers may attribute all the costs to one location.

Our feature-specific profiler overcomes both of these problems. It provides process accounting for their VMs and processes and maps time costs to individual processes, e.g., the authentication process for an individual SSH connection, rather than the authentication code shared among all processes. For VMs, it reports aggregate costs and presents their execution time broken down by children.

2.3 Parser Backtracking

The Parsack parsing library[3] provides a disjunction operator that attempts to parse alternative non-terminals in sequence. The operator backtracks in each case unless the non-terminal successfully matches. When the parser backtracks, however, any work it did for matching that non-terminal does not contribute to the final result and is wasted.

For this reason, ordering non-terminals within disjunctions to minimize backtracking, e.g., by putting infrequently matched non-terminals at the end, can significantly improve parser performance. Our feature-specific profiler reports time spent on each disjunction branch from which the parser ultimately backtracks.

3 The Profiler's Architecture

Because programmers may create new features, our feature-specific profiler consists of two parts: the core framework and feature-specific plug-ins. The core is a sampling profiler with an API that empowers the implementors of linguistic features to create plug-ins for their creations.

The core part of our profiler employs a sampling-thread architecture to detect when programs are executing certain pieces of code. When a programmer turns on the profiler, a run of the program spawns a separate sampling thread, which inspects the stack of the main thread at regular intervals. Once the program terminates, an offline analysis deals with the collected stack information, looking for feature-specific stack markers and producing programmer-facing reports.

The feature-specific plug-ins exploit this core by placing markers on the control stack that are unique to that construct. Each marker indicates when a feature executes its specific code. The offline analysis can then use these markers to attribute specific slices of time consumption to a feature.

For our Racket-based prototype, the plug-in architecture heavily relies on Racket's continuation marks, an API for stack inspection (Clements et al. 2001). Since this API differs from stack inspection protocols in other languages, the first subsection recalls the idea. The second explains how the implementor of a feature uses continuation marks to interact with the profiler framework for structurally simple constructs. The last subsection presents the offline analysis.

---

[3] https://github.com/stchang/parsack

3.1   Inspecting the Stack with Continuation Marks

Any program may use continuation marks to attach key-value pairs to stack frames and retrieve them later. Racket's API provides two main operations:

- (with-continuation-mark *key value expr*), which attaches (*key*, *value*) to the current stack frame and evaluates *expr*.
- (current-continuation-marks [*thread*]), which walks the stack and retrieves all key-value pairs from the stack of an optionally specified thread, which defaults to the current thread. This allows one thread to inspect the stack of another.

Programs can also filter marks to consider only those with relevant keys using

- (continuation-mark-set->list *marks key*), which returns the list of values with that key contained in *marks*.

Outside of these operations, continuation marks do not affect a program's semantics.[4] Figure 2 illustrates the working of continuation marks with a function that traverses binary trees and records paths from roots to leaves. Whenever the function reaches an internal node, it leaves a continuation mark recording that node's value. When it reaches a leaf, it collects those marks, adds the leaf to the path and returns the completed path.

```
; Tree = Number | [List Number Tree Tree]
; paths : Tree -> [Listof [Listof Number]]
(define (paths t)
  (cond
    [(number? t)
     (list (cons t (continuation-mark-set->list (current-continuation-marks) 'paths)))]
    [else
     (with-continuation-mark 'paths (first t)
       (append (paths (second t)) (paths (third t))))]))

> (paths '(1 (2 3 4) 5))
'((3 2 1) (4 2 1) (5 1))
```

Fig. 2. Recording paths in a tree with continuation marks

Continuation marks are extensively used in the Racket ecosystem, notably for the generation of error messages in the DrRacket IDE (Findler et al. 2002), an algebraic stepper (Clements et al. 2001), the DrRacket debugger, for thread-local dynamic binding, and for exception handling. Serializable continuations in the PLT web server (McCarthy 2010) are also implemented using continuation marks.

Beyond Racket, continuation marks have also been implemented on top of Microsoft's CLR (Pettyjohn et al. 2005) and JavaScript (Clements et al. 2008). Other languages provide similar mechanisms, such as stack reflection in Smalltalk and the stack introspection used by the GHCi debugger (Marlow et al. 2007) for Haskell.

---

[4] Continuation marks also preserve proper tail call behavior.

3.2 Feature-Specific Data Gathering

During program execution, feature-specific plug-ins leave feature markers on the stack. The core profiler gathers these markers concurrently, using a sampling thread.

Marking. The author of a plug-in for the feature-specific profiler must change the implementation of the feature so that instances mark themselves with *feature marks*. It suffices to wrap the relevant code with `with-continuation-mark`. These marks allow the profiler to observe whether a thread is currently executing code related to a feature.

Figure 3 shows an excerpt from the instrumentation of Typed Racket assertions. The underlined conditional is responsible for performing the actual assertion. The feature mark's key should uniquely identify the construct. In this case, we use the symbol `'TR-assertion` as key. Unique choices avoid false reports and interference by distinct plug-ins. As a consequence, our feature-specific profiler can present a unified report to users; it also implies that users need not select in advance the constructs they deem problematic.

The mark value—or *payload*—can be anything that identifies the instance of the feature to which the cost should be assigned. In figure 3, the payload is the source location of a specific assertion in the program, which allows the profiler to compute the cost of individual assertions.

Writing such plug-ins, while simple and non-intrusive, requires access to the implementation of the feature of interest. Because it does not require any specialized profiling knowledge, however, it is well within the reach of the authors of linguistic constructs.

```
(define-syntax (assert stx)
  (syntax-case stx ()
    [(assert v p) ; the compiler rewrites this to:
     (quasisyntax
       (let ([val v] [pred p])
         (with-continuation-mark 'TR-assertion (unsyntax (source-location stx))
           (if (pred val) val (error "Assertion failed.")))))]))
```

Fig. 3. Instrumentation of assertions (excerpt)

Antimarking. Features are seldom "leaves" in a program; feature code usually runs user code whose execution time may not have to count towards the time spent in the feature. For example the profiler must not count the time spent in function bodies towards the function call protocol for keyword arguments.

To solve this problem, a feature-specific profiler expects *antimarks* on the stack. Such antimarks are continuation marks with a distinguished value that delimit a feature's code. Our protocol dictates that the continuation mark key used by an antimark is the same as that of the feature it delimits and that they use the `'antimark` symbol as payload. Figure 4 illustrates the idea with code that instruments a simplified version of Racket's optional and keyword argument protocol. In contrast, assertions do not require antimarks because user code evaluation happens outside the marked region.

```
(define-syntax (lambda/keyword stx)
  (syntax-case stx ()
    [((lambda/keyword formals body) ; the compiler rewrites this to:
     (quasisyntax
      (lambda (unsyntax (handle-keywords formals))
        (with-continuation-mark 'kw-opt-protocol (unsyntax (source-location stx))
          (; parse keyword arguments, compute default values, ...
           (with-continuation-mark 'kw-opt-protocol 'antimark
             body)))))]))  ; body is use-site code
```

Fig. 4. Use of antimarks in instrumentation

The analysis phase recognizes antimarks and uses them to cancel out feature marks. Time is attributed to a feature only if the most recent mark is a feature mark. If it is an antimark, the program is currently executing user code, which should not be counted.

Sampling. During program execution, our profiler's sampling thread periodically collects and stores continuation marks from the main thread. The sampling thread has knowledge of the keys used by feature marks and collects marks for all features at once.

3.3   Analyzing Feature-Specific Data

After the program execution terminates, the core profiler analyzes the data collected by the sampling thread to produce a feature cost report.

Cost assignment. The profiler uses a standard sliding window technique to assign a time cost to each sample based on the elapsed time between the sample, its predecessor and its successor. Only samples with a feature mark as the most recent mark contribute time towards features.

Payload grouping. As explained in section 3.2, payloads identify individual feature instances. Our accounting algorithm groups samples by payload and adds up the cost of each sample; the sums correspond to the cost of each feature instance. Our profiler then generates reports for each feature, using payloads as keys and time costs as values.

Report composition. Finally, after generating individual feature reports, our profiler combines them into a unified report. Constructs absent from the program or those inexpensive enough to never be sampled are pruned to avoid clutter. The report lists features in descending order of cost, and does likewise for instances within feature reports.

Figure 5 shows a feature profile for a Racket implementation of the FizzBuzz[5] program with an input of 10,000,000. Most of the execution time is spent printing numbers not divisible by either 3 or 5 (line 16), which includes most numbers. About a second is spent in generic sequence dispatch; the range function produces a list, but the for iteration form accepts all sequences and must therefore process its input generically.

---

[5] http://imranontech.com/2007/01/24/

```
10  (define (fizzbuzz n)
11    (for ([i (range n)])
12      (cond
13        [(divisible i 15) (printf "FizzBuzz\n")]
14        [(divisible i 5)  (printf "Buzz\n")]
15        [(divisible i 3)  (printf "Fizz\n")]
16        [else             (printf "~a\n" i)])))
17
18  (feature-profile
19    (fizzbuzz 10000000))
```

```
Output accounts for 68.22% of
running time (5580 / 8180 ms)
  4628 ms : fizzbuzz.rkt:16:24
   564 ms : fizzbuzz.rkt:15:24
   232 ms : fizzbuzz.rkt:14:24
   156 ms : fizzbuzz.rkt:13:24

Generic sequences account for 11.78%
of running time (964 / 8180 ms)
   964 ms : fizzbuzz.rkt:11:11
```

Fig. 5. Feature profile for FizzBuzz

4 Profiling Rich Features

The basic architecture assumes that the placement of a feature and the location where it incurs a run-time costs are the same or in one-to-one correspondence. In contrast to such *structurally simple* features, some, such as contracts, cause time consumption in many different places, and in other cases, such as Marketplace processes, several different instances of a construct contribute to a single cost center. We call the latter kind of linguistic features *structurally rich*.

While the creator of a structurally rich feature can use a basic plug-in to measure some aspects of its cost, it is best to adapt a different strategy for evaluating such features. This section shows how to go about such an adaptation. Section 6.2 illustrates with an example how to migrate from a basic plug-in to one appropriate for a structurally rich feature.

4.1 Custom Payloads

Instrumentation for structure-rich features uses arbitrary values as mark payloads instead of locations.

Contracts. Our contract plug-in uses *blame objects* as payloads. A blame object explains contract violations and pinpoints the faulty party; every time an object traverses a higher-order contract boundary, the contract system attaches a blame object. Put differently, a blame object holds enough information—the contract to check, the name of the contracted value, and the names of the components that agreed to the contract—to reconstruct a complete picture of contract checking events.

Marketplace processes. The Marketplace plug-in uses process names as payloads. Since current-continuation-marks gathers all the marks currently on the stack, the sampling thread can gather *core samples*.[6] Because Marketplace VMs are spawned and transfer control using function calls, these core samples include not only the current process but also all its ancestors—its parent VM, its grandparent, etc.

---

[6] In analogy to geology, a core sample includes marks from the entire stack.

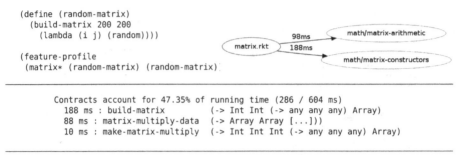

```
(define (random-matrix)
  (build-matrix 200 200
    (lambda (i j) (random))))

(feature-profile
  (matrix* (random-matrix) (random-matrix))
```

```
Contracts account for 47.35% of running time (286 / 604 ms)
  188 ms : build-matrix          (-> Int Int (-> any any any) Array)
   88 ms : matrix-multiply-data  (-> Array Array [...]))
   10 ms : make-matrix-multiply  (-> Int Int Int (-> any any any) Array)
```

Fig. 6. Module graph and by-value views of a contract boundary

Parser backtracking. The Parsack plug-in combines three values into a payload: the source location of the current disjunction, the index of the active branch within the disjunction, and the offset in the input where the parser is currently matching. Because parsing a term may require recursively parsing sub-terms, the Parsack plug-in gathers core samples that allow it to attribute time to all active non-terminals.

While storing rich payloads is attractive, plug-in writers must avoid excessive computation or allocation when constructing payloads. Even though the profiler uses sampling, payloads are constructed every time feature code is executed, whether or not the sampler observes it.

4.2   Analyzing Rich Features

Programmers usually cannot directly digest information generated via custom payloads. If a feature-specific plug-in uses such payloads, its creator should implement an analysis pass that generates user-facing reports.

Contracts. The goal of the contract plug-in is to report which pairs of parties impose contract checking, and how much the checking costs. Hence, the analysis aims to provide an at-a-glance overview of the cost of each contract and boundary.

To this end, our analysis generates a *module graph* view of contract boundaries. This graph shows modules as nodes, contract boundaries as edges and contract costs as labels on edges. Because typed-untyped boundaries are an important source of contracts, the module graph distinguishes typed modules (in green) from untyped modules (in red). To generate this view, our analysis extracts component names from blame objects. It then groups payloads that share pairs of parties and computes costs as discussed in section 3.3. The top-right part of figure 6 shows the module graph for a program that constructs two random matrices and multiplies them. This code resides in an untyped module, but the matrix functions of the math library reside in a typed module. Hence linking the client and the library introduces a contract boundary between them.

In addition to the module graph, our feature-specific profiler provides other views as well. For example, the bottom portion of figure 6 shows the *by-value* view, which provides fine-grained information about the cost of individual contracted values.

Marketplace Processes. The goal of our feature-specific analysis for Marketplace processes is to assign costs to individual processes and VMs, as opposed to the code they execute. Marketplace feature marks use the names of processes and VMs as payloads, which allows the plug-in to distinguish separate processes executing the same code.

Our analysis uses full core samples to attribute costs to VMs based on the costs of their children. These core samples record the entire ancestry of processes in the same way the call stack records function calls. We exploit that similarity and reuse standard edge profiling techniques to attribute costs to the entire ancestry of a process.

```
===============================================================
Total Time  Self Time      Name                           Local%
===============================================================
100.0%        32.3%         ground
                            (tcp-listener 5999 ::1 53588)  33.7%
                            tcp-driver                      9.6%
                            (tcp-listener 5999 ::1 53587)   2.6%
                            [...]
33.7%         33.7%         (tcp-listener 5999 ::1 53588)
2.6%           2.6%         (tcp-listener 5999 ::1 53587)
[...]
```

Fig. 7. Marketplace process accounting (excerpt)

Figure 7 shows the accounting from a Marketplace-based echo server. The first entry of the profile shows the ground VM, which spawns all other VMs and processes. The rightmost column shows how execution time is split across the ground VM's children. Of note are the processes handling requests from two clients. As reflected in the profile, the client on port 53588 is sending ten times as much input as the one on port 53587.

Parser backtracking. The feature-specific analysis for Parsack determines how much time is spent backtracking for each branch of each disjunction. The source locations and input offsets in the payload allows the plug-in to identify each unique visit that the parser makes to each disjunction during parsing.

We detect backtracking as follows. Because disjunctions are ordered, the parser must have backtracked from branches 1 through $n - 1$ once it reaches the nth branch of a disjunction. Therefore, whenever the analysis observes a sample from branch n of a disjunction at a given input location, it attributes backtracking costs to the preceding branches. It computes that cost from the samples taken in these branches at the same input location. As with the Marketplace plug-in, the Parsack plug-in uses core samples and edge profiling to handle the recursive structure of the parsing process.

Figure 8 shows a simple parser that first attempts to parse a sequence of bs followed by an a, and in case of failure, backtracks in order to parse a sequence of bs. The right portion of figure 8 shows the output of the feature-specific profiler when running the parser on a sequence of 9,000,000 bs. It confirms that the parser had to backtrack from the first branch after spending almost half of the program's execution attempting it. Swapping the $a and $b branches in the disjunction eliminates this backtracking.

```
26 (define $a (compose $b (char #\a)))
27 (define $b (<or> (compose (char #\b) $b)        Parsack Backtracking
28                  (nothing)))                     =================================
29 (define $s (<or> (try $a) $b))                   Time (ms / %)   Disjunction   Branch
30                                                   =================================
31 (feature-profile (parse $s input))               2076    46%    ab.rkt:29:12    1
```

Fig. 8. An example Parsack-based parser and its backtracking profile

5   Instrumentation Control

As described, plug-ins insert continuation marks regardless of whether a programmer wishes to profile or not. We refer to this as *active marking*. For features where individual instances perform a significant amount of work, such as contracts, the overhead of active marks is usually not observable. For other features, such as fine-grained console output where the aggregate cost of individually inexpensive instances is significant, the overhead of marks can be problematic. In such situations, programmers want to control *when* marks are applied on a by-execution basis.

In addition, programmers may also want to control *where* mark insertion takes place to avoid reporting costs in code that they cannot modify or wish to ignore. For instance, reporting that some function in the standard library performs a lot of pattern matching is useless to most programmers; they cannot fix it.

To establish control over the *when* and *where* of continuation marks, our framework introduces the notion of *latent marks*. A latent mark is an annotation that, on demand, can be turned into an active mark by a preprocessor or a compiler pass. We distinguish between *syntactic latent marks* for use with features implemented using metaprogramming and *functional latent marks* for use with library or runtime functions.

5.1   Syntactic Latent Marks

Syntactic latent marks exist as annotations on the intermediate representation (IR) of user code. To add a latent mark, the implementation of a feature leaves tags[7] on the residual program's IR instead of directly inserting feature marks. These tags are discarded after compilation and thus have no run-time effect on the program. Other metaprograms or the compiler can observe latent marks and turn them into active marks.

Our implementation uses Racket's *compilation handler* mechanism to interpose the activation pass between macro-expansion and the compiler's front end with a command-line flag that enables the compilation handler. The compilation handler then traverses the input program, replacing any syntactic latent mark it finds with an active mark. Because latent marks are implicitly present in user code, no library recompilation is necessary. The programmer must merely recompile the code to be profiled.

---

[7] We use Racket's syntax property mechanism, but any IR tagging mechanism would apply.

This method applies only to features implemented using meta-programming. Because Racket relies heavily on syntactic extension, most of our plug-ins use syntactic latent marks.

5.2 Functional Latent Marks

Functional latent marks offer an alternative to syntactic latent marks. Instead of tagging the programmer's code, a preprocessor or compiler pass recognizes calls to feature-related functions and rewrites the programmer's code to wrap such calls with active marks. Like syntactic latent marks, functional latent marks require recompilation of user code that uses the relevant functions. They do not, however, require recompiling libraries that *provide* feature-related functions, which makes them appropriate for functions provided as runtime primitives.

6   Evaluation

Our evaluation addresses two promises concerning feature-specific profiling: that measuring in a feature-specific way supplies useful insights into performance problems, and that it is easy to implement new plug-ins. This section first presents case studies that demonstrate how feature-specific profiling improves the performance of programs. Then it reports on the amount of effort required to implement plug-ins. The online version of this paper[8] includes an appendix that discusses run-time overhead.

6.1   Case Studies

To be useful, a feature-specific profiler must accurately identify specific uses of features that are responsible for significant performance costs in a given program. Furthermore, an ideal profiler must provide *actionable* information, that is, its reports must point programmers towards solutions. Ideally, it will also provide *negative* information, i.e., confirm that some constructs need not be investigated.

We present three case studies suffering from the overhead of specific features. Each subsection describes a program, summarizes the feature-specific profiler's feedback, and explains the changes that directly follow from the report. Figure 9 presents the results of comparing execution times before and after the changes. It also includes results from two additional programs—a sound synthesis engine and a Shill-based automatic grading script—which we do not discuss due to a lack of space.

Maze Generator. Our first case study employs a Typed Racket version of a maze generator, due to Olin Shivers. For scale, the maze generator is 758 lines of code. The program generates a maze on a hexagonal grid, ensures that it is solvable, and prints it.

According to the feature profile, 55% of the execution time is spent performing output. Three calls to display, each responsible for printing part of the bottom of hexagons, stand out as especially expensive. Printing each part separately results in a

---

[8] http://www.ccs.neu.edu/racket/pubs/#cc15-saf

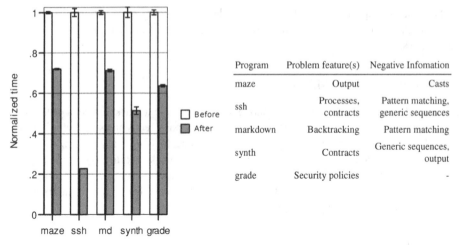

Program	Problem feature(s)	Negative Infomation
maze	Output	Casts
ssh	Processes, contracts	Pattern matching, generic sequences
markdown	Backtracking	Pattern matching
synth	Contracts	Generic sequences, output
grade	Security policies	-

Results are the mean of 30 executions on a 6-core 64-bit Debian GNU/Linux system with 12GB of RAM. Because Shill only supports FreeBSD, results for *grade* are from a 6-core FreeBSD system with 6GB of RAM. Error bars are one standard deviation on either side.

Fig. 9. Execution time after profiling and improvements (lower is better)

large number of single-character output operations. This report suggests fusing all three output operations into one. Following this advice results in a $1.39\times$ speedup.

Inside an inner loop, a dynamic type assertion enforces an invariant that the type system cannot guarantee statically. Even though this might raise concerns with a cost-conscious programmer, the profile reports that the time spent in the cast is negligible.

Marketplace-Based SSH Server. Our second case study involves an SSH server[9] written using the Marketplace library. For scale, the SSH server is 3,762 lines of code. To exercise it, a driver script starts the server, connects to it, launches a Racket read-eval-print-loop on the host, evaluates the expression `(+ 1 2 3 4 5 6)`, disconnects and terminates the server.

As figure 10 shows, our feature-specific profiler brings out two useful facts. First, two *spy* processes—the `tcp-spy` process and the boot process of the `ssh-session` VM—account for over 25% of the total execution time. In Marketplace, spies are processes that observe other processes for logging purposes. The SSH server spawns these spy processes even when logging is ignored, resulting in unnecessary overhead.

Second, contracts account for close to 67% of the running time. The module view, of which figure 11 shows an excerpt, reports that the majority of these contracts lie at the boundary between the typed Marketplace library and the untyped SSH server. We can selectively remove these contracts in one of two ways: by adding types to the SSH server or by disabling typechecking in Marketplace.

Disabling spy processes and type-induced contracts results in a speedup of around $4.41\times$. In addition to these two areas of improvement, the feature profile also provides

---

[9] https://github.com/tonyg/marketplace-ssh

negative information: pattern matching and generic sequences, despite being used pervasively, account for only a small fraction of the server's running time.

```
Marketplace Processes
=================================================================
Total Time  Self Time     Name                             Local%
=================================================================
100.0%      3.8%          ground
                          ssh-session-vm                   51.2%
                          tcp-spy                          19.9%
                          (tcp-listener 2322 ::1 44523)    19.4%
                          [...]
51.2%       1.0%          ssh-session-vm
                          ssh-session                      31.0%
                          (#:boot-process ssh-session-vm)  14.1%
                          [...]
19.9%       19.9%         tcp-spy
7.2%        7.2%          (#:boot-process ssh-session-vm)
[...]

Contracts account for 66.93% of running time (3874 / 5788 ms)
   1496 ms : add-endpoint  (-> pre-eid? role? [...] add-endpoint?)
   1122 ms : process-spec  (-> (-> any [...]) any)
   [...]

Pattern matching accounts for 0.76% of running time (44 / 5788 ms)
   [...]

Generic sequences account for 0.35% of running time (20 / 5788 ms)
   [...]
```

Fig. 10. Profiling results for the SSH server (excerpt)

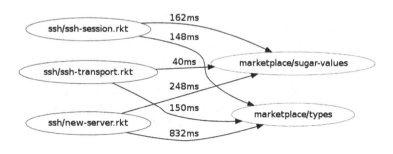

Fig. 11. Module graph view for the SSH server (excerpt)

Markdown Parser. Our last case study involves a Parsack-based Markdown parser,[10] due to Greg Hendershott. For scale, the Markdown parser is 4,058 lines of Racket code. To profile the parser, we ran it on 1,000 lines of sample text.[11]

As figure 12 shows, backtracking from three branches took noticeable time and accounted for 34%, 2%, and 2% of total execution time, respectively. Based on the tool's

---

[10] https://github.com/greghendershott/markdown
[11] An excerpt from "The Time Machine" by H.G. Wells.

report, we moved the problematic branches further down in their enclosing disjunction, which produced a speedup of 1.40×.

For comparison, Parsack's author, Stephen Chang, manually optimized the same version of the Markdown parser using ad-hoc, low-level instrumentation and achieved a speedup of 1.37×. Using our tool, the second author, with no knowledge of the parser's internals, was able to achieve a similar speedup in only a few minutes of work.

The feature-specific profiler additionally confirmed that pattern matching accounted for a negligible amount of the total running time.

```
Parsack Backtracking
========================================================
Time (ms / %)   Disjunction                  Branch
========================================================
5809.5  34%     markdown/parse.rkt:968:7       8
366.5    2%     parsack/parsack.rkt:449:27     1
313.5    2%     markdown/parse.rkt:670:7       2
[...]

Pattern matching accounts for 0.04% of running time (6 / 17037 ms)
   6 ms : parsack/parsack.rkt:233:4
```

Fig. 12. Profiling results for the Markdown parser (excerpt)

6.2   Plug-in Implementation Effort

Writing feature-specific plug-ins is a low-effort endeavor. It is easily within reach for the authors of linguistic libraries because it does not require advanced profiling knowledge. To support this claim, we start with anecdotal evidence from observing the author of the Marketplace library implement feature-specific profiling support for it.

Mr. Garnock-Jones, an experienced Racket programmer, implemented the plug-in himself, with the first author acting as interactive documentation of the framework. Implementing the first version of the plug-in took about 35 minutes. At that point, Mr. Garnock-Jones had a working process profiler that performed the basic analysis described in section 3.3. Adding a feature-specific analysis took an additional 40 minutes. Less experienced library authors may require more time for a similar task. Nonetheless, we consider this amount of effort to be quite reasonable.

Feature	Instrumentation LOC	Analysis LOC
Output	11	-
Generic sequences	18	-
Type casts and assertions	37	-
Shill security policies	23	-
Pattern matching	18	-
Optional and keyword arguments	50	-
Method dispatch	12	-
Contracts	183	672
Marketplace processes	7	9
Parser non-terminals	18	60

Fig. 13. Instrumentation and analysis LOC per feature

For the remaining features, we report the number of lines of code for each plug-in in figure 13. The third column reports the number of lines of domain-specific analysis code. The basic analysis is provided as part of the framework. The line counts for Marketplace and Parsack do not include the portions of Racket's edge profiler that are re-linked into the plug-ins, which account for 506 lines. With the exception of contract instrumentation—which covers multiple kinds of contracts and is spread across the 16,421 lines of the contract system—instrumentation is local and non-intrusive.

7 Limitations

Our specific approach to feature-specific profiling applies only to certain kinds of linguistic constructs. This section describes cases that our feature-specific profiler should but cannot support. Those limitations are not fundamental to the idea of feature-specific profiling and could be addressed by different approaches to data gathering.

Control features. Because our instrumentation strategy relies on continuation marks, it does not support features that interfere with marks. This rules out non-local control features that unroll the stack, such as exception raising.

Non-observable features. The sampler must be able to observe a feature in order to profile it. This rules out uninterruptible features, e.g., struct allocation, or FFI calls, which do not allow the sampling thread to be scheduled during their execution. Other obstacles to observability include sampling bias (Mytkowicz et al. 2010) and instances that execute too quickly to be reliably sampled.

Diffuse features. Some features, such as garbage collection, have costs that are diffused throughout the program. This renders mark-based instrumentation impractical. An event-based approach, such as Morandat et al.'s (2012), would fare better. The use of events would also make feature-specific profiling possible in languages that do not support stack inspection.

8 Related Work

Programmers already have access to a wide variety of performance tools that are complementary to feature-specific profilers. This section compares our work to those approaches that are closely related.

8.1 Traditional Profiling

Profilers have been successfully used to diagnose performance issues for decades. They most commonly report on the consumption of time, space and I/O resources. Traditional profilers group costs according to program organization, be it static—e.g., per function—or dynamic—e.g., per HTTP request. Feature-specific profilers group costs according to linguistic features and specific feature instances.

Each of these views is useful in different contexts. For example, a feature-specific profiler's view is most useful when non-local feature costs make up a significant portion of a program's running time. Traditional profilers may not provide actionable information in such cases. Furthermore, by identifying costly features, feature-specific profilers point programmers towards potential solutions, namely correcting feature usage. In contrast, traditional profilers often report costs without helping find solutions. Conversely, traditional profilers may detect a broader range of issues than feature-specific profilers, such as inefficient algorithms, which are invisible to feature-specific profilers.

8.2   Vertical Profiling

A vertical profiler (Hauswirth et al. 2004) attempts to see through the use of high-level language features. It therefore gathers information from multiple layers—hardware performance counters, operating system, virtual machine, libraries—and correlates them into a gestalt of program performance.

Vertical profiling focuses on helping programmers understand how the interaction between layers affects their program's performance. By comparison, feature-specific profiling focuses on helping them understand the cost of features per se. Feature-specific profiling also presents information in terms of features and feature instances, which is accessible to non-expert programmers, whereas vertical profilers report low-level information, which requires a deep understanding of the compiler and runtime system.

Hauswirth et al.'s work introduces the notion of *software performance monitors*, which are analogous to hardware performance monitors but record software-related performance events. These monitors could possibly be used to implement feature-specific profiling by tracking the execution of feature code.

8.3   Alternative Profiling Views

A number of profilers offer alternative views to the traditional attribution of time costs to program locations. Most of these views focus on particular aspects of program performance and are complementary to the view offered by a feature-specific profiler. Some recent examples include Singer and Kirkham's (2008) profiler, which assigns costs to programmer-annotated code regions, listener latency profiling (Jovic and Hauswirth 2011), which reports high-latency operations, and Tamayo et al.'s (2012) tool, which provides information about the cost of database operations.

8.4   Dynamic Instrumentation Frameworks

Dynamic instrumentation frameworks such as Valgrind (Nethercote and Seward 2007) or Javana (Maebe et al. 2006) serve as the basis for profilers and other kinds of performance tools. These frameworks resemble the use of continuation marks in our framework and could potentially be used to build feature-specific profilers. These frameworks are much more heavy-weight than continuation marks and, in turn, allow more thorough instrumentation, e.g., of the memory hierarchy, of hardware performance counters, etc., though they have not been used to measure the cost of linguistic features.

8.5 Optimization Coaching

Like a feature-specific profiler, an optimization coach (St-Amour et al. 2012) aims to help non-experts improve the performance of their programs. Where coaches focus on enabling compiler optimizations, feature-specific profilers focus on avoiding feature misuses. The two are complementary.

Optimization coaches operate at compile time whereas feature-specific profilers, like other profilers, operate at run time. Because of this, feature-specific profilers require representative program input to operate, whereas coaches do not. On the other hand, by having access to run time data, feature-specific profilers can target actual program hot spots, while coaches must rely on static heuristics to prioritize reports.

9 Conclusion

This paper introduces feature-specific profiling, a technique that reports program costs in terms of linguistic features. It also presents an architecture for feature-specific profilers that allows the authors of libraries to implement plug-ins in their libraries.

The alternative view on program performance offered by feature-specific profilers allows easy diagnosis of performance issues due to feature misuses, especially those with distributed costs, which might go undetected using a traditional profiler. By pointing to the specific features responsible, feature-specific profilers provide programmers with actionable information that points them towards solutions.

Acknowledgements. Tony Garnock-Jones implemented the Marketplace plug-in and helped us perform the SSH case study. Stephen Chang assisted with the Parsack plug-in and the Markdown case study. Christos Dimoulas and Scott Moore collaborated on the Shill plug-in and the grading script experiment. Robby Findler provided assistance with the contract system. We thank Eli Barzilay, Matthew Flatt, Asumu Takikawa, Sam Tobin-Hochstadt and Jan Vitek for helpful discussions.

This work was partially supported by Darpa, NSF SHF grants 1421412, 1421652, and Mozilla.

References

Clements, J., Flatt, M., Felleisen, M.: Modeling an algebraic stepper. In: Sands, D. (ed.) ESOP 2001. LNCS, vol. 2028, pp. 320–334. Springer, Heidelberg (2001)

Clements, J., Sundaram, A., Herman, D.: Implementing continuation marks in JavaScript. In: Proc. Scheme Works., pp. 1–10 (2008)

Findler, R.B., Clements, J., Flanagan, C., Flatt, M., Krishnamurthi, S., Steckler, P., Felleisen, M.: DrScheme: A programming environment for Scheme. JFP 12(2), 159–182 (2002)

Findler, R.B., Felleisen, M.: Contracts for higher-order functions. In: Proc. ICFP, pp. 48–59 (2002)

Matthew Flatt and PLT. Reference: Racket. PLT Inc., PLT-TR-2010-1 (2010), http://racket-lang.org/tr

Garnock-Jones, T., Tobin-Hochstadt, S., Felleisen, M.: The network as a language construct. In: Shao, Z. (ed.) ESOP 2014. LNCS, vol. 8410, pp. 473–492. Springer, Heidelberg (2014)

Hauswirth, M., Sweeney, P.F., Diwan, A., Hind, M.: Vertical profiling. In: Proc. OOPSLA, pp. 251–269 (2004)

Jovic, M., Hauswirth, M.: Listener latency profiling. SCP 19(4), 1054–1072 (2011)

Maebe, J., Buytaert, D., Eeckhout, L., De Bosschere, K.: Javana: A system for building customized Java program analysis tools. In: Proc. OOPSLA, pp. 153–168 (2006)

Marlow, S., Iborra, J., Pope, B., Gill, A.: A lightweight interactive debugger for Haskell. In: Proc. Haskell Works., pp. 13–24 (2007)

McCarthy, J.: The two-state solution: native and serializable continuations accord. In: Proc. OOPSLA, pp. 567–582 (2010)

Moore, A.S., Dimoulas, C., King, D., Chong, S.: SHILL: A secure shell scripting language. In: Proc. OSDI (2014)

Morandat, F., Hill, B., Osvald, L., Vitek, J.: Evaluating the Design of the R Language. In: Noble, J. (ed.) ECOOP 2012. LNCS, vol. 7313, pp. 104–131. Springer, Heidelberg (2012)

Mytkowicz, T., Diwan, A., Hauswirth, M., Sweeney, P.F.: Evaluating the accuracy of Java profilers. In: Proc. PLDI, pp. 187–197 (2010)

Nethercote, N., Seward, J.: Valgrind: A framework for heavyweight dynamic binary instrumentation. In: Proc. PLDI, pp. 89–100 (2007)

Pettyjohn, G., Clements, J., Marshall, J., Krishnamurthi, S., Felleisen, M.: Continuations from generalized stack inspection. In: Proc. ICFP, pp. 216–227 (2005)

Singer, J., Kirkham, C.: Dynamic analysis of Java program concepts for visualization and profiling. SCP 70(2-3), 111–126 (2008)

St-Amour, V., Tobin-Hochstadt, S., Felleisen, M.: Optimization coaching: Optimizers learn to communicate with programmers. In: Proc. OOPSLA, pp. 163–178 (2012)

Strickland, T.S., Felleisen, M.: Contracts for first-class classes. In: Proc. DLS, pp. 97–112 (2010)

Strickland, T.S., Tobin-Hochstadt, S., Findler, R.B., Flatt, M.: Chaperones and impersonators. In: Proc. OOPSLA, pp. 943–962 (2012)

Tamayo, J.M., Aiken, A., Bronson, N., Sagiv, M.: Understanding the behavior of database operations under program control. In: Proc. OOPSLA, pp. 983–996 (2012)

Tobin-Hochstadt, S., Felleisen, M.: Interlanguage refactoring: From scripts to programs. In: Proc. DLS, pp. 964–974 (2006)

A Synchronous-Based Code Generator
for Explicit Hybrid Systems Languages[*]

Timothy Bourke[1,3], Jean-Louis Colaço[2], Bruno Pagano[2], Cédric Pasteur[2], and
Marc Pouzet[4,3,1]

[1] INRIA Paris-Rocquencourt
[2] ANSYS/Esterel-Technologies, Toulouse
[3] DI, École normale supérieure, Paris
[4] Université Pierre et Marie Curie, Paris

Abstract. Modeling languages for hybrid systems are cornerstones of
embedded systems development in which software interacts with a physical environment. Sequential code generation from such languages is important for simulation efficiency and for producing code for embedded
targets. Despite being routinely used in industrial compilers, code generation is rarely, if ever, described in full detail, much less formalized.
Yet formalization is an essential step in building trustable compilers for
critical embedded software development.

This paper presents a novel approach for generating code from a hybrid systems modeling language. By building on top of an existing synchronous language and compiler, it reuses almost all the existing infrastructure with only a few modifications. Starting from an existing synchronous data-flow language conservatively extended with Ordinary Dif-
ferential Equations (ODEs), this paper details the sequence of source-to-
source transformations that ultimately yield sequential code. A generic
intermediate language is introduced to represent transition functions.
The versatility of this approach is exhibited by treating two classical
simulation targets: code that complies with the FMI standard and code
directly linked with an off-the-shelf numerical solver (Sundials CVODE).

The presented material has been implemented in the ZÉLUS compiler
and the industrial SCADE Suite KCG code generator of SCADE 6.

1   Introduction

Hybrid systems modeling languages allow models to include both software and
elements of its physical environment. Such models serve as references for simulation, testing, formal verification, and the generation of embedded code. Explicit
hybrid systems languages like SIMULINK/STATEFLOW[1] combine Ordinary Dif-
ferential Equations (ODEs) with difference and data-flow equations, hierarchical
automata in the style of Statecharts [15], and traditional imperative features.

---

[*] Examples in ZÉLUS and the extension of SCADE 6 with hybrid features are available
at http://zelus.di.ens.fr/cc2015/.

[1] http://mathworks.org/simulink

© Springer-Verlag Berlin Heidelberg 2015
B. Franke (Ed.): CC 2015, LNCS 9031, pp. 69–88, 2015.
DOI: 10.1007/978-3-662-46663-6_4

Models in these languages mix signals that evolve in both discrete and continuous time. While the formal verification of hybrid systems has been extensively studied [8], this paper addresses the different, but no less important, question of generating sequential code (typically C) for efficient simulations and embedded real-time implementations.

Sequential code generation for synchronous languages [5] like LUSTRE [14] has been extensively studied. It can be formalized as a series of source-to-source and traceable transformations that progressively reduce high-level programming constructs, like hierarchical automata and activation conditions, into a minimal data-flow kernel [10]. This kernel is further simplified into a generic intermediate representation for transition functions [6], and ultimately turned into C code. Notably, this is the approach taken in the SCADE Suite KCG code generator of SCADE 6[2], which is used in a wide range of critical embedded applications.

Yet synchronous languages only manipulate discrete-time signals. Their expressiveness is deliberately limited to ensure determinacy, execution in bounded time and space, and simple, traceable code generation. The cyclic execution model of synchronous languages does not suffer the complications that accompany numerical solvers. Conversely, a hybrid modeling language allows discrete and continuous time behaviors to interact. But this interaction together with unsafe constructs, like side effects and while loops, is not constrained enough, nor specified with adequate precision in tools like SIMULINK/STATEFLOW. It can occasion semantic pitfalls [9,4] and compiler bugs [1]. A precise description of code generation, that is, the actual implemented semantics, is mandatory in safety critical development processes where target code must be trustworthy. Our aim, in short, is to increase the expressiveness of synchronous languages without sacrificing any confidence in their code generators.

Benveniste et al. recently proposed a novel approach for the design and implementation of a hybrid modeling language that reuses synchronous language principles and an existing compiler infrastructure. They proposed an ideal synchronous semantics based on non standard analysis [4] for a LUSTRE-like language with ODEs [3], and then extended the kernel language with hierarchical automata [2] and a modular causality analysis [1]. These results form the foundation of ZÉLUS [7]. This paper describes their validation in an industrial compiler.

Paper Contribution and Organisation Our first contribution is to precisely describe the translation of a minimal synchronous language extended with ODEs into sequential code. Our second contribution is the experimental validation in two different compilers: the research prototype ZÉLUS [7] and the SCADE Suite KCG code generator. In the latter it was possible to reuse all the existing infrastructure like static checking, intermediate languages, and optimisations, with little modification. The extensions for hybrid features require only 5% additional lines of code. Moreover, the proposed language extension is conservative in that regular synchronous functions are compiled as before—the same synchronous code is used both for simulation and for execution on target platforms.

---

[2] http://www.esterel-technologies.com/products/scade-suite/

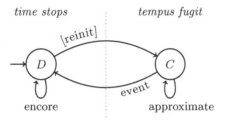

Fig. 1. Basic structure of a hybrid simulation algorithm

The paper is organised as follows. Section 2 recalls the classical simulation loop of hybrid systems. Section 3 describes the overall compiler architecture as implemented in KCG. Section 4 defines the input language, Section 5 defines a clocked intermediate language, and Section 6 defines the target imperative language. Code generation is defined in Section 6.1. We illustrate the versatility of the compiler in two typical practical situations: generating code that complies with the FMI standard and generating code that incorporates an off-the-shelf numerical solver (Sundials CVODE). Practical experiments in KCG and ZÉLUS are presented in Section 7. Section 8 discusses extensions and related work. We conclude in Section 9.

2   The Simulation Loop of Hybrid Systems

The first choice to make in implementing a hybrid system is how to solve ODEs. Creating an efficient and numerically accurate numerical solver is a daunting and specialist task. Reusing an existing solver is more practical, with two possible choices: either (a) generate a *Functional Mock-Up Unit* (FMU) using the standardized *Functional Mock-Up Interface* (FMI) and rely on an existing simulation infrastructure [19]; or (b) use an off-the-shelf numerical solver like CVODE [16] and program the main simulation loop. The latter corresponds to the *co-simulation* variant (CS) of FMI, where each FMU embeds its own solver.

The simulation loop of a hybrid system is the same no matter which option is chosen. It can be defined formally as a *synchronous function* that defines four streams $t(n)$, $lx(n)$, $y(n)$, and $z(n)$, with $n \in \mathbb{N}$. $t(n) \in \mathbb{R}$ is the increasing sequence of instants at which the solver stops.[3] $lx(n)$ is the value at time $t(n)$ of the *continuous state variables*, that is, of all variables defined by their derivatives in the original model. $y(n)$ is the value at time $t(n)$ of the *discrete state*. $z(n)$ indicates any *zero-crossings* at instant $t(n)$ on signals monitored by the solver, that is, any signals that become equal to or pass through zero.

The synchronous function has two modes: the discrete mode (D) contains all computations that may change the discrete state or that have side effects. The continuous mode (C) is where ODEs are solved. The two modes alternate according to the execution scheme summarized in Figure 1.

---

[3] In SIMULINK, these are called *major time steps*.

The Continuous Mode (C). In this mode, the solver computes an approximation of the solution of the ODEs and monitors a set of expressions for zero-crossings. Code generation is independent of the actual solver implementation. We abstract it by introducing a function $solve(f)(g)$ parameterized by f and g where:

- $x'(\tau) = f(y(n), \tau, x(\tau))$ defines the derivatives of continuous state variables x at instant $\tau \in \mathbb{R}$;
- $upz(\tau) = g(y(n), \tau, x(\tau))$ defines the current values of a set of zero-crossing signals upz, indexed by $i \in \{1, \ldots, k\}$.

The continuous mode C computes four sequences s, lx, z and t such that:

$$(lx, z, t, s)(n + 1) = solve(f)(g)(s, y, lx, t, step)(n)$$

where

$s(n)$ is the internal state of the solver at instant $t(n) \in \mathbb{R}$. Calling $solve(f)(g)$ updates the state to $s(n + 1)$.

x is an approximation of a solution of the ODE,

$$x'(\tau) = f(y(n), \tau, x(\tau))$$

It is parameterized by the current discrete state $y(n)$ and initialized at instant $t(n)$ with the value of $lx(n)$, that is, $x(t(n)) = lx(n)$.

$lx(n+1)$ is the value of x at $t(n + 1)$, that is:

$$lx(n + 1) = x(t(n + 1))$$

lx is a discrete-time signal whereas x is a continuous-time signal.

$t(n + 1)$ is bounded by the horizon $t(n) + step(n)$ that the solver has been asked to reach, that is:

$$t(n) \leq t(n + 1) \leq t(n) + step(n)$$

$z(n+1)$ signals any zero-crossings detected at time $t(n + 1)$. An event occurs with a transition to the discrete mode D when horizon $t(n) + step(n)$ is reached, or when at least one of the zero-crossing signals $upz(i)$, for $i \in \{1, \ldots, k\}$ crosses zero,[4] which is indicated by a true value for the corresponding boolean output $z(n + 1)(i)$.

$$event = z(n + 1)(0) \vee \cdots \vee z(n + 1)(k) \vee (t(n + 1) = t(n) + step(n))$$

If the solver raises an error (for example, a division by zero or an inability to find a solution), we consider that the simulation fails.

---

[4] The function $solve(f)(g)$ abstracts from the actual implementation of zero-crossing detection. To account for a possible zero-crossing at the horizon $t(n) + step(n)$, the solver may integrate over a strictly larger interval $[t(n), t(n) + step(n) + margin]$, where *margin* is a solver parameter.

$$z(n + 1)(i) = \begin{array}{l} (\forall T \in [t(n), t(n + 1)[\, . \, upz(T)(i) < 0) \\ \wedge \, \exists m \leq margin \, . \, (\forall T \in [t(n + 1), t(n + 1) + m] \, . \, upz(T)(i) \geq 0) \end{array}$$

This definition assumes that the solver also stops whenever a zero-crossing expression passes through zero from positive to negative.

The Discrete Mode (D). All discrete changes occur in this mode. It is entered when an event is raised during integration. During a discrete phase, the function *next* defines y, lx, *step*, *encore*, z, and t:

$$(y, lx, step, encore)(n + 1) = next(y, lx, z, t)(n)$$
$$z(n + 1) = false$$
$$t(n + 1) = t(n)$$

where

$y(n + 1)$ is the new discrete state; outside of mode D, $y(n + 1) = y(n)$.

$lx(n + 1)$ is the new continuous state, which may be changed directly in the discrete mode.

$step(n + 1)$ is the new step size.

$encore(n+1)$ is true if an additional discrete step must be performed. Function *next* can decide to trigger instantaneously another discrete event causing an *event cascade* [4].

$t(n)$ (the simulation time) is unchanged during discrete phases.

The initial values for $y(0)$, $lx(0)$ and $s(0)$ are given by an initialization function *init*. Finally, $solve(f)(g)$ may decide to reset its internal state if the continuous state changes. If $init\_solve(lx(n), s(n))$ initializes the solver state, we have:

$$reinit = (lx(n + 1) \neq lx(n))$$
$$s(n + 1) = if\ reinit\ then\ init\_solve(lx(n + 1), s(n))\ else\ s(n)$$

Taken together, the definitions from both modes give a synchronous interpretation of the simulation loop as a stream function that computes the sequences lx, y and t at instant $n + 1$ according to their values at instant n and an internal state. Writing $solve(f)(g)$ abstracts from the actual choice of integration method and zero-crossing detection algorithm. A more detailed description of $solve(f)(g)$ would be possible (for example, an automaton with two states: one that integrates, and one that detects zero-crossings) but with no influence on the code generation problem which must be independent of such simulation details.

Given a program written in a high-level language, we must produce the functions *init*, f, g, and *next*. In practice, they are implemented in an imperative language like C. Code generation for hybrid models has much in common with code generation for synchronous languages. In fact, the following sections show how to extend an existing synchronous language and compiler with ODEs.

3   Compiler Architecture

The compiler architecture for hybrid programs is based on those of existing compilers for data-flow synchronous languages like Scade 6 or Lucid Synchrone, as described for instance in [6]. After initial checks, it consists in successive

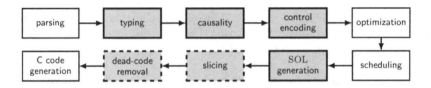

Fig. 2. Compiler architecture (modified passes are gray; new ones are also dashed)

rewritings of the source program into intermediate languages, and ending with sequential code in the target language (typically C). The different passes are shown in Figure 2:

1. Parsing transforms code in the source language, described in Section 4, into an abstract syntax tree;
2. Typing checks programs according to the system of [3]. In the language extended with ODEs, this system distinguishes continuous and discrete blocks to ensure the correct separation of continuous and discrete behaviors;
3. Causality analysis verifies the absence of causality loops [1]. It is readily extended to deal with the new constructs;
4. Control structures are encoded into the purely data-flow kernel with clocks defined in Section 5, using an extension of the clock-based compilation of [6]. A small modification accounts for the fact that transitions are executed in a discrete context whereas the bodies of states are continuous;
5. Traditional optimizations (dead-code removal, common sub-expression elimination, etc.) are performed;
6. Scheduling orders equations according to data dependencies, as explained in Section 5.2;
7. Code is translated into an intermediate sequential object language called SOL, defined in Section 6 together with the translation. This language extends the one presented in [6] to deal with the new constructs (continuous states, zero-crossings) which translation to sequential code must be added;
8. Slicing specializes the sequential function generated for each node into functions f, g, and *next*, as described in Section 6.2;
9. Dead-code removal eliminates useless code from functions. For instance, derivatives need not be computed by the *next* function and values of zero-crossings are surely false during integration;
10. The sequential code is translated to C code.

The compiler passes in gray in Figure 2 are those that must be modified in, or added to (dashed borders), a traditional synchronous language compiler. The modifications are relatively minor—around 10% of each pass—and do not require major changes to the existing architecture. Together with the new passes, they amount to 5% of the total code size of the compiler.

$d ::= \text{let } x = e \mid \text{let } k\ f(pi) = pi \text{ where } E \mid d; d$

$e ::= x \mid v \mid op(e, \ldots, e) \mid \text{pre}(e) \mid e \rightarrow e \mid \text{last } x \mid f(e, \ldots, e) \mid (e, \ldots, e) \mid \text{up}(e)$

$p ::= x \mid (x, \ldots, x)$

$pi ::= xi \mid xi, \ldots, xi$

$xi ::= x \mid x \text{ last } e \mid x \text{ default } e$

$E ::= p = e \mid \text{der } x = e \mid \text{if } e \text{ then } E \text{ else } E \mid \text{present } e \text{ then } E \text{ else } E$
$\qquad \mid \text{reset } E \text{ every } e \mid \text{local } pi \text{ in } E \mid \text{do } E \text{ and} \ldots E \text{ done}$

$k ::= \text{D} \mid \text{C} \mid \text{A}$

Fig. 3. A synchronous kernel with ODEs

4   A Synchronous Language Kernel with ODEs

We consider a synchronous language extended with control structures and ODEs. The synchronous sub-language, that is, with ODEs removed, is the subset of SCADE 6 [13] described in [10]. Compared to ZÉLUS [7], the language considered here does not include hierarchical automata, but they can be translated into the presented kernel [2]. The abstract syntax given in Figure 3 is distilled from the two concrete languages on which this material is based.

A program is a sequence of definitions (d), of either a value ($\text{let } x = e$) that binds the value of expression e to x, or a function ($\text{let } k\ f(pi) = pi \text{ where } E$). In a function definition, k is the kind of the function f, pi denotes formal parameters, and the result is the value of an expression e which may contain variables defined in the auxiliary equations E. There are three kinds: $k = \text{A}$ (omitted in the concrete syntax) signifies a *combinational* function like, for example, addition; $k = \text{D}$ (written node in the concrete syntax) signifies a function that must be activated at discrete instants (typically a LUSTRE or SCADE node); $k = \text{C}$ (written hybrid in the concrete syntax) signifies a function that may contain ODEs and which must be activated in continuous-time. An expression e is either a variable (x), an immediate value (v), for example, a boolean, integer or floating point constant, the point-wise application of an imported function (op) like $+$, $*$, or $\text{not}(\cdot)$, an uninitialized delay $(\text{pre}(e))$, an initialization $(e_1 \rightarrow e_2)$, the previous value of a state variable $(\text{last } x)$, a function application $(f(e))$, a tuple $(e, \ldots, e)$ or a rising zero-crossing detection $(\text{up}(e))$. A pattern p is a list of identifiers. pi is a list of parameters where a variable x can be assigned a default value e ($x \text{ default } e$) or declared as a state initialized with e ($x \text{ last } e$). An equation (E) is either an equality between a pattern and an expression which must hold at every instant $(p = e)$; the definition of the current derivative of x ($\text{der } x = e$); a conditional that activates a branch according to the value of a boolean expression ($\text{if } e \text{ then } E_1 \text{ else } E_2$), or a variant that operates on event expressions ($\text{present } e \text{ then } E_1 \text{ else } E_2$); a reset on a condition e ($\text{reset } E \text{ every } e$); a localization of variables ($\text{local } xi \text{ in } E$); or a synchronous composition of zero or more equations ($\text{do } E \text{ and} \ldots E \text{ done}$).

In this language kernel, a synchronous function taking input streams `tick` and `res`, and returning the number of instants when `tick` is true, reset every time `res` is true, is written: ♣[5]

```
let node counting(tick, res) = o where
  reset
    local c last 0 in
    do if tick then do c = last c + 1 done and o = c done
  every res
```

The `if`/`then` abbreviates a conditional with an empty `else` branch. `c` is declared to be a local variable initialized to 0 (the notation is borrowed from SCADE 6). Several streams are defined in `counting` such that $\forall n \geq 0, o(n) = c(n)$ with:

1. $(\text{last c})(0) = 0$ and $\forall n > 0, \text{last c}(n) = \textit{if } \text{res}(n) \textit{ then } 0 \textit{ else } c(n-1)$
2. $c(n) = \textit{if } \text{tick}(n) \textit{ then } \text{last c}(n) + 1 \textit{ else } \text{last c}(n)$

The `node` keyword $(k = \text{D})$ in the definition signals that this program is purely synchronous. As a first program in the extended language we write the classic 'bouncing ball' program with a `hybrid` $(k = \text{C})$ declaration: ♣

```
let hybrid bouncing(y0, y'0) = (y last y0) where
  local y' last y'0 in
  do  der y = y'
  and present up(-. last y) then do y' = -0.8 *. last y' done
      else do der y' = -. g done
```

where `g` is a global constant for gravity. Given initial position `y0` and speed `y'0`, this program returns the current position `y`. The derivative of `y'` is $-g$ and `y'` is reset to $-0.8 \cdot \text{last } y'$ when $\text{last } y'$, the left-limit of the signal `y`, becomes zero.

In the following, we suppose that programs have passed the static checking defined in [3] and that they are causally correct [1].

5   A Clocked Data-Flow Internal Language

We now introduce the internal clocked data-flow language into which the input language is translated. Its syntax is defined in Figure 4. Compared to the previous language, the body of a function is now a set of equations of the form $(x_i = a_i)_{x_i \in I}$ where the x_i are pairwise distinct variables and each a_i is an expression e annotated with a clock ck: e is only evaluated when the boolean formula ck evaluates to true. The base clock is denoted `base`; it is the constant `true`. ck `on` a is true when both ck and a are true. An expression e^{ck} with clock $ck = (\text{base on } a_1 \cdots) \text{ on } a_n$ is evaluated only when for all $1 \leq i \leq n$, a_i is true. An expression e is either a variable (x), an immediate value (v), the application of an operator $(op(a, \ldots, a))$, the i-th element of a tuple a $(\text{get}(a, i))$, a delay initialized with a constant $(v \text{ fby } a)$, an uninitialized delay $(\text{pre}(a))$, an integrator whose derivative is a_1 and whose output is a_2 $(\text{integr}(a_1, a_2))$, a function

---

[5] The ♣'s link to http://zelus.di.ens.fr/cc2015/, which contains both examples in ZÉLUS and SCADE hybrid, and the C code generated by the latter's compiler.

$$d ::= \mathtt{let}\ x = c\ |\ \mathtt{let}\ k\ f(p) = a\ \mathtt{where}\ C\ |\ d; d$$

$$a ::= e^{ck}$$

$$e ::= x\ |\ v\ |\ op(a, \ldots, a)\ |\ \mathtt{get}(a, i)\ |\ v\ \mathtt{fby}\ a\ |\ \mathtt{pre}(a)\ |\ \mathtt{integr}(a, a)$$
$$|\ f(a, \ldots, a)\ \mathtt{every}\ a\ |\ (a, \ldots, a)\ |\ \mathtt{up}(a)\ |\ \mathtt{merge}(a, a, a)\ |\ a\ \mathtt{when}\ a$$

$$p ::= x\ |\ (x, \ldots, x)$$

$$C ::= (x_i = a_i)_{x_i \in I}$$

$$ck ::= \mathtt{base}\ |\ ck\ \mathtt{on}\ a$$

$$k ::= \mathtt{D}\ |\ \mathtt{C}\ |\ \mathtt{A}$$

Fig. 4. A clocked data-flow internal language

application reset when a signal a is true ($f(a_1, \ldots, a_n)\ \mathtt{every}\ a$), an n-tuple of values ($a_1, \ldots, a_n$), the zero-crossing detection operator ($\mathtt{up}(a)$), the combination of signals a_1 and a_2 according to the boolean signal a ($\mathtt{merge}(a, a_1, a_2)$), or a signal a_1 sampled on condition a_2 ($a_1\ \mathtt{when}\ a_2$),

This clocked internal representation is a Single Static Assignment (SSA) representation [11]. Every variable x has a single definition and the clock expression defines when it is computed.

The main novelty with respect to the clocked internal language of [6] is the introduction of operators $\mathtt{integr}(a_1, a_2)$ and $\mathtt{up}(a)$.

5.1 Translation

The translation from a synchronous data-flow language with the control structures if/then/else, present/else and reset/every into clocked data-flow equations is defined in [10]. The SCADE Suite KCG code generator follows the same algorithm. We illustrate the translation on three kinds of examples.

Translation of Delays and Conditionals. In the example below, z is an input, x_1 and x_2 are local variables, and the last value of x_1 is initialized with 42:

```
local x₁ last 42, x₂ in
if  z then do x₁ = 1 + last x₁ and x₂ = 1 + (0 fby (x₂ + 2)) done
else do x₂ = 0 done
```

The translation of the above program returns the following set of clocked equations. To simplify the notation, we only expose the clocks of top-level expressions.

$$x_1 = \mathtt{merge}(z, 1 + (m_1\ \mathtt{when}\ z), m_1\ \mathtt{when}\ \mathtt{not}(z))^{\mathtt{base}}$$

$$m_1 = (42\ \mathtt{fby}\ x_1)^{\mathtt{base}}$$

$$x_2 = \mathtt{merge}(z, 1 + m_2, 0)^{\mathtt{base}}$$

$$m_2 = (0\ \mathtt{fby}\ ((x_2\ \mathtt{when}\ z) + 2))^{\mathtt{base\ on}\ z}$$

In this translation, the conditional branch for when z is false is implicitly completed with the equation $x_1 = $ last x_1, that is, x_1 is maintained. The value of last x_1 is stored in m_1. It is the previous value of x_1 on the clock where x_1 is defined: here, the base clock. The initialized delay 0 fby x_2 is local to a branch, and thus equal to the last value that was observed on x_2. This observation is made only when z is true, that is, when clock base on z is true.

Translation of Nested Resets. The second example illustrates the translation of the reset construct and its effect on unit delays.

```
reset
    if c then do x₁ = 1 else x₁ = (0 fby x₁) + 1 done
    reset
        x₂ = (1 fby x₂) + 1
    every k₂
every k₁
```

The condition of a reset is propagated recursively to every stateful computation within the reset. This is the case for unit delays and applications of stateful functions. The above program is first translated into:

$$x_1 = \mathtt{merge}(c, 1, m_1 + 1)^{\mathtt{base}}$$
$$x_2 = (m_2 + 1)^{\mathtt{base}}$$
$$m_1 = (0 \ \mathtt{fby} \ x_1)^{\mathtt{base \ on \ not}(c)} \ every \ k_1{}^{\mathtt{base}}$$
$$m_2 = (1 \ \mathtt{fby} \ x_2)^{\mathtt{base}} \ every \ k_1{}^{\mathtt{base}} \ or \ k_2{}^{\mathtt{base}}$$

The notation $(0 \ \mathtt{fby} \ x_1)^{\mathtt{base \ on \ not}(c)} \ every \ k_1{}^{\mathtt{base}}$ defines the sequence m_1 whose value is reset to 0 every time k_1 is true. Resets of unit delays are translated into regular clocked equations. We replace the equations for m_1 and m_2 with:

$$m_1 = \mathtt{merge}(k_1, 0, r_1 \ \mathtt{when} \ \mathtt{not}(k_1))^{\mathtt{base}}$$
$$r_1 = (0 \ \mathtt{fby} \ \mathtt{merge}(c, m_1 \ \mathtt{when} \ c, x_1 \ \mathtt{when} \ \mathtt{not}(c)))^{\mathtt{base}}$$
$$m_2 = \mathtt{merge}(k_1, 1, \mathtt{merge}(k_2, 1, r_2) \ \mathtt{when} \ \mathtt{not}(k_1))^{\mathtt{base}}$$
$$r_2 = (1 \ \mathtt{fby} \ x_2)^{\mathtt{base}}$$

Translation of Integrators. The bouncing ball program from Section 4 becomes:

$$y = (y_0 \ \text{->} \ ly)^{\mathtt{base}}$$
$$ly = \mathtt{integr}(y', y)^{\mathtt{base}}$$
$$ly' = \mathtt{integr}(t_1, y')^{\mathtt{base}}$$
$$y' = \mathtt{merge}(z, -0.8 {*}. ly' \ \mathtt{when} \ z, ly' \ \mathtt{when} \ \mathtt{not}(z))^{\mathtt{base}}$$
$$t_1 = \mathtt{merge}(z, 0.0, -.g)^{\mathtt{base}}$$
$$z = \mathtt{up}(-. \ ly)^{\mathtt{base}}$$

The variable y' changes only when z is true and keeps its last value ly' otherwise. The operation $\mathtt{integr}(a_1, a_2)$ defines a signal as the integration of a_1 in the continuous mode (C) and as a_2 in the discrete mode (D). The derivative of ly' is $-.g$ when z is false and otherwise it is 0.0 (constant ly').

5.2   Static Data-Flow Dependencies and Well Formed Schedules

Code is generated in two steps: (a) equations are first statically scheduled according to data-flow dependencies, (b) every equation is translated into an imperative statement in a target sequential language. Data-flow dependencies are defined as in LUSTRE [14]: an expression a which reads a variable x, must be scheduled after x. The dependency relation is reversed when x is defined by a delay like, for example, $x = v\ \mathtt{fby}\ a_1$. In this case a must be scheduled before x. In other words, delays break dependency relations. The integrator $x = \mathtt{integr}(a_1, a_2)$ plays the role of a delay: x does not depend instantaneously on variables in a_1 or in a_2, and any read of x must be performed before x is defined.

Equations are normalized so that unit delays, integrators, function calls, and zero-crossings appear only at the roots of defining expressions. We partition expressions into three classes: *strict* (se), *delayed* (de) and *controlled* (ce). An expression is strict if its output depends instantaneously on its inputs, otherwise it is delayed. A controlled expression ce is strict.

$$
\begin{aligned}
eq &::= x = ce^{ck} \mid x = f(sa, \ldots, sa)\,\mathtt{every}\,sa^{ck} \mid x = de^{ck} \\
sa &::= se^{ck} \\
ca &::= ce^{ck} \\
se &::= x \mid v \mid op(sa, \ldots, sa) \mid \mathtt{get}(sa, i) \mid (sa, \ldots, sa) \mid sa\,\mathtt{when}\,sa \\
ce &::= se \mid \mathtt{merge}(sa, ca, ca) \mid ca\,\mathtt{when}\,sa \\
de &::= \mathtt{pre}(ca) \mid v\,\mathtt{fby}\,ca \mid \mathtt{integr}(ca, ca) \mid \mathtt{up}(ca)
\end{aligned}
$$

A controlled expression is essentially a tree of $\mathtt{merge}(\cdot, \cdot, \cdot)$ expressions terminated by the application of a primitive, a variable, or a constant. Merges are implemented as nested conditionals.

Let $Read(a)$ denote the set of variables read by a. Given a set of normalized equations $C = (x_i = a_i)_{x_i \in I}$, a valid schedule $Schedule(\cdot) : I \to \{1 \ldots |I|\}$ is a one-to-one function such that, for all $x_i \in I$ and $x_j \in Read(a_i) \cap I$:

1. if a_i is strict, $Schedule(x_j) < Schedule(x_i)$, and,
2. if a_i is delayed, $Schedule(x_i) \le Schedule(x_j)$.

Checking that a given sequence of equations fulfills the well formation rules can be done in polynomial time. Schedules can be obtained by topological sorting but the resulting code is poor. Finding a schedule that minimizes the number of openings and closings of control structures is NP-hard [22]. In the following, if $C = (x_i = a_i)_{x_i \in I}$, we suppose the existence of a scheduling function $SchedEq(C)$ that returns a sequence of scheduled equations.

We are now ready to define the sequential target language.

$$md \quad ::= \mathtt{let}\, x = c \mid \mathtt{let}\, f = \mathtt{class}\langle M, I, (method_i(p_i) = e_i \,\mathtt{where}\, S_i)_{i \in [1..n]}\rangle \mid md; md$$

$$M \quad ::= [x : m[= v]; \ldots; x : m[= v]]$$

$$I \quad ::= [o : f; \ldots; o : f]$$

$$m \quad ::= Discrete \mid Zero \mid Cont$$

$$e \quad ::= v \mid lv \mid \mathtt{get}(e, i) \mid op(e, \ldots, e) \mid o.method(e, \ldots, e) \mid (e, \ldots, e)$$

$$S \quad ::= () \mid lv \leftarrow e \mid S\,;\,S \mid \mathtt{var}\, x, \ldots, x\, \mathtt{in}\, S \mid \mathtt{if}\, c\, \mathtt{then}\, S\, \mathtt{else}\, S$$

$$R, L ::= S; \ldots; S$$

$$lv \quad ::= x \mid lv.field \mid \mathtt{state}\,(x)$$

Fig. 5. A simple object-based language

6   A Sequential Object Language

We define a simple object-based language called SOL to serve as an intermediate language in the translation. It is designed to be easily translatable into target languages like C and JAVA and resembles the language introduced in [6] and used in KCG. Each stateful function in the source language is translated into a class with an internal memory that a collection of methods act on. The syntax is given in Figure 5.

A program is a sequence of constant and class definitions (md). Class definitions take the form $\mathtt{class}\langle M, I, (method_i(p_i) = e_i \,\mathtt{where}\, S_i)_{i \in [1..n]}\rangle$ and comprise a list M of memories, a list I of instances and a list of methods. A memory entry $[x : m[= v]]$ defines a variable x of kind m, optionally initialized to a constant v. A memory x is either a discrete state variable $(Discrete)$, a zero-crossing $(Zero)$, or a continuous state variable $(Cont)$. An instance entry $[o : f]$ stores the internal memory of a nested function f. The memories, instances, and methods in a class must be pair-wise distinct.

An expression (e) is either an immediate value (v), an access to the value of a variable (lv), an access to a tuple $(\mathtt{get}(e, i))$, an application of an operation to an argument $(op(e, \ldots, e))$, a method invocation $(o.method(e, \ldots, e))$, or a tuple $((e_1, \ldots, e_n))$. An instruction (S) is either void $(())$, an assignment of the value of e to a left value lv $(lv \leftarrow e)$, a sequence $(S_1\,;\,S_2)$, the declaration of local variables $(\mathtt{var}\, x_1, \ldots, x_n\, \mathtt{in}\, S)$, or a conditional $(\mathtt{if}\, e\, \mathtt{then}\, S_1\, \mathtt{else}\, S_2)$.

To make an analogy with object-oriented programming, memories are instance variables of a class. The value of a variable x of kind $Discrete$ is read from $\mathtt{state}\,(x)$ and is modified by writing $\mathtt{state}\,(x) \leftarrow c$. Variables x of kind $Zero$ are used to compile $\mathtt{up}(e)$ expressions. Each x has two fields: $\mathtt{state}\,(x).zin$ is a boolean set to true only when a zero-crossing on x has been detected, and $\mathtt{state}\,(x).zout$ stores the current value of the expression for monitoring during integration. A variable x of kind $Cont$ is a continuous state variable: $\mathtt{state}\,(x).der$ is its instantaneous derivative and $\mathtt{state}\,(x).pos$ its value.

We do not present the translation from SOL to C code (see [6] for details).

6.1   Producing a Single Step Function

We now describe the translation of the clocked internal language into SOL code. Every function definition is translated into a class with two methods: a method *reset* which initializes the internal memory and a method *step* which, given an internal memory and current input value, returns an output and updates the internal memory. The translation follows the description given in [6] and implemented in KCG. Here we describe the novelties related to ODEs and zero-crossings. Given an environment ρ, an expression e, and an equation E:

- $TrExp(\rho)(e)$ returns an expression of the target language.
- $TrIn(\rho)(lv)(a)$ translates a and returns an assignment S that stores the result of a into the left value lv.
- $TrEq(\rho)(eq) = \langle I, R, L \rangle$ translates an equation eq and returns a set of instances I, a sequence of instructions R to be executed at initialization, and a sequence of instructions L to be executed at every step.
- $TrEq(\rho)(eq_1 \cdots eq_n) = \langle I, R, L \rangle$ translates sequences of equations $eq_1 \cdots eq_n$.

An environment ρ associates a name and a kind to every local name in the source program. A name is either a variable (kind *Var*) or a memory (kind *Mem(m)*). We distinguish three kinds of memories: discrete (*Discrete*), zero-crossing (*Zero*), and continuous (*Cont*). Memories can optionally be initialized.

$$\rho ::= [\,] \mid \rho, x : s \qquad s ::= Var \mid Mem(m) \mid Mem(m) = v$$

The main function translates global definitions of values and functions into global values and classes. It uses auxiliary functions whose definitions follow.[6]

$TrDef(\text{let } k\, f(p) = a \text{ where } C) =$
   $\quad \text{let } \rho = Env(C) \text{ in let } M, (x_1, \ldots, x_n) = mem(\rho) \text{ in}$
   $\quad \text{let } [eq_1 \cdots eq_n] = SchedEq(C) \text{ in}$
   $\quad \text{let } (\langle I_i, R_i, L_i \rangle = TrEq(\rho)(eq_i))_{i \in [1..n]} \text{ in}$
   $\quad \text{let } e = TrExp(\rho)(a) \text{ in}$
   $\quad \text{let } I = I_1 + \cdots + I_n \text{ and } R = R_1; \ldots; R_n \text{ and } L = L_1; \ldots; L_n \text{ in}$
   $\quad \text{let } f = \text{class}\langle M, I, reset = R \; step(p) = e \text{ where var } x_1, \ldots, x_n \text{ in } L\rangle$

$TrDef(\text{let } x = e) = \text{let } x = TrExp([\,])(e)$

First of all, equations in C must conform to the well formation rules defined in Section 5.2. $Env(C)$ builds the environment associated to C and $\rho(x_i)$ defines the kind associated to a defined variable from C:

$$Env(\{x_1 = a_1, \ldots, x_n = a_n\}) = Env(x_1 = a_1) + \cdots Env(x_n = a_n)$$
$$Env(x = \text{pre}(a)^{ck}) = [x : Mem(Discrete)]$$
$$Env(x = \text{up}(e)^{ck}) = [x : Mem(Zero)]$$
$$Env(x = \text{integr}(a_1, a_2)^{ck}) = [x : Mem(Cont)]$$
$$Env(x = a) = [x : Var] \text{ otherwise}$$

---

[6] The *let* used in defining the translation function is not the syntactic **let** of programs.

$$
\begin{aligned}
TrExp(\rho)(v) &= v \\
TrExp(\rho)(x) &= state(\rho)(x) \\
TrExp(\rho)(\mathbf{get}(a,i)) &= \mathbf{get}(TrExp(\rho)(a),i) \\
TrExp(\rho)(op(a_1,\ldots,a_n)) &= let\ (c_i = TrExp(\rho)(a_i))_{i\in[1..n]}\ in\ op(c_1,\ldots,c_n) \\
TrExp(\rho)((a_1,\ldots,a_n)) &= let\ (c_i = TrExp(\rho)(a_i))_{i\in[1..n]}\ in\ (c_1,\ldots,c_n) \\
TrExp(\rho)(a_1\ \mathbf{when}\ a_2) &= TrExp(\rho)(a_1) \\
TrIn(\rho)(lv)(a_1\ \mathbf{when}\ a_2) &= TrIn(\rho)(lv)(a_1) \\
TrIn(\rho)(lv)(\mathbf{merge}(a_1,a_2,a_3)) &= \mathbf{if}\ TrExp(\rho)(a_1)\ \mathbf{then}\ TrIn(\rho)(lv)(a_2) \\
&\quad\ \mathbf{else}\ TrIn(\rho)(lv)(a_3) \\
TrIn(\rho)(lv)(a) &= lv \leftarrow TrExp(\rho)(a) \quad \text{otherwise}
\end{aligned}
$$

Fig. 6. The translation function for combinatorial expressions

$mem(\rho)$ returns a pair $M,(x_1,\ldots,x_n)$ where M is an environment of memories (kind $Mem(m)$), and $(x1,\ldots,x_n)$ is a set of variables (kind Var).

The set of equations C is statically scheduled with an auxiliary function $SchedEq(C)$. Every equation is translated into a triple $\langle I_i, R_i, L_i\rangle$. The set of instances $I_1,\ldots,I_n$ are gathered, checking that defined names appear only once. Finally, the code associated to f is a class with a set of memories M, a set of instances I and two methods: *reset* is the initialization method used to reset all internal states, and *step* is the step function parameterized by p.

Given a clock expression ck and an instruction S, $Control(ck)(S)$ returns an instruction that executes S only when ck is true. We write **if** e **then** S as a shortcut for **if** e **then** S **else** $()$.

$$
\begin{aligned}
Control(\mathbf{base})(S) &= S \\
Control(ck\ \mathbf{on}\ e)(S) &= Control(ck)(\mathbf{if}\ e\ \mathbf{then}\ S)
\end{aligned}
$$

The translation function for expressions is defined in Figure 6 and raises no difficulties. It uses the auxiliary function $state(\rho)(x)$:

$$
state(\rho)(x) = \begin{cases}
\mathbf{state}\,(x) & \text{if}\ \rho(x) = Mem(Discrete) \\
\mathbf{state}\,(x).zin & \text{if}\ \rho(x) = Mem(Zero) \\
\mathbf{state}\,(x).pos & \text{if}\ \rho(x) = Mem(Cont) \\
x & \text{otherwise}
\end{cases}
$$

Access to a discrete state variable is written $\mathbf{state}\,(x)$. The current value of a zero-crossing event (kind $= Zero$) is stored into $\mathbf{state}\,(x).zin$ while the current value of a continuous state variable (kind $= Cont$) is stored into $\mathbf{state}\,(x).pos$.

The translation function for equations is given in Figure 7:

$$TrEq(\rho)(x = (f(\boldsymbol{a}) \text{ every } e^{ck'})^{ck}) = let\ (e_i = TrExp(\rho)(a_i))_{i \in [1..n]}\ in$$

$$let\ e = TrExp(\rho)(e^{ck'})\ in$$

$$let\ L = Control(ck')(\text{if } e \text{ then } o.reset);$$
$$Control(ck)(x \leftarrow o.step(e_1, \ldots, e_n))$$
$$in\ \langle [o : f], o.reset, L \rangle$$

$$TrEq(\rho)(x = \mathbf{pre}(a)^{ck}) \quad = let\ S = TrIn(\rho)(\mathbf{state}\,(x))(a)\ in$$
$$\langle [\,], [\,], Control(ck)(S) \rangle$$

$$TrEq(\rho)(x = v \text{ fby } a^{ck}) \quad = let\ S = TrIn(\rho)(\mathbf{state}\,(x))(a)\ in$$
$$\langle [\,], \mathbf{state}\,(x) \leftarrow v, Control(ck)(S) \rangle$$

$$TrEq(\rho)(x = \mathbf{integr}(a_1, a_2)^{ck}) \quad = let\ S_1 = TrIn(\rho)(\mathbf{state}\,(x).der)(a_1)\ in$$
$$let\ S_2 = TrIn(\rho)(\mathbf{state}\,(x).pos)(a_2)\ in$$
$$\langle [\,], [\,], Control(ck)(S_1; S_2) \rangle$$

$$TrEq(\rho)(x = \mathbf{up}(a)^{ck}) \quad = Control(ck)(TrIn(\rho)(\mathbf{state}\,(x).zout)(a))$$

$$TrEq(\rho)(x = e^{ck}) \quad = Control(ck)(TrIn(\rho)(state(\rho)(x))(a))\ \text{otherwise}$$

Fig. 7. The translation function for equations

1. The translation of a function application $(f(a_1, \ldots, a_n) \text{ every } e^{ck'})^{ck}$ defines a fresh instance $[o : f]$. This instance is reset by calling method $o.reset$ every time ck' on e is true. It is activated by calling method $o.step$ when ck is true.
2. A unit delay $\mathbf{pre}(a)$ or v fby a is translated into a clocked assignment to a state variable.
3. An integrator is translated into two assignments: one defining the current derivative $\mathbf{state}\,(x).der$, and the other defining the current value of the continuous state $\mathbf{state}\,(x).pos$.
4. A zero-crossing is translated into an equation that defines the current value of the signal to observe $(\mathbf{state}\,(x).zout)$.

6.2   Slicing

The translation to SOL generates a *step* method for each function declaration. Functions declared to be discrete-time $(k = \mathtt{D})$ are regular synchronous functions and they require no additional treatment. But functions declared to be continuous-time $(k = \mathtt{C})$ require specializing the method *step* to obtain the three functions f, g and *next* introduced in Section 2:

– The *next* function is obtained by copying the body of *step* and removing the computation of derivatives, that is, writes to the $\mathbf{state}\,(x).der$ field of memories of kind *Cont*, and the computation of zero-crossings, that is, writes to the $\mathbf{state}\,(z).zout$ field of memories of kind *Zero*.

- A method called *cont* is added to compute the values of derivatives and zero-crossing signals. Functions f and g call this method and then return, respectively, the computed derivatives and the computed zero-crossings. The *cont* method is obtained by removing all code activated on a discrete clock, that is, by replacing all reads of the state $(z).zin$ fields of memories of kind *Zero* with *false*. Indeed, we know that the status z of zero-crossings is always false in the continuous mode C. Writes to the state $(x).pos$ field of memories of kind *Cont* can also be removed. Finally, all conditions on an event (variables of type zero) are replaced with the value *false*.

The goal of this transformation is to optimize the generated code and to avoid useless computation. The behavior of the generated code is not changed—the code removed, for a given mode, is either never activated or computes values that are never read. Traditional optimizations like constant propagation and dead-code removal can be applied after slicing to further simplify each method.

6.3   Transferring Data to and from a Solver

The transformations described above scatter the values of continuous states and zero-crossings across the memories of the objects that comprise a program. Numerical solvers must able to read and write these memories in order to perform simulations. A simple solution is to augment each object with new methods that copy values to and from the memory fields and arrays provided by a solver. When generating C code, another approach is to define a global array of pointers to the continuous states that can be used to read and write directly to memory fields. ZÉLUS implements the first solution; KCG implements the second.

7   Practical Experiments

7.1   Zélus with SUNDIALS

ZÉLUS is, at its core, essentially the language defined in Section 4. It is compiled into the intermediate language defined in Section 6, which is, in turn, translated directly into OCaml. To produce working simulations, the loop described at a high-level in Section 2 is implemented in two parts: (a) additional methods in the intermediate language, and, (b) a small run-time library.

The additional methods derivatives and crossings are specializations of the generated step function that present the interface expected by the run-time library. These functions contain assignments that copy between the vectors passed by a numerical solver and the internal variables described in Section 6.1.

Another additional method implements the looping implied by the transition labelled 'encore' in Figure 1. It makes an initial step that only updates the internal values of 'last' variables, then a discrete step with zero-crossings from the solver, and then further discrete steps, without solver zero-crossings, until the calculated horizon exceeds the current simulation time. There is a trade-off to make between code generated by the compiler and code implemented in the run-time library. In this case, looping within the generated code allows us to exploit several invariants on the values of internal variables.

The run-time library implements the other transitions of Figure 1 and manages numerical solver details. The library declares generic interfaces for 'state solvers' and 'zero-crossing solvers'. The state solver interface comprises functions for initialization, reinitialization, advancing the solution by one step, and interpolating between the last step and the current step. The zero-crossing solver interface includes almost the same functions, but with different arguments, except that interpolation between steps is replaced by a function for finding instants of zero-crossing between two steps. Modules satisfying these two interfaces are combined by generic code to satisfy the 'solver' interface described in Section 2.

7.2   SCADE with FMIs

In a second experiment, we extended the Scade Suite KCG code generator of SCADE 6 using the ideas presented in earlier sections. This generator produces a C code instantiation of a 'Functional Mockup Unit' (FMU) that respects the *FMI for Model Exchange 1.0 standard* [19]. An FMU describes a mix of ODEs and discrete events. It is simulated, with or without other components, by an external solver provided by a host. The execution model of FMI [19, Section 2.9] resembles the scheme described in Section 2 and is readily adapted to give the behavior described by Figure 1.

The code generated by the compiler is linked to a run-time library which implements the functions required by the FMI standard. There are generic functions to instantiate and terminate the FMU, to enable logging, to set the simulation time, and so on. The implementation of the set function for continuous states (`fmiSetContinuousStates`), called by the host before an event, copies the given inputs to the corresponding continuous states lx. The get function (`fmiGetContinuousStates`) returns the new value of lx to the solver after an event. Similar functions exist for inputs, outputs, and zero-crossings (termed *event indicators* in FMI). At any instant, the first of these set or get functions calls the *cont* method of the root node; subsequent calls used cached values. In response to a discrete event (`fmiEventUpdate`), the *step* method is called once, and then repeatedly while $encore(n+1)$ is true. For the additional calls, the status of $z(n)$ is computed by comparing the current value of zero-crossing signals with their values after the previous discrete step. The *reinit* flag, which is set if a continuous state is reset, corresponds to the `stateValuesChanged` field of the `fmiEventInfo` input structure of `fmiEventUpdate`.

8   Discussion and Related Works

This work is related to the definition of an operational semantics for block diagram languages that mix discrete and continuous time behaviors [17]. A unified semantics is given to PTOLEMYII [21] in which basic operators are characterized by four atomic step functions that depend on input, internal state, and simulation time and that act on an internal state according to a calling policy [23].

This semantics is modular in the sense that any composition of operators results in the same four functions. It generalizes the operational semantics of explicit hybrid modelers presented in [17] and [12]. The idea that a state transformer can be represented by a collection of atomic functions is much older and has been implemented since the late 1990s in SIMULINK s-functions[7]. It is also the basis of the FMI and FMU standards for model exchange and co-simulation. In our compiler organization, the four functions would correspond to four methods of a SOL machine. The novelty is not the representation of a state transformer as a set of methods but rather the production of those methods in a traceable way that recycles an existing synchronous compiler infrastructure. The result is not an interpreter, as in [23], but a compiler that produces statically scheduled sequential code.

The observation that the synchronous model could be leveraged to model the simulation engine of hybrid systems was made by Lee and Zheng [18]. Our contribution is the use of a synchronous compiler infrastructure to effectively build a hybrid modeling language.

The present work deliberately avoids considering the early compiler stages that perform static typing and causality analysis. These stages are defined in [3,1] for a similar language kernel. Presented with a program that has not passed static checking and causality analysis, code generation either fails or generates incorrect code. For instance, the equation x = x + 1 cannot be statically scheduled according to Section 5.2 and code generation thus fails. Activating an equation x = 0 -> pre x + 1 in a continuous block would produce imperative code that increments x during integration.

Previous work on ZÉLUS [7] compiled ODEs to purely synchronous code by adding new inputs and outputs to each continuous node. For each continuous state, the node takes as input the value computed by the solver and returns the derivative and the new value of the continuous state. We have chosen here to delay this translation to the generation of sequential code. This approach is much easier to integrate into more complex languages like SCADE 6 with higher-order constructs like iterators [20]. It also avoids the cost of copying the added arguments at every function call.

9   Conclusion

This full-scale experimental validation confirms the interest of building a hybrid systems modeling language on top of a synchronous language. We were surprised to discover that the extension of SCADE 6 with hybrid features required only 5% extra lines of code in total. It confirms the versatility of the compiler architecture of SCADE 6, which is based on successive rewritings of the source program into several intermediate languages.

Moreover, while sequential code generation in hybrid modeling tools is routinely used for efficient simulation, it is little used or not used at all to produce target embedded code in critical applications that are submitted to strong safety

---

[7] http://www.mathworks.com/help/pdf_doc/simulink/sfunctions.pdf

requirements. This results in a break in the development chain: parts of applications must be rewritten into either sequential or synchronous programs, and all properties verified on the source model cannot be trusted and have to be re-verified on the target code. The precise definition of code generation, built on the proven compiler infrastructure of a synchronous language avoids the rewriting of control software and may also increase confidence in simulation results.

Acknowledgments. We warmly thank Albert Benveniste and the anonymous reviewers for their helpful remarks on this paper.

References

1. Benveniste, A., Bourke, T., Caillaud, B., Pagano, B., Pouzet, M.: A type-based analysis of causality loops in hybrid systems modelers. In: Int. Conf. Hybrid Systems: Computation and Control (HSCC 2014). ACM Press, Berlin (2014)
2. Benveniste, A., Bourke, T., Caillaud, B., Pouzet, M.: A Hybrid Synchronous Language with Hierarchical Automata: Static Typing and Translation to Synchronous Code. In: ACM SIGPLAN/SIGBED Conf. on Embedded Software (EMSOFT 2011), Taipei, Taiwan (October 2011)
3. Benveniste, A., Bourke, T., Caillaud, B., Pouzet, M.: Divide and recycle: types and compilation for a hybrid synchronous language. In: ACM SIGPLAN/SIGBED Conf. on Languages, Compilers, Tools and Theory for Embedded Systems (LCTES 2011), Chicago, USA (April 2011)
4. Benveniste, A., Bourke, T., Caillaud, B., Pouzet, M.: Non-Standard Semantics of Hybrid Systems Modelers. Journal of Computer and System Sciences (JCSS) 78(3), 877–910 (2012), Special issue in honor of Amir Pnueli
5. Benveniste, A., Caspi, P., Edwards, S., Halbwachs, N., Le Guernic, P., de Simone, R.: The synchronous languages 12 years later. Proc. IEEE 91(1) (January 2003)
6. Biernacki, D., Colaco, J.-L., Hamon, G., Pouzet, M.: Clock-directed modular code generation of synchronous data-flow languages. In: ACM Int. Conf. Languages, Compilers and Tools for Embedded Systems (LCTES), Tucson, Arizona (June 2008)
7. Bourke, T., Pouzet, M.: Zélus, a Synchronous Language with ODEs. In: Int. Conf. on Hybrid Systems: Computation and Control (HSCC 2013). ACM, Philadelphia (2013)
8. Carloni, L., Benedetto, M.D.D., Pinto, A., Sangiovanni-Vincentelli, A.: Modeling Techniques, Programming Languages, Design Toolsets and Interchange Formats for Hybrid Systems. Technical report, IST-2001-38314 WPHS, Columbus Project (March 2004)
9. Caspi, P., Curic, A., Maignan, A., Sofronis, C., Tripakis, S.: Translating Discrete-Time Simulink to Lustre. ACM Trans. on Embedded Computing Systems (2005), Special Issue on Embedded Software
10. Colaço, J.-L., Pagano, B., Pouzet, M.: A Conservative Extension of Synchronous Data-flow with State Machines. In: ACM Int. Conf. on Embedded Software (EMSOFT 2005), Jersey city, New Jersey, USA (September 2005)
11. Cytron, R., Ferrante, J., Rosen, B.K., Wegman, M.N., Zadeck, F.K.: Efficiently computing static single assignment form and the control dependence graph. ACM Trans. Program. Lang. Syst. 13(4), 451–490 (1991)

12. Denckla, B., Mosterman, P.: Stream and state-based semantics of hierarchy in block diagrams. In: Proc. of the 17th IFAC World Congress, pp. 7955–7960 (2008)
13. Esterel-Technologies. Scade language reference manual. Technical report, Esterel-Technologies (2014)
14. Halbwachs, N., Raymond, P., Ratel, C.: Generating efficient code from data-flow programs. In: 3rd Int. Symp. on Programming Language Implementation and Logic Programming, Passau, Germany (August 1991)
15. Harel, D.: StateCharts: A Visual Approach to Complex Systems. Science of Computer Programming 8(3), 231–275 (1987)
16. Hindmarsh, A.C., Brown, P.N., Grant, K.E., Lee, S.L., Serban, R., Shumaker, D.E., Woodward, C.S.: SUNDIALS: Suite of nonlinear and differential/algebraic equation solvers. ACM Trans. Mathematical Software 31(3), 363–396 (2005)
17. Lee, E.A., Zheng, H.: Operational semantics of hybrid systems. In: Morari, M., Thiele, L. (eds.) HSCC 2005. LNCS, vol. 3414, pp. 25–53. Springer, Heidelberg (2005)
18. Lee, E.A., Zheng, H.: Leveraging synchronous language principles for heterogeneous modeling and design of embedded systems. In: Int. Conf. on Embedded Software (EMSOFT 2007), Salzburg, Austria (September/October 2007)
19. MODELISAR. Functional Mock-up Interface for Model Exchange v1.0 (2010)
20. Morel, L.: Array iterators in Lustre: From a language extension to its exploitation in validation. EURASIP Journal on Embedded Systems (2007)
21. Ptolemaeus, C. (ed.): System Design, Modeling, and Simulation using Ptolemy II. Ptolemy.org (2014)
22. Raymond, P.: Compilation efficace d'un langage déclaratif synchrone: le générateur de code Lustre-v3. PhD thesis, Institut National Polytechnique de Grenoble (1991)
23. Tripakis, S., Stergiou, C., Shaver, C., Lee, E.A.: A modular formal semantics for Ptolemy. Mathematical Structures in Computer Science 23(04), 834–881 (2013)

Faster, Practical GLL Parsing

Ali Afroozeh and Anastasia Izmaylova

Centrum Wiskunde & Informatica, 1098 XG Amsterdam, The Netherlands
{ali.afroozeh, anastasia.izmaylova}@cwi.nl

Abstract. Generalized LL (GLL) parsing is an extension of recursive-descent (RD) parsing that supports all context-free grammars in cubic time and space. GLL parsers have the direct relationship with the grammar that RD parsers have, and therefore, compared to GLR, are easier to understand, debug, and extend. This makes GLL parsing attractive for parsing programming languages.

In this paper we propose a more efficient Graph-Structured Stack (GSS) for GLL parsing that leads to significant performance improvement. We also discuss a number of optimizations that further improve the performance of GLL. Finally, for practical scannerless parsing of programming languages, we show how common lexical disambiguation filters can be integrated in GLL parsing.

Our new formulation of GLL parsing is implemented as part of the Iguana parsing framework. We evaluate the effectiveness of our approach using a highly-ambiguous grammar and grammars of real programming languages. Our results, compared to the original GLL, show a speedup factor of 10 on the highly-ambiguous grammar, and a speedup factor of 1.5, 1.7, and 5.2 on the grammars of Java, C#, and OCaml, respectively.

1   Introduction

Developing efficient parsers for programming languages is a difficult task that is usually automated by a parser generator. Since Knuth's seminal paper [1] on LR parsing, and DeRemer's work on practical LR parsing (LALR) [2], parsers of many major programming languages have been constructed using LALR parser generators such as Yacc [3].

Grammars of most real programming languages, when written in their most natural form, are often ambiguous and do not fit deterministic classes of context-free grammars such as LR(k). Therefore, such grammars need to be gradually transformed to conform to these deterministic classes. Not only is this process time consuming and error prone, but the resulting derivation trees may also considerably differ from those of the original grammar. In addition, writing a deterministic grammar for a programming language requires the grammar writer to think more in terms of the parsing technology, rather than the intended grammar. Finally, maintaining a deterministic grammar is problematic. A real-world example is the grammar of Java. In the first version of the Java Language Specification [4], the grammar was represented in an LALR(1) form, but this format

© Springer-Verlag Berlin Heidelberg 2015
B. Franke (Ed.): CC 2015, LNCS 9031, pp. 89–108, 2015.
DOI: 10.1007/978-3-662-46663-6_5

has been abandoned in later versions, most likely due to the difficulties of maintaining an LALR(1) grammar as the language evolved.

Generalized LR (GLR) [5] is an extension of LR parsing that effectively handles shift/reduce conflicts in separate stacks, merged as a Graph Structured Stack (GSS) to trim exponentiality. As GLR parsers can deal with any context-free grammar, there is no restriction on the grammar. Moreover, GLR can behave linearly on LR grammars, and therefore, it is possible to build practical GLR parsers for programming languages [6,7].

Although GLR parsers accept any context-free grammar, they have a complicated execution model, inherited from LR parsing. LR parsing is based on the LR-automata, which is usually large and difficult to understand. As a result, LR parsers are hard to modify, and it is hard to produce good error messages. Many major programming languages have switched from LR-based parser generators, such as Yacc, to hand-written recursive-descent parsers. For example, GNU's GCC and Clang, two major C++ front-ends, have switched from LR(k) parser generators to hand-written recursive-descent parsers[1].

Recursive-descent (RD) parsers are a procedural interpretation of a grammar, directly encoded in a programming language. The straightforward execution model of RD parsers makes them easy to understand and modify. However, RD parsers do not support left-recursive rules and have worst-case exponential runtime. Generalized LL (GLL) [8] is a generalization of RD parsing that can deal with any context-free grammar, including the ones with left recursive rules, in cubic time and space. GLL uses GSS to handle multiple function call stacks, which also solves the problem of left recursion by allowing cycles in the GSS. GLL parsers maintain the direct relationship with the grammar that RD parsers have, and therefore, provide an easy to understand execution model. Finally, GLL parsers can be written by hand and can be debugged in a programming language IDE. This makes GLL parsing attractive for parsing programming languages.

Contributions. We first identify a problem with the GSS in GLL parsing that leads to inefficient sharing of parsing results, and propose a new GSS that provides better sharing. We show that the new GSS results in significant performance improvement, while preserving the worst-case cubic complexity of GLL parsing. Second, we discuss a number of other optimizations that further improve the performance of GLL parsing. Third, we demonstrate how common lexical disambiguation filters, such as follow restrictions and keyword exclusion, can be implemented in a GLL parser. These filters are essential for scannerless parsing of real programming languages. The new GSS, the optimizations, and the lexical disambiguation filters are implemented as part of the Iguana parsing framework, which is available at `https://github.com/cwi-swat/iguana`.

Organization of the paper. The rest of this paper is organized as follows. GLL parsing is introduced in Section 2. The problem with the original GSS in GLL

---

[1] `http://clang.llvm.org/features.html#unifiedparser`
`http://gcc.gnu.org/wiki/New_C_Parser`

parsing is explained in Section 2.3, and the new, more efficient GSS is introduced in Section 3. Section 4 gives a number of optimizations for implementing faster GLL parsers. Section 5 discusses the implementation of common lexical disambiguation mechanisms in GLL. Section 6 evaluates the performance of GLL parsers with the new GSS, compared to the original GSS, using a highly ambiguous grammar and grammars of real programming languages such as Java, C# and OCaml. Section 7 discusses related work on generalized parsing and disambiguation. Finally, Section 8 concludes this paper and discusses future work.

2   GLL Parsing

2.1   Preliminaries

A context-free grammar is composed of a set of nonterminals N, a set of terminals T, a set of rules P, and a start symbol S which is a nonterminal. A rule is written as $A ::= \alpha$, where A (head) is a nonterminal and α (body) is a string in $(T \cup N)^*$. Rules with the same head can be grouped as $A ::= \alpha_1 \mid \alpha_2 \mid \ldots \mid \alpha_p$, where each α_k is called an *alternative* of A. A *derivation step* is written as $\alpha A \beta \Rightarrow \alpha \gamma \beta$, where $A ::= \gamma$ is a rule, and α and β are strings in $(T \cup N)^*$. A *derivation* is a possibly empty sequence of derivation steps from α to β and is written as $\alpha \overset{*}{\Rightarrow} \beta$. A derivation is left-most if in each step the left most nonterminal is replaced by its body. A *sentential* form is a derivation from the start symbol. A *sentence* is a sentential form that only consists of terminal symbols. A sentence is called *ambiguous* if it has more than one left-most derivation.

2.2   The GLL Parsing Algorithm

The Generalized LL (GLL) parsing algorithm [8] is a fully general, worst-case cubic extension of recursive-descent (RD) parsing that supports all context-free grammars. In GLL parsing, the worst-case cubic runtime and space complexities are achieved by using a Graph-Structured Stack (GSS) and constructing a binarized Shared Packed Parse Forest (SPPF). GSS allows to efficiently handle multiple function call stacks, while a binarized SPPF solves the problem of unbounded polynomial complexity of Tomita-style SPPF construction [9]. GLL solves the problem of left recursion in RD parsing by allowing cycles in the GSS.

GLL parsing can be viewed as a grammar traversal process guided by the input string. At each point during execution, a GLL parser is at a grammar slot (grammar position) L, and maintains three variables: c_I for the current input position, c_U for the current GSS node, and c_N for the the current SPPF node. A grammar slot is of the form $X ::= \alpha \cdot \beta$ and corresponds to a grammar position before or after any symbol in the body of a grammar rule, similar to LR(0) items. A GSS node corresponds to a function call in an RD parser, and is of the form (L, i), where L is a grammar slot of the form $X ::= \alpha A \cdot \beta$, i.e., after a nonterminal, and i is the current input position when the node is created. Note that the grammar slot of a GSS node effectively records the return grammar position, needed to continue parsing after returning from a nonterminal. A GSS edge is of the form (v, w, u), where v and u are the source and target GSS nodes, respectively, and w is an SPPF node recorded on the edge.

GLL parsers produce a binarized SPPF. In an SPPF, nodes with the same subtrees are shared, and different derivations of a node are attached via packed nodes. A binarized SPPF introduces *intermediate* nodes, which effectively group the symbols of an alternative in a left-associative manner. An example of a binarized SPPF, resulting from parsing `"abc"` using the grammar $S ::= aBc \,|\, Ac$, $A ::= ab$, $B ::= b$ is as follows:

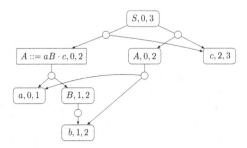

A binarized SPPF has three types of nodes. *Symbol* nodes of the form (x, i, j), where x is a terminal or nonterminal, and i and j are the left and right extents, respectively, indicating the substring recognized by x. *Intermediate* nodes of the form $(A ::= \alpha \cdot \beta, i, j)$, where $|\alpha|, |\beta| > 0$, and i and j are the left and right extents, respectively. Terminal nodes are leaf nodes, while nonterminal and intermediate nodes have *packed nodes* as children. A packed node (shown as circles in the SPPF above) is of the form $(A ::= \alpha \cdot \beta, k)$, where k, the *pivot*, is the right extent of the left child. A packed node has at most two children, both non-packed nodes. A packed node represents a derivation, thus, a nonterminal or intermediate node having more than one packed node is ambiguous.

As mentioned before, a GLL parser holds a pointer to the current SPPF node, c_N, and at the beginning of each alternative, c_N is set to the dummy node, $. As the parser traverses an alternative, it creates terminal nodes by calls **getNodeT**(t, i, j), where t is a terminal, and i and j are the left and right extents, respectively. Nonterminal and intermediate nodes are created by calls **getNodeP**$(A ::= \alpha \cdot \beta, w, z)$, where w and z are the left and right children, respectively. This function first searches for an existing nonterminal node (A, i, j), if $|\beta| = 0$, or intermediate node $(A ::= \alpha \cdot \beta, i, j)$, where i and j are the left extent of w and the right extent of z, respectively. If such a node exists, it is retrieved, otherwise created. Then, w and z are attached to the node via a packed node, if such a packed node does not exist.

In GLL parsing, when the parser reaches a non-deterministic point, e.g., a nonterminal with multiple alternatives, it creates *descriptors*, which capture the parsing states corresponding to each choice, and adds them to a set, so that they can be processed later. A descriptor is of the form (L, u, i, w), where L is a grammar slot, u is a GSS node, i is an input position, and w is an SPPF node. A GLL parser maintains two sets of descriptors: $\mathcal{R}$ for pending descriptors, and $\mathcal{U}$ for storing all the descriptors created during the parsing, to eliminate the duplicate descriptors. A descriptor is added to $\mathcal{R}$, via a call to function **add**, only if it does not exist in $\mathcal{U}$. In addition, a set $\mathcal{P}$ is maintained to store and reuse the results of parsing associated with GSS nodes, i.e., the elements of the form (u, z), where z is an SPPF node. A GLL parser has a main loop that in each iteration, removes a descriptor from $\mathcal{R}$, sets c_U, c_I, and c_N to the respective values in the descriptor, and jumps to execute the code associated with the grammar slot of the descriptor. An example of a GLL parser is given below for the grammar Γ_0: $A ::= aAb \,|\, aAc \,|\, a$.

$$\mathcal{R} := \varnothing; \mathcal{P} := \varnothing; \mathcal{U} := \varnothing$$
$$c_U := (L_0, 0); c_I := 0; c_N := \$$$

L_0 :**if**$(\mathcal{R} \neq \varnothing)$
    remove(L, u, i, w) **from** $\mathcal{R}$
    $c_U := u;\; c_I := i;\; c_N := w$; **goto** L
  else if (there exists a node $(A, 0, n)$)
    report success
  else report failure

L_A :**add**$(A ::= .aAb, c_U, c_I, \$)$
  add$(A ::= .aAc, c_U, c_I, \$)$
  add$(A ::= .a, c_U, c_I, \$)$
  goto L_0

$L_{.aAb}$:**if**$(I[c_I] = a)$
  $c_N := \mathbf{getNodeT}(a, c_I, c_I + 1)$
  else goto L_0
  $c_I := c_I + 1$
  $c_U := \mathbf{create}(A ::= aA \cdot b, c_U, c_I, c_N)$
  goto L_A

$L_{.aAc}$:**if**$(I[c_I] = a)$
  $c_N := \mathbf{getNodeT}(a, c_I, c_I + 1)$
  else goto L_0
  $c_I := c_I + 1$
  $c_U := \mathbf{create}(A ::= aA \cdot c, c_U, c_I, c_N)$
  goto L_A

$L_{aA.b}$:**if**$(I[c_I] = b)$
  $c_R := \mathbf{getNodeT}(b, c_I, c_I + 1)$
  else goto L_0
  $c_I := c_I + 1$
  $c_N := \mathbf{getNodeP}(A ::= aAb\cdot, c_N, c_R)$
  pop(c_U, c_I, c_N); **goto** L_0

$L_{aA.c}$:**if**$(I[c_I] = c)$
  $c_R := \mathbf{getNodeT}(c, c_I, c_I + 1)$
  else goto L_0
  $c_I := c_I + 1$
  $c_N := \mathbf{getNodeP}(A ::= aAc\cdot, c_N, c_R)$
  pop(c_U, c_I, c_N); **goto** L_0

We describe the execution of a GLL parser by explaining the steps of the parser at different grammar slots. Here, and in the rest of the paper, we do not include the check for first/follow sets in the discussion. We also assume that the input string, of length n, is available as an array I. Parsing starts by calling the start symbol at input position 0. At this moment, c_U is initialized by the default GSS node $u_0 = (L_0, 0)$, where L_0 does not correspond to any actual grammar position. Let X be a nonterminal defined as $X ::= \alpha_1 \,|\, \alpha_2 \,|\, \ldots \,|\, \alpha_p$. A GLL parser starts by creating and adding descriptors, each corresponding to the beginning of an alternative: $(X ::= \cdot\alpha_k, c_U, c_I, \$)$. Then, the parser goes to L_0.

Based on the current grammar slot, a GLL parser continues as follows. If the grammar slot is of the form $X ::= \alpha \cdot t\beta$, the parser is before a terminal. If $I[c_I] \neq t$, the parser jumps to L_0, terminating this execution path, otherwise a terminal node is created by $\mathbf{getNodeT}(t, c_I, c_I + 1)$. If $|\alpha| \geq 1$, the terminal node is assigned to c_R, and an intermediate or nonterminal node is created by

getNodeP$(X ::= \alpha t \cdot \beta, c_N, c_R)$, and assigned to c_N. The parser proceeds with the next grammar slot.

If the grammar slot is of the form $X ::= \alpha \cdot A\beta$, i.e., before a nonterminal, the **create** function is called with four arguments: the grammar slot $X ::= \alpha A \cdot \beta$, c_U, c_I, and c_N. First, **create** either retrieves a GSS node $(X ::= \alpha A \cdot \beta, c_I)$ if such a node exists, or creates one. Let v be $(X ::= \alpha A \cdot \beta, c_I)$. Then, a GSS edge (v, c_N, c_U) is added from v to c_U, if such an edge does not exists. If v was retrieved, the currently available results of parsing A at c_I are reused to continue parsing: for each element (v, z) in $\mathcal{P}$, a descriptor $(X ::= \alpha A \cdot \beta, c_U, h, y)$ is added, where y is the SPPF node returned by **getNodeP**$(X ::= \alpha A \cdot \beta, c_N, z)$, and h is the right extent of z. Finally, the call to **create** returns v, which is assigned to c_U. Then, the parser jumps to the definition of A and adds a descriptor for each of its alternatives.

If the grammar slot is of the form $A ::= \alpha\cdot$, the parser is at the end of an alternative, and therefore, should return from A to the calling rule and continue parsing. This corresponds to the return from a function call in an RD parser. The **pop** function is called with three arguments: c_U, c_I, c_N. Let (L, j) be the label of c_U. First, the element (c_U, c_N) is added to set $\mathcal{P}$. Then, for each outgoing edge (c_U, z, v) from c_U, a descriptor of the form (L, v, c_I, y) is created, where y is the SPPF node returned by **getNodeP**(L, z, c_N). Parsing terminates and reports success if all descriptors in $\mathcal{R}$ are processed and an SPPF node labeled $(S, 0, n)$, corresponding to the start symbol and the whole input string, is found, otherwise reports failure.

2.3   Problems with the Original GSS in GLL Parsing

To illustrate the problems with the original GSS in GLL parsing, we consider the grammar Γ_0 (Section 2.2) and the input string `"aac"`. Parsing this input string results in the GSS shown in Figure 1(a). The resulting GSS has two separate GSS nodes for each input position, 1 and 2, and each GSS node corresponds to an instance of A in one of the two alternatives: aAb or aAc. This implies that, for example, the following two descriptors, corresponding to the beginning of the first alternative of A, are created and added to $\mathcal{R}$: $(A ::= \cdot aAb, u_1, 1, \$)$, which is added after creating u_1, and $(A ::= \cdot aAb, u_2, 1, \$)$, which is added after creating u_2. Although both descriptors correspond to the same grammar position and the same input position, they are distinct as their parent GSS nodes, u_1 and u_2, are different. The same holds for the following descriptors corresponding to the other alternatives of A: $(A ::= \cdot aAc, u_1, 1, \$)$, $(A ::= \cdot aAc, u_2, 1, \$)$ and $(A ::= \cdot a, u_1, 1, \$)$, $(A ::= \cdot a, u_2, 1, \$)$. This example demonstrates that, although the results of parsing A only depend on the alternatives of A and the current input position, GLL creates separate descriptors for each instance of A, leading to multiple executions of the same parsing actions.

However, the calls corresponding to different instances of A at the same input position are not completely repeated. As can be seen, sharing happens one level deeper in GSS. For example, processing $(A ::= \cdot aAb, u_1, 1, \$)$ or $(A ::= \cdot aAb, u_2, 1, \$)$ matches `a`, increases input position to 2 and moves the grammar

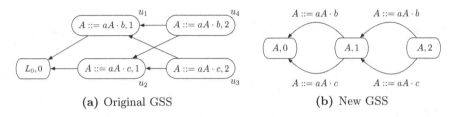

Fig. 1. Original and new GSS for parsing "aac" using $A ::= aAb \,|\, aAc \,|\, a$

pointer before A, leading to the call to the same instance of A at input position 2, which is handled by the same GSS node u_4 connected to u_1 and u_2. This sharing, however, happens per nonterminal instance. For example, if we consider the input string "aaacc", a can be matched at input position 2, and therefore, the same result but associated with different instances of A will be stored in set $\mathcal{P}$ as $(u_3, (A, 2, 3))$ and $(u_4, (A, 2, 3))$. Both nodes u_3 and u_4 will pop with the same result $(A, 2, 3)$, and given that both u_3 and u_4 are shared by u_1 and u_2, descriptors that, again, encode the same parsing actions, but account for different parent GSS nodes, will be created: $(A ::= aA \cdot b, u_1, 3, w_1)$, $(A ::= aA \cdot b, u_2, 3, w_1)$ and $(A ::= aA \cdot c, u_1, 3, w_2)$, $(A ::= aA \cdot c, u_2, 3, w_2)$, where $w_1 = (A ::= aA \cdot b, 0, 3)$ and $w_2 = (A ::= aA \cdot c, 0, 3)$.

3   More Efficient GSS for GLL Parsing

In this section, we propose a new GSS that, compared to the original GSS, provides a more efficient sharing of parsing results in GLL parsing. We use the fact that all calls corresponding to the same nonterminal and the same input position should produce the same results, and therefore, can be shared, regardless of a specific grammar rule in which the nonterminal occurs. The basic idea is that, instead of recording return grammar positions in GSS nodes, i.e., grammar slots of the form $X ::= \alpha A \cdot \beta$, names of nonterminals are recorded in GSS nodes, and return grammar positions are carried on GSS edges. Figure 1(b) illustrates the new GSS resulting from parsing "aac" using Γ_0.

First, we introduce new forms of GSS nodes and edges. Let $X ::= \alpha \cdot A\beta$ be the current grammar slot, i be the current input position, u be the current GSS node, and w be the current SPPF node. As in the original GLL, at this point, a GSS node is either retrieved, if such a node exists, or created. However, in our setting, such a GSS node is of the form (A, i), i.e., with the label that consists of the name of a nonterminal, in contrast to $X ::= \alpha A \cdot \beta$ in the original GSS, and the current input position. Let v be a GSS node labeled as (A, i). As in the original GLL, a new GSS edge is created from v to u. However, in our setting, a GSS edge is of the form (v, L, w, u), where, in addition to w as in the original GSS, the return grammar position L, i.e., $X ::= \alpha A \cdot \beta$, is recorded.

Second, we remove the default GSS node $u_0 = (L_0, 0)$, which requires a special label that does not correspond to any grammar position. In our setting, the initial GSS node is of the form $(S, 0)$ and corresponds to the call to the grammar start symbol S at input position 0, e.g., $(A, 0)$ in Figure 1(b).

Finally, we re-define the **create** and **pop** functions of the original GLL to accommodate the changes to GSS. We keep the presentation of these functions similar to the ones of the original GLL algorithm [8], so that the difference between the definitions can be easily seen. The new definitions of the **create** and **pop** functions are given below, where L is of the form $X ::= \alpha A \cdot \beta$, $|\alpha|, |\beta| \geq 0$, u and v are GSS nodes, and w, y, z are SPPF nodes.

```
create(L, u, i, w) {
    if (there exists a GSS node labeled (A, i)) {
        let v be the GSS node labeled (A, i)
        if (there is no GSS edge from v to u labeled L, w) {
            add a GSS edge from v to u labeled L, w
            for ((v, z) ∈ P) {
                let y be the SPPF node returned by getNodeP(L, w, z)
                add(L, u, h, y) where h is the right extent of y
            }
        }
    } else {
        create a new GSS node labeled (A, i)
        let v be the newly-created GSS node
        add a GSS edge from v to u labeled L, w
        for (each alternative αk of A) { add(A ::= ·αk, v, i, $) }
    }
    return v
}


pop(u, i, z) {
    if ((u, z) is not in P) {
        add (u, z) to P
        for (all GSS edges (u, L, w, v)) {
            let y be the SPPF node returned by getNodeP(L, w, z)
            add(L, v, i, y)
        }
    }
}
```

The **create** function takes four arguments: a grammar slot L of the form $X ::= \alpha A \cdot \beta$, a GSS node u, an input position i, and an SPPF node w. If a GSS node (A, i) exists (if-branch), the alternatives of A are not predicted at i again. Instead, after a GSS edge (v, L, w, u) is added, if such an edge does not exist, the currently available results of parsing A at i, stored in $\mathcal{P}$, are reused. For each result (v, z) in $\mathcal{P}$, an SPPF node y is constructed, and a descriptor (L, u, h, y) is added to continue parsing with the grammar slot $X ::= \alpha A \cdot \beta$ and the next input position h, corresponding to the right extent of y. If a GSS node (A, i) does not exist (else-branch), such a node is first created, then an edge (v, L, w, u) is added, and finally, a descriptor for each alternative of A with the input position i and parent node v is created and added.

The **pop** function takes three arguments: a GSS node u, an input position i, and an SPPF node z. If an entry (u, z) exists in $\mathcal{P}$, the parser returns from the function. Otherwise, (u, z) is added to $\mathcal{P}$, and, for each outgoing GSS edge of u, a descriptor is added to continue parsing with the grammar slot recorded on the edge, the current input position and the SPPF node constructed from w and z.

As the signatures of the **create** and **pop** functions stay the same as in the original GLL, replacing the original GSS with the new GSS does not require any modification to the code generated for each grammar slot in a GLL parser. Also note that the new GSS resembles the memoization of function calls used in functional programming, as a call to a nonterminal at an input position is represented only by the name of the nonterminal and the input position.

3.1   Equivalence

As illustrated in Sections 2 and 3, in the original GLL, sharing of parsing results for nonterminals is done at the level of nonterminal instances. On the other hand, in GLL with the new GSS, the sharing is done at the level of nonterminals themselves, which is more efficient as, in general, it results in less descriptors being created and processed. In Section 6 we present the performance results showing that significant performance speedup can be expected in practice. In this section we discuss the difference between GLL parsing with the original and new GSS for the general case, and show that the two GLL versions are semantically equivalent.

The use of the new GSS, compared to the original one, prevents descriptors of the form (L, u_1, i, w) and (L, u_2, i, w) to be created. These descriptors have the same grammar slot, the same input position, the same SPPF node, but different parent GSS nodes. In GLL with the original GSS, such descriptors may be added to $\mathcal{R}$ when, in the course of parsing, calls to different instances of a nonterminal, say A, at the same input position, say i, are made. Each such call corresponds to a parsing state where the current grammar slot is of the form $X ::= \tau \cdot A\mu$ (i.e., before A), and the current input position is i. To handle these calls, multiple GSS nodes of the form $(X ::= \tau A \cdot \mu, i)$, where the grammar slot corresponds to a grammar position after A, are created during parsing. We enumerate all such grammar slots with L_k, and denote GSS nodes (L_k, i) as u_k.

When a GSS node u_k is created, descriptors of the form $(A ::= \cdot\gamma, u_k, i, \$)$ are added. If $a_1 a_2 \ldots a_n$ is the input string and $A \overset{*}{\Rightarrow} a_{i+1} \ldots a_j$, u_k will pop at j, and processing descriptors of the form $(A ::= \cdot\gamma, u_k, i, \$)$ will lead to creation of descriptors of the form $(A ::= \alpha B \cdot \beta, u_k, l, w)$, $i \leq l \leq j$, i.e., in an alternative of A, and of the form $(A ::= \gamma\cdot, u_k, j, (A, i, j))$, i.e., at the end of an alternative of A. All these descriptors encode the parsing actions that do not semantically depend on a specific u_k. Indeed, starting from the same grammar position in an alternative of A, say $A ::= \alpha \cdot \beta$, regardless of a specific u_k, the parsing continues with the next symbol in the alternative and the current input position, and either produces an (intermediate) SPPF node, which does not depend on u_k, moving to the next symbol in the alternative, or fails. Finally, when descriptors of the form $(A ::= \gamma\cdot, u_k, j, (A, i, j))$ are processed, the same SPPF node (A, i, j) will be recorded in set $\mathcal{P}$ for each u_k.

In the original GLL, when u_k is being popped, for each (u_k, z) in set $\mathcal{P}$, where z is of the form (A, i, j), and each outgoing edge (u_k, w, v), a descriptor (L_k, v, j, y), where y is the SPPF node returned by **getNodeP**(L_k, w, z), is added to continue parsing after A. Let v be a GSS node with index h, then h and j are the left and right extents of y, respectively. In the following we show how using the new GSS, descriptors equivalent to (L_k, v, j, y) are created, but at the same time, the problem of repeating the same parsing actions is avoided.

In GLL with the new GSS, when calls to different instances of a nonterminal, say A, at the same input position, say i, are made, a GSS node $u = (A, i)$ is retrieved or created. Similar to the original GLL, when u is created, descriptors of the form $(A ::= \cdot\gamma, u, i, \$)$ are added, and if $A \stackrel{*}{\Rightarrow} a_{i+1} \ldots a_j$, descriptors of the form $(A ::= \alpha B \cdot \beta, u, l, w)$, $i \leq l \leq j$, and of the form $(A ::= \gamma\cdot, u, j, (A, i, j))$ will also be added. The essential difference with the original GLL is that the label of u is A, and therefore, the descriptors corresponding to parsing A at i are independent of the context in which A is used. Upon the first call to A at i, regardless of its current context, such descriptors are created, and the results are reused for any such call in a different context. Finally, when descriptors of the form $(A ::= \gamma\cdot, u, j, (A, i, j))$ are processed, the SPPF node $z = (A, i, j)$ is recorded as a single element (u, z) in set $\mathcal{P}$.

In GLL parsing with the new GSS, whenever the parser reaches a state with a grammar slot of the form $X ::= \tau \cdot A\mu$, and the input position i, there will be an edge (u, L_k, w, v) added to u, where L_k is of the form $X ::= \tau A \cdot \mu$. Finally, for each (u, z) in set $\mathcal{P}$ and each edge (u, L_k, w, v), the descriptor (L_k, v, j, y) will be added, where y is the SPPF node returned by **getNodeP**(L_k, w, z).

3.2 Complexity

In this section we show that replacing the original GSS with the new GSS does not affect the worst-case cubic runtime and space complexities of GLL parsing. To introduce the new GSS into GLL parsing, we changed the forms of GSS nodes and edges. We also re-defined the **create** and **pop** functions to accommodate these changes. However, all these modifications had no effect on the SPPF construction, the **getNode** functions, and the code of GLL parsers that uses **create** and **pop** to interact with GSS. Specifically, this implies that when the main loop of a GLL parser executes, and the next descriptor is removed from $\mathcal{R}$, the execution proceeds in the same way as in the original GLL parsing until the call to either **create** or **pop** is made.

First, we show that the space required for the new GSS is also at most $O(n^3)$. In the new GSS, all GSS nodes have unique labels of the form (A, i), where $0 \leq i \leq n$. Therefore, the new GSS has at most $O(n)$ nodes. In the new GSS, all GSS edges have unique labels of the form (u, L, w, v), where L is of the form $X ::= \alpha A \cdot \beta$, the source GSS node u is of the form (A, i), and the target GSS node v is of the form (X, j). The label of an edge in the new GSS consists of L and w, where w has j and i as the left and right extents, which are also the indices of v and u, respectively. Given that $0 \leq j \leq i \leq n$, the number of outgoing edges for any source GSS node u is at most $O(n)$, and the new GSS has at most $O(n^2)$ edges. Thus the new GSS requires at most $O(n)$ nodes and at most $O(n^2)$ edges.

The worst-case $O(n^3)$ runtime complexity of the original GLL follows from the fact that there are at most $O(n^2)$ descriptors, and processing a descriptor may take at most $O(n)$ time, by calling **pop** or **create**. Now, we show that the worst-case complexity of both **create** and **pop** is still $O(n)$, and the total number of descriptors that can be added to $\mathcal{R}$ is still at most $O(n^2)$. All elements in set $\mathcal{P}$ are of the form (v, z), where v is of the form (A, i), and z has i and j as the left and right extents, respectively, where $0 \leq i \leq j \leq n$. Therefore, the number of elements in $\mathcal{P}$, corresponding to the same GSS node, is at most $O(n)$. Since a GSS node has at most $O(n)$ outgoing edges, $\mathcal{P}$ has at most $O(n)$ elements corresponding to a GSS node, and the new GSS and $\mathcal{P}$ can be implemented using arrays to allow constant time lookup, both **create** and **pop** have the worst-case complexity $O(n)$.

Finally, a descriptor is of the form (L, u, i, w), where w is either $ or has j and i as the left and right extents, respectively, and j is also the index of u. Thus the total number of descriptors that can be added to $\mathcal{R}$ is at most $O(n^2)$.

4   Optimizations for GLL Implementation

The GLL parsing algorithm [8] is described using a set view, e.g., $\mathcal{U}$ and $\mathcal{P}$, which eases the reasoning about the worst-case complexity, but leaves open the challenges of an efficient implementation. The worst-case $O(n^3)$ complexity of GLL parsing requires constant time lookup, e.g., to check if a descriptor has already been added. Constant time lookup can be achieved using multi-dimensional arrays of size $O(n^2)$, however, such an implementation requires $O(n^2)$ initialization time, which makes it impractical for near-linear parsing of real programming languages, whose grammars are nearly deterministic.

For near-linear parsing of real programming languages we need data structures that provide amortized constant time lookup, without excessive overhead for initialization. One way to achieve this is to use a combination of arrays and linked lists as described in [10]. In this approach the user needs to specify, based on the properties of the grammar, which dimensions should be implemented as arrays or linked lists.

In this section we propose an efficient hash table-based implementation of GLL parsers. We show how the two most important lookup structures, $\mathcal{U}$ and $\mathcal{P}$, can be implemented using local hash tables in GSS nodes. The idea is based on the fact that the elements stored in these data structures have a GSS node as a property. Instead of having a global hash table, we factor out the GSS node and use hash tables that are local to a GSS node. In an object-oriented language, we can model a GSS node as an object that has pointers to its local hash tables. In the following, we discuss different implementations of $\mathcal{U}$ and $\mathcal{P}$. We consider GLL parsing with new GSS, and assume that n is the length of the input, and $|N|$ and $|L|$ are the number of nonterminals and grammar slots, respectively.

Descriptor elimination set $(\mathcal{U})$: set $\mathcal{U}$ is used to keep all the descriptors created during parsing for duplicate elimination. A descriptor is of the form (L, u, i, w), where L is of the form $A ::= \alpha \cdot \beta$, u is of the form (A, j), and w is either a dummy node, or a symbol node of the form (x, j, i), when $\alpha = x$, or an intermediate node of the form (L, j, i). As can be seen, in a descriptor, the input index of the GSS node is the same as the left extent of the SPPF node, and the input index of the descriptor is the same as the right extent of the SPPF node. Also note that the label of the GSS and SPPF node is already encoded in L. Thus we can effectively consider a descriptor as (L, i, j). We consider three implementations of $\mathcal{U}$:

- *Global Array*: $\mathcal{U}$ can be implemented as an array of size $|L| \times n \times n$, which requires $O(n^2)$ initialization time.
- *Global hash table*: $\mathcal{U}$ can be implemented as a single global hash table holding elements of the form (L, i, j).
- *Local hash table in a GSS node*: $\mathcal{U}$ can be implemented as a local hash table in a GSS node. This way, we only need to consider a descriptor as (L, i).

Popped elements $(\mathcal{P})$: The set of popped elements, $\mathcal{P}$, is defined as a set of (u, w), where u is a GSS node of the form (A, i), and w is an SPPF node of the form (A, i, j). For eliminating duplicates, $\mathcal{P}$ can effectively be considered as a set of (A, i, j). We consider three implementations of $\mathcal{P}$:

- *Global Array*: $\mathcal{P}$ can be implemented as an array of size $|N| \times n \times n$, which requires $O(n^2)$ initialization time.
- *Global hash table*: $\mathcal{P}$ can be implemented as a global hash table holding elements of the form (A, i, j).
- *Local hash table in a GSS node*: $\mathcal{P}$ can be implemented as a local hash table in a GSS node. This way we can eliminate duplicate SPPF nodes using a single integer, the right extent of the SPPF node (j).

Hash tables do not have the problem of multi-dimensional arrays, as the initialization cost is constant. However, using a global hash table is problematic for parsing large input files as the number of elements is in order of millions, leading to many hash collisions and resizing. For example, for a C# source file of 2000 lines of code, about 1,500,000 descriptors are created and processed.

Using local hash tables in GSS nodes instead of a single global hash table provides considerable speedup when parsing large inputs with large grammars. First, by distributing hash tables over GSS nodes, we effectively reduce the number of properties needed for hash code calculation. Second, local hash tables will contain fewer entries, resulting in fewer hash collisions and requiring fewer resizing. In the Iguana parsing framework we use the standard `java.util.HashSet` as the implementation of hash tables. Our preliminary results show that, for example, by using a local hash table for implementing $\mathcal{U}$ instead of a global one, we can expect speedup of factor two. Detailed evaluation of the optimizations presented in this section, and their effect on memory usage, is future work.

There are two algorithmic optimizations possible that further improve the performance of GLL parsers. These optimizations remove certain runtime checks that can be shown to be redundant based on the following properties:

*1) There is at most one call to the **create** function with the same arguments. Thus no check for duplicate GSS edges is needed.*
The properties of a GSS edge (v, L, w, u) are uniquely identified by the arguments to **create**: L, u, i, w, where L is of the form $X ::= \alpha A \cdot \beta$, and $v = (A, i)$. Therefore, if it can be shown that there is at most one call to **create** with the same arguments, the check for duplicate GSS edges can be safely removed.

Let us consider a call **create**$(X ::= \alpha A \cdot \beta, u, i, w)$. This call can only happen if a descriptor of one of the following forms has been processed, where τ is a possibly empty sequence of terminals and $j \leq i$: (1) $(X ::= \cdot \alpha A \beta, u, j, \$)$ when $\alpha = \tau$; or (2) $(X ::= \gamma B \cdot \tau A \beta, u, j, z)$ when $\alpha = \gamma B \tau$, $|\gamma| \geq 0$. Therefore, for the call to happen more than once, the same descriptor has to be processed again. However, this can never happen as all the duplicate descriptors are eliminated.

*2) There is at most one call to the **getNodeP** function with the same arguments. Thus no check for duplicate packed nodes is needed.*
Let us consider a call **getNodeP**$(A ::= \alpha \cdot \beta, w, z)$, where w is either $\$$ or a non-packed node having i and k as the left and right extents, and z is a non-packed node having k and j as the left and right extents. This call may create and add a packed node $(A ::= \alpha \cdot \beta, k)$ under the parent node, which is either (A, i, j) when $|\beta| = 0$, or $(A ::= \alpha \cdot \beta, i, j)$ otherwise. Clearly, the same call to **getNodeP** will try to add the same packed node under the existing parent node.

Now suppose that the same call to **getNodeP** happens for the second time. Given that a GSS node is ensured to pop with the same result at most once (set $\mathcal{P}$ and **pop**), the second call can only happen if a descriptor of one of the following forms has been processed for the second time, where $u = (A, i)$ and τ is a possibly empty sequence of terminals: (1) $(A ::= \cdot \alpha \beta, u, i, \$)$ when either $\alpha = \tau$ or $\alpha = \tau X$; or (2) $(A ::= \gamma B \cdot \sigma \beta, u, l, y)$, $i \leq l \leq k$, when $\alpha = \gamma B \sigma$, $|\gamma| \geq 0$, and either $\sigma = \tau$ or $\sigma = \tau X$. This can never happen as all the duplicate descriptors are eliminated.

Note that the second optimization is only applicable for GLL parsers with the new GSS. In the original GLL, u can be of the form $(X ::= \mu A \cdot \nu, i)$, and therefore, multiple descriptors with the same grammar slot, the same input position, the same SPPF node, but different parent nodes, corresponding to multiple instances of A, can be added, resulting in multiple calls to **getNodeP** with the same arguments.

5   Disambiguation Filters for Scannerless GLL Parsing

Parsing programming languages is often done using a separate scanning phase before parsing, in which a scanner (lexer) first transforms a stream of characters to a stream of tokens. Besides performance gain, another important reason for a separate scanning phase is that deterministic character-level grammars are virtually nonexistent. The main drawback of performing scanning before parsing is that, in some cases, it is not possible to uniquely identify the type of tokens without the parsing context (grammar rule in which they appear). An example is nested generic types in Java, e.g., `List<List<T>>`. Without the parsing context, the scanner cannot unambiguously detect the type of `>>` as it can be either a right-shift operator or two closing angle brackets.

Scannerless parsing [11,12] eliminates the need for a separate scanning phase by treating the lexical and context-free definitions the same. A scannerless parser solves the problems of identifying the type of tokens by parsing each character in its parsing context, and provides the user with a unified formalism for both syntactical and lexical definitions. This facilitates modular grammar development at the lexical level, which is essential for language extension and embedding [13].

A separate scanning phase usually resolves the character-level ambiguities in favor of the longest matched token and excludes keywords from identifiers. In absence of a separate scanner, such ambiguities should be resolved during parsing. In the rest of this section we show how most common character-level disambiguation filters [14] can be implemented in a GLL parser.

To illustrate character-level ambiguities, we use the grammar below, which is adapted from [14]. This grammar defines a `Term` as either a sequence of two terms, an identifier, a number, or the keyword `"int"`. `Id` is defined as one or more repetition of a single character, and `WS` defines a possibly empty blank.

```
Term  ::= Term WS Term | Id | Num | "int"
Id    ::= Chars
Chars ::= Chars Char | Char
Char  ::= 'a' | .. | 'z'
Num   ::= '1' | .. |'9'
WS    ::= ' ' | ε
```

This grammar is ambiguous. For example, the input string `"hi"` can be parsed as either `Term(Id("hi"))`, or `Term(Term(Id("h")),Term(Id("i")))`. Following the longest match rule, the first derivation is the intended one, as in the second one `"h"` is recognized as an identifier, while it is followed by `"i"`. We can use a *follow restriction* ($\nrightarrow$) to disallow an identifier to be followed by another character: `Id ::= Chars -/- Char`. Another ambiguity occurs in the input string `"intx"` which can be parsed as either `Term(Id("intx"))` or `Term(Term("int"), Term(Id("x")))`. We can solve this problem by adding a *precede restriction* ($\nleftarrow$) as follows: `Id ::= Char -\- Chars`, specifying that `Id` cannot be preceded by a character. Finally, we should exclude the recognition of `"int"` as `Id`. For this, we use an exclusion rule: `Id ::= Chars \"int"`.

Below we formally define each of these restrictions and show how they can be integrated in GLL parsing. For follow and precede restrictions we only consider the case where the restriction is a single character, denoted by c. This can be trivially extended to other restrictions such as character ranges or arbitrary regular expressions. We assume that I represents the input string as an array of characters and i holds the current input position.

Follow restriction. For a grammar rule $A ::= \alpha x \beta$, a follow restriction for the symbol x is written as $A ::= \alpha x \not\rightarrow c\beta$, meaning that derivations of the form $\gamma A \sigma \Rightarrow \gamma \alpha x \beta \sigma \stackrel{*}{\Rightarrow} \gamma \alpha x c \tau$ are disallowed. For implementing follow restrictions, we consider the grammar position $A ::= \alpha x \cdot \beta$. If x is a terminal, the implementation is straightforward: if $i < |I|$ and $I[i] = c$, the control flow returns to the main loop, effectively terminating this parsing path. If x is a nonterminal, we consider the situation where a GLL parser is about to create a descriptor for $A ::= \alpha x \cdot \beta$. This happens when pop is executed for a GSS node (x, j) at i. While iterating over the GSS edges, if a GSS edge labeled $A ::= \alpha x \cdot \beta$ is reached, the condition of the follow restriction associated with this grammar position will be checked. If $I[i] = c$, no descriptor for this label will be added.

Precede Restriction. For a grammar rule $A ::= \alpha x \beta$, a precede restriction for the symbol x is written as $A ::= \alpha c \nleftarrow x\beta$, meaning that derivations of the form $\gamma A \sigma \Rightarrow \gamma \alpha x \beta \sigma \stackrel{*}{\Rightarrow} \tau c x \beta \sigma$ are disallowed. The implementation of precede restrictions is as follows. When a GLL parser is at the grammar slot $A ::= \alpha \cdot x\beta$, if $i > 0$ and $I[i-1] = c$, the control flow returns to the main loop, effectively terminating this parsing path.

Exclusion. For a grammar rule $A ::= \alpha X \beta$, the exclusion of string s from the nonterminal X is written as $A ::= \alpha X \backslash s \beta$, meaning that the language accepted by the nonterminal X should not contain the string s, i.e., $L(X \backslash s) = L(X) - \{s\}$, where L defines the language accepted by a nonterminal. Similar to the implementation of follow restrictions for a nonterminal, when a GSS node (X, j) is popped at i, and the parser iterates over the outgoing GSS edges, if an edge $A ::= \alpha X \cdot \beta$ is found, the condition of the exclusion is checked. If the substring of the input from j to i matches s, no descriptor for the grammar position $A ::= \alpha X \cdot \beta$ is added, which effectively terminates this parsing path.

6   Performance Evaluation

To evaluate the efficiency of the new GSS for GLL parsing, we use a highly ambiguous grammar and grammars of three real programming languages: Java, C# and OCaml. We ran the GLL parsers generated from Iguana in two different modes: *new* and *original*, corresponding to the new and original GSS, respectively. Iguana is our Java-based GLL parsing framework that can be configured to run with the new or original GSS, while keeping all other aspects of the algorithm, such as SPPF creation, the same. The optimizations given in Section 4, with the exception of removing checks for packed nodes, which is only applicable to GLL parser with the new GSS, are applied to both modes.

We ran the experiments on a machine with a quad-core Intel Core i7 2.6 GHz CPU and 16 GB of memory running Mac OS X 10.9.4. We executed the parsers on a 64-Bit Oracle HotSpot^{TM} JVM version 1.7.0_55 with the `-server` flag. To allow for JIT optimizations, the JVM was first warmed up, by executing a large sample data, and then each test is executed 10 times. The median running time (CPU user time) is reported.

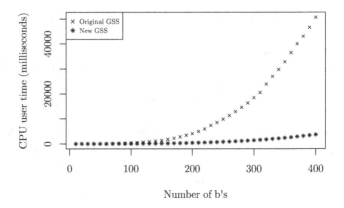

Fig. 2. Running the GLL parsers for grammar $S ::= SSS \mid SS \mid b$

Table 1. The result of running highly ambiguous grammar on strings of b's

size	time (ms)		# GSS nodes		# GSS edges	
	new	original	new	original	new	original
50	6	35	51	251	3877	18 935
100	45	336	101	501	15 252	75 360
150	151	1361	151	751	34 127	169 285
200	386	4080	201	1001	60 502	300 710
250	791	9824	251	1251	94 377	469 635
300	1403	18 457	301	1501	135 752	676 060
350	2367	32 790	351	1751	184 627	919 985
400	3639	50 648	401	2001	241 002	1 201 410

6.1 Highly Ambiguous Grammar

To measure the effect of the new GSS for GLL parsing on highly ambiguous
grammars, we use the grammar $S ::= SSS \mid SS \mid b$. The results of running a
GLL parser with the new and original GSS for this grammar on strings of b's
is shown in Figure 2. As can be seen, the performance gain is significant. The
median and maximum speedup factors for the highly ambiguous grammar, as
shown in Figure 3, are 10 and 14, respectively. To explain the observed speedup,
we summarize the results of parsing the strings of b's in Table 1. Note that
the number of nodes and edges for the original GSS are slightly more than the
numbers reported in [8], as we do not include the check for first and follow sets.
As can be seen, GLL with the new GSS has $n + 1$ GSS nodes for inputs of length
n, one for each call to S at input positions 0 to n. For GLL with the original
GSS, there are 5 grammar slots that can be called: $S ::= S \cdot SS$, $S ::= SS \cdot S$,
$S ::= SSS\cdot$, $S ::= S \cdot S$, and $S ::= SS\cdot$, which lead to $5n + 1$ GSS nodes. In
such a highly ambiguous grammar, most GSS nodes are connected, therefore,
the iteration operations over edges in the create and pop functions will take
much more time, as explained in Section 3.1.

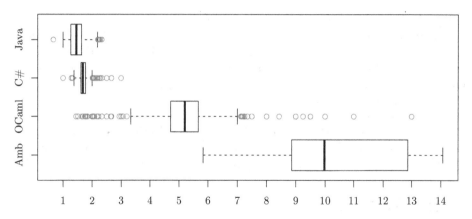

Fig. 3. Comparing the speedup factor of the new and original GSS

6.2   Grammars of Programming Languages

To measure the effect of the new GSS on the grammars of real programming languages, we have chosen the grammars of three programming languages from their language reference manual.

Java: We used the grammar of Java 7 from the Java Language Specification [15] (JLS). The grammar contains 329 nonterminals, 728 rules, and 2410 grammar slots. We have parsed 7449 Java files from the source code of JDK 1.7.0_60-b19. As shown in Figure 3, the median and maximum speedup factors for Java are 1.5 and 2.3, respectively.

C#: We used the grammar of C# 5 from the C# Language Specification [16]. The grammar contains 534 nonterminals, 1275 rules, and 4195 grammar slots. The main challenge in parsing C# files was dealing with C# directives, such as #if and #region. C# front ends, in contrast to C++, do not have a separate preprocessing phase for directives. Most C# directives can be ignored as comment, with the exception of the conditional ones, as ignoring them may lead to parse error. As the purpose of this evaluation was to measure the performance of GLL parsers on C# files, and not configuration-preserving parsing, we ran the GNU C preprocessor on the test files to preprocess the conditional directives. The rest of the directives were treated as comments. We have parsed 2764 C# files from the build-preview release of the Roslyn Compiler. As shown in Figure 3, the median and maximum speedup factors for C# are 1.7 and 3, respectively.

OCaml: We used the grammar of OCaml 4.0.1 from the OCaml reference manual [17]. The grammar of OCaml is different from Java and C# in two aspects. First, OCaml is an expression-based language, as opposed to Java and C#. This provides us with a grammar with different characteristics for testing the effectiveness of the new GSS. Second, the reference grammar of OCaml is highly ambiguous, having numerous operators with different associativity and priority levels. We used a grammar rewriting technique [18] to obtain an unambiguous grammar. The rewritten grammar contains 685 nonterminals, 5728 rules, and 27294 grammar slots. We have parsed 871 files from the OCaml 4.0.1 source release. As shown in Figure 3, the median and maximum speedup factors for OCaml are 5.2 and 13, respectively. The rewriting technique used in [18] to encode precedence rules leads to more rules. This can be one reason for the more significant speedup for the OCaml case, compared to Java and C#. The other possible reason is the nature of OCaml programs that have many nested expressions, requiring high non-determinism. The case of OCaml shows that the new GSS is very effective for parsing large, complex grammars, such as OCaml.

7 Related Work

For many years deterministic parsing techniques were the only viable option for parsing programming languages. As machines became more powerful, and the need for developing parsers in other areas such as reverse-engineering and source code analysis increased, generalized parsing techniques were considered for parsing programming languages. In this section we discuss several related work on applying generalized parsing to parsing programming languages.

Generalized parsing. Generalized parsing algorithms have the attractive property that they can behave linearly on deterministic grammars. Therefore, for the grammars that are nearly deterministic, which is the case for most programming languages, using generalized parsing is feasible [19]. For example, the ASF+SDF Meta-Environment [7] uses a variation of GLR parsing for source code analysis and reverse engineering.

The original GLR parsing algorithm by Tomita [5] fails to terminate for some grammars with ϵ rules. Farshi [20] provides a fix for ϵ rules, but his fix requires exhaustive GSS search after some reductions. Scott and Johnstone [21] provide an alternative to Farshi's fix, called Right Nulled GLR (RNGLR), which is more elegant and more efficient. GLR parsers have worst-case $O(n^{k+1})$ complexity, where k is the length of the longest rule in the grammar [9]. BRNGLR is a variation of RNGLR that uses binarized SPPFs to enable GLR parsing in cubic time. Elkhound [6] is a GLR parser, based on Farshi's version, that switches to the machinery of an LR parser on deterministic parts of the grammar, leading to significant performance improvement. Another faster variant of GLR parsing is presented by Aycock and Horspool [22], which uses a larger LR automata, trading space for time.

Disambiguation. Disambiguation techniques that are used in different parsing technologies can be categorized in two groups: implicit or explicit disambiguation. Implicit disambiguation is mostly used in parsing techniques that return at most one derivation tree. Perhaps the name nondeterminism-reducer is a more correct term, as these techniques essentially reduce non-determinism during parsing, regardless if it leads to ambiguity or not. Yacc [3], PEGs [23] and

ANTLR [24] are examples of parsing techniques that use implicit disambiguation rules. For example, in Yacc, shift/reduce conflicts are resolved in favor of shift, and PEGs and ANTLR use the order of the alternatives. These approaches do not work in all cases and may lead to surprises for the language engineer.

Explicit disambiguation is usually done using declarative disambiguation rules. In this approach, the grammar formalism allows the user to explicitly define the disambiguation rules, which can be applied either during parsing, by pruning parsing paths that violate the rules, or be applied after the parsing is done, as a parse forest processing step. Post-parse filtering is only possible when using a generalized parser that can return all the derivations in form of a parse forest. Aho et. al show how to modify LR(1) parsing tables to resolve shift/reduce conflicts based on the the priority and associativity of operators [25]. In Scannerless GLR (SGLR) which is used in SDF2 [26], operator precedence and character-level restrictions such as keyword exclusion are implemented as parse table modifications, but some other disambiguation filters such as `prefer` and `avoid` as post-parse filters [14]. Economopoulos et al. [27] investigate the implementation of SDF disambiguation filters in the RNGLR parsing algorithm and report considerable performance improvement.

8   Conclusions

In this paper we presented an essential optimization to GLL parsing, by proposing a new GSS, which provides a more efficient sharing of parsing results. We showed that GLL parsers with the new GSS are worst-case cubic in time and space, and are significantly faster on both highly ambiguous and near-deterministic grammars. As future work, we plan to measure the effect of the new GSS and the optimizations presented in Section 4 on memory, and to compare the performance of our GLL implementation with other parsing techniques.

Acknowledgments. We thank Alex ten Brink who proposed the modification to the GSS in GLL recognizers. Special thanks to Elizabeth Scott and Adrian Johnstone for discussions on GLL parsing, and to Jurgen Vinju for his feedback.

References

1. Knuth, D.E.: On the Translation of Languages from Left to Right. Information and Control 8(6), 607–639 (1965)
2. Deremer, F.L.: Practical Translators for LR(k) Languages. PhD thesis, Massachusetts Institute of Technology (1969)
3. Johnson, S.C.: Yacc: Yet Another Compiler-Compiler AT&T Bell Laboratories, http://dinosaur.compilertools.net/yacc/
4. Gosling, J., Joy, B., Steele, G.L.: The Java Language Specification, 1st edn. Addison-Wesley Longman Publishing Co., Inc, Boston (1996)
5. Tomita, M.: Efficient Parsing for Natural Language: A Fast Algorithm for Practical Systems. Kluwer Academic Publishers, Norwell (1985)
6. McPeak, S., Necula, G.C.: Elkhound: A Fast, Practical GLR Parser Generator. In: Duesterwald, E. (ed.) CC 2004. LNCS, vol. 2985, pp. 73–88. Springer, Heidelberg (2004)

7. van den Brand, M., Heering, J., Klint, P., Olivier, P.A.: Compiling language definitions: The ASF+SDF compiler. ACM Trans. Program. Lang. Syst. 24 (2002)

8. Scott, E., Johnstone, A.: GLL parse-tree generation. Science of Computer Programming 78(10), 1828–1844 (2013)

9. Johnson, M.: The Computational Complexity of GLR Parsing. In: Tomita, M. (ed.) Generalized LR Parsing, pp. 35–42. Springer US (1991)

10. Johnstone, A., Scott, E.: Modelling GLL parser implementations. In: Malloy, B., Staab, S., van den Brand, M. (eds.) SLE 2010. LNCS, vol. 6563, pp. 42–61. Springer, Heidelberg (2011)

11. Salomon, D.J., Cormack, G.V.: Scannerless NSLR(1) Parsing of Programming Languages. In: Programming Language Design and Implementation, PLDI 1989, pp. 170–178 (1989)

12. Visser, E.: Scannerless Generalized-LR Parsing. Technical report, University of Amsterdam (1997)

13. Bravenboer, M., Tanter, É., Visser, E.: Declarative, Formal, and Extensible Syntax Definition for AspectJ. In: Object-Oriented Programming, Systems, Languages, and Applications, OOPSLA 2006, pp. 209–228 (2006)

14. den van Brand, M.G.J., Scheerder, J., Vinju, J.J., Visser, E.: Disambiguation Filters for Scannerless Generalized LR Parsers. In: Nigel Horspool, R. (ed.) CC 2002. LNCS, vol. 2304, pp. 143–158. Springer, Heidelberg (2002)

15. Gosling, J., Joy, B., Steele, G., Bracha, G., Buckley, A.: The Java Language Specification Java SE 7 Edition (February 2013)

16. Microsoft Corporation: C# Language Specification Version 5.0 (2013)

17. Leroy, X., Doligez, D., Frisch, A., Garrigue, J., Rémy, D., Vouillon, J.: The OCaml system release 4.01: Documentation and user's manual (September 2013)

18. Afroozeh, A., van den Brand, M., Johnstone, A., Scott, E., Vinju, J.: Safe Specification of Operator Precedence Rules. In: Erwig, M., Paige, R.F., Van Wyk, E. (eds.) SLE 2013. LNCS, vol. 8225, pp. 137–156. Springer, Heidelberg (2013)

19. Johnstone, A., Scott, E., Economopoulos, G.: Generalised parsing: Some costs. In: Duesterwald, E. (ed.) CC 2004. LNCS, vol. 2985, pp. 89–103. Springer, Heidelberg (2004)

20. Nozohoor-Farshi, R.: GLR Parsing for ϵ-Grammers. In: Tomita, M. (ed.) Generalized LR Parsing, pp. 61–75. Springer US (1991)

21. Scott, E., Johnstone, A.: Right Nulled GLR Parsers. ACM Trans. Program. Lang. Syst. 28(4), 577–618 (2006)

22. Aycock, J.: Faster Generalized LR Parsing. In: Jähnichen, S. (ed.) CC 1999. LNCS, vol. 1575, pp. 32–46. Springer, Heidelberg (1999)

23. Ford, B.: Parsing Expression Grammars: A Recognition-Based Syntactic Foundation. In: Principles of Programming Languages, POPL 2004, pp. 111–122 (2004)

24. Parr, T., Harwell, S., Fisher, K.: Adaptive LL(*) Parsing: The Power of Dynamic Analysis. In: Object Oriented Programming Systems Languages and Applications, OOPSLA 2014, pp. 579–598. ACM (2014)

25. Aho, A.V., Johnson, S.C., Ullman, J.D.: Deterministic Parsing of Ambiguous Grammars. In: Principles of Programming Languages, POPL 1973, pp. 1–21 (1973)

26. Visser, E.: Syntax Definition for Language Prototyping. PhD thesis, University of Amsterdam (1997)

27. Economopoulos, G., Klint, P., Vinju, J.: Faster Scannerless GLR Parsing. In: de Moor, O., Schwartzbach, M.I. (eds.) CC 2009. LNCS, vol. 5501, pp. 126–141. Springer, Heidelberg (2009)

Analysis and Optimisation

A Backend Extension Mechanism for PQL/Java with Free Run-Time Optimisation

Hilmar Ackermann[1], Christoph Reichenbach[1], Christian Müller[1],
and Yannis Smaragdakis[2]

[1] Goethe University Frankfurt
{hilmar.ackermann,creichen}@gmail.com
[2] University of Athens
yannis@smaragd.org

Abstract. In many data processing tasks, declarative query programming offers substantial benefit over manual data analysis: the query processors found in declarative systems can use powerful algorithms such as query planning to choose high-level execution strategies during compilation. However, the principal downside of such languages is that their primitives must be carefully curated, to allow the query planner to correctly estimate their overhead. In this paper, we examine this challenge in one such system, PQL/Java. PQL/Java adds a powerful declarative query language to Java to enable and automatically parallelise queries over the Java heap. In the past, the language has not provided any support for custom user-designed datatypes, as such support requires complex interactions with its query planner and backend.

We examine PQL/Java and its intermediate language in detail and describe a new system that simplifies PQL/Java extensions. This system provides a language that permits users to add new primitives with arbitrary Java computations, and new rewriting rules for optimisation. Our system automatically stages compilation and exploits constant information for dead code elimination and type specialisation. We have re-written our PQL/Java backend in our extension language, enabling dynamic and staged compilation.

We demonstrate the effectiveness of our extension language in several case studies, including the efficient integration of SQL queries, and by analysing the run-time performance of our rewritten prototype backend.

1 Introduction

Modern CPUs are equipped with increasingly many CPU cores. Consequently, parallel execution is becoming more and more important as a means for higher software performance. However, traditional general-purpose mechanisms for parallel programming (such as threads and locks) come with complex semantics [17] and may increase code size substantially, raising the risk of program bugs. Hence, modern languages are beginning to provide language facilities that simplify common parallel patterns.

© Springer-Verlag Berlin Heidelberg 2015
B. Franke (Ed.): CC 2015, LNCS 9031, pp. 111–130, 2015.
DOI: 10.1007/978-3-662-46663-6_6

Our past work, PQL/Java [14], presented one such system, implemented as a language extension that adds a Parallel Query Language (PQL) on top of Java. PQL/Java provides easy access to embarrassingly parallel computations (computations that can be completed in constant time with enough CPU cores) and *fold*-like reductions, both constructing and querying Java containers. Unlike other parallel language extensions such as Java 8 Streams and Parallel LINQ, PQL/Java *automatically* decides which part of a query to parallelise, and how.

Consider a simple example: a user wishes to compute the intersection of two hash sets, s1 and s2, and at the same time eliminate all set elements e that have some property, such as e.x < 0. In Java 8 streams, such a computation can be parallelised with a parallel stream and a filter, as follows:

```
s1.parallelStream()
  .filter(e -> s2.contains(e) && e.x >= 0).collect(Collectors.toSet());
```

This prescribes the following execution: Java will iterate over s1, possibly in parallel (after partitioning the set), and for each set element (a) check if it is also contained in s2, and, if so, (b) also check if it satisfies the filtering condition. All elements that pass are then collected in an output set.

The same intent can be expressed in PQL as the following:

```
query(Set.contains(e)):
    s1.contains(e) && s2.contains(e) && e.x >= 0;
```

PQL, unlike Java Streams, *does not prescribe an execution strategy* for the above. The PQL/Java system may choose to evaluate the above query exactly as in the Java Streams example, or it may choose to test e.x >= 0 before s2.contains(e) (since the former will typically be much faster and will eliminate some of the latter checks), it may choose to iterate over s2 instead of s1, and it may even choose to execute the query sequentially if it predicts that the overhead for parallel execution would be too high.

PQL can thus perform complex strategic optimisations over parallel queries that are beyond the scope of other parallel language extensions. Partly this is due to more restricted semantics of operations (e.g., guarantee of no side-effects, which allows the order of two conditions to be exchanged).

However, even within a more restricted semantic framework, the ability to optimise comes at a price:

- PQL must be aware of different *execution strategies* for language constructs. For our example above, it must be aware both of the *iteration* strategy and of the *is-contained-check* strategy.
- PQL requires a *cost model* for each execution strategy in order to be able to choose between different implementation alternatives.

For example, if a user wishes to query a custom matrix datatype, PQL will not be able to help, as PQL has no built-in knowledge about this type. The user can at best convert the datatype, but support for custom queries (such as 'sum up all matrix elements for all rows at column 2') or for parallelism would require changes to the compiler.

We have therefore designed an *extension specification language* PQL-ESL that simplifies the task of extending PQL, to allow programmers to easily add support for their own datatypes and computations. In addition to providing PQL-ESL for language extensions, we have re-implemented the PQL/Java backend in PQL-ESL. This has allowed us to perform additional optimisations, particularly *run-time query optimisation*.

Run-time query optimisation applies common ideas from staged execution to query processing: we re-optimise queries as new information becomes available. In our earlier example, the dynamic execution system may determine the sizes of s1 and s2 before deciding which execution strategy to apply. This is critical for efficient execution: recall that we iterate over one set and check for containment in the other. Iteration is $O(n)$ over the size of the set, but containment checks are $O(1)$ for hash sets. Iterating over the smaller set therefore provides substantial performance benefits.

Our contributions in this paper are as follows:

- We describe PQL-ESL, an extension specification language for our parallel declarative query programming language PQL/Java. PQL-ESL allows programmers to provide compact, human-readable implementations of execution strategies, while exploiting static and dynamic information about the program (static and dynamic types of query parameters).
- We show how PQL-ESL can be used to facilitate run-time query optimisation in PQL/Java.
- We describe an implementation of PQL mostly in PQL-ESL, and compare the performance of the PQL/Java system with and without PQL-ESL.
- We provide five case studies to show how PQL-ESL allows users to quickly extend PQL with new primitives, including an SQL connector.

Section 2 provides background to our PQL/Java system and summarises relevant aspects, with a focus on our intermediate language. Section 3 then describes our extension specification language, and Section 4 describes how we process and compile the language. Section 5 evaluates our new backend. Section 6 discusses related work, and Section 7 concludes.

2   Background

PQL/Java consists of several layers: The query language PQL itself, which we summarise in Section 2.1, the intermediate language PQIL, basis for our optimisations, which we describe in section 2.2, and the PQL runtime, which supports all of the above. We expand the description of our pre-existing work from [14] in this section before discussing our new extension mechanism in Section 3.

2.1   PQL

With parallelism becoming increasingly important, we designed the Parallel Query Language (PQL) to guarantee that everything written in the language can be parallelised effectively. As we learned from the research area of "Descriptive Complexity" [12], the complexity class that most closely corresponds to our notion of 'embarrassingly parallel' problems matches first-order logic over finite structures. We thus designed PQL on top of first-order logic, with an extension to support *fold*-like reductions (which are not embarrassingly parallel, but are present in most practical parallel frameworks, such as Map-Reduce).

Our goal is to guarantee that any computation expressed in PQL is either trivial or highly parallelisable. This is certainly the case with our original set of primitives. While user extensions and convenience support for user data types may violate this guarantee, our compiler can be set up to issue suitable warnings.

Below is a brief PQL example:

```
exists int x: s1.contains(x) && x > 0;
```

Here, x is a logically quantified variable of type **int**. This query tests whether there exists any element in set s1 that is greater than zero and returns **true** or **false** accordingly. Analogously, we provide universal queries via **forall**.

PQL queries may include Java expressions as logical constants, as long as these expressions do not depend on logically quantified variables. For example:

```
exists int x: s1.contains(x) && x > arbitraryMethod();
```

Here, we treat the subexpression arbitraryMethod() as a logical constant—we execute it precisely once, and supply its constant result to the query. Note that we do not allow PQL programs to use arbitraryMethod(x), as x is a logically quantified variable. This is a design decision to ensure that programmers don't have to worry about the order of side effects if arbitraryMethod is not pure.

We further provide **query**, which constructs a container; we have already seen it used to construct sets, but it can also construct arrays and maps:

```
query(Map.get(int x) = int y): s1.contains(x) && y==x*x;
```

constructs a map from all values in s1 to their square values.

reduce signifies a value reduction:

```
reduce(addInt) int x: s1.contains(x);
```

sums up all values from set s1. Here, addInt can be a user-defined static binary method that we require to be associative, and annotated with a neutral element (0 in this case, to be returned in case s1 is empty). We require the method to be associative, to permit parallel computation with subsequent merging. Note that in the above we will reduce all viable x values, meaning that x determines both the set of possibilities we consider and the bag of values we combine. In some cases, these are not the same and x may occur more than once; to support this scenario, we provide the following syntax:

```
reduce(addInt) int x over int y: x = a[y] * b[y];
```

which computes a vector dot product over all vector indices y.

Our query constructions may be nested freely. For example,

```
query(Map.get(int x) = int y):
        s1.contains(x) && y = reduce(mulInt) int z: range(0, x, z);
```

would compute a map from all values in s1 to their factorial values. Here, range is a method that constructs a set of values from 0 to x and tests whether z is contained within; our system has special support for evaluating this method efficiently (i.e., without generating an intermediate set).

In addition, our query expressions may contain any Java expressions, though only some of them may contain logical variables. Specifically, logical variables may occur in any primitive computation or expression (i.e., we model all unary and binary operators, including **instanceof** and the **?:** ternary operator), as well as .contains(), get(), and array index accesses on sets, maps, and arrays. We further simplify syntax so that map and array accesses can use the same notation.

2.2   The PQL Intermediate Language, PQIL

Our focus in this paper is on our system's backend, which operates on our relational intermediate language, PQIL. Every operator in the language can be viewed as a predicate, i.e., a virtual (not necessarily physically materialised) database table. Our system performs computations as a generalised version of a database join. We use the term 'join operators' for the PQIL primitives, and each operator takes a number of parameter variables. For example, the PQL expression s1.contains(x) && s2.contains(x) may be represented by the following PQIL program, consisting of two primitive operators in sequence within a block:

$$\{ \quad \text{CONTAINS}(s_1, x); \quad \text{CONTAINS}(s_2, x); \quad \}$$

The above will compute a join over s_1 and s_2, with $\text{CONTAINS}(s_1, x)$ iterating over all possible values for x, and $\text{CONTAINS}(s_2, x)$ filtering out all values that are not also in s_2. We thus translate logical expressions that would have a **boolean** value in Java into queries that search for the exact values that will make the expression come true.

In the above example, $\text{CONTAINS}(s_1, x)$ *writes* x and $\text{CONTAINS}(s_2, x)$ *reads* x. PQIL can make this distinction explicit by marking the variables as '$?x$' for reading and '$!x$' for writing, i.e., $\{\text{CONTAINS}(?s_1, !x); \text{CONTAINS}(?s_2, ?x); \}$. Variables being in 'read mode' or 'write mode' thus describes the operational behaviour of each join operator: $\text{CONTAINS}(?s_1, !x)$ must write $!x$ and thus iterates over $?s_1$, while $\text{CONTAINS}(?s_2, ?x)$ only reads its parameters and thus performs a containment check. For optimisation purposes, we support a further variable mode, '$\_$', which stands for 'ignore': this can be useful e.g. in the PQL query

```
query(Set.contains(x)): exists y: a[x] = y;
```

where y is immaterial and we only care about the index values of array a. Here, our PQIL representation is $\text{ARRAYLOOKUP}\langle int \rangle(?a, !x, \_)$ which our backend can exploit to generate efficient code that never dereferences any array elements.

Each PQIL program has a *program context* that assigns each variable v a type $\tau(v)$ and a value binding $val(v)$. Whenever the value is not a known constant, we set $val(v) = \top$. For example, when performing a range check range(1, 10, x), the numbers 1 and 10 will be represented by variables with such a known value.

Join operators are typed; for example, $\text{RANGE}(x : int, y : int, z : int)$ joins over three integer variables. PQIL allows mismatching actual parameter types; our backend generates implicit conversion code, including (un)boxing, as needed.

PQL provides join operators to support all of Java's unary, binary, and ternary operators, as well as operators to interface with sets, maps, and arrays, as well as to support conversions, field accesses, and container accesses. Each operator is monomorphic, so we use different variants for all viable types. Figure 1 lists some of our operators.

$\text{FIELD}\langle \tau, f \rangle(o_1, o_2)$	$o_2 = ((\tau)o_1).f$
$\text{CONTAINS}(s, v)$	$s.\text{contains}(v)$
$\text{RANGECONTAINS}\langle \tau \rangle(s, e, v)$	for τ in int, long: $s \leq v \leq e$
$\text{ARRAYLOOKUP}\langle \tau \rangle(a, k, v)$	$a[k] = v$
$\text{TYPE}\langle \tau \rangle(v)$	Checks that v has type τ; checks bounds for integral types

Fig. 1. List of five of our primitive PQIL predicates ("join operators"). The remaining operators are analogous.

The semantics of each operator is that it will attempt to produce all viable bindings for all parameter variables $!x$ that match any given, previously bound variables $?y$ and then *proceed*. We may later backtrack to the same operator, at which point it may proceed again. If no more bindings are available, the operator *aborts*. For example, $\text{CONTAINS}(?s, !x)$ on a set with three elements will succeed three times, then abort. We treat (_) as write-mode variables with fresh names.

We permit duplicate variable bindings where appropriate, so that PQIL observes a Bag semantics. For most primitive operators, such as $\text{ADD}\langle int \rangle(?x, ?y, !z)$, variables can only be bound once (there is only one z for any given x and y such that integer addition yields $z = x + y$), but for other operators, especially container accesses, multiple bindings are possible (as in CONTAINS).

The alternative $\text{ADD}\langle int \rangle(?x, ?y, ?z)$ reads and compares z and produces one binding (succeeds, if $z = x + y$) or zero bindings (aborts, otherwise).

In addition to the above primitive operators, PQIL provides a number of control structures: boolean materialisation (translating successful/failed bindings into **true**/**false** values), disjunctive and conjunctive blocks, and reductions.

We have already used conjunctive blocks in our earlier examples (denoted by curly braces, $\{ j_0, \ldots, j_k \}$). The semantics of such a block are $j_0 \bowtie \ldots \bowtie j_k$, i.e., we join each primitive with its neighbour (again with bag semantics). PQIL also supports a disjunctive block to model the semantics of the 'or' operator.

Finally, we use the reduction operator REDUCE to express generalised reductions, which include map, set, and array construction. For example, we express the PQL query **reduce(Map.get(x) == y) : s1.contains(x) && y == x+1** as:

$$\text{REDUCE}[\text{MAP}(?x, ?y, !m)] \{\text{CONTAINS}(?s_1, !x); \text{ADD}\langle int \rangle(?x, 1, !y); \}$$

Here, $\text{MAP}(?x, ?y, !m)$ is a *reductor* that specifies that for each viable binding produced by the body of the reduction (the block containing CONTAINS and

ADD), the fresh map m obtains a mapping from x to y. Multiple mismatching bindings for x cause an exception. The reduction provides a singular binding of variable m. Reductions can construct sets, maps, maps with default values, and arrays, or *fold* (**reduce**) values through a user-supplied method.

2.3   Optimising PQIL

Before compiling PQIL to Java bytecode, we perform high-level optimisations:

- *Nested Block Flattening* splices conjunctive blocks into their parent conjunctive block, if it exists (analogously with disjunctive blocks).
- *Common Sub-Join Elimination* combines redundant primitive join operators within the same conjunctive block, if one is equal to *or generalises* the other.
- *Type Bound Elimination* eliminates unnecessary occurrences of $\text{TYPE}\langle\tau\rangle(x)$.
- *Access Path Selection* re-orders join primitives (see below).
- *Map Reduction Nesting* merges nested reductions that are part of a map/array construction into a single reduction [14].
- *Read/Write Assignment* assigns each variable occurrence a flag to determine whether the variable is read, written, or ignored (Section 2.2). The accompanying must-define flow analysis is an important subroutine in Access Path Selection, and it enables Common Sub-Join Elimination.

Access path selection (or 'query planning') is a standard database optimisation [15] that we apply to each conjunctive block. This technique searches for the most efficient strategy for satisfying a sequence of constraints (as expressed in our join operators). PQL uses a single-phase access path selector that re-orders individual join operators within a conjunctive block. This optimisation is mandatory in our compilation process, as it assigns variables' read/write modes.

Consider the intermediate code in Figure 2 ('Unoptimised'). The reduction here contains five primitive join operators, of which Type Bound Elimination can eliminate one ($\text{TYPE}\langle Point\rangle(e)$). Access path selection can re-order the remaining four. Our access path selection employs a beam search strategy (retaining the best partial access paths found so far) to limit the search space.

We model the cost for executing each join operator in four *cost attributes*:

- *size*: how many bindings do we expect the operator to generate?
- *cost*: how much does generating one binding cost?
- *selectivity*: what fraction of past bindings will our current join not filter out?
- *parallel*: is this join operator parallelisable?

Not all of this information is available at compile time, and estimate where necessary. This can lead to sub-optimal decisions (Section 5), highlighting the need for staged compilation.

We use the *parallel* flag to discount *size*, but only if the join operator occurs in the head of its block, which is where our backend can parallelise the operator.

Each join operator can have different sets of cost attributes depending on its variables' access modes. For example, the *size* of $\text{CONTAINS}(?s, ?v)$ is always 1,

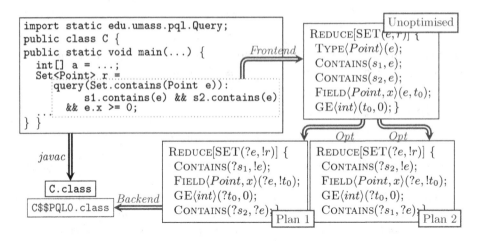

Fig. 2. An example of PQL compilation. Here, GE is the join operator for greater-than-or-equal. The frontend emits PQIL (Section 2.2), which we then optimise (Section 2.3). Access path selection identifies multiple query plans (Plan 1, Plan 2) and chooses the most efficient one. The backend generates Java bytecode either to disk (depicted) or into memory at runtime (Section 4).

whereas the *size* of CONTAINS$(?s, !v)$ is exactly the size of the set s. Some combinations of access modes are disallowed, if our system lacks an implementation.

Each variable x is marked as 'write' $(!x)$ precisely the first time it appears (or never, if it is a logical constant and $val(x) \neq \top$), so our search algorithm can unambiguously determine access modes and the correct cost from our model. In our example, the possible solutions cannot start with FIELD$\langle Point, x \rangle(e, t_0)$ because e is not bound yet. Similarly, we cannot start with GE$\langle int \rangle(t_0, 0)$ because t_0 is not bound yet. Our algorithm will only consider CONTAINS$(?s_i, !e)$ (for $i \in \{1, 2\}$) as initial join operation in the block. Filtering by set is slower yet equally selective to loading and comparing an integer field, so our access path selector will generate either Plan 1 or Plan 2 here.

3   PQL Extension Specification Language

Reflecting PQL, our intermediate language PQIL is a powerful language with a large degree of variability in how each of its join operators might be implemented. This poses a challenge for implementing new join operators or extending existing ones. We thus opted for an extension specification language, PQL-ESL, which allows us to compactly (re-)implement old and new operators.

We designed PQL-ESL so that it should be (a) easy to compile to efficient Java bytecode, (b) simplify the implementation of PQIL and future extensions, and (c) be compact and expressive. To that end, we based our language syntax and semantics on Java's, for expressions, statements, and method definitions, and borrowed from Java's annotation syntax for special attributes. The language includes a number of changes and adds several features:

- Reference semantics for operator parameters
- Type inference (parameters and locals need not be explicitly typed)
- Access mode specifications and tests
- *sections*
- Control operators to signal successful variable binding, or binding failure
- PQIL property tests for parameters
- Templates
- Explicit parallelism support
- Cost model attribute computations

Figure 3 summarises the most salient features of our grammar. In the following, we discuss some of the more interesting features from the above list by looking at examples from our specifications.

3.1   Access Mode Specifications

Consider the following example:

```
1 @accessModes{rr}
2 lt(val1, val2) {
3     local:
4         if ( @type{int} val1 < val2) proceed;
5         else abort;
6 }
```

This program describes the implementation of the PQIL operator for 'less than'. The first line describes the possible access modes for all parameter variables, which we here restrict to be read mode (r) for both. We permit listing multiple access modes, with read, write (w), and wildcard mode (_) annotations, plus a meta-wildcard (.) operator for any of r, w, _.

Line 2 specifies the operator and its parameters. PQL-ESL infers variable types automatically in most cases, so users need not specify them here.

3.2   Sections

Line 3 is a *section* specifier. Each PQL-ESL program can describe up to four sections: *global*, which marks one-time initialisation code (which we don't need here), *local*, which marks code that must be executed each time we start evaluating the PQIL operator, *iterate*, which marks code that we must evaluate every time we backtrack to this operator due to the failure of a subsequent operator, and *model*, which computes cost model attributes (Section 3.7). Section markers may be conditional: we use this to permit conditionally moving computations from the local to the global section.

Lines 4 and 5 contain a standard Java conditional. The only noteworthy feature is the use of @type{int}, which can resolve type ambiguity in overloaded operators. This is *optional* (Section 3.5); omitting the specification would permit our implementation to compare any numeric type.

```
opdef    ::= ⟨generic⟩* (⟨init⟩ '{' ⟨stmt⟩* '}')?
init     ::= ⟨accessm⟩ ID '(' (ID (',' ID )*)? ')'
generic  ::= '@generic' '{' ID '}' '{' STR (',' STR)* '}'
accessm  ::= '@accessModes' '{' (ACC (',' ACC)*)? '}'
stmt     ::= ⟨if⟩ | ⟨section⟩ | ⟨goto⟩ | ⟨return⟩ | ⟨while⟩ | ⟨do⟩ | ⟨assign⟩ | ⟨call⟩
return   ::= 'abort' ';' | 'proceed' ';' | 'proceed' 'on' ID '?=' ⟨expr⟩ ';'
assign   ::= ⟨typeinfo⟩? ID '=' ⟨expr⟩ ';'
typeinfo ::= '@type' '{' TYPE '}'
```

Fig. 3. Partial EBNF grammar for PQL-ESL, eliding more standard language constructions (nested expressions, **while** loops, new object constructions, method calls, etc.) that are syntactically similar or identical to Java

3.3 Special Control Operators

Finally, lines 4 and 5 also describe what we should do if the comparison succeeds (**proceed**) and what we should do if it fails (**abort**). Here, **proceed** signals a successful evaluation of the PQIL operator, proceeding e.g. to the next nested operator in a conjunctive block or to a reductor that aggregates a successful conclusion of a reduction body. **abort**, meanwhile, signals that the reductor cannot produce any (or any more) bindings and must backtrack. It then backtracks to the most closely nested operator that provides an `iterate` section. All control flow must end with an explicit **abort** or **proceed**; we do not permit leaving the body of an PQL-ESL program implicitly.

3.4 Property Tests on Parameter Variables

Since each operator may supply multiple access modes, PQL-ESL code provides a means for testing these access modes, using the operator `isMode(` $(a_1, \ldots, a_n)$`,` $(m_1$ `||` $\ldots$ `||` $m_k)$ `)`, which evaluates to 'true' iff the access modes for variables a_1 to a_n match one of the access modes m_i $(1 \leq i \leq k)$.

As an example, consider the following (slightly simplified) fragment from our original implementation of negation, $\text{NEG}(a, b)$:

```
if (isMode( (b), (r) )) {
    tmp = !a;
if (b == tmp) proceed;
    else abort;
} else {
b = !a;
proceed; }
```

This shows the variability when dealing with two access modes (read vs. write) for the second parameter: if b is in read mode, we must compare to determine if we should proceed or abort, if it is in write mode, we assign to it. Wildcard mode would require another **isMode** check.

We have found the above to be a very common pattern expression and function operators so we provide a short form, **proceed on** v ?= expr, that expands to the above and also handles wildcard mode. The proceed-on operator simplifies the above example to `proceed on b ?= !a;`

We provide a second test on parameters, `isConst(x)`, which evaluates to 'true' iff $val(x) \neq \top$; we use it to move initialisations related to x from the *local* section to the *global* section to reduce initialisation overhead to constant time.

3.5   Templates

Our earlier definition of `lt` is not the actual code that we use, as that would require a substantial amount of repetition both to support PQL's primitive numeric types and to support similar operations. Instead, PQL-ESL provides a template programming mechanism that allows us to re-use such specifications, as in the example below:

```
@generic{operator}{"<=", "<"}
@generic{type}{"int", "long", "double"}
@accessModes{rr}
lt_lte(val1, val2) {
      local:
      if ( @type{#type#} val1 #operator# val2)
            proceed;
      else abort;
}
```

This program has two template parameters: `operator`, which can be 'less-than or equal' (`<=`) or 'less-than' (`<`), and `type`, which can be int, long, and double. The PQL-ESL template processor generates all 6 possible pairs of substitutions for the two parameters. Such instantiation is critical for performance, as each of the 6 different operations uses different bytecode operations. Note that we could omit `@type{#type#}` and the explicit template specification for `type`, as type inference will implicitly introduce suitable template parameters as needed.

3.6   Explicit Parallelism

Support for parallel execution is a central PQL feature, so PQL-ESL provides a special interface for parallel access. Operator specifications call **isParallelMode()** to detect whether the operator should run in parallel. In parallel mode, two predefined variables are available: `__thread_index` (indicating the current operator's thread ID) and `__threads_nr` (indicating the total number of threads in use).

For example, an implementation of ARRAYLOOKUP($?a, !i, !v$) may explore the array a in parallel on multiple cores. It reads `__thread_index` and `__threads_nr` and computes the beginning and end of the array indices it should explore; the perspective of the individual operator is that it will explore only that fraction of the index space. Each operator implementation provides its own solution for parallel execution.

3.7   Cost Attributes

Effective language extensions for PQL must also be able to provide cost models to our access path selection mechanism; otherwise we may use them ineffectively (i.e., pick a less efficient access path over a more efficient one). We therefore provide a special section, *model*, that only serves to compute cost attributes. This *model* section is divided into three subsections: *size*, *cost* and *selectivity* (cf. Section 2.3). Let's have a look at the formulas to calculate the cost of an entire given conjunctive block:

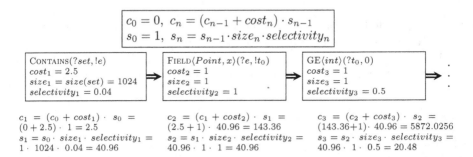

In this example we calculated the cost for the earlier example Plan 1 of figure 2. The cost till operator i is respectively in c_i. Assignments to distinguished variables in these sections (e.g., $\texttt{size}$), are handed to the access path selector. Note that the *parallel* cost attribute need not be specified, as we can infer it from uses of **isParallelMode()**.

Since this section is part of the specification body, it can take advantage of access mode, constantness, and parallelism information, as well as dynamic properties (such as actual container sizes).

4   Translation with PQL-ESL

PQL-ESL allows us to specify what bytecode we should generate for which join operator. However, the exact bytecode can vary substantially based on (a) access modes for each parameter x, (b) type information $\tau(x)$ and value bindings $val(x)$, as provided by the program context (where known), and (c) whether we are generating code for parallel execution or for sequential execution.

We first *precompile* all PQL-ESL specifications into Java code; this step is only required to add or change PQIL operators. Precompilation reads PQL-ESL specifications, performs name and type analysis as well as template expansion, and generates the PQL-ESL static compiler backend.

At static compile time (invoking our extended $\texttt{javac}$), we process any PQL source code as per Figure 2, then feed the resultant PQIL into this PQL-ESL backend. Static compilation determines all compilation possibilities for each of our PQIL operators in the given context. For each viable configuration of each operator, it generates a *snippet*, consisting of bytecode (via ASM [3]) and metadata for linking. The dynamic compiler later chooses between snippets.

4.1 Static Compilation and Snippets

The static compiler backend takes in a PQIL program (passed down from the compiler frontend, Figure 2) and compiles it to a dynamic code generator. Since each PQIL operator may be compiled in one of several alternative ways (depending on access modes, etc.), the static compiler performs various checks to determine which compilation patterns to apply. We derive these checks directly from each PQL-ESL specification. Consider compiling CONTAINS(s, v). To provide a correct translation, we must check for numerous alternatives:

(a) What is the mode of v? Read, write, or wildcard? (b) What is the type of s? An unknown/user-defined set type that we cannot parallelise, or a known set type whose internal representation we know how to parallelise? (c) Are we performing parallel access in write or wildcard mode?

As we discussed in the previous section, PQL-ESL can capture all possibilities concisely. Consider the following example:

```
1 local:
2     if (isConst(s))
3         global:
4     if (s instanceof PSet) ...
```

First, consider line 4. Here, we check whether s is of type PSet or a general set, where PSet is PQL's set implementation, specially optimised for parallel evaluation. Additional parallelisable set types can be supported easily.

The default interpretation of the above **instanceof** check is that we should perform it locally, i.e., every time we enter the operator for the first time (possibly with a new s). This correctly captures the possibility that s might change frequently. Lines 2 and 3 capture a first optimisation: if we know that s is going to be constant during the evaluation of the query, we only need to execute this code once (which we accomplish by moving it into the *global* section).

Thus, the code explicitly handles the distinction between evaluation at operator execution vs. evaluation at query execution start time. Our system handles remaining distinctions automatically: if the dynamic compiler knows whether s is constant and/or whether its dynamic type will be a subtype of PSet, it will perform constant folding/dead code elimination, though we precompute this optimisation at *static* compile time. That is, the static compiler compiles the same operator multiple times under different assumptions, such as *known PSet* (only compiling the **true** branch), *known not PSet* (only compiling the **false** branch), and *unknown whether PSet* (compiling both branches and a dynamic check).

The result of static compilation is a multitude of different bytecode sequences that contains all of the variations that are plausible from the static compiler's perspective. We further separate this bytecode into the *static* and *local+iterate* sections, as these need to be executed at different times. We accompany the resultant bytecode sections with a brief relocation table, to resolve back-tracking jumps to the *iterate* section start. Each such combination we refer to as a *snippet*. Simultaneously, our static compiler generates a *composition scaffold* for each operator, which is effectively a nested **switch** table to pick the optimal snippet.

4.2   Dynamic Compilation

Of our PQIL optimisations (Section 2.3), two (Type Bound Elimination and Access Path Selection) potentially benefit from run-time information. Since access path selection can have a substantial impact on the execution time of a query, our dynamic compiler re-runs access path selection before dynamic code generation, factoring in newly available information (e.g., run-time container sizes).

The result is a re-ordered PQIL specification, which we then pass into the composition scaffold. The scaffold examines each operator parameter's access modes and may further examine constantness, dynamic types, and whether the operator is to be compiled for parallel execution. It then picks the optimally specialised snippet for each operator and configuration, and links it against its neighbouring snippets, emitting bytecode that is ready for execution.

5   Evaluation

To test the utility of our PQL-ESL language, we used it to re-implement our PQL/Java bytecode backend. We found the language to be entirely suitable to this task, though implementing the FIELD operator's field access operation required the addition of a single PQL-ESL feature.

To further evaluate our language, we performed three forms of evaluation: We evaluated the usability of PQL-ESL by implementing four new extensions, we examined in detail the performance of our dynamic compiler with four pre-existing PQL benchmarks [14] and two new synthetic benchmarks and we implemented support for communicating with SQL data sources via JDBC.

5.1   Case Studies

To evaluate the generality of our language, we selected four language extensions that we did not previously support in PQL and added them to our system.

sqrt: Our first extension was a square-root function on doubles. This addition permits two access modes, one for computing and one for testing the square root.

primes: We further added support for prime numbers. We added two extensions, PRIMECHECK, which determines whether a number is prime by trying to divide by all smaller non-even numbers up to the number's square root, and PRIMERANGE, which computes all prime numbers in a given range, using the Sieve of Eratosthenes. Our rewriting engine automatically introduces PRIMERANGE when PRIMECHECK and RANGE affect the same variable.

Java 8 streams: To bridge the gap between Java 8 streams and PQL, we added a STREAMCONTAINS(s, v) operator analogous to our CONTAINS(s, v) operator. In access mode CONTAINS$(?s, ?v)$, it uses a Java 8 `EqualityPredicate` to text whether v is contained in the stream s. For access mode CONTAINS$(?s, !v)$, it iterates over all stream elements and binds them to v, again unifying two mechanisms into a single interface.

Extension	LOC	Snippets
SQRT	5	4
PRIMECHECK	20	2
PRIMERANGE	42	4
STREAMCONTAINS	21	4
MODULO	8→61	16→32

Benchmark	Snippets	Bytes
threegrep	16	1155
wordcount	8	1747
bonus	18	1773
webgraph	16	1608
setnested	8	1407
arraynested	10	993

Fig. 4. Sizes of our new operators, counting global, local, and iterate sections. The arrows for the pre-existing MODULO operator indicate changes due to our extensions.

Fig. 5. Snippet statistics for our benchmarks. Here, **total bytes** is the size of all bytecodes in the final linked bytecode for the query, in bytes.

modulo: For our last extension, we modified the existing $\text{MODULO}(x, y, z)$ operator, for int and long parameters, to permit access modes $\text{MODULO}(?x, !y, ?z)$ and $\text{MODULO}(!x, ?y, ?z)$, allowing users to find all x for a given y and z such that $x \bmod y = z$ (analogously for y).

Figure 4 summarises the sizes of our extensions, counting their lines of code and number of snippets. Despite the large amount of variability in many of the extensions, we found the code sizes to be very manageable.

5.2 JDBC Link

Our JDBC link adds three new user-facing operators: one that represent a database, one that represents a table in the database, and one that represents access to a field in the database. In an approach comparable to that of Cheung et al.'s QBS [7] we then automatically promote PQL operators to database operators where possible, using our rewriting engine. We further filter expected/required result fields automatically through a custom PQIL analysis. In total, this link uses ten custom operators with 9–53 lines of code. Operators include a single highly-polymorphic operator that represents all numeric comparisons between fields and constants, operators for simplified access to three particular database systems, and the SQL LIKE operator. Automatic promotion to joins between tables is not supported yet, though the PQL-ESL-specified *operators* are as expressive as JDBC permits them to be.

While database access via JDBC can inherently not be parallelised, our JDBC link allows users to take advantage of our query language and to optimise interactions with data sources on the Java heap.

5.3 Performance Evaluation

We examined our system with the following benchmarks:

- *threegrep*, which find all strings (in a set of 100-character strings) that contain the substring "012" [8].

- *wordcount*, which computes the absolute numbers of occurrences of words in documents. We represent words by unique integer IDs. The result is a map from word IDs to the number of times they occur in a set of documents.
- *bonus*, which is a well-known example from the databases literature [19] that computes employee salary boni, given each employee's department, the department's bonus policy, and the employee's accumulated bonus. The result is again a map, from each employee to their aggregate bonus.
- *webgraph*, as defined by Yang et al. [19], in which we compute the set of all documents in a graph structure that point to themselves via one point of indirection.
- *setnested*, which computes the intersection of two random sets of integers, plus a size bound (similar to our initial motivating example, but without a field access). One of the sets contains only a single element, while the other contains 500,000.
- *arraynested*, which computes the set intersection of two random arrays, again with a size bound. Sizes of the arrays are identical to *setnested*.

Figure 5 summarises the number of snippets for each benchmark. Even for our four more complex benchmarks, our static compiler is effective at keeping the number of relevant alternatives small. While some important snippets can reach a substantial size (up to around 650 bytes for a snippet in wordcount that represents a nested reduction into a default map, to aggregate the total counts), the size of the ultimately generated bytecode remains below $2kB$, within the size of what we might expect for such a computation.

We took each benchmark's PQL implementation and compiled it both with our original backend [14] and with the new PQL-ESL backend. For comparison, we also ran best-effort manual implementations. We ran all benchmarks 13 times, discarding the first 3 runs as warm-up runs. Compared to our earlier backend, we configured our benchmarks to '50% mode', which reduces the workload for each benchmark by at least 50%, thereby making the dynamic compilation overhead more easily visible and putting our original system at a deliberate advantage.

We ran all benchmarks on the Oracle JDK 1.8.0_05, on a Sun SPARC64 (Sparc v9) Enterprise-T5120 system, with 8 cores at 8 SMT threads each. We left all system configuration at its defaults, other than increasing the default heap size to 13200 MiB. Access path selection used a search window size of 16.

Our current PQL-ESL backend does not yet serialise snippets to class files. For our experiments, we therefore ran the static and dynamic compilation phases in the same JVM, taking care to separate the execution phases. We avoided including the rest of the PQL/Java compiler by separately compiling all PQL source code into PQIL and feeding the result directly into our backend.

Figure 6 shows our total execution time, *excluding* dynamic recompilation time. The quality of the code generated by our new backend is competitive with our existing backend for all existing benchmarks, outperforming it in *webgraph* and, for small and large numbers of threads, in *bonus*.

Figure 6 separately shows dynamic recompilation time, which is currently in the millisecond range, meaning that dynamic recompilation is only effective

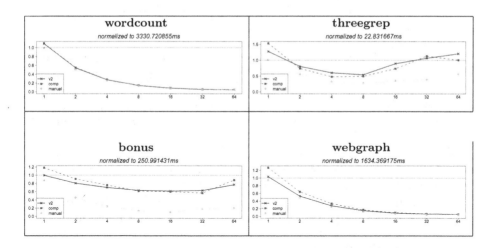

Fig. 6. Benchmark execution times: Execution time (y axis) by number of threads (x axis). The figure shows manual java implementation (*manual*), the new backend (*v2*) and the original backend (*comp*).

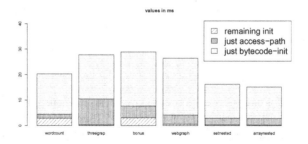

Fig. 7. Dynamic compilation overhead, split into snippet-based code generation, access path selection, and remaining initialisation (allocating supporting data structures)

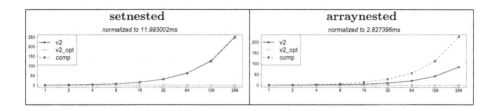

Fig. 8. Execution times (y axis) for queries with increasing workloads (x axis), in benchmarks that rely on dynamic access path selection, running single-threaded

for large data sets. We can leverage this insight to use suitable heuristics that determine whether dynamic optimisation is warranted from the size of any input containers, and default to execution without dynamic compilation for small workloads, where sub-optimal access paths are not critical.

Dynamic compilation overhead is the price we pay for dynamic optimisation. We see the value that we gain for this price in Figure 8, which again shows our benchmarks *setnested* and *arraynested*. Both benchmarks operate over two containers with substantially different sizes. Performance depends on picking the larger container to iterate over, and the smaller container to check containment in; this is only possible with run-time information.

For each benchmark, we scale the sizes of both containers by the factor on the x axis. In our graphs, *comp* and *v2* show our old and new backend, respectively. As we can see, our new backend outperforms the old backend even without recompilation. However, execution time increases exponentially for both implementations if they choose the less optimal container for iteration. *v2_opt* shows our new backend with dynamic re-compilation, with near constant-time performance. Initialisation overheads are again shown separately, in Figure 6.

Overall, we found performance of PQL-ESL to be on par with our current system when not factoring in dynamic optimisation. With dynamic optimisation, our PQL-ESL backend can greatly outperform our existing system. At the same time, re-writing our backend in PQL-ESL has given us the flexibility to re-target compilation to static or dynamic compile time, to add new language features quickly, and to apply further language-based optimisations in the future.

6   Related Work

Extensible query languages are widely known in the literature. For example, the Meteor language for the Stratosphere platform [11] can be extended with new operators, as can PigLatin [13]. FlumeJava [5], PLINQ [9] and Java 8 Streams, which act as internal DSLs, can be extended by implementing predefined interfaces. All of the above systems thus permit users to add new operators.

However, to the best of our knowledge none of these systems utilise a special-purpose extension language to simplify optimisation, multi-stage or otherwise. Similarly, none of the above systems will automatically select between different modes of user-defined operators, as permitted by our read/write mode distinction. The only optimisations they can apply to language extensions are therefore optimisations provided by the host language compiler. As we have shown, this suggests that these systems may be missing optimisation opportunities.

Delite, a framework for highly-optimised domain-specific languages, includes a query language, OptiQL [16] that can conceptually integrate with other domain-specific languages, performing parallelisation and other optimisations across DSLs. However, we are not aware of OptiQL supporting custom operators. StreamJIT [2], a commensal compiler framework, treats IRs as libraries and permits IR-level optimisation. Instead of code generation, commensal compilation relies on compiler optimisations; however, it is unclear that complex control flow between operators such as ours could be inlined automatically (and without inline guards) by standard JVM JIT inlining.

Meanwhile, general-purpose Turing-complete languages geared at easing access to parallelism, such as Chapel [4], Fortress [1], and X10 [6] allow user-defined extensions through standard abstractions (functions, classes). However, these languages provide control over parallel primitives (task distribution, atomic regions) rather than automating parallelisation, and being Turing-complete, they may be too powerful for effective automatic parallelisation. By contrast, PQL/-Java strives first to be easy to parallelise, foregoing expressivity to achieve this goal, with PQL-ESL bridging the gap to our Turing-complete host language.

Our focus in this paper has been on extending the PQL/Java backend. Complementary frontend extensions could be based on techniques from the literature, such as those found in Sugar [10] or Silver [18].

7   Conclusion

PQL-ESL is a mechanism for extending the PQL/Java backend with support for new primitives and for more effectively optimising existing primitives. Leveraging PQL-ESL with a two-stage compiler permits us to compile PQL queries statically and dynamically re-optimising as new information becomes available.

We have shown that PQL-ESL is effective at describing PQL primitives by re-implementing our compiler backend in it, and effective at describing new primitives by adding four extensions to PQL. Furthermore, our experiments demonstrate that our execution performance is competitive with our previous backend. For some queries, dynamic compilation enables optimisations that permits the PQL-ESL backend to outperform our previous backend by reducing the algorithmic overhead from $O(n)$ to $O(1)$. Our implementation is publicly available[1].

References

1. Allen, E., Chase, D., Hallett, J., Luchangco, V., Maessen, J.W., Ryu, S., Steele, G., Tobin-Hochstadt, S.: The Fortress Language Specification. Tech. rep., Sun Microsystems (2008)
2. Bosboom, J., Rajadurai, S., Wong, W.F., Amarasinghe, S.: StreamJIT: A Commensal Compiler for High-performance Stream Programming. In: OOPSLA 2014, pp. 177–195. ACM, New York (2014)
3. Bruneton, E., Lenglet, R., Coupaye, T.: ASM: a code manipulation tool to implement adaptable systems. Adaptable and Extensible Component Systems (2002)
4. Callahan, D., Chamberlain, B., Zima, H.: The cascade high productivity language. In: Proceedings of the Ninth International Workshop on High-Level Parallel Programming Models and Supportive Environments, pp. 52–60 (April 2004)
5. Chambers, C., Raniwala, A., Perry, F., Adams, S., Henry, R.R., Bradshaw, R., Weizenbaum, N.: FlumeJava: easy, efficient data-parallel pipelines. In: Programming Language Design and Implementation (PLDI), pp. 363–375. ACM, New York (2010)

---

[1] http://sepl.cs.uni-frankfurt.de/pql.html

6. Charles, P., Grothoff, C., Saraswat, V., Donawa, C., Kielstra, A., Ebcioglu, K., von Praun, C., Sarkar, V.: X10: an object-oriented approach to non-uniform cluster computing

7. Cheung, A., Solar-Lezama, A., Madden, S.: Optimizing database-backed applications with query synthesis. SIGPLAN Not. 48(6), 3–14 (2013)

8. Dean, J., Ghemawat, S.: MapReduce: simplified data processing on large clusters. In: Operating Systems Design & Implementation (OSDI). USENIX Association (2004)

9. Duffy, J., Essey, E.: Parallel LINQ: Running queries on multi-core processors. MSDN Magazine (October 2007)

10. Erdweg, S., Rieger, F.: A framework for extensible languages. In: Järvi, J., Kästner, C. (eds.) GPCE, pp. 3–12. ACM (2013)

11. Heise, A., Rheinländer, A., Leich, M., Leser, U., Naumann, F.: Meteor/sopremo: An extensible query language and operator model. In: Proceedings of the International Workshop on End-to-end Management of Big Data (BigData) in Conjunction with VLDB, Istanbul, Turkey (2012)

12. Immerman, N.: Descriptive Complexity. Springer (1998)

13. Olston, C., Reed, B., Srivastava, U., Kumar, R., Tomkins, A.: Pig latin: A not-so-foreign language for data processing. In: Proc. ACM SIGMOD International Conference on Management of Data (SIGMOD), pp. 1099–1110. ACM (2008)

14. Reichenbach, C., Smaragdakis, Y., Immerman, N.: PQL: A purely-declarative Java extension for parallel programming. In: Noble, J. (ed.) ECOOP 2012. LNCS, vol. 7313, pp. 53–78. Springer, Heidelberg (2012)

15. Selinger, P.G., Astrahan, M.M., Chamberlin, D.D., Lorie, R.A., Price, T.G.: Access path selection in a relational database management system. In: ACM SIGMOD Int. Conf. on Management of Data, SIGMOD 1979, pp. 23–34. ACM, New York (1979), http://doi.acm.org/10.1145/582095.582099

16. Sujeeth, A., Rompf, T., Brown, K., Lee, H., Chafi, H., Popic, V., Wu, M., Prokopec, A., Jovanovic, V., Odersky, M., Olukotun, K.: Composition and reuse with compiled domain-specific languages. In: Castagna, G. (ed.) ECOOP 2013. LNCS, vol. 7920, pp. 52–78. Springer, Heidelberg (2013)

17. Vafeiadis, V., Narayan, C.: Relaxed separation logic: A program logic for C11 concurrency. In: Hosking, A.L., Eugster, P.T., Lopes, C.V. (eds.) OOPSLA, pp. 867–884. ACM (2013)

18. Van Wyk, E., Bodin, D., Gao, J., Krishnan, L.: Silver: an extensible attribute grammar system. Science of Computer Programming 75(1-2), 39–54 (2010)

19. Yang, H.C., Dasdan, A., Hsiao, R.L., Parker, D.S.: Map-reduce-merge: simplified relational data processing on large clusters. In: ACM SIGMOD Int. Conf. on Management of Data, SIGMOD 2007, pp. 1029–1040. ACM, New York (2007)

Staged Points-to Analysis for Large Code Bases

Nicholas Allen, Bernhard Scholz, and Padmanabhan Krishnan

Oracle Labs
Brisbane, Australia
{nicholas.allen,bernhard.scholz,paddy.krishnan}@oracle.com

Abstract. Bug checker tools for Java require fine-grained heap abstractions including object-sensitive call graphs, field information for objects, and points-to sets for program variables to find bugs in source codes. However, heap abstractions coined commonly as points-to analysis, have high runtime-complexity especially when the points-to analysis is context-sensitive, and, hence, state-of-the-art points-to analyses do not scale for large code bases.

In this paper, we introduce a new points-to framework that facilitates the computation of context-sensitive points-to analysis for large code bases. The framework is demand-driven, i.e., a client queries the points-to information for some program variables. The novelty of our approach is a pre-analysis technique that is a combination of staged points-to analyses with program slicing and program compaction. We implemented the proposed points-to framework in Datalog for a proprietary bug checker that could identify security vulnerabilities in the OpenJDK^{TM} library which has approximately 1.3 million variables and 500,000 allocation-sites. For the clients that we have chosen, our technique is able to eliminate about 73% of all variables and about 95% of allocation-sites. Thus our points-to framework scales for code bases with millions of program variables and hundreds of thousands of methods.

1 Introduction

With the wide-spread use of bug checking and productivity tools [4,8,5], the scalability of static program analysis for large code bases is imminent. Object-oriented languages heavily rely on the state of the heap and for static program analyses it is crucial to reason about the state by using a heap abstraction. For most bug checking tools one cannot consider software components in isolation [19] easily. For example, Octeau et al. [19] argue that a high-fidelity analysis of component interaction is required for a comprehensive security analysis, and hence a comprehensive heap abstraction is required. A heap abstraction over-approximates the connectivity of the objects on the heap, which program variables may point to which objects, and resolves virtual dispatches to construct a call-graph. Static program analysis for object-oriented languages relies on the precision of the heap abstraction, i.e., how the effect of heap operations are abstracted including object creations, variable references, and read/write

© Springer-Verlag Berlin Heidelberg 2015
B. Franke (Ed.): CC 2015, LNCS 9031, pp. 131–150, 2015.
DOI: 10.1007/978-3-662-46663-6_7

operations on object fields. The heap abstraction is computed via a points-to analysis, for which there exists a cornucopia of methods [21,18,12,24,23,17].

The standard context-insensitive points-to algorithm [2] has insufficient precision for many applications including security analysis [19,11]. To improve the precision of points-to, context sensitive analyses have been introduced [15,23]. There are various notions of contexts. For instance, method invocations on different receiver objects are treated differently. One could also combine the receiver object with the caller object to create the context to distinguish invocations. In the context of computing a precise points-to relation Smaragdakis et al. [23] present a number of context-sensitive analyses and identify situations where the various context-sensitive analysis can be used. In their experimental study, the authors show that the 2-Object+1-Heap context sensitive points-to relation is the most precise for object-oriented programs.

Computing the context-sensitive points-to sets for large-scale software is not viable due to high computational costs. Scalable points-to analysis for object-oriented languages such as Java has attracted a lot of attention. To overcome the performance bottleneck of context-sensitive points-to analysis, approaches that rely on refinement, demand-driven analysis and pre-analysis have been explored [24,25,22,27]. For example, to overcome the precision versus scalability trade-off for large-scale software, demand-driven analysis [28,25] is one of the most popular approaches that computes a points-to analysis for a client. The client issues specific points-to queries and for only parts of the program that affect the points-to queries, a points-to set is computed. Other approaches include preprocessing the input [22] which may increase the efficiency of context-sensitive analysis. But the presented approach is unable to compute the 2-Object+1-Heap context-sensitive points-to relations for the programs *hsqld* and *jython* from the DaCapo benchmark suite [6] which are much smaller than real-world code bases including the source code of the JDK library. Similarly, pre-analysis to measure potential impact on the final result [20] could also increase the overall efficiency. But the results reported in the paper are on relatively small programs.

The problem we address in this paper is how to compute a precise but expensive demand-driven context-sensitive points-to analysis, such as the 2-Object+1-Heap, for very large code-bases. A client issues a query that refers to variables located in a method, for which the client queries the points-to set. Thus only parts of the program that affect the client's queries are considered. However, converting a context-sensitive points-to analysis into a demand-driven analysis is challenging even for alias analysis [27]. The main issues in converting a context-sensitive points-to analysis to a demand-driven problem stems from the nature of the problem: context-sensitivity is obtained in a forward fashion (from the program start to a location) and hence can only be converted to a backward problem for the demand-driven approach with great difficulties.

Our approach overcomes this issue by employing static program slicing and program compaction for given points-to queries. The program slicing and compaction that we employ reduces the input program to a semantically equivalent for the points-to queries[1], for which the context-sensitive points-to analysis is exhaustively run in a forward-fashion. The program compaction is a program transformation that eliminates variables and their assignments that can be expressed by other variables. Since context-sensitive analysis are sensitive to the number of statements and variables in a method, program compaction is a key ingredients for scalable context-sensitive points-to.

However, program slicing and compaction is insufficient on its own for achieving scalability for input programs used in our experimental study. To achieve scalability for programs with millions of program variables, points-to analysis has to be performed in stages. A lightweight (context-insensitive) points-to analysis is performed on the reduced input program. The lightweight points-to analysis enables the construction of a more precise call graph, since virtual dispatches can rely on a may-points-to analysis rather than the pure syntactic type information. With the improved call-graph, another round of program slicing and compaction is performed, which further reduces the input program. We refer to the first stage, i.e., program slicing and compaction with the light-weight points-to analysis as a pre-analysis, since its points-to result is not actually used beside construction a refined reduced input program. One of the advantages of our framework is that existing state-of-the-art points-to analyses can be employed.

For our experimental case study, we use Java's OpenJDK library, that consists of approximately 1.3 millions of variables, 200 thousand methods, 600 method invocations, and 400 thousand object creation sites. We have chosen clients that produce points-to query sets for tasks related to security analysis for a proprietary security analysis tool for Java. We are able to compute context-sensitive points-to relation with our points-to framework under 8 hours. Without our staged points-to framework, deep context-sensitive points-to analysis is not computable for problem sizes in the scale of Java's OpenJDK library.

The main contributions of our work are:

– We introduce a points-to framework that can use off-the-shelf exhaustive context-sensitive points-to analysis for large-scale code bases. The framework uses a refinement approach, i.e., points-to analyses of various complexity are performed in stages in conjunction with static program slicing and compaction. A preceding stage produces points-to information to further reduce the input program by refining the call-graph.
– We introduce the notion of program compaction that compacts a flow-sensitive program representation.
– We perform experiments on a large-scale code to show that our points-to framework is feasible.

This paper is organised as follows. In Section 2 we give an overview of our approach. In Section 3 we illustrate our technique by an example. In Section 4 the details of our staged approach is explained. Our implementation of the approach as well as its usefulness is described in Section 5. We conclude the paper by

---

[1] Note that the reduced input program may not be executable and may not produce semantically correct information for other queries which were not specified.

comparing our work with related work in the literature and highlighting the novelty of our work in Section 6.

2   Staged Points-To Framework

Our framework produces high-precision points-to analysis results for large-scale software. To overcome the complexity issue of high-precision points-to analysis, we specialise the points-to analysis for a client that issues points-to queries. Points-to queries concern variables for which the client desires the points-to set. The specialisation is performed by using static program slicing and program compaction such that an off-the-shelf points-to analysis is performed on the reduced input program. The reduced input program produces for the points-to query set the same results as the original input. However, specialisation is not sufficient on its own. For large-scale software we observed that a refinement is necessary, i.e., the points-to analysis is performed in stages. In each stage a more refined reduced input-program is produced. The refined input-program is smaller than the previous one due to the points-to analysis of the stage such that a later points-to analysis has less work to perform.

The process to obtain a context-sensitive points-to information in stages using specialisation and refinement is illustrated in Figure 1. First, the client provides the set of points-to queries that are passed on to the step that computes the initial slice of the program. The initial slice is computed based on syntax information only rather than performing any points-to analysis. After this the slice is compacted, i.e., variables that are not of interest or are not actual/formal parameters, and return values are eliminated. The compacted slice is passed on a flow-insensitive and field-sensitive points-to analysis. The points-to analysis builds a heap-abstraction and hence field sensitivity is taken into account. A related issue is the construction of the call-graph [26]. Virtual method resolution could be done in conjunction with the points-to analysis. This leads to a mutual dependency between the points-to analysis and the construction of the call-graph. The context-insensitive analysis thus builds a call-graph that is more precise than the initial call-graph constructed using the Class Hierarchy Analysis (CHA).

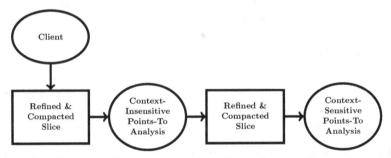

Fig. 1. Staged process of slicing and analysis for context-sensitive points-to analysis

The points-to and the call-graph relations are used to compute the final slice to refine the virtual dispatch of call-sites. The final slice is passed on to perform the context-sensitive analysis. The use of the less expensive points-to analysis and slicing can be viewed as a particular instance of pre-analysis for the final context sensitive points-to analysis. The pre-analysis enables us to compute the context-sensitive points-to set in an effective fashion. Note that we are able to use the context-insensitive points-to results to further slice the program as it is an over-approximation of the desired result. In general, we can use any points-to relation that is computable on the initial slice provided it is a sound over-approximation of the desired points-to relation. Thus, context-insensitive and 2-Object+1-Heap can be seen as an instance of our approach.

3   Motivating Example

In this section we present an example program and show the effect of the syntactic based and context-insensitive based slicing. The aim is to remove unnecessary variables and objects. This example is representative of actual code fragments on which our analysis is performed. Consider the program in Listing 1.1. It has trusted and untrusted objects which can be used in a secure or an insecure setting. The client's query is only interested in the use of untrusted objects in a secure setting. Thus non-security related actions and trusted objects are removed by our analysis.

Listing 1.1. Original Program

```
 1  class SecurityApplication {
 2      public static void main(String[] args) {
 3          String result = setup(args);
 4          System.out.println(result);
 5
 6          SecurityFactory uFactory = new UntrustedSecurityFactory();
 7          SecurityFactory tFactory = new TrustedSecurityFactory();
 8
 9          SecurityObject uObject = uFactory.getSecurityObject();
10          SecurityObject tObject = tFactory.getSecurityObject();
11
12          doSecurity(uObject, tObject);
13      }
14
15      private static void doSecurity(SecurityObject secObj1,
16                                     SecurityObject secObj2) {
17          SecurityAction action1 = new SecurityAction();
18          SecurityAction action2 = new SecurityAction();
19          action1.object = secObj1;
20          action2.object = secObj2;
21
22          Object res1 = action1.invoke();
23          Object res2 = action2.invoke();
24
25          doOtherThings(res1, res2);
26      }
27
28      private static String setup(String[] args) { ··· }
29
30      private static void doOtherThings(Object result1, Object result2) { ··· }
31  }
32
```

```
33   interface SecurityFactory {
34       public SecurityObject getSecurityObject();
35   }
36
37   class UntrustedSecurityFactory implements SecurityFactory {
38       public SecurityObject getSecurityObject() {
39           SecurityObject newObj = new UntrustedSecurityObject();
40           return newObj;
41       }
42   }
43
44   class TrustedSecurityFactory implements SecurityFactory {
45       public SecurityObject getSecurityObject() {
46           SecurityObject newObj = new TrustedSecurityObject();
47           return newObj;
48       }
49   }
50
51   class SecurityAction {
52       public SecurityObject object;
53       public Object invoke() {
54           SecurityObject storedObject = this.object;
55           return invoke0(storedObject);
56       }
57       private static native Object invoke0(SecurityObject obj);
58   }
59
60   class SecurityObject {···}
61   class UntrustedSecurityObject extends SecurityObject {···}
62   class TrustedSecurityObject extends SecurityObject {···}
```

Specifically, assume that the client's query is: "whether at the invocation of invoke0 (at line 55) the parameter storedObject points-to an untrusted heap object of type UntrustedSecurityObject." In the example, the only allocation of the untrusted object is on line 39. It can be seen that variables such as args, result, res1, res2 and methods such as setup and doOtherThings have no influence on the desired result. Hence they can be removed from the initial slice.

Given the initial slice, the points-to analysis needs to determine if the variable storedObject at line 55 can point to the new object created at line 39. The variable uObject on line 9 will point to the untrusted object as it holds the return value of the invocation to the getSecurityObject method. The value now flows from uObject to secObj1 and then to action1.object on line 19. The method action1.invoke results in the untrusted object being used in the call of invoke0. As there is no other value flow, we can safely ignore the other variables. That is, the context-insensitive points-to indicates that variables such as tFactory (on line 7), tObject (on line 10) and action2 (on line 20) do not point to an untrusted heap object. Hence these variables and the allocation sites they point-to can be removed from the slice. Note that the method doSecurity now has only one parameter in the computed slice. The main points-to relation where the variables are in rectangular boxes and allocation-sites are in circles is shown in Figure 2. The figure also shows objects that are pruned (indicated via being crossed out) by the slicing operation. The resulting slice is shown in Listing 1.2.   •

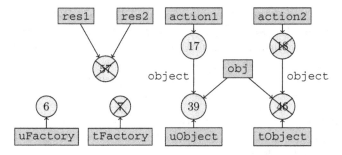

Fig. 2. Removal of Objects

Listing 1.2. Final Slice

```
1   class SecurityApplication {
2       public static void main() {
3           SecurityFactory uFactory = new UntrustedSecurityFactory();
4           SecurityObject uObject = uFactory.getSecurityObject();
5           doSecurity(uObject);
6       }
7
8       private static void doSecurity(SecurityObject secObj1) {
9           SecurityAction action1 = new SecurityAction();
10          action1.object = secObj1;
11          action1.invoke();
12      }
13  }
14
15  interface SecurityFactory {
16      public SecurityObject getSecurityObject();
17  }
18
19  class UntrustedSecurityFactory implements SecurityFactory {
20      public SecurityObject getSecurityObject() {
21          SecurityObject newUObj = new UntrustedSecurityObject();
22          return newUObj;
23      }
24  }
25
26  class SecurityAction {
27      public SecurityObject object;
28      public Object invoke() {
29          SecurityObject storedObject = this.object;
30          return invoke0(storedObject);
31      }
32      private static native Object invoke0(SecurityObject obj);
33  }
34
35  class SecurityObject {···}
36  class UntrustedSecurityObject extends SecurityObject {···}
```

4   Steps of the Staged Points-To Framework

In order to express the key aspects of our staged points-to analysis, we first
define a small flow-insensitive object-oriented language that includes core Java
features. The language has types so that class and sub-class relationships and
interfaces can be expressed. We also use the notion of types for object-fields,

call-sites and method signatures to model virtual dispatch. We assume variables reside in a single method and are unique. A variable has attached a declared type that may not be identical to object type of the object it is referring to. Each method has a special variable *self* that denotes the instance object itself. Every method is defined in a class, and is inherited by its sub-class (if not overridden). A method may consist of one or more of the following statements:

[L1] Heap allocations: $x = new\ C()$ creates a new instance of variable C.
[L2] Assignment: $x = y$ assigns variable x the value of variable y. Note that the variable *self* is pre-defined and cannot be assigned a value.
[L3] Assignment Cast: $x = (T)y$ assigns variable x the value of variable y by casting the value to type T.
[L4] Loading of a field: $x = y.f$ loads a value from the field f from the value in variable y and assigns the loaded to the variable x.
[L5] Storing of a field: $x.f = y$ stores the value present in variable y in the field f of the value in variable x.
[L6] Return Statement: *return u* returns the value u.
[L7] Call-Site: $y = o.s(x_1, \ldots, x_k)$ calls method a method m that is declared in type of variable o or any suitable super-class.

Note that we do not consider control-flow constructs in the language, since it was shown that flow sensitive analysis is less important than a context sensitive analysis [14,16]. Note that for real implementation we need to consider static fields, static method calls, calls to super, etc. For sake of simplicity, we do not discuss them here. In addition, we do not consider reflection mechanisms either.

4.1   Computing the Initial Slice

Here we describe the computation of a slice. The initial slice is computed by tracing the dataflow of the client specified query variables backwards by the assignment relation. The slice S is a multi-set containing variables, field types, and methods of a program. We use the auxiliary function $\tau(x)$ which identifies the type of a variable. Initially, the slice contains the query variables and the methods where the variables reside in. We use a model theoretic approach to describe the set that contains the initial slice. We search for the smallest set S for which following conditions hold:

[S1] All query variables v and methods m that contain variable v are in S.
[S2] If there is an object creation $x = newC()$ and $x \in S$, then $\{C, cons_C\} \subseteq S$ where $cons_C$ is the object constructor for the type C.
[S3] If there is an assignment $x = y$ and $x \in S$, then $y \in S$.
[S4] If there is an assignment cast $x = (T)y$ and $x \in S$, then $y \in S$.
[S5] If there is a load $x = y.f$ and $x \in S$, then $\tau(y).f \in S$, and $y \in S$.
[S6] If there is a store $x.f = y$ in method m, and there is $t'.f \in S$ that is compatible with $\tau(x).f$, then $\{m, x, y\} \subseteq S$.
[S7] If there is a callsite $y = o.s(x_1, \ldots, x_k)$ residing in method m, and callsite $o.s$ is compatible with a method $m' \in S$, then $m \in S$ and $o \in S$.

[S8] If there is a callsite $y = o.s(x_1, \ldots, x_k)$ residing in method m, callsite $o.s$ is compatible with a method $m'(z_1, \ldots, z_k) \in S$, and $z_i \in S$, then $x_i \in S$.

[S9] If there is a callsite $y = o.s(x_1, \ldots, x_k)$, $y \in S$, then for all methods m that are compatible with the call-site $o.s$ and for all *return* z residing in m, then $\{m, z\} \subseteq S$.

Rule [S2] extends the slice to include types and the constructors methods of objects that are created. Rule [S3] extends the slice to the source of the assignment, if the destination of the assignment is in the slice. Rule [S4] extends the slice for assignment casts. Rule [S5] adds the field $\tau(y).f$ if the result of the load operation on a field is in the slice. Note that we add all variables whose type is compatible with the loading of the field f. Rule [S6] adds the method m and the variables x and y to the slice, if a compatible field type can be found in the slice. Rule [S7] adds the caller to the slice and the instance object. Rule [S8] adds the actual parameters to a slice, if the formal parameter of a method are in the slice. Rule [S9] adds the return variables to the slice if the result variable is in the slice.

4.2   Compaction

The compaction process eliminates variables that do not contribute directly or indirectly to the points-to query. In addition, variables that store intermediate results can be eliminated. For example, in a method without points-to queries, the only variables which should remain are variables of object-creation sites, actual/formal parameters, instance variables, and return variables. The compaction reduces the size of the data-flow graph of a method, and, hence speeds up the convergence of the points-to analysis. The compaction can be perceived as an orthogonal process to slicing.

The implementation of compaction is based on standard techniques such as reaching-definitions, copy propagation and dead and redundant code elimination schemes [3,10] suitably adapted for object-oriented programs. Since there is no control-flow, the computation reduces to the computation of equivalence classes via the assign relation. This assign relation builds a value flow graph and involves the query variables, formal arguments/actual arguments, return statements, object creation sites, receiver objects of method invocations at call-sites.

The example on the left in Figure 3 is rewritten to the example on the right. The intermediate variables z and y are eliminated as assignments to them are redundant. That is, the assignment z = x is not necessary as all occurrences of z can be replaced by x. Formally, the variables x, y and z are in the same equivalence class while the variables a and b are in another equivalence class.

In the above example only one definition reached the use. That is, only x reaches z and only a reaches b. In general, various definitions could reach a point of use. Our solution is to maintain a subset of definitions that reach a variable. The subset in then used to identify all the assignments that are necessary. An example of this situation is shown in Figure 4.

```
1  int foo(int x) {          1  int foo(int x) {
2      z = x;                 2      a = goo(x);
3      y = x;                 3      return a;
4      a = goo(z);            4  }
5      b = a;
6      return b;
7  }
```

Fig. 3. Example of Compaction

```
1  int foo(int arg0, int arg1,      1  int foo(int arg0, int arg1,
2            int arg2) {                     int arg2) {
3      x = arg0;                     2      arg0arg1arg2 = arg0;
4      y = arg1;                     3      arg0arg1arg2 = arg1;
5      z = x;                        4      arg0arg1arg2 = arg2;
6      z = y; z:{arg0, arg1}         5      goo(arg0arg1arg2);
7      a = arg2;                     6      return arg0arg1arg2;
8      a = z; a:{arg0, arg1, arg2}   7  }
9      goo(a);
10     z = a; z:{arg0, arg1, arg2}
11     return z;
12 }
```

Fig. 4. Multiple values: Compaction

In general we replace variables by reusing subsets of reaching definitions. Note that this is sound in our context as we are computing a may-point-to relation. The subsets of reaching definitions can be arranged in a Hasse-diagram representing the partial order. The assignments can then be derived by reusing the assignments used for the relevant subsets and taking into account the variables from the reaching definitions that have been covered. An example of a partial order and the generated assignments is given in Figure 5. The emphasised variables are those that are introduced by compaction whereby variables a to d are program variables of the input program. All other intermediate variables that contributed to the partial order are elided.

```
1  ab = a; ab = b;
2  cd = c; cd = d;
3  bd = b; bd = d;
4  abcd = ab; abcd = cd;
```

Fig. 5. Partial Order and Assignments

4.3   Context-Insensitive Points-To Analysis

The improvement of the context-insensitive field-sensitive point-to analysis is the heap-abstraction, i.e., fields are analysed and hence more precise information is obtained for resolving virtual method dispatches. For each instance variable, the points-to set consisting of object-creation sites is computed, which we denote by $pt(v)$. For each field of an object-creation site, a set of object-creation sites that this field may point to, which we denote by $fpt(o, f)$, is also computed. An object-creation site has associated an actual type that is used to compute more precise virtual method dispatches. We search for the smallest points-to set for the current slice such that following points-to rules hold:

[P1] If there exists a heap allocation $a : x = new\ C(\ldots)$ in a method $m \in S$, then $a \in pt(x)$.

[P2] If there exists an assignment $x = y$ in a method $m \in S$, then $pt(y) \subseteq pt(x)$.

[P3] If there exists an assignment cast $x = (T)y$ in a method $m \in S$, then $o \in pt(x)$, for all $o \in pt(y)$ and $\tau(o) \leq T$.

[P4] If there exists a load statement $x = y.f$ in a method $m \in S$, then $pt(o.f) \subseteq pt(x)$ for all $o \in pt(y)$.

[P5] If there exists a store statement $x.f = y$ in a method $m \in S$, then $pt(y) \subseteq fpt(o, f)$ for all $o \in pt(x)$.

[P6] If there exists a call-site $y = o.s(x_1, \ldots, x_k)$ in a method $m \in S$, and for all methods $m'(z_1, \ldots, z_k)$ that are compatible with s and the types in $pt(o)$, then $pt(x_i) \subseteq pt(z_i)$ for all i, $1 \leq i \leq k$, $pt(o) \subseteq pt(m'.self)$, and $pt(y) \subseteq pt(u)$ for all *return* u residing in $m'(z_1, \ldots, z_k)$.

Note that the above rules are standard [21] for a field-sensitive context-insensitive points-to analysis. The points-to relation is used to obtain the final slice. The slice produced by using the context-insensitive points-to analysis will include variables, methods, heap allocation sites along with points-to facts for the client's query. While the rules are similar in structure as the rules in the variable-based slicing, there are some subtle differences as we now have the actual object creation sites for each variable and field-sensitivity.

[S'1] If $o \in pt(v)$ such that (v, o) is part of the facts for the client's query and m is the method that contains v, then $\{(o, v), m\} \subseteq S$.

[S'2] If $(v, h) \in S$, then $\{v, h\} \subseteq S$. Similarly if $(o, f, o') \in S$ then $\{o, f, o'\} \subseteq S$.

[S'3] If there is an assignment $x = y$ and $(x, o) \in S$, and $o \in pt(y)$ then $y \in S$.

[S'4] If there is a load $x = y.f$ and $(x, o) \in S$ and $o' \in pt(y)$ such that $o \in fpt(o', f)$, then $\{(o', f, o), (y, o')\} \subseteq S$.

[S'5] If there is a store $x.f = y$ in method m, and $o \in pt(x)$, $o' \in pt(y)$, $(o, f, o') \in S$, then $\{m, (x, o), (y, o')\} \subseteq S$.

The rule [S'1] adds all the facts that are relevant to the client's query to the slice. The rule [S'2] adds all the constituent elements of the points to and field-points-to relation in the slice to the slice. The rule [S'3] extends the slice with the variable on the right hand side of the assignment provided it points-to an object in the slice. The rule [S'4] adds the points-to facts related to a load operation to the slice provided the variable which has result of the load operation is in the slice. The rule [S'5] adds the method m and the points-to facts for the variables x and y to the slice, if a field is stored into and the field-points-to relation is part of the slice.

4.4   Context-Sensitive Points-To Analysis

The context-sensitive points-to analysis is the final stage of the analysis. It uses the last slice to compute the most precise points-to information. The contexts as well as the points-to relation is computed only on the slice and thus the analysis can use the standard techniques [23]. The construction of the slice guarantees that if o belongs to $cpt(c, x)$, then o will also belong to $pt(x)$ where cpt represents the context-sensitive points-to relation and c the context. So as long as the result of our context-sensitive analysis is a strict refinement of the results of the context-insensitive analysis, the result of the pre-analysis can be used for the context-sensitive analysis. The context-sensitive analysis further refines the call-graph. The points-to analysis will use the notion of a method being reachable in a context and use it to compute the points-to set. As noted in Section 1, one can use a method's receiver object and the object that allocates this receiver object as the context. As the resolution of the virtual method being invoked will depend on the type of the receiver object, certain methods will not be reachable in certain contexts. More details on this is available in the literature [7,23]. We use $reach(c, m)$ to indicate that method m is reachable in context c. Contexts are updated when a method is invoked or when an object is created. We use $extend(c, st)$ to identify the new context, where st is a statement that represents an invocation or an object creation. The rules for assignment and the linking of actual to formal parameters in a method invocation is shown below.

[CSP1] If there exists an assignment $x = y$ in a method $m \in S$, and $reach(c, m)$
    then $cpt(c, y) \subseteq cpt(c, x)$.

[CSP2] If there exists a call-site $y = o.s(x_1, \ldots, x_k)$ in a method $m \in S$ with
    $reach(c, m)$ and for all methods $m'(z_1, \ldots, z_k)$ that are compatible with s
    and $cpt(c, o)$, then $cpt(c, x_i) \subseteq cpt(c', z_i)$ for all i, $1 \leq i \leq k$ where $c' = extend(c, o.s(x_1, \ldots, x_k))$

One can show that for any program P, if v is a variable in a client's query then $cpt_P(c, x) = cpt_S(c, x)$ where cpt_P and cpt_S represent the context-sensitive points-to set computed for the entire program P and slice S respectively. That is, our slicing technique does not lose any relevant information.

5   Implementation and Results

In this section we demonstrate both the ineffectiveness of using off-the-shelf context-sensitive points-to analysis and the effectiveness of our staged points-to

Table 1. Context Sensitive Analysis: Not computable over the JDK

Context Sensitive Analysis	Outcome
1-Call-site-sensitive	Does not terminate after 20 hours
1-Object-sensitive	Does not terminate after 20 hours
2-Call-site-sensitive+1-Heap	Does not terminate after 20 hours
2-Object-sensitive+1-Heap	Out of memory

framework using specialisation (i.e. program slicing and compaction) and refinement (i.e. staging points-to). We have implemented our technique with Datalog [1] based on the DOOP [7] framework. We use OpenJDK 7 build 147 (rt.jar) as the artefact that is subject to various analyses. We ran our experiments on an Intel Xeon E5-2660 (2.2GHz) machine with 256GB RAM using the LogicBlox engine [13].

We report results of our experiments with some of the existing context-sensitive points-to analysis that was *not* computable *in general* for the OpenJDK library without specialisation and refinement. OpenJDK 7 (rt.jar) has more than 2 million lines of Java code. Note that lines of code is not necessarily an accurate indication of the complexity for the points-to analysis. The number of variables and allocation sites is a better indication of the effort required to perform points-to analysis. The OpenJDK 7 library has close to 1.3 million variables and about 500,000 heap allocation sites and goes well beyond the largest benchmarks sizes such as DaCapo [6] mainly used for points-to research in literature.

The results of points-to without specialisation and refinement are shown in Table 1. We terminated many of the analyses after 20 hours as that was well over our self-imposed time budget of 8 hours.

Choice of Client. As results of our analysis is dependent on the client's query, we choose different security analysis clients. We choose four security analysis that relate to access control and are derived from section 9 of the Java Secure Coding guidelines (JSCG) [9]. The guidelines specify certain properties where security sensitive methods are invoked. Examples of security sensitive methods include `AccessController.doPrivileged()`, `Class.forName()` and `Class.newInstance()`. The restrictions on the invocation of such methods require appropriate permissions, use of untainted objects and escaping of results from the JDK to the application.

Typically a client is interested in identifying locations in the program that violate the Java Security Guidelines. For this purpose the client identifies invocations to the security sensitive methods that are potential violations. Points-to information is required to determine properties such as taintedness of any of the arguments and results escaping from the JDK to the application. From a security view point other invocations that do not influence the security related invocations are not relevant. Note that although security is the principal motivation, we do not report any security specific results here. The focus here is purely on client driven calculation of a suitable context-sensitive points-to set.

5.1 Staged Points-To Framework Results

In this section we present the results of our analysis. We show that

(a) the reduction in the number of variables and allocation-sites due to program slicing and compaction,
(b) the size of the various points-to relations and
(c) the size of the call-graph

Table 2. Number of Variables

Client	Variables in Client's Query	Variables in Initial Slice	Variables after Context Insensitive Analysis
CSM	3,885	895,100	228,054
CSM-Escape	1,321	891,641	224,707
CSM-Taint	847	797,217	222,192
doPrivileged	12,202	799,484	266,558

The reduction in the number of program variables using our pre-analysis is given in Table 2. The behaviour is uniform across all clients (see Figure 6(a)) and there is no obvious link between the number of variables in the client's query and the number of variables in the various reduced input programs. The variables used either as parameters or as the base in the relevant invocations yields the variables that are in the client's query. The variable based slicing reduces the number of potentially relevant variables by approximately 30%. The context insensitive analysis on the slice further reduces the number of relevant variables by approximately 73%. This results in a slice with only about 18% of the original set of variables. The reduction in the number of allocation-sites is shown in Table 3. The variable based slice does not significantly reduce the number of allocation sites. But the context insensitive analysis marks only around 5.0% of the original set of allocation sites as relevant (shown in Figure 6(b)). This

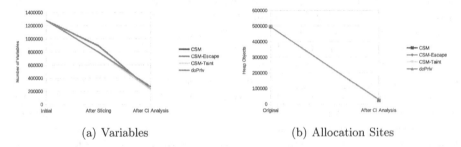

(a) Variables   (b) Allocation Sites

Fig. 6. Size Reduction

Table 3. Number of Allocation Sites

Client	Allocation Sites in Initial Slice	Allocation Sites after Context-Sensitive Analysis
CSM	494,560	23,215
CSM-Escape	494,111	22,928
CSM-Taint	492,821	22,850
doPrivileged	494,560	28,298

Table 4. Size of Points-To Relation

Client	Context-Insensitive	Context-Sensitive	Context-Sensitive (No Context)
CSM	115,470,090	435,721,445	1,895,206
CSM-Escape	115,374,473	434,238,551	1,885,825
CSM-Taint	107,538,308	296,998,797	1,585,422
doPrivileged()	141,053,434	413,813,791	1,952,346

massive reduction in the number of allocation sites combined with a significant reduction in the number of variables is the key reason for the success of our technique.

The size of the points-to relation is shown in Table 4. For all the clients there are more than 100 million points-to relations in the context-insensitive points-to set. They are refined to more than 400 million points-to relations, except in the case of CSM-Taint where 296 million facts are generated, an increase by a factor of more than 3.5. If the contexts from the context-sensitive relation are elided, there are about 1.9 million facts, except in the case of CSM-Taint where there are about 1.6 million facts. The sheer size indicates the memory required to hold these relations.

The average number of objects a variable points to gives insight to the problem. In the context-insensitive case it is about 140 objects per variable while in the context-sensitive case it is only about 8 objects per variable. This is shown in Table 5.

Table 5. Average Number of Allocation Sites Per Variable

Client	Context-Insensitive	Context-Sensitive
CSM	129.0	8.3
CSM-Escape	129.4	8.4
CSM-Taint	134.9	7.1
doPrivileged()	176.4	7.3

The call-graph relation generated by the context-insensitive points-to analysis contains approximately 300,000 points-to relations. This is refined to more than 80 million facts, except in the case of CSM-Taint where close to 59 million facts are generated. This represents an increase in the size by a factor of 247. However, if just the call-graph edges are (without the contexts) examined, there are approximately 140,000 edges. So the context-sensitive analysis reduces the number of edges from the context-insensitive relation by about 60%.

Table 6. Size of Call-Graph Relation

Client	Context-Insensitive	Context-Sensitive	Context-Sensitive (No Context)
CSM	337,658	83,472,063	141,066
CSM-Escape	337,482	83,415,055	140,535
CSM-Taint	332,135	58,926,898	137,809
doPrivileged()	373,991	77,723,735	153,079

Despite the size of the call-graph edges and the context-sensitive points-to set, slicing enables the computation of the context-sensitive points-to and call-graph relations in under 4 hours and 45 minutes which is well under our limit of about 8 hours. The break up of the time taken by each stage is shown in Table 7. All times are given in seconds.

Table 7. Timing Information

Client	Initial Slice	Context Insensitive	Context Sensitive	Total
CSM	285	1,913	14,936	17,134 (4.76hrs)
CSM-Escape	293	1,903	14,790	16986 (4.72hrs)
CSM-Taint	233	1,694	5,959	7886 (4.05hrs)
doPriv()	256	2,508	11,844	7886 (4.05hrs)

To summarise, our experiments show that the reduction in the number of variables and allocation sites using our points-to framework. Our experiments provides insight into the sizes of the various relations that are computed on the reduced input program. From our experimentation it is hard to establish a relationship between number of variables specified by client and performance. Ultimately it depends on the size of the reduced input program, which is hard to estimate purely from the client's query.

Limitation of the Experiment

Firstly, all experiments are conducted on various versions of JDK. Although we have reported results only on the OpenJDK 7, the results on other versions of JDK are similar. All large code bases may not have the same characteristics as the JDK. Hence our analysis might produce different results. But given that we have analysed the JDK in its entirety gives us confidence that the staged approach can be applied to other large systems. The second issue relates to the security related queries. All of them were related to access control and derived from the Java Security Coding Guidelines. While the coding guidelines cover key security related situations, there are many aspects of security that we have not covered. However, an initial analysis of the JDK shows that the security sensitive operations are related to each other which is why the number of variables and allocation sites are in the initial slice are independent on the client. We believe that clients derived from other secure coding guidelines will produce similar results.

6   Related Work

The novelty of our approach is using well known demand-driven points-to analyses and the notion of slicing and combining them in the right order to obtain a scalable demand-driven refinement technique to compute context sensitive points-to relations for large systems. We have demonstrated that our approach can compute the 2-Object-sensitive+1-Heap context-sensitive points-to set for security related analysis of the JDK. No existing work has reported results on any program that is as large as the JDK.

Most of the existing works report results on programs from standard benchmarking suites such as DaCapo [6]. All the programs in these suites are much smaller than the JDK. Jython, which is part of the DaCapo suite [6] is used as an example of a typically large example for static analysis [24,23]. Smaragdakis et al. [23] report that they were *unable* to compute the entire 2-Object+1-Heap sensitive points-to relation for Jython. As the JDK has about 10 times the number of heap allocation sites and about 6 times the number of variables of Jython, the standard DOOP technique cannot be used to compute the context-sensitive points-to relation for the JDK.

It is difficult to perform an accurate comparison of our approach with other approaches. This is because the analysis depends on both the size of the input program as well as the query that is used in the demand-driven refinement process. For instance, [22] achieve a 30% reduction in the number of variables; but that is independent of any client query. But they do not reduce the number of heap objects as they do not compute a relevant slice. None of the existing work use security analysis for their refinement nor do they use slicing to get a handle on complexity.

Sridharan and Bodík [24] use refinement with cast checking and disjoint analysis of factory methods as the criteria. Yan et al. [27] do not use refinement – they compute the may alias relation directly in a demand driven fashion using

CFL reachability. They develop a specific context-sensitive analysis based on reachability and summarisation and do not compute the points-to relation.

Pre-analysis is used to selectively compute the context-sensitive points-to set [20]. They use the pre-analysis to estimate the potential benefit before they compute context-sensitive facts. Thus for the same program they have context-insensitive facts for some program fragments while other fragments have context-sensitive facts. Our approach is orthogonal to their work as we compute the context-sensitive facts for the *entire slice* where the slice is identified using a demand-driven approach. Furthermore, their approach is for C programs and it is not clear how easily it can be applied to object-oriented programs. Finally, their results are on all relatively small programs (the largest program they use is `a2ps-4.14` which has fewer than 65K lines of code).

Table 8 summarises the key differences between the different approaches.

Table 8. Comparison of Different Approaches

Approach	CFL Based Alias or Variable Reduction	Heap reduction	Client Based Reduction or Selective Contexts
Set based pre-processing [22]	✓	✗	✗
Demand-driven alias analysis [27]	✓	✗	✓
Selective context-sensitive analysis [20]	✗	✗	✓
Our Work	✓	✓	✓

7   Conclusion

In this paper we introduced a staged demand-driven points-to framework that uses specialisation and refinement. The specialisation is achieved by static program slicing and program compaction. The refinement is achieved by staging the points-to analysis, i.e., a pre-analysis refines the reduced input program for the later stage. We have implemented our technique using the DOOP framework and have presented our results on the OpenJDK version 7 build 147 using 4 security related client queries. We have observed that our technique is able to reduce the number of variables and allocation sites which enables the computation of the 2-Object+1-Heap context-sensitive points-to well within our time bound of 8 hours. Our technique produces high-precision points-to analysis information for code bases with million of program variables and thousands of invocation sites going beyond the state-of-the-art.

References

1. Abiteboul, S., Hull, R., Vianu, V.: Foundations of Databases. Addison-Wesley (1995)
2. Andersen, L.O.: Program Analysis and Specialization for the C Programming Language. Ph.D. thesis, DIKU, University of Copenhagen (Fall 1994)
3. Appel, A.W.: Modern Compiler Implementation in Java. Cambridge University Press (1998)
4. Ball, T., Rajamani, S.K.: The SLAM toolkit. In: Berry, G., Comon, H., Finkel, A. (eds.) CAV 2001. LNCS, vol. 2102, pp. 260–264. Springer, Heidelberg (2001)
5. Bessey, A., Block, K., Chelf, B., Chou, A., Fulton, B., Hallem, S., Henri-Gros, C., Kamsky, A., McPeak, S., Engler, D.: A few billion lines of code later – using static analysis to find bugs in the real world. Comm. ACM 53, 66–75 (2010)
6. Blackburn, S.M., Garner, R., Hoffmann, C., Khan, A.M., McKinley, K.S., Bentzur, R., Diwan, A., Feinberg, D., Frampton, D., Guyer, S.Z., Hirzel, M., Hosking, A., Jump, M., Lee, H., Moss, J.E.B., Phansalkar, A., Stefanovic, D., VanDrunen, T., von Dincklage, D., Wiedermann, B.: The DaCapo benchmarks: Java benchmarking development and analysis. In: OOPSLA 2006: Proceedings of the 21st Annual ACM SIGPLAN Conference on Object-Oriented Programming, Systems, Languages, and Applications (2006)
7. Bravenboer, M., Smaragdakis, Y.: Strictly declarative specification of sophisticated points-to analyses. In: Proceeding of the 24th ACM SIGPLAN Conference on Object Oriented Programming Systems Languages and Applications, OOPSLA 2009, pp. 243–262. ACM (2009), http://doi.acm.org/10.1145/1640089.1640108
8. Cifuentes, C., Keynes, N., Li, L., Hawes, N., Valdiviezo, M.: Transitioning Parfait into a development tool. IEEE Security and Privacy 10(3), 16–23 (2012)
9. Corporation, O.: Secure coding guidelines for java se (April 2014), http://www.oracle.com/technetwork/java/seccodeguide-139067.html
10. Debray, S.K., Evans, W., Muth, R., De Sutter, B.: Compiler techniques for code compaction. ACM Transactions on Programming Languages and Systems 22(2), 378–415 (2000)
11. Feng, Y., Anand, S., Dillig, I., Aiken, A.: Apposcopy: Semantics-based detection of android malware through static analysis. In: International Symposium on Foundations of Software Engineering (2014) (to appear)
12. Gotsman, A., Berdine, J., Cook, B.: Interprocedural shape analysis with separated heap abstractions. In: Yi, K. (ed.) SAS 2006. LNCS, vol. 4134, pp. 240–260. Springer, Heidelberg (2006)
13. Green, T.J., Aref, M., Karvounarakis, G.: Logicblox, platform and language: A tutorial. In: Barceló, P., Pichler, R. (eds.) Datalog 2.0 2012. LNCS, vol. 7494, pp. 1–8. Springer, Heidelberg (2012)
14. Hind, M., Pioli, A.: Which pointer analysis should i use? In: Proceedings of the ACM SIGSOFT International Symposium on Software Testing and Analysis (ISSTA), pp. 113–123. ACM (2000)
15. Lhoták, O., Hendren, L.J.: Context-sensitive points-to analysis: Is it worth it? In: Mycroft, A., Zeller, A. (eds.) CC 2006. LNCS, vol. 3923, pp. 47–64. Springer, Heidelberg (2006)
16. Lhoták, O., Hendren, L.J.: Evaluating the benefits of context-sensitive points-to analysis using a BDD-based implementation. ACM Transactions on Software Engineering Methodology 18(1) (2008)

17. Lu, Y., Shang, L., Xie, X., Xue, J.: An incremental points-to analysis with cfl-reachability. In: Jhala, R., De Bosschere, K. (eds.) Compiler Construction. LNCS, vol. 7791, pp. 61–81. Springer, Heidelberg (2013)

18. Milanova, A., Rountev, A., Ryder, B.G.: Parameterized object sensitivity for points-to analysis for Java. ACM Transaction on Software Engineering Methodolology 14(1), 1–41 (2005), http://doi.acm.org/10.1145/1044834.1044835

19. Octeau, D., McDaniel, P., Jha, S., Bartel, A., Bodden, E., Klein, J., Le Traon, Y.: Effective inter-component communication mapping in android with epicc: An essential step towards holistic security analysis. In: Proceedings of the 22nd USENIX Conference on Security (SEC), pp. 543–558. USENIX Association (2013), http://dl.acm.org/citation.cfm?id=2534766.2534813

20. Oh, H., Lee, W., Heo, K., Yang, H., Yi, K.: Selective context-sensitivity guided by impact pre-analysis. In: ACM SIGPLAN Conference on Programming Language Design and Implementation (PLDI), pp. 475–484. ACM (2014)

21. Ryder, B.G.: Dimensions of precision in reference analysis of object-oriented programming languages. In: Hedin, G. (ed.) CC 2003. LNCS, vol. 2622, pp. 126–137. Springer, Heidelberg (2003)

22. Smaragdakis, Y., Balatsouras, G., Kastrinis, G.: Set-based pre-processing for points-to analysis. In: ACM SIGPLAN International Conference on Object Oriented Programming Systems Languages and Applications (OOPSLA), pp. 253–270 (2013)

23. Smaragdakis, Y., Bravenboer, M., Lhoták, O.: Pick your contexts well: understanding object-sensitivity. In: Proceedings of the 38th Annual ACM SIGPLAN-SIGACT Symposium on Principles of Programming Languages, POPL 2011, pp. 17–30. ACM (2011), http://doi.acm.org/10.1145/1926385.1926390

24. Sridharan, M., Bodík, R.: Refinement-based context-sensitive points-to analysis for Java. In: Proceedings of the 2006 ACM SIGPLAN Conference on Programming Language Design and Implementation, PLDI 2006, pp. 387–400. ACM (2006), http://doi.acm.org/10.1145/1133981.1134027

25. Sridharan, M., Gopan, D., Shan, L., Bodik, R.: Demand-driven points-to analysis for Java. In: Proceedings of the 20th Annual ACM Conference on Object-Oriented Programming, Systems, Languages, and Applications (OOPSLA), pp. 59–76. ACM (2005), http://doi.acm.org/10.1145/1094811.1094817

26. Tip, F., Palsberg, J.: Scalable propagation-based call graph construction algorithms. In: Rosson, M.B., Lea, D. (eds.) OOPSLA 2000, pp. 281–293. ACM (2000)

27. Yan, D., Xu, G., Rountev, A.: Demand-driven context-sensitive alias analysis for Java. In: Proceedings of the 2011 International Symposium on Software Testing and Analysis (ISSTA), pp. 155–165. ACM (2011), http://doi.acm.org/10.1145/2001420.2001440

28. Zheng, X., Rugina, R.: Demand-driven alias analysis for C. In: Proceedings of the 35th Annual ACM SIGPLAN-SIGACT Symposium on Principles of Programming Languages, POPL 2008, pp. 197–208 (2008), http://doi.acm.org/10.1145/1328438.1328464

Exact and Approximated Data-Reuse Optimizations for Tiling with Parametric Sizes*

Alain Darte and Alexandre Isoard

Compsys, Computer Science Lab (LIP), CNRS, INRIA, ENS-Lyon, UCB-Lyon
`firstname.lastname@ens-lyon.fr`

Abstract. Loop tiling is a loop transformation widely used to improve spatial and temporal data locality, to increase computation granularity, and to enable blocking algorithms, which are particularly useful when offloading kernels on computing units with smaller memories. When caches are not available or used, data transfers and local storage must be software-managed, and some useless remote communications can be avoided by exploiting data reuse between tiles. An important parameter of tiling is the sizes of the tiles, which impact the size of the required local memory. However, for most analyzes involving several tiles, which is the case for inter-tile data reuse, the tile sizes induce non-linear constraints, unless they are numerical constants. This complicates or prevents a parametric analysis with polyhedral optimization techniques.

This paper shows that, when tiles are executed in sequence along tile axes, the parametric (with respect to tile sizes) analysis for inter-tile data reuse is nevertheless possible, i.e., one can determine, at compile-time and in a parametric fashion, the copy-in and copy-out data sets for all tiles, with inter-tile reuse, as well as sizes for the induced local memories. When approximations of transfers are performed, the situation is much more complex, and involves a careful analysis to guarantee correctness when data are both read and written. We provide the mathematical foundations to make such approximations possible. Combined with hierarchical tiling, this result opens perspectives for the automatic generation of blocking algorithms, guided by parametric cost models, where blocks can be pipelined and/or can contain parallelism. Previous work on FPGAs and GPUs already showed the interest and feasibility of such automation with tiling, but in a non-parametric fashion.

1 Introduction

Todays' hardware diversity increases the need for optimizing compilers and runtime systems. A difficulty when using hardware accelerators (FPGA, GPU, dedicated boards) is to automatically perform kernel/function offloading (a.k.a. outlining as opposed to inlining) between the host and the accelerator, and to organize data transfers between the different memory layers (e.g., in a GPU, from remote to global memory, and from global to shared memory, or even registers).

---

* Improved version of IMPACT'14 paper (`impact.gforge.inria.fr/impact2014`).

© Springer-Verlag Berlin Heidelberg 2015
B. Franke (Ed.): CC 2015, LNCS 9031, pp. 151–170, 2015.
DOI: 10.1007/978-3-662-46663-6_8

This requires static analysis to identify the kernel input (data read) and output (data produced), and code generation for transfers, synchronizations, and computations. In general, such tasks are done by the programmer who has to express the communications, to allocate and size the intermediate buffers, and to decompose the kernel into fitting chunks of computation. When each kernel is offloaded in a three-phase process (i.e., upload, compute, store back), such programming remains feasible. For GPUs, developers can use OpenCL or CUDA, or they can rely on higher-level abstractions (e.g., compilation directives as in OpenACC or garbage collector mechanisms as in [9]), static analysis as in OpenMPC [24], runtime approaches as in [23], or mixed compile/runtime optimizations as in [26]. These approaches mainly work at the granularity of variable names, still defined by the programmer, but they can be used to optimize remote transfers when several kernels are successively launched. Things get more complicated when a given kernel is decomposed into smaller kernels (and the initial arrays into array regions) to get blocking algorithms, thanks to *loop tiling*. Indeed, iteration-wise loop analysis and element-wise array analysis are needed to enable intra- and inter-tile data reuse. Moreover, the choice of tile sizes is driven by hardware capabilities such as memory bandwidth, size, and organization, computational power, and such codes are very hard to obtain without automation and some cost model. With this objective, our contribution is a **parametric** (w.r.t. tile sizes) polyhedral analysis technique for **inter-tile data reuse** and a mathematical framework to reason with **approximations** of data accesses and transfers.

Loop tiling is a well-known transformation used to improve data locality [35], increase computation granularity, and control the use and size of local memories for out-of-core computations (see [37] for details on semantics, validity conditions, and code generation). It was first introduced for a set of perfectly nested loops, as a grouping of iterations into *supernodes* [20], which are atomic (i.e., can be executed without any communication/synchronization with other supernodes except for live-in/live-out data at beginning/end of a tile execution), identical by translation, bounded, and form a partition of the whole iteration space. Validity conditions were given in terms of dependence cones and hyperplane partitioning, which define tiles as hyper-rectangles (after some possible change of basis) and establish a link with affine scheduling and the generation of permutable loops. Now, tiling is also used for non-perfectly nested loops [7], thanks to multidimensional affine loop transformations: as in the perfectly nested case, some permutable dimensions can be used to perform tiling, even if not all instructions have the same iteration domain. Analysis and code generation may involve more complex sets, but the principles are similar. Today, loop tiling is still a key loop transformation for performance (speed, memory, locality) and the subject of many new advanced developments, including non-rectangular tiling.

Loop tiling can be viewed as a composition of strip-mining and loop interchange, after a preliminary change of basis. It transforms n nested loops into n *tile loops* iterating over the tiles, surrounding n *intra-tile loops* iterating within a tile. Dependence analysis and code generation for loop tiling is well-established in the polyhedral model [14], i.e., for a set of nested **for** loops, writing and reading multi-dimensional arrays and scalar variables, where loop bounds, if conditions, and array access functions are affine expressions of surrounding loop counters and structure parameters. In this case, loop iterations can be represented by a *polyhedral iteration domain*. When tile sizes are numerical constants, parametric (w.r.t. program counters and structural parameters) polyhedral optimizations (e.g., linear programming) can be used although loop tiling transforms n loops into $2n$ loops. Indeed, the image by tiling of an n-dimensional polyhedral iteration domain can be expressed as a $2n$-dimensional polyhedral iteration domain, because the set of points after tiling with fixed sizes can be described by affine inequalities.[1] In general, **parametric tiling** refers to the case where tile sizes are parameters too. Parametric analysis within a tile is in general feasible as the set of points in a tile is defined with affine constraints from the tile sizes and the *tile origin* (first corner of the tile). However, when an analysis involves several tiles, it becomes more intricate, if not unsolvable, as *a priori* expressing the tiled space with tile sizes as parameters induces quadratic constraints. For example, the tiling theory developed in [36], the code generation schemes of [20,15,7], the data movement and scratch-pad optimizations of [22,21,6,4,28,34] are not parametric. Recently, efficient code generation for parametric tiling [30,19] as well as some form of symbolic scheduling for tiled codes [8] have been developed.

In the context of high-level synthesis (HLS), inter-tile data reuse was proposed [2] (then automated [4]), as a source-to-source process on top of Altera C2H HLS tool, to offload small computation kernels to FPGAs while optimizing communications from a remote (in this case external) DDR memory. Similar results with data reuse between two successive tiles only were then demonstrated for AutoESL Xilinx tool [28]. Different (and more restricted) forms of inter-tile data reuse were also designed for programmable accelerators such as GPUs [5,17,34]. None of these approaches are parametric w.r.t. tile sizes. In this paper, we show that maximal inter-tile data reuse can be expressed in the parametric case, even in an approximated situation. The trick to get around a quadratic formulation is to work with all possible tiles – not just the tiles that are part of the iteration space partitioning and whose origins belong to a lattice – but the difficulty is to make sure that exactness and correctness are maintained. Our contributions, mostly at the level of code analysis, are the following:

- When read/write accesses can be described in an exact way using polyhedral representations, we show how to derive, thanks to manipulations of integer sets, the copy-in and copy-out sets for each tile, with parametric tile sizes. This gives a full parametric generalization of the inter-tile data reuse of [4].
- We extend this parametric analysis to handle approximations, which make the analysis more complex when some data may be both read and written by the tiles, as loading too much may not be safe. We introduce the concept of *pointwise functions* for which no additional loss of accuracy is induced.
- Using similar analysis principles, we show how such a parametric analysis can be exploited in the following steps of the compilation, in particular to perform parametric array contraction for the definition of local arrays.

---

[1] However, difficulties due to large coefficients are possible.

2   Prerequisites

2.1   Notations and Definitions

We write all vectors with bold letters such as i, with components $i_1, \ldots, i_n$. The vector $\mathbf{0}$ (resp. $\mathbf{1}$) has all components equal to 0 (resp. 1) and $a \circ b$ is the product (component-wise) of a and b. We denote by $\preceq$ the lexicographic total order on vectors of arbitrary size and by $\leq$ the component-wise partial order on vectors with same size, defined by $i \leq j$ if and only if (iff) $i_k \leq j_k$ for all k.

We will not elaborate on how to build and interpret the different affine functions for tiling non-perfectly nested loops. To simplify the discussion and notations, we only focus on the n dimensions to be tiled. We assume that each statement S with polyhedral iteration domain $\mathcal{D}_S$ (scanned with the iteration vector i) is tiled, after a first affine mapping $i \mapsto i' = \theta(S, i)$, by canonical tiles whose sizes are specified by a vector s. In other words, a point i is mapped to the tile indexed by $\boldsymbol{T}$ where $T_k = \lfloor \frac{i'_k}{s_k} \rfloor$, or equivalently $s_k T_k \leq (\theta(S, i))_k < s_k(T_k + 1)$, for $k \in [1..n]$, i.e., $0 \leq \theta(S, i) - s \circ \boldsymbol{T} \leq s - 1$. Also, we restrict to the case where the original and the tiled programs are both executed sequentially.[2] Several orders of iterations in the tiled program are possible, we consider that the tiled code is executed following the lexicographic order on the $2n$-dimensional vectors $(\boldsymbol{T}, i')$. The tiled iteration domain for statement S is then:

$$\mathcal{T}_S = \{(\boldsymbol{T}, i') \mid \exists i \in \mathcal{D}_S, \; i' = \theta(S, i), \; 0 \leq i' - s \circ \boldsymbol{T} \leq s - 1\}$$

If θ is a one-to-one mapping and $\mathcal{D}_S$ the set of integer points in a polyhedron, then i can be eliminated and $\mathcal{T}_S$ is also the set of integer points in a polyhedron.

Example We illustrate the concepts and steps of our technique with the kernel `jacobi_1d_imper` from PolyBench [29], with a time loop, and tiled in 2D. For the code in Fig. 1, the Pluto compiler [27] generates the following mapping:

$$\theta(S_1, (t, i)) = (t, 2t + i, 0) \quad \theta(S_2, (t, j)) = (t, 2t + j + 1, 1)$$
$$\mathcal{D}_{S_1} = \mathcal{D}_{S_2} = \{(t, i) \mid 0 \leq t \leq M - 1, 0 \leq i \leq N - 2\}$$

```
for (t = 0; t < M; t++) {
    for (i = 1; i < N - 1; i++)
        S1: B[i] =
            (A[i-1] + A[i] + A[i+1])/3;
    for (j = 1; j < N - 1; j++)
        S2: A[j] = B[j];
}
```

Fig. 1. Original kernel.

```
for (t = 0; t < M; t++)
    for (i' = 2t+1; i' < 2t + N; i'++) {
        S0: i = i'-2t;
        S1: if (i<N-1) B[i] =
            (A[i-1] + A[i] + A[i+1])/3;
        S2: if (i>1) A[i-1] = B[i-1];
    }
```

Fig. 2. Transformed kernel.

---

[2] However, parallelism inside a tile is possible, as well as hierarchical tiling, which enables to play with the extent of the tiled domain. Parallel execution are also possible by defining a partial execution order, if execution follows the axes defining tiles. Other cases seem possible but with additional complications and approximations.

This means shifting S_2 by 1 in the j loop, fusing the i and j loops, then skewing by 2 the inner loop, to get the code of Fig. 2. Then, several tiled code generations are possible depending on how iterators are defined and how tiles are aligned, i.e., what the underlying lattice of the tiling is. With the relation $T_k = \lfloor \frac{i_k}{s_k} \rfloor$, tiles are aligned with the canonical basis obtained after the transformation θ (see Fig. 3 for tiles of size 2×3, drawn in the original basis to save space). With the "outset" code generation scheme of [30], for tile sizes $s_1 \times s_2$, we get:

```
for (T1 = 0; T1 < M; T1+=s1) {
  lb = 2T1+1-(s2-1); lb = s2*ceiling(lb/s2);
  for (T2 = lb; T2 < 2T1 + N + 2(s1 - 1); T2+=s2)
    for (t=max(0,T1); t<min(M,T1+s1); t++)
      for (i'=max(2t+1,T2); i'<min(2t+N,T2+s2); i'++) {
        S0: i = i'-2t;
        S1: if (i<N-1) B[i] = (A[i-1] + A[i] + A[i+1])/3;
        S2: if (i>1) A[i-1] = B[i-1];
      }
}
```

For our scheme, it would also be valid to shift, after tiling, the inner tile-loop w.r.t. the outer tile-loop, i.e., to move up or down each column in Fig. 3.   □

2.2   Inter-Tile Data Reuse

The inter-tile reuse problem we formalize here is the kernel offloading with optimized remote accesses presented in [2,4], even if other variations are possible. A kernel is tiled and offloaded, tile by tile, to a computing accelerator (a FPGA in [2,4]). Initially, all data are in remote memory, while all computations are performed on the accelerator. Each tile T consists of three *successive* phases: a *loading* phase where data are copied from remote memory to local memory, enabling burst communications, then a *compute* phase where the original computations corresponding to the tile are performed on the local memory, and finally a *storing* phase where data are copied to remote memory. In addition, all compute (resp. loading and storing) phases are performed in sequence, following the lexicographic order on tile indices. Nevertheless, loads and stores can be done

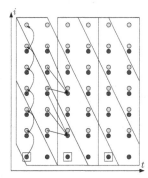

Non-empty 2×3 tiles drawn w.r.t the original space. Instruction S_1 in red. Instruction S_2 in green.

Are also shown some flow dependences, due to reads of B, at distance $(0,1)$, and reads of A, at distance $(1,0)$, $(1,-1)$, $(1,-2)$ in the (t,i) space.

Fig. 3. jacobi1d kernel and skewed tiling.

concurrently with the computations of other tiles, enabling pipelining, compu-tation/communication overlapping, and execution similar to double buffering. *Inter-tile reuse* makes this possible even when data are both read and written.[3]

Then, the "maximal inter-tile data reuse problem" is to define the loading and storing sets Load(T) and Store(T) for each tile T so that a data element is never loaded from remote memory if it is already available in local memory, i.e., if it has already been loaded or computed (as, in this latter case, the remote memory is not necessarily up-to-date). This inter-tile reuse is performed for each *tile strip* (subspace of tiles corresponding to inner tile dimensions). In [4], a tile strip is one-dimensional, but the technique can be applied to multi-dimensional strips. This choice however impacts the size of the local memory.

Note: there are some similarities with the reuse analysis of [16]. Given a "slid-ing window" of iterations, one analyzes the data that each iteration needs to bring because they were not already present due to previous iterations in the sliding window. But the communications are not coalesced out of the tile, they are still at the iteration level. In other words, this is a reuse analysis at constant (possibly parametric) distance (the sliding window), but with no granularity or scheduling (through tiling) reorganization, which makes the problem different.

The technique of [4], based on parametric linear programming [13], consists in performing loads (resp. stores) as late (resp. as soon) as possible, i.e., a data element is loaded just before the first tile that accesses it, if this access is a read, and is stored just after the last tile that writes it. Among all schemes that exploit a full inter-tile reuse in a strip, this tends to reduce the size of the local memory. We illustrate this technique again on the `jacobi_1d_imper` example.

Example (cont'd) For the tiling of Fig. 3, a 1D tile strip is vertical, indexed by $T_1 = \lfloor \frac{t}{s_1} \rfloor$. To simplify explanations, we only consider the array A (the ar-ray B is not live-in of a tile strip). We compute the first operation (following the order defined by the tiling) that accesses A[m]. This means computing, with $(i_1, i_2) = (t, i)$ and parameters M, N, m, T_1, the lexicographic minimum of $(T_2, i'_1, i'_2, k, i_1, i_2)$ in a set defined by a disjunction of two conjunctions of affine inequalities derived from the program (iteration domains and access functions):

$$\begin{cases} -1 \leq m - i_2 \leq 1, \ 0 \leq i_1 \leq M - 1, \ 1 \leq i_2 \leq N - 2, \ k = 0, \\ i'_1 = i_1, \ i'_2 = 2i_1 + i_2, \ 0 \leq i'_1 - 2T_1 \leq 1, \ 0 \leq i'_2 - 3I_2 \leq 2 \end{cases}$$
$$\vee$$
$$\begin{cases} m = i_2, \ 0 \leq i_1 \leq M - 1, \ 1 \leq i_2 \leq N - 2, \ k = 1, i'_1 = i_1, \\ i'_2 = 2i_1 + i_2 + 1, \ 0 \leq i'_1 - 2T_1 \leq 1, \ 0 \leq i'_2 - 3T_2 \leq 2 \end{cases}$$

The first set of constraints corresponds to reads in S_1 and specifies that A[m] is A[i-1], A[i], or A[i+1], that iterations in tiles are valid $((T_1, T_2, i'_1, i'_2) \in \mathcal{T}_S)$, and $k = 0$ is the third component of $\theta(S_1, (t, i))$ (i.e., S_1 is the first executed statement in the loop body). The second set of constraints corresponds to writes

---

[3] Without inter-tile reuse, full pipelining of tiles is not always possible if a data is locally written, then read in a subsequent tile. Indeed, one would then need to wait for the data to be stored in remote memory before loading it again. Inter-tile reuse enables to break such a cycle of synchronizations and avoid considering latencies.

in S_2 (with $k = 1$, i.e., second executed statement in the loop body). The lexicographic minimum is expressed as a disjunction of cases (a QUAST or quasi affine solution tree [13]). Then, all solutions (i.e., leaves of the tree) that correspond to a write operation are removed. Here, all first accesses are reads, no simplification is needed. It remains to project out the variables i'_1, i'_2, i_1, i_2, k, to get a relation between tile index T and array element m, which describes $\text{Load}(T)$ as a union:

$$\text{Load}(T) = \begin{array}{c} \{m \mid 0 \leq 2T_1 \leq M - 1, 2 \leq m \leq N - 1, 1 \leq m + 4T_1 - 3T_2 \leq 3\} \\ \cup \\ \{m \mid 0 \leq m \leq 1, 3 \leq N, 0 \leq 2T_1 \leq M - 1, -1 \leq 4T_1 - 3T_2 \leq 1\} \end{array}$$

The second set loads the additional A[0] and A[1] for the unique tile in the strip that contains an iteration $(t, 1)$ on its first column (squares in Fig. 3). □

As can be seen from the inequalities involved in the previous example with $s = (2, 3)$ (and in the definition of $\mathcal{T}_S$), considering the components of the size vector s as parameters generates **quadratic constraints**. In other words, this formulation is inherently not linear in the tile sizes. The goal of this paper is to show that, surprisingly, the problem can nevertheless be solved, both for exact inter-tile reuse (as in the previous example) and with approximations.

3   Dealing with Unaligned Tiles

The first key idea to break the non-linearity constraint is to represent each tile not with its tile index T defined earlier, but with the index I of its *origin* (first element in the tile in the lexicographic order). The first difference is that tiles are scanned with loops with increments equal to 1 when T is used and equal to s when I is used. The second difference is that, when I is used instead of T, the set of elements i in a tile is affine in s: this is the set of all i such that $I \leq i \leq I + s - 1$. In other words, parametric analysis inside a tile is possible. This representation is not new, it is used for analysis in PIPS [18, Fig. 6] and for the parametric code generation [30] used for the tiled code of Section 2.1. However, when reasoning with different tiles, the non-linearity is coming back. Indeed, in a given execution, the tile origins I are restricted to the lattice $\mathcal{L}$ defined by $I \in \mathcal{L}$ iff $I = s \circ J$ for some integer vector J. The second key idea is to show how these quadratic constraints can nevertheless be ignored, by reasoning on the set of all tiles of size s, not just those restricted to $\mathcal{L}$. The inter-tile reuse problem then becomes (piece-wise) affine in s as we will show.

Note that, with standard conditions for tiling (i.e., when all dependence distances are non-negative along the dimensions being tiled [20]), if a tiling is valid, any translation of it is valid too. In other words, considering all tile origins $I = s \circ J + I_0$ for some vector I_0 defines a valid tiling too. This has the same effect as defining the tiling from the shifted mapping $i \mapsto \sigma(S, i) - I_0$ for all S. Hereafter, we say that two tiles are *aligned* if they belong to the same tiling.

3.1   Exact Approach with Set Equations

In Section 2.2, maximal inter-tile data reuse was expressed as a linear programming optimization, following [4]. It can be equivalently formulated with set equations [3], expressed in terms of $\text{In}(T)$ and $\text{Out}(T)$, the standard *live-in* and *live-out* sets for tile T, as defined for example for array region analysis [10]:

$$\text{Load}(T) = \text{In}(T) \setminus \bigcup_{T' \prec T} (\text{In} \cup \text{Out})(T') = \text{In}(T) \setminus (\text{In} \cup \text{Out})(T' \prec T)\}$$

$$\text{Store}(T) = \text{Out}(T) \setminus \bigcup_{T' \succ T} \text{Out}(T') = \text{Out}(T) \setminus \text{Out}(T' \succ T)$$

Here, as indicated in the previous formulas, $X(T' \prec T)$ is a shortcut to denote the union of all sets $X(T')$ for all tiles T' executed before T (lexicographic order) in the same tile strip as T. Expressing $X(T' \prec T)$ from $X(T')$ is done simply by adding the constraint $T' \prec T$ and specifying that T' is in the strip where reuse is exploited. The previous set equations state that we load what is live-in for T and not previously live-in (redundant load) or live-out (defined locally), and we store what is live-out, but not again live-out later (redundant store). One could expect to rather subtract $\text{Load}(T' \prec T)$ from $\text{Load}(T)$ and $\text{Store}(T' \succ T)$ from $\text{Store}(T)$, but such recursive implicit definitions are not usable.

We now rephrase these equations when tiles T are represented by their tile origins I as previously explained. We also consider *all* tiles with size s, not just those whose origins belong to the lattice $\mathcal{L}$, i.e., even those that will not be executed in a given tiling. These tiles contain valid iterations (which will be executed as part of an *aligned* tile), but their Load and Store sets will not generate transfers during the execution. We define two relations on tiles:

- $I' \sqsubset_s I$ iff $I' \prec I$ and $I - I' \in \mathcal{L}$. This is equivalent to the lexicographic order $T' \prec T$ for the corresponding tile indices.
- $I' \prec_s I$ iff, for some $k \in [1..n]$, $I'_i \leq I_i$ for all $i < k$ and $I'_k \leq I_k - s_k$ where n is the dimension of I and I'. This is a variation of the lexicographic order.

The standard reflexive extensions $\sqsubseteq_s$ and $\preceq_s$ of these relations are clearly partial orders. Fig. 4 shows all tile origins I' strictly smaller (in blue) or strictly larger (in red) than the tile origin I (in yellow), for the orders $\sqsubseteq_s$ and $\preceq_s$. Note that tiles comparable for $\sqsubseteq_s$ are always aligned with each other. An alternate, maybe more intuitive, definition of $\prec_s$ is as follows: $I' \prec_s I$ iff, in the tiling induced by I (the same is true with I', this is symmetric), every point in the tile I' is executed before any point in the tile I (but I and I' may not be aligned).

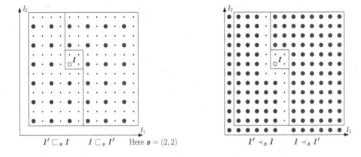

Fig. 4. Orders $\sqsubseteq_s$ and $\preceq_s$. Points are tile origins.

With tile origins, the previous Load/Store equations can be rewritten as:

$$\text{Load}(\boldsymbol{I}) = \text{In}(\boldsymbol{I}) \setminus (\text{In} \cup \text{Out})(\boldsymbol{I}' \sqsubset_{\boldsymbol{s}} \boldsymbol{I}) \tag{1}$$

$$\text{Store}(\boldsymbol{I}) = \text{Out}(\boldsymbol{I}) \setminus \text{Out}(\boldsymbol{I}' \sqsupset_{\boldsymbol{s}} \boldsymbol{I}) \tag{2}$$

The key is now to show that these sets can also be defined equivalently as:

$$\text{Load}(\boldsymbol{I}) = \text{In}(\boldsymbol{I}) \setminus (\text{In} \cup \text{Out})(\boldsymbol{I}' \prec_{\boldsymbol{s}} \boldsymbol{I}) \tag{3}$$

$$\text{Store}(\boldsymbol{I}) = \text{Out}(\boldsymbol{I}) \setminus \text{Out}(\boldsymbol{I}' \succ_{\boldsymbol{s}} \boldsymbol{I}) \tag{4}$$

This is not obvious as the contribution of unaligned tiles (i.e., not in the same tiling as $\boldsymbol{I}$) is also subtracted, thus the Load/Store sets could now be too small. Nicely, these sets **only involve affine constraints** as the relation $\prec_{\boldsymbol{s}}$ is, by definition, piece-wise affine (this is also the case for a similar "happens-before" relation defined on iteration points). They can thus be computed with a library such as isl [32]. Before proving these formulas, we first illustrate their use.

Example (cont'd) The following sets were computed thanks to the isl calculator iscc [33] with the generic script of Fig. 5, for jacobi_1d_imper (see Fig. 3).

$$\begin{aligned}
\text{Load}(\boldsymbol{I}) = \ & \{A(m) \mid 1 \le m + 2I_1 - I_2 \le s_2,\, s_1 \ge 1,\, I_1 \ge 0,\, m \ge 1,\, I_1 \le -1 + M, \\
& \quad I_2 \ge 2 - s_2 + 2I_1,\, m \le -1 + N,\, N \ge 3\} \\
\cup \ & \{A(m) \mid m \ge 1 + I_2,\, m \ge 1,\, M \ge 1,\, m \le -1 + N,\, I_1 \le -1, \\
& \quad I_1 \ge 1 - s_1,\, I_2 \ge 2 - s_2,\, N \ge 3,\, m \le s_2 + I_2\} \\
\cup \ & \{A(1) \mid I_2 = 1 + 2I_1 \wedge 0 \le I_1 \le -1 + M,\, N \ge 3,\, s_1 \ge 1,\, s_2 \ge 1\} \\
\cup \ & \{A(m) \mid 0 \le m \le 1,\, I_2 = 1 \le s_2,\, 1 - s_1 \le I_1 \le -1,\, M \ge 1,\, N \ge 3\} \\
\cup \ & \{A(0) \mid 0 \le I_1 \le M - 1,\, N \ge 3,\, s_1 \ge 1,\, 1 \le I_2 - 2I_1 \ge 2 - s_2\} \\
\cup \ & \{A(0) \mid 1 - s_1 \le I_1 \le -1,\, M \ge 1,\, N \ge 3,\, I_2 \ge 2 - s_2,\, I_2 \le 0\}
\end{aligned}$$

$$\begin{aligned}
\text{Store}(\boldsymbol{I}) = \ & \{B(m) \mid m \ge 1,\, m \ge 2 - 2M + s_2 + I_2,\, m \le -2 + N, \\
& \quad I_1 \ge 1 - s_1,\, 2 \le m + 2s_1 + 2I_1 - I_2 \le 1 + s_2,\, s_1 \ge 1\} \\
\cup \ & \{B(m) \mid m \ge 1,\, s_1 \ge 1,\, m \le -2 + N,\, I_1 \le -1 + M,\, m \le 1 - 2M + s_2 + I_2, \\
& \quad m \ge 2 - 2s_1 - 2I_1 + I_2,\, I_1 \ge 1 - s_1,\, M \ge 1,\, m \ge 2 - 2M + I_2\} \\
\cup \ & \{A(m) \mid m \ge 1,\, m \ge 1 - 2M + s_2 + I_2,\, m \le -2 + N, \\
& \quad I_1 \ge 1 - s_1,\, 1 \le m + 2s_1 + 2I_1 - I_2 \le s_2,\, s_1 \ge 1\} \\
\cup \ & \{A(m) \mid m \ge 1,\, s_1 \ge 1,\, m \le -2 + N,\, I_1 \le -1 + M,\, m \le -2M + s_2 + I_2, \\
& \quad m \ge 1 - 2s_1 - 2I_1 + I_2,\, I_1 \ge 1 - s_1,\, M \ge 1,\, m \ge 1 - 2M + I_2\}
\end{aligned}$$

The fact that the array B appears in the Store set may be surprising as B is recomputed in each tile strip (this is why it does not appear in the Load set). This is because the script of Fig. 5 considers each tile strip in isolation. To be able to remove B from the Store set, one would need a similar analysis on tile strips to discover that B is actually overwritten by subsequent tile strips. Then, only the last tile strip should store B, in case it is live-out of the program.

It can be checked (e.g., with iscc) that the set $\text{Load}(\boldsymbol{I})$ above is indeed a generalization of the set $\text{Load}(\boldsymbol{T})$ derived earlier for the canonical tiling with $\boldsymbol{s} = (2, 3)$. It is the complete expression, parameterized by $\boldsymbol{s}$, of all cases, including incomplete tiles, and even tilings obtained by translation of $\mathcal{L}$. Note that simply changing the object Strip (see Fig. 5) from {[I_1,I_2]->[I_1,I_2']} to {[I_1,I_2]->[I_1',I_2']} gives 2D inter-tile reuse, i.e., in the whole space, as

```
# Inputs
Params := [M, N, s_1, s_2] -> { : s_1 >= 0 and s_2 >= 0 };
Domain := [M, N] -> { # Iteration domains
    S_1[i_1, i_2] : 1 <= i_2 <= N-2 and 0 <= i_1 <= M-1;
    S_2[i_1, i_2] : 1 <= i_2 <= N-2 and 0 <= i_1 <= M-1; } * Params;
Read := [M, N] -> { # Read access functions
    S_1[i_1, i_2] -> A[m] : -1 + i_2 <= m <= 1 + i_2;
    S_2[i_1, i_2] -> B[i_2]; } * Domain;
Write := [M, N] -> { # Write access functions
    S_1[i_1, i_2] -> B[i_2];
    S_2[i_1, i_2] -> A[i_2]; } * Domain;
Theta := [M, N] -> { # Preliminary mapping
    S_1[i_1, i_2] -> [i_1, 2 i_1 + i_2, 0];
    S_2[i_1, i_2] -> [i_1, 1 + 2 i_1 + i_2, 1]; };
# Tools for set manipulations
Tiling := [s_1, s_2] -> { # Two dimensional tiling
    [[I_1, I_2] -> [i_1, i_2, k]] -> [i_1, i_2, k] :
        I_1 <= i_1 < I_1 + s_1 and I_2 <= i_2 < I_2 + s_2 };
Coalesce := { [I_1, I_2] -> [[I_1, I_2] -> [i_1, i_2, k]] };
Strip := { [I_1, I_2] -> [I_1, I_2'] };
Prev := { # Lexicographic order
    [[I_1, I_2] -> [i_1, i_2, k]] -> [[I_1, I_2] -> [i_1', i_2', k']] :
        i_1' <= i_1 - 1 or (i_1' <= i_1 and i_2' <= i_2 - 1)
        or (i_1' <= i_1 and i_2' <= i_2 and k' <= k - 1) };
TiledPrev := [s_1, s_2] -> { # Special ''lexicographic'' order
    [I_1, I_2] -> [I_1', I_2'] : I_1' <= I_1 - s_1 or
        (I_1' <= I_1 and I_2' <= I_2 - s_2) } * Strip;
TiledNext := TiledPrev^-1;
TiledRead := Tiling.(Theta^-1).Read;
TiledWrite := Tiling.(Theta^-1).Write;
# Set/relation computations
In := Coalesce.(TiledRead - (Prev.TiledWrite));
Out := Coalesce.TiledWrite;
Load := In - ((TiledPrev.In) + (TiledPrev.Out));
Store := Out - (TiledNext.Out);
print coalesce (Load % Params); print coalesce (Store % Params);
```

Fig. 5. Script iscc for the Jacobi1D example.

the first dimension is not a fixed parameter anymore. The strict order $\prec_s$ is defined by TiledPrev while Load and Store, at the end of the script, express Eqs. (3) and (4). Constraints on parameters or on I can be added in Params, e.g., to get simplified Load/Store sets for complete tiles, for large tiles, etc. Note however that isl uses coalescing heuristics to simplify expressions and, depending on the constraints, the outcome can be simpler or more complicated (although equivalent). Here, replacing $s_1 \geq 0$ by $s_1 > 0$ changes the final expression. $\square$

To prove that we can use $\prec_s$ (in Eqs. (3) and (4)) instead of $\sqsubset_s$ (in Eqs. (1) and (2)), we define the concept of *pointwise functions*. This is a bit more than what we need for the proofs, but this concept makes easier to understand the underlying problems, related to the equality (or not) of some unions of images of sets, which will be even more subtle when dealing with approximations.

3.2 Pointwise Functions

If $\mathcal{A}$ is a set, $\mathcal{P}(\mathcal{A})$ denotes the set of subsets of $\mathcal{A}$ (sometimes also written $2^{\mathcal{A}}$). Hereafter, the function F is typically a function such as Out, which maps a tile, i.e., a subset of the tile strip ($\mathcal{A}$), to a subset of all data elements ($\mathcal{B}$).

Definition 1. *Let $\mathcal{A}$ and $\mathcal{B}$ be two sets, $\mathcal{C} \subseteq \mathcal{P}(\mathcal{A})$. The function $F : \mathcal{C} \to \mathcal{P}(\mathcal{B})$ is* **pointwise** *iff there exists $f : \mathcal{A} \to \mathcal{P}(\mathcal{B})$ such that $\forall X \in \mathcal{C}$, $F(X) = \bigcup_{x \in X} f(x)$.*

In other words, a function F is pointwise if the image of any set where F is defined (not necessarily all sets) can be summarized by the contributions (through f) of the points it contains. In our case, $\mathcal{A}$ is the set of iterations in the tile strip to be analyzed and $\mathcal{C}$ is the set of all tiles (aligned or unaligned) intersected with $\mathcal{A}$.

If all written values are live-out, then $\mathrm{Out}(\boldsymbol{I}) = \mathrm{Write}(\boldsymbol{I})$, the values written in $\boldsymbol{I}$. Otherwise, this set should be intersected with Liveout, the set of all elements live-out of the tile strip. The function Write is, by definition, pointwise, because it is the union, for all points i in $\boldsymbol{I}$, of the set of values $\mathrm{write}(i)$ written at iteration i. Also, even if $\boldsymbol{I} \mapsto \mathrm{In}(\boldsymbol{I})$ may not be pointwise, any element read but not written in $\boldsymbol{I}$ is live-in for $\boldsymbol{I}$, thus $(\mathrm{In} \cup \mathrm{Write})(\boldsymbol{I}) = (\mathrm{Read} \cup \mathrm{Write})(\boldsymbol{I})$, which is pointwise, by introducing $\mathrm{read}(i)$ the set of points read at iteration i. We get:

$$\mathrm{Load}(\boldsymbol{I}) = \mathrm{In}(\boldsymbol{I}) \setminus (\mathrm{In} \cup \mathrm{Write})(\boldsymbol{I}' \sqsubset_{\boldsymbol{s}} \boldsymbol{I}) = \mathrm{In}(\boldsymbol{I}) \setminus \bigcup_{\boldsymbol{I}' \sqsubset_{\boldsymbol{s}} \boldsymbol{I}} \bigcup_{i \in \boldsymbol{I}'} (\mathrm{read} \cup \mathrm{write})(i)$$

$$= \mathrm{In}(\boldsymbol{I}) \setminus \bigcup_{\boldsymbol{I}' \prec_{\boldsymbol{s}} \boldsymbol{I}} \bigcup_{i \in \boldsymbol{I}'} (\mathrm{read} \cup \mathrm{write})(i) = \mathrm{In}(\boldsymbol{I}) \setminus (\mathrm{In} \cup \mathrm{Write})(\boldsymbol{I}' \prec_{\boldsymbol{s}} \boldsymbol{I})$$

This is because $\cup_{\boldsymbol{I}' \prec_{\boldsymbol{s}} \boldsymbol{I}} \boldsymbol{I}' = \cup_{\boldsymbol{I}' \sqsubset_{\boldsymbol{s}} \boldsymbol{I}} \boldsymbol{I}'$. Indeed, since all tiles aligned with $\boldsymbol{I}$ form a partition of $\mathcal{A}$, the points covered by the two unions are the same: these are all the points executed before any point in $\boldsymbol{I}$. The same is true for $\mathrm{Store}(\boldsymbol{I})$, which is equal to $\mathrm{Liveout} \cap (\mathrm{Write}(\boldsymbol{I}) \setminus \mathrm{Write}(\boldsymbol{I}' \sqsupset_{\boldsymbol{s}} \boldsymbol{I}))$, or equivalently equal to $\mathrm{Liveout} \cap (\mathrm{Write}(\boldsymbol{I}) \setminus \mathrm{Write}(\boldsymbol{I}' \succ_{\boldsymbol{s}} \boldsymbol{I}))$. This concludes the proof in the exact case.

In summary, because tiles represent points exactly and because the "happens-before" relation (the fact that a point, resp. a tile, happens, during tiled execution, before another point, resp. tile) can be represented by a piece-wise affine relation, it is possible to perform a parametric analysis of inter-tile data reuse.

The equality of the unions of the images for $\boldsymbol{I}' \sqsubset_{\boldsymbol{s}} \boldsymbol{I}$ and for $\boldsymbol{I}' \prec_{\boldsymbol{s}} \boldsymbol{I}$ is actually a general property, and even a characterization, of pointwise functions. As the following theorem shows, pointwise functions are exactly those that induce the desired "stability" property on union of sets, i.e., if two unions of sets cover the same points, then the union of their contributions through F are the same. This a more general property than *distributive functions* (for $\cup$), those for which $F(A \cup B) = F(A) \cup F(B)$ because, in our case, $F(A \cup B)$ may not be defined.

Theorem 1. *$F : \mathcal{C} \to \mathcal{P}(\mathcal{B})$ is pointwise if and only if $\forall \mathcal{C}' \subseteq \mathcal{C}$, $\forall \mathcal{C}'' \subseteq \mathcal{C}$, $\bigcup_{X \in \mathcal{C}'} X = \bigcup_{X \in \mathcal{C}''} X \Rightarrow \bigcup_{X \in \mathcal{C}'} F(X) = \bigcup_{X \in \mathcal{C}''} F(X)$.*

Note that the previous property on unions is equivalent to $\forall X \in \mathcal{C}$, $\forall \mathcal{C}' \subseteq \mathcal{C}$, $X \subseteq \bigcup_{X' \in \mathcal{C}'} X' \Rightarrow F(X) \subseteq \bigcup_{X' \in \mathcal{C}'} F(X')$, i.e., if a set is covered by a union of sets, then its image is contained in the union of the images of these sets.

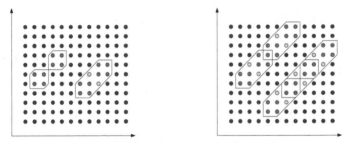

Fig. 6. "Double squares" (red), F (image of red & green), non pointwise situations.

A third equivalent characterization is possible, which explicitly builds a function f for a pointwise function F. If F and G are from $\mathcal{C}$ to $\mathcal{P}(\mathcal{B})$, we write $F \subseteq G$ if $\forall X \in \mathcal{C}$, $F(X) \subseteq G(X)$. Theorem 2 also identifies the "largest" pointwise under-approximation of F. All missing proofs are provided in [11] (appendix).

Theorem 2. *For $F : \mathcal{C} \subseteq \mathcal{P}(\mathcal{A}) \to \mathcal{P}(\mathcal{B})$, let $F_\circ$ be the pointwise function defined from $f_\circ(x) = \bigcap_{Y \in \mathcal{C},\, x \in Y} F(Y)$. Then $F_\circ$ is the largest pointwise under-approximation of F, i.e., $F_\circ \subseteq F$ and, if F' is pointwise, $F' \subseteq F \Rightarrow F' \subseteq F_\circ$. In particular, F is pointwise if and only if $F = F_\circ$.*

To get the intuition for these concepts, it is simpler to consider objects more general than rectangular tiles. Let $\mathcal{C}$ be the set of all possible "double squares" (in 2D) defined as two diagonally-neighboring squares as depicted on the left of Fig. 6 (red points in two boxes). Suppose each point i has an image $f(i)$. If $F(I)$ is defined for a "double-square" I as the union of all $f(i)$ for $i \in I$, it is pointwise by definition. Now, suppose $F(I)$ is defined as the union of all $f(i)$ for i in the convex hull of I (red + green points). The first situation on the right of Fig. 6 shows that each point i is included in two "double-squares" whose images by F have only $f(i)$ in common. Thus F_0 is not equal to F (the image of green points are missing) unless f has some additional property and, according to Theorem 2, F is not pointwise. The second situation on the right of Fig. 6 shows that a "double-square" is fully contained in two "double-squares", but the image of its green points (if f is injective) is not covered by the image of these two "double-squares" so, according to Theorem 1, F is not pointwise.

3.3 The Case of Approximations

We will use the previous properties of pointwise functions for approximations. There are at least four reasons why approximations of the various sets In, Out, Load, and Store may be used in an automatic code analyzer and optimizer.

- The execution of S at iteration i is not guaranteed, for example when it depends on a non-analyzable (e.g., data-dependent) `if` condition.
- The access functions are not fully analyzable (e.g., indirect accesses).
- The In/Out sets are approximated on purpose (e.g., they are restricted to polyhedra or hyper-rectangles) due to the algorithms used for analysis.
- The Load/Store sets are approximated to make them simpler, or to get transfer sets of some special form (e.g., vector/array communications).

In the first two cases, the approximation is pointwise, so the Read/Write functions remain pointwise. In the last two cases, it is more likely that In ∪ Out is not pointwise anymore. We first recall and extend the principles stated in [3] for approximations, assuming that the sets $\overline{\text{In}}$, $\underline{\text{Out}}$, and $\overline{\text{Out}}$ are given such that $\text{In}(I) \subseteq \overline{\text{In}}(I)$ and $\underline{\text{Out}}(I) \subseteq \text{Out}(I) \subseteq \overline{\text{Out}}(I)$. Here, the under-approximations (that could benefit from [10,31]) are not used for correctness, only for accuracy.

Non-Parametric Case. The first step is to define the Store sets, as exactly as possible from the $\overline{\text{Out}}$ sets, i.e., the sets of data possibly written:

$$\text{Store}(I) = \text{Liveout} \cap (\overline{\text{Out}}(I) \setminus \overline{\text{Out}}(I' \sqsupseteq_s I)) \tag{5}$$

Then, any over-approximation $\overline{\text{Store}}(I)$ of $\text{Store}(I)$ can be used. Eq. (5) means that a possibly-defined element is always stored to remote memory, in case it is indeed written at runtime. But what if this is not the case? We add it to the set of input elements so that its initial value is stored back instead of garbage:

$$\overline{\text{In}}'(I) = \overline{\text{In}}(I) \cup (\overline{\text{Store}}(I) \setminus \underline{\text{Out}}(I)) \tag{6}$$

Following [3, Thm. 3], loads are defined, as exactly as possible, from the sets $\underline{\text{Out}}$, $\overline{\text{Out}}$, and $\overline{\text{In}}'$ (i.e., after $\overline{\text{Store}}$ is defined). They are valid if for any tile I:

$$\text{Load}(I' \sqsubseteq_s I) \text{ contains } \overline{\text{Ra}}(I) = \overline{\text{In}}'(I) \setminus \underline{\text{Out}}(I' \sqsubset_s I) \tag{7}$$

$$\text{Load}(I) \cap \overline{\text{Out}}(I' \sqsubset_s I) = \emptyset \tag{8}$$

Eq. (7) means that all data possibly defined outside of the tile strip – the remote accesses $\overline{\text{Ra}}(I)$ – have to be loaded before I. Eq. (8) means that data possibly defined earlier in the tile strip should not be loaded, as this could overwrite some valid data. Eq. (9) below gives a non-recursive definition of $\text{Load}(I)$, simpler (and more usable) than the formula of [3, Thm. 6] (although it is equivalent):

$$\text{Load}(I) = \overline{\text{Ra}}_I \cap ((\overline{\text{In}}' \cup \overline{\text{Out}})(I) \setminus (\overline{\text{In}}' \cup \overline{\text{Out}})(I' \sqsubset_s I)) \tag{9}$$

where $\overline{\text{Ra}}_I$ denotes all remote accesses for the tile strip w.r.t. I, i.e., the union of all $\overline{\text{Ra}}(I')$, as defined in Eq. (7), for all I' that belong to the same tiling as I. The mechanism of Eq. (9) is actually simple: unlike for the exact case, a remote access live-in for I (i.e., in $\overline{\text{In}}'(I)$) cannot be loaded just before I if it *may* be written earlier (i.e., in $\overline{\text{Out}}(I' \sqsubset_s I)$). Otherwise, the load will erase the right value if, at runtime, it was indeed written earlier. Instead, the trick is to load the element before the first tile I' that may write it. This way, either the value is defined locally and the read in I gets this value, or it is not defined and the read gets the original value. Thm. 3 (see the proof in [11]) states more formally the correctness and exactness of Eq. (9). Then, any over-approximation $\overline{\text{Load}}(I)$ of this "exact" $\text{Load}(I)$ can be used (even if it may induce some useless loads) as long as it still satisfies $\overline{\text{Load}}(I) \cap \overline{\text{Out}}(I' \sqsubset_s I) = \emptyset$, as required by Eq. (8).

Theorem 3. *Eq. (9) defines valid loads, which are "exact" w.r.t. the $\overline{\text{In}}'$, $\underline{\text{Out}}$, and $\overline{\text{Out}}$ sets (no useless or redundant loads) and performed as late as possible.*

We write ΔF the function defined from F by $\Delta F(I) = F(I) \setminus F(I' \sqsubset_s I)$. Then, with $F = \overline{\text{In}}' \cup \overline{\text{Out}}$, we get $\text{Load}(J) = \overline{\text{Ra}}_I \cap \Delta F(J)$ for all J aligned with I.

Parametric Case. Our goal is to reformulate Eqs. (5) and (9) so that the Store and Load sets can be computed with the tile sizes s as parameter. Can we just replace the order $\sqsubseteq_s$ by $\preceq_s$ as in the exact case (Section 3.1)? No. Doing so may, in general, be incorrect, resulting in missing loads or stores for I, if subtracting the contribution of unaligned tiles (i.e., those that will not be executed) remove additional elements. This is where pointwise functions come, again, into play.

The easy case is when approximations are at the level of iterations, i.e., the accesses of each iteration i are approximated with $\underline{\text{write}}(i) \subseteq \text{write}(i) \subseteq \overline{\text{write}}(i)$ and $\text{read}(i) \subseteq \overline{\text{read}}(i)$, resulting in pointwise functions $\underline{\text{Write}}$, $\overline{\text{Write}}$, and $\overline{\text{Read}}$. If the sets $\overline{\text{Out}}$, $\overline{\text{In}}$, then Store are derived from $\overline{\text{Write}}$ and $\overline{\text{Read}}$ with no further approximation, then, as for the exact case, $\overline{\text{Out}}$ and $\overline{\text{In}}' \cup \overline{\text{Out}}$ are pointwise too. Thus, a Store(I) can be computed with Eq. (5), in a parametric way, with $\succ_s$ instead of $\sqsupseteq_s$. The same is true for the central part of Load(I) in Eq. (9) with $\prec_s$ instead of $\sqsubseteq_s$. It remains to compute $\overline{\text{Ra}}_I$ from $\overline{\text{Ra}}(I) = \overline{\text{In}}'(I) \setminus \overline{\text{Out}}(I' \sqsubseteq_s I)$. As the tiles in $\mathcal{L}$ cover the whole iteration space, $\overline{\text{Ra}}_I$ is the set of all data that are maybe read (or written for stores) and possibly not written before, i.e., live-in for the tile strip, for the schedule induced by the tiling aligned with I. But if the mapping θ used for tiling was considered legal with the same pointwise approximation of reads and writes, then any shifted tiling (with standard validity conditions) preserves anti, flow, and output dependences, thus $\overline{\text{Ra}}_I$ does not depend on I. It is even equal to the live-in data for the tile strip when considering the original order of the code and, thus, can be computed, independently on s.

The previous approach can be used when Load/Store sets are computed "exactly" but from a pointwise approximation of accesses. We now consider the case where, in addition to this pointwise approximation, even the sets $\overline{\text{Out}}$, $\overline{\text{In}}$, $\overline{\text{Store}}$, and $\overline{\text{Load}}$ can be over-approximated further, for whatever reason. For example, $\overline{\text{Store}}(I)$ can contain data that are not even in $\overline{\text{Out}}$ or $\overline{\text{In}}$, and thus not remote in the strict sense. However, transfers still need to be correct. We first consider how to handle $\overline{\text{Out}}$ in Eq. (5) and $\overline{\text{In}}' \cup \overline{\text{Out}}$ in Eq. (9), which, *a priori*, have no reason to be pointwise. We deal with the computation of $\overline{\text{Ra}}_I$ later.

We first mention an interesting intermediate situation that works with no further difficulties, even if the approximations are not pointwise. If a pointwise function F is over-approximated through its domain (the iterations) instead of its range (the data), i.e., $\overline{F}(I) = F(\overline{I})$ with $I \subseteq \overline{I}$, then it may be the case that, when computing the unions (either with $\sqsubseteq_s$ or $\prec_s$), no new iterations are added with the approximated domains. This is what happens with the approximated "double-squares" of Fig. 6, typical from parallel tiles. Then $\overline{F}(I' \sqsubseteq_s I)$ equals:

$$\bigcup_{I' \sqsubseteq_s I} \bigcup_{i \in \overline{I'}} f(i) = \bigcup_{I' \sqsubseteq_s I} \bigcup_{i \in I'} f(i) = \bigcup_{I' \prec_s I} \bigcup_{i \in I'} f(i) = \bigcup_{I' \prec_s I} \bigcup_{i \in \overline{I'}} f(i) = \overline{F}(I' \prec_s I)$$

In this case, even without pointwise functions, parametric approximations can be designed, with a careful analysis of the "shape" (the sets $\overline{I}$) of approximations. But, this situation does not cover the case where approximations are made in the range of F and cannot be converted into approximations in the domain of F, as it is the case for pointwise functions. We now address this general case.

The key point for approximation is that loading earlier and storing later always keeps correctness. As noticed earlier, Load(I) has the form $\overline{\mathrm{Ra}}_I \cap \Delta F(I)$ with $\Delta F(I) = F(I) \setminus F(I' \sqsubseteq_s I)$, thus $\Delta F(I' \sqsubseteq_s I) = F(I' \sqsubseteq_s I)$. If we define F° pointwise such that $F \subseteq F^\circ$, then $\Delta F(I' \sqsubseteq_s I) \subseteq \Delta F^\circ(I' \sqsubseteq_s I)$, i.e., possibly more data are loaded (but no load is delayed), thus the validity condition of Eq. (7) is satisfied with $\overline{\mathrm{Ra}}_I \cap \Delta F^\circ$. The same is true for Store(I) with $\sqsupseteq_s$: possibly more data are stored but no store is advanced. Finally, Eq. (8) is satisfied too as $\overline{\mathrm{Out}}(I' \sqsubseteq_s I) \subseteq F(I' \sqsubseteq_s I) \subseteq F^\circ(I' \sqsubseteq_s I)$, which is subtracted in ΔF°. Thus, such an over-approximation mechanism (making F bigger) is always valid.

Thm. 4 below shows how to build such a function F° with the additional property that loads in ΔF that correspond to "pointwise loads" are still loaded for the same tile with ΔF°, i.e., not earlier (thus with no lifetime increase). Indeed, the goal is to try to avoid the naive solution where all data are loaded (resp. stored) before (resp. after) the whole computation of the tile strip.

Theorem 4. *Let $\mathcal{C}$ be the set of all tiles of size s and $F : \mathcal{C} \to \mathcal{P}(\mathcal{B})$. Define F° by $F^\circ(I) = \cup_{J,\, I \in J} F(J)$, where $I \in J$ means that I is in the tile with origin J. Then $F \subseteq F^\circ$ and F° is pointwise. Moreover, if y is such that $\forall I,\, y \in F(I) \Rightarrow y \in F_\circ(I)$ ($F_\circ$ is defined in Thm. 2), then $\forall I,\, y \in \Delta F^\circ(I) \Rightarrow y \in \Delta F(I)$, i.e., over-approximating F by F° does not load "pointwise" elements earlier.*

The same technique can be used for Store(I) but with an expression such as $F^\circ(I) = \cup_{J,\, J \in I} F(J)$. It remains to see what to do with the set $\overline{\mathrm{Ra}}_I$. We can compute, with s as parameter, $\overline{\mathrm{Ra}}(I) = \overline{\mathrm{In}}(I) \setminus \underline{\mathrm{Out}}(I' \prec_s I)$, thus replacing $\sqsubseteq_s$ by $\prec_s$. We get *a priori* a smaller set, which could be problematic because of the intersection in Eq. (9). However, it is still correct and, actually, even more precise. Indeed, as Out is exact, we have $\overline{\mathrm{In}}'(I) \setminus \mathrm{Out}(I' \sqsubseteq_s I) = \overline{\mathrm{In}}'(I) \setminus \mathrm{Out}(I' \prec_s I)$ and what is actually important in Eq. (7) is that this set is indeed loaded. Thus, considering $\overline{\mathrm{Ra}}(I) = \overline{\mathrm{In}}(I) \setminus \underline{\mathrm{Out}}(I' \prec_s I)$ in Eq. (7) is fine as it is a superset. Finally, to compute $\overline{\mathrm{Ra}}_I = \bigcup_{J,\, J - I \in \mathcal{L}} \overline{\mathrm{Ra}}(J)$, we drop the lattice constraint. If $\overline{\mathrm{Ra}}$ is not pointwise, we get a possibly larger set: this is suboptimal, but correct.

This completes the theory for parametric tiling with inter-tile reuse and approximations. In practice, it needs to be adapted to each approximation scheme but it still provides some general mathematical means to reason on the correctness of approximations for parametric tiling. A possible approximation (to reduce complexity) consists in removing, in all intermediate computations such as Out, Store, In', all existential variables (projection) and to manipulate only integer points in polyhedra. Another possibility is to rely on array region analysis techniques [10]. This is left for future work. We point out however that generalizing such a parametric inter-tile reuse to more general tilings, where tiles (rectangular or not) are not executed following the axes that define them, will be more difficult if the iteration space covered by tiles that "happen before" a given tile cannot be defined by a piece-wise affine relation. One can still define approximations, even not necessarily pointwise, as long as $(\overline{\mathrm{In}}' \cup \overline{\mathrm{Out}})(I' \prec_s I) = (\overline{\mathrm{In}}' \cup \overline{\mathrm{Out}})(I' \sqsubseteq_s I)$ (and similar equalities), as illustrated with the "double-squares" of Fig. 6. However such approximations are more difficult to define systematically and may require unacceptable (i.e., too rough) additional over-approximations.

4   Next Step: Deriving Local Memory Sizes

One of the interests of computing the Load/Store sets in a parametric fashion is that, now, the size of the resulting local memory (e.g., obtained by bounding boxes or lattice-based array contraction [12]) can also be computed in a parametric fashion. Such a parametric scheme seems almost mandatory in a context such as described in [4,28], for HLS from C to FPGA. Indeed, as explained in [4], some manual (though systematic) changes must be done to the tiled code so that it is accepted by the HLS tool. Doing these changes for all interesting tile sizes is not reasonable. Also, as explained in [28], identifying the right tile sizes may require executions of multiple scenarios. Parametric code generation would help speeding up such a design space exploration. With this parametric inter-tile reuse, combined with parametric code generation [30] and buffer sizing [1], one should be able to derive a fully automatic scheme, with parametric tile sizes. This also makes the design and use of analytical cost models possible, in particular to explore hierarchical tiling, which impacts the local memory size.

To illustrate such applications, we extended the buffer sizing of [1] – which requires lifetime information of array elements to use memory reuse for array contraction – to the case where s is a parameter, and for partial orders of computations, e.g., those expressing pipeline executions. As for inter-tile reuse, we consider all tiles, not just those aligned w.r.t. a given lattice. Again, one can make sure that no rough approximation is performed that would result in an overestimated memory size. These results are out of the scope of this paper. We only report here some examples, for two schedules, as illustration. The first schedule performs all computations in sequence: tiles are serialized and each tile performs its loads, then its computations, then its stores before a new tile is computed. The second one is a double-buffering-style schedule (in each tile strip) defined with the following precedences: a) if I_1, I_2, I_3 are three successive tiles for $\sqsubseteq_s$, transfer requests are serialized as $\mathrm{Load}(I_2) \to \mathrm{Store}(I_1) \to \mathrm{Load}(I_3) \to \mathrm{Store}(I_2) \to \ldots$, b) tile computations are done sequentially following $\sqsubseteq_s$, and c) each tile I loads its set $\mathrm{Load}(I)$, then computes, then stores its set $\mathrm{Store}(I)$. All other overlappings (in particular parallelism between computations and transfers) can arise at runtime, achieving a kind of double-buffering-style computation.

Example (cont'd) The `jacobi_1d_imper` code of Fig. 1 has two parameters N and M defining the loop bounds. The proposed tiling has also two tile size parameters s_1 and s_2. There could be a 5th parameter to specify each tile strip, but we chose to derive mappings valid for all tile strips (as for all examples hereafter). After Load/Store analysis and memory folding with modulos, we get (after simplification) to following sizes for A and B, for the sequential schedule:

- size(B) $= \min(N - 2, 2M + s_2 - 1, 2s_1 + s_2 - 1)$.
- size(A) $= \min(N, 2M + s_2, 2s_1 + s_2)$.

and, with the pipeline schedule:

- size(B) $= \min(N - 2, 2M + 2s_2 - 2, 2s_1 + 2s_2 - 2)$.
- size(A) $= \min(N, 2M + 2s_2, 2s_1 + 2s_2)$.

These expressions are actually expressed as disjunctions, each term that contributes to the minimum being specified by conditions on parameters. One can also of course easily retrieve (this time in a parametric fashion) the expression of the memory size for the product of 2 polynomials analyzed in [4].   □

We are still working on an automated implementation of our algorithms with isl, to be integrated into PPCG [34], an optimizer for GPUs. For the moment, we manually adapted an iscc script for some PolyBench [29] examples. The reader interested in the details can consult the table provided in the appendix of [11]. The transformations θ were given by the isl scheduler, which gives results similar to those of Pluto [27]. We tiled the largest consecutive tilable dimensions (underlined in the table) for which dependences are nonnegative. Some examples were omitted, either because the isl scheduler did not exhibit any "tileability"[4] – at least without preliminary transformations such as array expansion –, or because they had too many instructions[5] or variables[6] and would not fit in the table (these examples were not tried: they may – but maybe not – reveal complexity issues, which will be explored with the automatic implementation in isl, as well as different approximation schemes). Moreover, parameters were restricted so that each kernel domain contains at least one strip with at least two consecutive full tiles, and tile sizes are at least 2: this avoids many special cases (their generation is possible however) that, again, would not fit in the table.

The results we provided in the table of [11] are the array sizes after memory folding. We computed a memory allocation compatible for all tile strips, depending on the program parameters and the counters of the loops surrounding the tiled loops. Another choice could have been to compute a memory allocation depending on the strip, potentially saving space for boundary strips. The memory size was computed for both sequential and pipelined (double buffering) execution with inter-tile data reuse, using the successive modulo approach of Lefebvre and Feautrier [25]. We are still working on the approximations, not provided in the table, as well as on techniques to speed-up and simplify both the expressions of intermediate sets such as $\overline{In}'$ and the final ones such as $\overline{Load}$ and memory sizes.

Double buffering, as expected, usually doubles the local memory size in terms of the innermost tile size. Some arrays require almost all data to be live during a strip, thus causing the whole array to be stored into local memory (e.g., x in trisolv). Furthermore, modulo allocation has limitations. It is really apparent on floyd_warshall where memory conflicts are spread in such a way that only a modulo bigger than $k + 1$ and $n - k$ on both dimensions is valid. Thus, while the number of conflicting memory addresses is proportional to the tile area, the allocation is not. A tighter memory allocation could be obtained with a piece-wise modulo allocation scheme, allocating accesses to path$[i, k]$ and path$[k, j]$ differently from the accesses to path$[i, j]$. More generally, it is more likely that automating such schemes, with pipelining, parallelism, and hierarchical transfers, will require more advanced communication and allocation strategies.

---

[4] Kernels durbin, ludcmp, cholesky, and symm
[5] Kernels adi, fdtd-apml, gramschmidt, 2mm, 3mm, correlation, and covariance
[6] Kernels bicg, gemver, and gesummv

5   Conclusion

This work provides the first parametric solution for generating memory transfers with data reuse when a kernel is offloaded to a distant accelerator, tile by tile after loop tiling, and when all intermediate results are stored locally on the accelerator. In this case, when a value has been loaded or defined in a previous tile, it is read from the local memory and not loaded from the remote memory, which is not yet up-to-date. Our solution is parametric in the sense that we can derive the copy-in/copy-out sets for each tile, exploiting both intra- and inter-tile data reuse, with tile sizes as parameters. Such a result is quite surprising as parametric tiling is often considered as necessarily involving quadratic constraints, i.e., not analyzable within the polyhedral model. We solve it in an affine way with a different reasoning that considers, in the analysis, all (unaligned) possible tiles obtained by translation and not just the tiles of a given tiling. A similar technique can be used to parameterize the computations of local memory sizes, thanks to parametric lifetime analysis and array contraction with parametric modulos (or bounded boxes), even for pipeline schedules similar to double buffering.

This reasoning can also be extended in the case of approximations, which are needed when dealing with kernels that are not fully affine, or because approximations of communications are desired for code simplicity, complexity issues, or architectural constraints (e.g., vector communication). The main difficulty with approximation is that, when some data can be both read and written, loading blindly from remote memory, in an over-approximate way, is not safe as it may not be up-to-date. We address the problem thanks to the introduction of the concept of pointwise functions, well suited to deal with unaligned tiles. This concept may be useful for other applications linked to extensions of the polyhedral model as it turns out to be fairly powerful. For the moment, our study provides the mathematical foundations to discuss the correctness of approximation techniques that still need to be designed, even if some simple schemes are already possible. The full implementation, from the analysis down to code generation, is still a development challenge. Full experiments will be needed to validate the approach and help designing cost models for tile size selection. Nevertheless, the different performance studies with inter-tile data reuse for GPUs [16,17,34] or FPGAs [4,28], for non-parametric tile sizes, already demonstrate its interest.

"Guessing" the right size of the tiles can be laborious, especially when dealing with multi-level tiling and multi-level caches. The search space can become so wide that even iterative compilation might not be sufficient. As said, our parametric technique provides a direct expression of the copy-in/copy-out sets for each tile, and can then be used for performing array contraction on the accelerator still in a parametric fashion. It is only with such a parametric description that we can hope to design cost models for compile-time tile size selection in the context of tiling with inter-tile data reuse. Such static compilation techniques could then be integrated on top of intermediate languages such as OpenACC or OpenCL, or directly generate lower-level code, providing an automatic way to derive blocking algorithms for accelerators. Other applications are certainly possible, as soon as data reuse among tiles or pages has to be analyzed.

Acknowledgements. We thank Sven Verdoolaege for his help in using isl/ iscc and for his suggestion that set differences and relations could solve the nonparametric problem as efficiently as linear programming optimizations [4]. This work was partly supported by the ManycoreLabs project PIA-6394 led by Kalray.

References

1. Alias, C., Baray, F., Darte, A.: Bee+Cl@k: An implementation of lattice-based array contraction in the source-to-source translator Rose. In: Int. Conf. on Languages, Compilers, and Tools for Embedded Systems (LCTES'07), ACM (2007)
2. Alias, C., Darte, A., Plesco, A.: Optimizing DDR-SDRAM communications at C-level for automatically-generated hardware accelerators. An experience with the Altera C2H HLS tool. In: 21st Int. Conf. on Application-specific Systems, Architectures and Processors (ASAP'10), pp. 329–332, IEEE, Rennes (2010)
3. Alias, C., Darte, A., Plesco, A.: Kernel offloading with optimized remote accesses. Tech. Rep. RR-7697, Inria (Jul 2011) http://hal.inria.fr/inria-00611179
4. Alias, C., Darte, A., Plesco, A.: Optimizing remote accesses for offloaded kernels: Application to HLS for FPGA. In: Design, Automation and Test in Europe (DATE'13), pp. 575–580, Grenoble (2013)
5. Baskaran, M.M., Bondhugula, U., Krishnamoorthy, S., Ramanujam, J., Rountev, A., Sadayappan, P.: Automatic data movement and computation mapping for multi-level parallel architectures with explicitly managed memories. In: Symp. on Principles and Practice of Parallel Programming (PPoPP'08), pp. 1–10 (2008)
6. Baskaran, M.M., Vasilache, N., Meister, B., Lethin, R.: Automatic communication optimizations through memory reuse strategies. In: Symp. on Principles and Practice of Parallel Programming (PPoPP'12), pp. 277–278, ACM (2012)
7. Bondhugula, U., Hartono, A., Ramanujam, J., Sadayappan, P.: A practical automatic polyhedral parallelizer and locality optimizer. In: Int. Conf. on Programming Languages Design and Implementation (PLDI'08), pp. 101–113, ACM (2008)
8. Boppu, S., Hannig, F., Teich, J.: Loop program mapping and compact code generation for programmable hardware accelerators. In: 24th Int. Conf. on Application-Specific Systems, Architectures and Processors (ASAP'13), pp. 10–17, IEEE (2013)
9. Bourgoin, M., Chailloux, E., Lamotte, J.L.: Efficient abstractions for GPGPU programming. International Journal of Parallel Programming 42(4), 583–600 (2014)
10. Creusillet, B., Irigoin, F.: Interprocedural array region analyses. In: Int. Workshop on Languages and Compilers for Parallel Computing (LCPC'96). LNCS, vol. 1033, pp. 46–60. Springer (1996)
11. Darte, A., Isoard, A.: Exact and approximated data-reuse optimizations for tiling with parametric sizes. RR-8671 (Jan 2015), http://hal.inria.fr/hal-01103460
12. Darte, A., Schreiber, R., Villard, G.: Lattice-based memory allocation. IEEE Transactions on Computers 54(10), 1242–1257 (Oct 2005)
13. Feautrier, P.: Parametric integer programming. RAIRO Recherche Opérationnelle 22(3), 243–268 (1988), corresponding software tool PIP: http://www.piplib.org/
14. Feautrier, P., Lengauer, C.: The polyhedron model. In: Padua, D. (ed.) Encyclopedia of Parallel Programming. Springer (2011)
15. Goumas, G.I., Athanasaki, M., Koziris, N.: An efficient code generation technique for tiled iteration spaces. IEEE TPDS 14(10), 1021–1034 (2003)
16. Größlinger, A.: Precise management of scratchpad memories for localising array accesses in scientific codes. In: Compiler Construction (CC'09), pp. 236–250 (2009)
17. Guelton, S., Amini, M., Creusillet, B.: Beyond do loops: Data transfer generation with convex array regions. In: Int. Workshop on Languages and Compilers for Parallel Computing (LCPC'13). LNCS, vol. 7760, pp. 249–263. Springer (2013)

18. Guelton, S., Keryell, R., Irigoin, F.: Compilation pour cible hétérogènes: automatisation des analyses, transformations et décisions nécessaires. In: 20èmes Rencontres Françaises du Parallélisme (Renpar'11), Saint Malo, France (May 2011)
19. Hartono, A., Baskaran, M.M., Ramanujam, J., Sadayappan, P.: DynTile: Parametric tiled loop generation for parallel execution on multicore processors. In: Int. Symp. on Parallel and Distributed Processing (IPDPS'10), pp. 1–12, IEEE (2010)
20. Irigoin, F., Triolet, R.: Supernode partitioning. In: Int. Symp. on Principles of Programming Languages (POPL'88), pp. 319–329, ACM, San Diego (1988)
21. Issenin, I., Borckmeyer, E., Miranda, M., Dutt, N.: DRDU: A data reuse analysis technique for efficient scratch-pad memory management. ACM Trans. on Design Automation of Electronics Systems (ACM TODAES) 12(2), article 15 (Apr 2007)
22. Kandemir, M., Kadayif, I., Choudhary, A., Ramanujam, J., Kolcu, I.: Compiler-directed scratch pad memory optimization for embedded multiprocessors. IEEE Transactions on VLSI Systems 12(3), 281–287 (Mar 2004)
23. Kim, J., Kim, H., Lee, J.H., Lee, J.: Achieving a single compute device image in OpenCL for multiple GPUs. In: Symp. on Principles and Practice of Parallel Programming (PPoPP'11), pp. 277–288, ACM (2011)
24. Lee, S., Eigenmann, R.: OpenMPC: Extended OpenMP programming and tuning for GPUs. In: ACM/IEEE International Conference for High Performance Computing, Networking, Storage and Analysis (SC'10), pp. 1–11, IEEE Comp. (2010)
25. Lefebvre, V., Feautrier, P.: Automatic storage management for parallel programs. Parallel Computing 24, 649–671 (1998)
26. Pai, S., Govindarajan, R., Thazhuthaveetil, M.J.: Fast and efficient automatic memory management for GPUs using compiler-assisted runtime coherence scheme. In: 21st International Conference on Parallel Architectures and Compilation Techniques (PACT'12), pp. 33–42, ACM (2012)
27. PLUTO: An automatic polyhedral parallelizer and locality optimizer for multicores. http://pluto-compiler.sourceforge.net
28. Pouchet, L.N., Zhang, P., Sadayappan, P., Cong, J.: Polyhedral-based data reuse optimization for configurable computing. In: ACM/SIGDA Int. Symp. on Field Programmable Gate Arrays (FPGA'13), pp. 29–38, ACM (2013)
29. Pouchet, L.N.: PolyBench/C, the polyhedral benchmark suite. http://sourceforge.net/projects/polybench/
30. Renganarayanan, L., Kim, D., Rajopadhye, S.V., Strout, M.M.: Parameterized tiled loops for free. In: Int. Conf. on Programming Language Design and Implementation (PLDI'07), pp. 405–414, San Diego, ACM (Jun 2007)
31. Upadrasta, R., Cohen, A.: Sub-polyhedral scheduling using (unit-)two-variable-per-inequality polyhedra. In: 40th Int. Symp. on Principles of Programming Languages (POPL'13), pp. 483–496, ACM, Roma (Jan 2013)
32. Verdoolaege, S.: isl: An integer set library for the polyhedral model. In: Mathematical Software - ICMS 2010, LNCS, vol. 6327, pp. 299–302. Springer (2010), http://freecode.com/projects/isl/
33. Verdoolaege, S.: Counting affine calculator and applications. In: 1st Int. Workshop on Polyhedral Compilation Techniques (IMPACT'11). Chamonix (Apr 2011)
34. Verdoolaege, S., Juega, J.C., Cohen, A., Gómez, J.I., Tenllado, C., Catthoor, F.: Polyhedral parallel code generation for CUDA. ACM Transactions on Architecture and Code Optimization (TACO) 9(4), 54 (2013)
35. Wolf, M., Lam, M.: A data locality optimizing algorithm. In: Int. Conf. on Programming Language Design and Implementation (PLDI'91), pp. 30–44, ACM (1991)
36. Xue, J.: On tiling as a loop transformation. Par. Proc. Letters 7(4), 409–424 (1997)
37. Xue, J.: Loop Tiling for Parallelism. Kluwer Academic Publishers (2000)

OptGen: A Generator for Local Optimizations

Sebastian Buchwald

Karlsruhe Institute of Technology
buchwald@kit.edu

Abstract. Every compiler comes with a set of local optimization rules, such as $x + 0 \rightarrow x$ and $x \& x \rightarrow x$, that do not require any global analysis. These rules reflect the wisdom of the compiler developers about mathematical identities that hold for the operations of their intermediate representation. Unfortunately, these sets of hand-crafted rules guarantee neither correctness nor completeness. OptGen solves this problem by generating *all* local optimizations up to a given cost limit. Since OptGen verifies each rule using an SMT solver, it guarantees correctness and completeness of the generated rule set. Using OptGen, we tested the latest versions of GCC, ICC and LLVM and identified more than 50 missing local optimizations that involve only two operations.

Keywords: Intermediate Representations, Local Optimizations, Superoptimization.

1 Introduction

Every compiler comes with a set of local optimization rules, like $x + 0 \rightarrow x$ or simple constant folding. By definition, such rules exhibit a left-hand side of limited size and require no global analysis. Thus, they can be applied at any time during the compile run.

So far, the local optimizations provided by state-of-the-art compilers are incomplete. For instance, GCC 4.9 and ICC 15 do not support the local optimization $x \mid (x \oplus y) \rightarrow x \mid y$[1] whereas LLVM 3.5 fails to perform the optimization $-((x - y) + z) \rightarrow y - (x + z)$. Furthermore, all three compilers miss some optimizations with non-trivial constants, like $x \& (\texttt{0x7FFFFFFF} - x) \rightarrow x \& \texttt{0x80000000}$ for 32-bit integer types. Moreover, the compiler does not guarantee the correctness of the supported optimization rules. This raises the question for a generator that systematically enumerates and verifies all local optimizations up to a given pattern size.

On the assembly level, superoptimizers solve a related problem: They try to generate a better version for a fixed sequence of instructions, while preserving the semantics of the sequence. In order to guarantee the correctness of their transformation, they transform the instruction sequences into SAT or SMT formulas. Then, they use the corresponding solver to verify the equivalence of the constructed formulas. Later, generators for peephole optimizers used the same

---

[1] $\oplus$ stands for bitwise exclusive or, $\mid$ for bitwise or, and $\&$ for bitwise and.

© Springer-Verlag Berlin Heidelberg 2015
B. Franke (Ed.): CC 2015, LNCS 9031, pp. 171–189, 2015.
DOI: 10.1007/978-3-662-46663-6_9

technique to verify correctness but also aim for completeness. However, they all used a limited set of constants, like $\{0, 1, -1\}$.

The dilemma of supporting all constants is revealed when creating constant folding rules. On a 32-bit architecture, we would create 2^{64} constant folding rules for every binary operation: $0 + 0 \rightarrow 0, 0 + 1 \rightarrow 1$, and so on. Obviously, enumerating all these rules is far too expensive and impractical for end users. Thus, the handling of constants is the key challenge when aiming for completeness of the generated rule set.

In contrast to peephole optimizations, local optimizations work on the intermediate representation (IR). Since modern IRs in static single assignment form model data dependencies explicitly, local optimizations match these data dependencies instead of instruction sequences. This allows to perform local optimizations on patterns that span the whole function.

In this paper, we present OPTGEN[2], a generator for local optimization rules. OPTGEN takes a set of operations, their costs, and a cost limit as input parameters. It then generates *all* local optimizations up to the given cost limit and provides them in textual or graphical form. Furthermore, it generates a test suite that finds missing local optimizations in existing compilers. The contributions of this paper are:

- A generator for *all* local optimization rules up to a given cost limit.
- An approach how to cope with constants that can be backported to generators for peephole optimizers.
- An optimization that combines local optimization rules with global analyses.
- An evaluation of state-of-the-art compilers that reveals more than 50 missing local optimizations that involve only two operations.

The remainder of the paper is structured as follows. In Section 2, we discuss preliminaries and related work. Section 3 presents design and implementation techniques of OPTGEN. In Section 4, we combine local optimization rules with global analysis information. In Section 5, we evaluate OPTGEN, state-of-the-art compilers, and the global optimization phase. Finally, Section 6 concludes and discusses future work.

2   Preliminaries and Related Work

The goal of OPTGEN is to generate a set of local optimization rules that is correct and complete. In this section, we present related work that mostly focuses on assembly level. Along the way, we learn the advantages and drawbacks of working on the IR level rather than on the assembly level.

2.1   Superoptimization Research

During the compilation of a program, the compiler performs many optimizations to improve the resulting code with respect to execution speed, code size, or some other criterion. Although the term *optimization* suggests optimal results, modern compilers fail to produce optimal code even for small inputs.

---

[2] http://pp.ipd.kit.edu/optgen/

In 1987, Massalin presented a program that can compute the shortest sequence of assembly instructions to realize a given instruction sequence [7]. Since his approach guarantees optimality and the term optimization was already occupied, he called his program *superoptimizer*. The superoptimizer takes a set of instructions and enumerates sequences of them. It then translates the sequence into a boolean expression and compares the resulting minterms with the minterms of the original instruction sequence to decide whether they are equivalent.

Massalin presented two techniques to speed up the superoptimizer. First, he created a set of test inputs and compared the results of the generated sequence and the original one. In his experience, this filters out almost all sequences that are not equivalent. The second speed-up technique is to reject generated sequences that contain a known non-optimal subsequence. With both techniques, the superoptimizer is able to generate sequences of up to 13 instructions in a reasonable amount of time.

In 2002, Joshi et al. presented their superoptimizer *Denali* that allows to find larger optimal sequences [4]. In contrast to Massalin's approach, Denali takes a set of equivalences that should be used to optimize the program. Thus, Denali's task is to find the optimal representation of the input program regarding the given equivalences.

Joshi et al. decided to use E-graphs for a very compact representation of multiple equivalent representations [8]. Denali iteratively applies the given equivalences until the E-graph contains all possible program realizations. Then, Denali constructs a boolean formula that is satisfiable if, and only if, the program can be computed within k cycles. If the formula is satisfiable, Denali can construct a program from the corresponding logical interpretation that uses exactly k cycles. Furthermore, if the formula for $k-1$ is not satisfiable, the previously constructed program uses the minimal number of cycles.

More recently, Schkufza et al. propose to use a Markov chain Monte Carlo sampler to find better versions of a given instruction sequence [9]. Their implementation STOKE sacrifices optimality for the capability to generate optimized sequences of more than 15 instructions. This allows to find sequences that differ algorithmically, which may result in larger speed-ups than an optimal approach that is limited to fewer instructions. In a follow-up paper, Schkufza et al. extended their approach to floating-point arithmetic [10].

2.2   Generators for Peephole Optimizers

Superoptimizers aim to optimize small performance-critical parts of a larger program. In particular, the runtime of a superoptimization run is too high to form an optimization phase of a general-purpose compiler. However, the idea of having some kind of fast superoptimization for arbitrary programs is very attractive.

Bansal and Aiken tackle this problem by using training programs to create a peephole optimization database [1]. The compiler's peephole optimization phase can then use a simple look-up to find an applicable optimization for the considered sequence of instructions. Their approach works as follows: First, they compile a set of training programs. Then, the *harvester* extracts all instruction sequences that are candidates for optimizations. The candidates are inserted into a hash table, where the hash is based on the execution of some fixed test inputs. In the second step, they enumerate all instruction sequences up to a given length. For each sequence they perform a look-up in the hash table. If the look-up succeeds, the generated sequence is an optimization candidate for the sequence in the hash table. Thus, they compare both sequences on a larger set of test inputs and finally use a SAT solver to decide whether both sequences are equivalent.

2.3   Generated Optimizations for Intermediate Representations

The tools discussed so far work on the assembly level. This allows to fully leverage the available instruction set and to formulate a precise cost model. However, if we generate optimizations for multiple target architectures, we notice some common optimizations. Following an idiom in compiler design, we should perform these common optimizations on the intermediate representation.

In fact, all compilers come with a set of *local optimizations*. These optimizations consist of small rules that require no global analysis. Thus, the compiler can use these rules at any time, even during construction of an SSA-based IR [2]. In contrast to peephole optimizations, local optimizations have a more global view on the program. They can follow the data dependencies and the sharing of values is not obscured by spilling and other backend phases. Figure 1 illustrates the advantages of working on the IR level. Due to the explicit data dependency, we can model the local optimization as a graph rewrite rule. Figure 1a shows the graph rewrite rule for the optimization $x \mid (x \oplus y) \rightarrow x \mid y$ that can be applied on the IR in Figure 1b. However, a peephole optimizer cannot apply this rule on the assembly level, since the instructions of basic blocks 2 and 3 occur between the instructions that belong to the optimization rule.

Currently, the compiler's local optimizations are handcrafted and reflect the knowledge of the compiler developers. Thus, the optimization rules guarantee

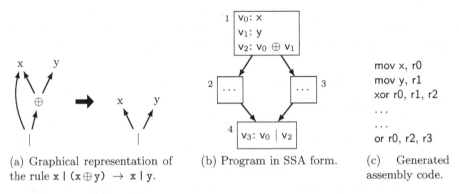

(a) Graphical representation of the rule $x \mid (x \oplus y) \rightarrow x \mid y$.

(b) Program in SSA form.

(c)   Generated assembly code.

Fig. 1. The local optimization of Figure 1a can be applied on the IR of Figure 1b. However, on the assembly level of Figure 1c, the generated code of basic blocks 2 and 3 prevent the application of the corresponding peephole optimization.

neither correctness nor completeness. Regarding correctness, the ALIVe tool [6] demonstrates a possible approach to verify local optimizations. A promising solution to get the completeness guarantee is to port the idea of a generator for peephole optimizations to the IR level. So far, there is only little research regarding this idea. For instance, Tate et al. pick up the ideas of Denali and apply them to their intermediate representation [12]. However, to the best of our knowledge, there is no approach that tackles the systematic generation of local optimizations.

3   Rule Generation

In this chapter, we present and discuss our tool OPTGEN that generates local optimizations. When creating OPTGEN, our idea was to generate *all* local optimizations up to a given cost limit. The main challenge for this purpose is the handling of constants: Since a 32-bit architecture has 2^{32} constants, enumerating all constant folding rules for a binary operation would result in 2^{64} rules. Obviously, this cannot be accomplished in a reasonable amount of time. In the following, we present the general design of OPTGEN and explain how we tackle the large amount of available constants.

3.1   General Design of OPTGEN

OPTGEN's task is to generate all local optimizations up to a given cost limit. Thus, OPTGEN takes the considered operations and their costs, as well as the cost limit, as input parameters. Furthermore, the user must specify the bit width of the operations. It then generates the local optimizations and outputs them in textual and graphical form. Furthermore, it can generate a test suite that can be used to find missing optimizations in existing compilers. Currently, OPTGEN supports the unary integer operations $\sim$ and -, as well as the binary integer operations +, &, |, - and $\oplus$. However, adding a new operation only requires a mapping to the SMT solver and a method to evaluate the operation for constant operands.

We use Figure 2 and a running example to demonstrate the work flow of OPTGEN: We want OPTGEN to generate all local optimizations up to cost 2 for the 8-bit operations & and |, which both have cost 1. Before OPTGEN starts the actual generation, it creates a number of random test inputs. Later, we will use these random tests to compute a *semantic hash* for each expression. The underlying idea is that if two expressions evaluate to different values for the test inputs, the considered expressions cannot be semantically equivalent.

OPTGEN now generates all expressions for each cost. For cost 0 the *generator* generates the variable x and the constants 0 to 255. The generator passes each of these expressions to the *matcher*. The matcher checks whether we have already found an optimization rule that applies to the given expression. Since we have found no optimization rule yet, the matcher passes the expression to the *semantic checker*. The semantic checker computes the semantic hash and looks up a list of possibly equivalent expressions in the *semantic hash table*. Assuming a perfect

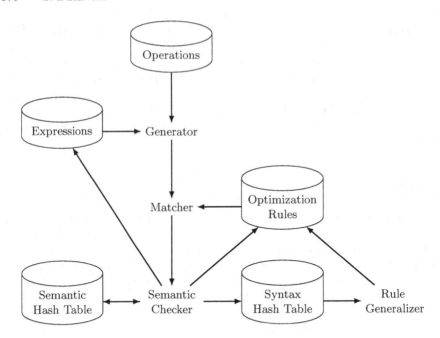

Fig. 2. General design of OPTGEN

hash function, the lookup finds no such expression in our example. Thus, the semantic checker inserts the expression into the list of expression as well as into the *semantic hash table.*

Before OPTGEN generates the expressions with cost 1, it realizes that we have a binary operation with cost 1 and introduces a new variable y. Then, it starts the actual generation process by applying the available operations to the already generated expressions. The first generated expression is x & x. Since we have found no optimization rule yet, the matcher passes the expression to the semantic checker. The semantic checker now computes the semantic hash and looks up a list of possibly equivalent expressions. Assuming a perfect hash function, our list only contains the expression x. The semantic checker now uses an SMT solver to determine whether both expressions are equivalent. In our case, the expressions are equivalent. Since x is cheaper than x & x, OPTGEN creates a new optimization rule x & x → x and inserts it into the list of rules. In the next step, OPTGEN creates the optimization rule x & 0 → 0 in a similar fashion.

The next generated expression is x & 1. Again, the matcher finds no existing optimization rule and passes the expression to the semantic checker that looks up possibly equivalent expressions in the semantic hash table. Let us assume the hash table lookup finds some candidate, e.g., the expression 1. In this case, the following SMT check fails. Thus, we insert the expression x & 1 into the list of candidates for the computed hash value.

When generating expressions with cost 2, another interesting case occurs: Processing the expression (x & y) & 0, the matcher finds the applicable optimization rule x & 0 → 0. In this case, we skip the generated expression. Otherwise, the semantic checker would create the optimization rule (x & y) & 0 → 0 that is subsumed by the existing optimization rule x & 0 → 0.

3.2 Handling Constants

For our running example, OPTGEN generates many similar constant folding rules like 1 & 2 → 0 and 1 & 3 → 1. Returning each of these rules to the user is inconvenient. Instead, the user is interested in a single constant folding rule for each operation. Thus, OPTGEN provides a *rule generalizer* that tries to generalize the generated rules. In our running example, we want to create a rule c0 & c1 → eval(c0 & c1), where c0 and c1 are *symbolic constants* and eval performs constant folding.

Before we can start the generalization, we need to find sets of syntactically equivalent rules. We solve this problem by computing a *syntax hash* for each expression that only depends on the structure of the expression, i.e., ignoring the values of the constants. Thus, we can use a *syntax hash table* to efficiently find syntactically equivalent rules. As shown in Figure 2, the semantic checker is responsible for filling the syntax hash table with rules that contain constants.

Given a set of syntactically equivalent rules, the rule generalizer first tries to find expressions that compute the constants of the right-hand side using the constants of the left-hand side. Currently, it does this by considering the already enumerated expressions. In our running example, we have one constant on the right-hand side and two constants on the left-hand side. Hence, the rule generalizer searches a function f(x,y) such that f(1,2) = 0, f(1,3) = 1 and so on. If it finds an appropriate function, it creates the corresponding rule and checks its correctness using an SMT solver. If the check succeeds, the rule generalizer found a rule that supersedes the considered rules. Otherwise, it continues the search for an appropriate function. In our running example, the rule generalizer finds f(x,y) = x & y and verifies the resulting rule c0 & c1 → eval(c0 & c1).

An interesting situation occurs for the rules (x | 2) & 1 → x & 1, (x | 1) & 2 → x & 2 and so on. In general, the optimization (x | c1) & c2 → x & c2 is not valid. However, it becomes valid if c1 and c2 are bitwise disjoint. OPTGEN tackles such cases by using *conditional rules*. By definition, a conditional rule is valid if the corresponding condition evaluates to **true**. Furthermore, the condition must be a function that only depends on the symbolic constants that appear on the left-hand side of the rule.

The rule generalizer solves the problem of finding a condition by searching a *condition expression* that evaluates to 0 if, and only if, the condition holds. Finding a condition expression is similar to finding the computations for constants on the right-hand side of a rule: We simply check the already enumerated expressions for an appropriate one. Since the enumerated expressions are sorted according to their costs, simpler condition expressions are considered before complex ones. For our example, OPTGEN finds the appropriate condition expression c1 & c2 and creates the conditional rule (c1 & c2) == 0 ⇒ (x | c1) & c2 → x & c2.

The main advantage of symbolic constants is their independence of the bit width. Thus, the SMT solver can verify the local optimization rule $(c1 \& c2) == 0 \Rightarrow (x \mid c1) \& c2 \rightarrow x \& c2$ for 8 bits as well as for 32 bits. If we generalize every non-trivial set of syntactically equivalent rules, we can easily extend the verification from 8 bits to 32 bits. For the remaining rules with particular constants, OPTGEN expands the 8-bit constants to 32 bits by padding the most significant or least significant bits with zeros or ones and checks all four resulting rules using an SMT solver. In our experience, this approach is sufficient to find the corresponding 32-bit rule. Thus, we can generate all local optimizations for 8 bits, extend the resulting rules to 32 bits, and verify them for the latter bit width. Whether the rule set of the extended bit width is also complete depends on the operations and the bit width used during generation. A proven approach to achieve completeness is to increase the generation bit width until the generated rule set for the extended bit width remains unchanged. For instance, generating all 3-bit rules with cost limit 3 for the bitwise operations $\sim$, $\&$, $\mid$ and $\oplus$ creates the same 32-bit rule set as generating all 4-bit rules.

Currently, OPTGEN can only generalize rules if the required condition expression and computations of the symbolic constants on the right-hand side are enumerated expressions. A more general solution would use superoptimization techniques to find the appropriate expressions. The basic idea is that the existing optimization rules define partial functions for the condition expression and computations of the symbolic constants that appear on the right-hand side of the generalized rule. These functions are partial, because we skip expressions that are matched by existing optimization rules. For instance, the generalized rule $(c1 \& c2) == 0 \Rightarrow (x \mid c1) \& c2 \rightarrow x \& c2$ covers the optimization rule $(x \mid 1) \& 0 \rightarrow x \& 0$. However, we will never create the latter one because we can apply $x \& 0 \rightarrow 0$ on its left-hand side.

Based on the partial functions, we can use superoptimization techniques to find the appropriate expressions. This may require to limit the cost of each expression to guarantee termination. If we found an expression for each partial function, we can use the SMT solver the verify the corresponding rule. If the SMT check fails, the SMT solver can generate a counterexample for these expressions. Thus, we can use this counterexample to refine our partial functions and continue the search for appropriate expressions.

3.3 Performance Tuning

In this section, we present some speed-up techniques implemented in OPTGEN.

The key insight regarding performance is that SMT checks are slow. Thus, we need to avoid them if possible. The main source of unnecessary SMT checks are collisions in the semantic hash table. In this case, a created expression could have multiple candidates of equivalent expressions that are compared via SMT checks. However, at most one of them can be equivalent to the expression at hand.

Our solution to this problem are *witnesses*: A set of test inputs such that each pair of expressions of the hash table bucket evaluates to a different result for at least one witness. Since each hash table bucket has it own set of witnesses, these sets are usually very small. For a new expression with multiple candidates, we first evaluate the witnesses and compare the results with the results of the available candidates. By definition, at most one candidate can compute the same results for all witnesses. Thus, we need at most one SMT check per generated expression. Whenever this SMT check fails, we insert the new expression into the hash table bucket. Hence, we need a new witness to distinguish the two expressions. Fortunately, the SMT solver also generates a counterexample as a result of the failing SMT check. Thus, we simply use this counterexample as a new witness for the checked expressions.

Another performance-critical task is to check the applicability of existing rules to expressions. OPTGEN performs such checks for each generated expression. Furthermore, OPTGEN uses these checks to identify rules that are covered by more general ones. For an efficient matching, we use an n-ary tree structure that can be indexed by the available operation types. If we find a new optimization rule, we traverse the nodes of the left-hand side in preorder and insert the corresponding nodes into the tree. The created leaf contains a reference to the inserted rule. Figure 3 shows the search tree after inserting the rules $x \& 0 \to 0$ and $(c1 \& c2) == 0 \Rightarrow (x \mid c1) \& c2 \to x \& c2$.

Assume we want to find a rule that matches $(x \mid 3) \& 1$. In order to use our data structure, we process our expression in preorder. The type of the first operation is $\&$. The matcher now descends into every child that corresponds to a type that matches $\&$. Thus, it visits node 1 and proceeds with the $\mid$ node of the expression. Since both existing children of the search tree are labeled with matching types, we must visit them both.

Let us assume the matcher first descends into node 2. Since the variable matches the whole subexpression $x \mid 3$, the matcher skips the corresponding nodes of the expression and proceeds with the constant 1. In the next step, the matcher reaches the leaf that contains the rule $x \& 0 \to 0$. Thus, it tries to apply the rule to the expression. Unfortunately, the constant 0 does not match the constant 1.

The matcher continues its search by descending from node 1 to node 3. Since the path to the second rule fits our expression, the matcher tries to apply the rule $(c1 \& c2) == 0 \Rightarrow (x \mid c1) \& c2 \to x \& c2$. This time the condition of the rule is not fulfilled. Thus, the matcher continues its search. Since the matcher has already processed the interesting paths of the search tree, it stops and reports that no matching rule exists.

3.4   Applications of OPTGEN

OPTGEN supports the compiler developer by providing an optimization test suite. The test suite helps to find missing optimizations of the developed compiler. Furthermore, it identifies optimization applications that should be prevented by the compiler in case of shared subexpressions. Figure 4 shows such a situation: Applying the local optimization $-((x - y) + z) \to y - (x + z)$ increases the global costs, because of the shared subexpression $(x - y) + z$. However, if the value $(x - y) + z$ is already present the optimization is worthwhile. A possible solution to this problem would be to conservatively prevent optimizations in case of shared subexpressions.

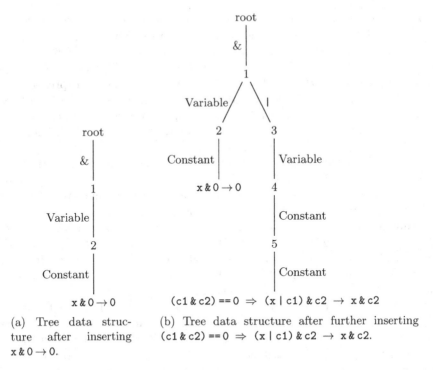

(a) Tree data struc-
ture after inserting
$x \& 0 \to 0$.

(b) Tree data structure after further inserting
$(c1 \& c2) == 0 \Rightarrow (x | c1) \& c2 \to x \& c2$.

Fig. 3. Tree data structure to find applicable rules for an expression. Each inner node can be indexed by the available operations types. For an insert or lookup operation the operation types of the expression are considered in preorder.

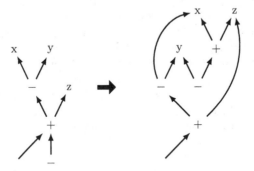

Fig. 4. The compiler should prevent the application of the local optimization rule $-((x - y) + z) \to y - (x + z)$, since the subexpression $(x - y) + z$ has another user

4   Combining Local Optimizations with Global Analyses

Local optimizations have the advantage that they do not require any prior analysis. Thus, they can be applied at any time, e.g., directly after the construction of an operation. In our experience, it is also worthwhile to have a compiler phase that applies all local optimizations until it reaches a fixpoint. During this phase, we can provide analysis information that improves the existing local optimizations.

In the following, we present two analyses that allow a compact and powerful implementation of the local optimizations generated by OPTGEN. As we will see, the generated local optimization rules with symbolic constants are crucial to our approach. We start with a simple optimization rule to motivate our idea: $(x + 2) \& 1 \rightarrow x \& 1$. OPTGEN covers this rule by the generalized rule $((c0 \mid -c0) \& c1) == 0 \Rightarrow (x + c0) \& c1 \rightarrow x \& c1$. The condition ensures that adding the constant $c0$ only influences bits that are masked out by the constant $c1$. Our plan is to stepwise relax the condition to apply this optimization in even more cases.

4.1   Constant-Bit Analysis

Our first insight to improve the optimization $(x + 2) \& 1 \rightarrow x \& 1$ is that the second operand of the addition can be an arbitrary expression as long as the rightmost bit is not set. For instance, $(x + (y \& 42)) \& 1 \rightarrow x \& 1$ is also a valid optimization rule.

This motivates us to implement a *constant-bit analysis* that indicates bits that are always set or not set, respectively. For the expression $y \& 42$, the analysis computes $00?0?0?0$ for the rightmost 8 bits, where 0 indicates bits that are guaranteed to be zero and ? indicates bits that are not constant. Similarly, $y \mid 42$ results in $??1?1?1?$. The bit information is stored in two bit vectors. The bit vector `zeros` contains a cleared bit if the corresponding bit is guaranteed to be cleared and a set bit otherwise. Likewise, the bit vector `ones` contains a set bit if the corresponding bit is guaranteed to be set and a cleared bit otherwise.

The Constant-bit analysis is a forward data flow analysis that generalizes sparse conditional constant propagation [13]. Since the data-flow analysis is optimistic, it initializes the `zeros` bit vector with zeros and the `ones` bit vector with ones. Then, it applies the transfer function until the analysis reaches the fixpoint.

Some of the transfer functions are straight-forward. For constants we set the bit vectors according to the bits of the constants. For loads from memory we set all bits of the `zeros` vector and clear the bits of the `ones` vector. The bitwise operations $\&$ and $\mid$ can be transformed by applying the same operation to corresponding bit vectors of the operands. For instance, $\mathtt{ones}(x \& y) = \mathtt{ones}(x) \& \mathtt{ones}(y)$. For the bitwise complement $\sim$ we must apply the operation to the other bit vector of the operand: $\mathtt{ones}(\sim x) = \sim\mathtt{zeros}(x), \mathtt{zeros}(\sim x) = \sim\mathtt{ones}(x)$. Contrarily, the transfer function for the exclusive or $\oplus$ is more complex:
$\mathtt{ones}(x \oplus y) = (\mathtt{ones}(x) \& \sim\mathtt{zeros}(y)) \mid (\mathtt{ones}(y) \& \sim\mathtt{zeros}(x))$,
$\mathtt{zeros}(x \oplus y) = (\mathtt{zeros}(x) \& \sim\mathtt{ones}(y)) \mid (\mathtt{zeros}(y) \& \sim\mathtt{ones}(x))$.

Transfer functions for arithmetic operations also reuse the operation itself. For the addition $x + y$, we first add the `ones` and `zeros` of the operands: $\mathtt{vo} = \mathtt{ones}(x) + \mathtt{ones}(y)$ and $\mathtt{vz} = \mathtt{zeros}(x) + \mathtt{zeros}(y)$. Then, we compute bit vectors that indicate which bits are not constant: $\mathtt{xnc} = \mathtt{ones}(x) \oplus \mathtt{zeros}(x)$, $\mathtt{ync} = \mathtt{ones}(y) \oplus \mathtt{zeros}(y)$ and $\mathtt{vnc} = \mathtt{vo} \oplus \mathtt{vz}$. This allows us to determine the non-constant bits of the result: $\mathtt{nc} = \mathtt{xnc} \mid \mathtt{ync} \mid \mathtt{vnc}$. Finally, we can compute the constant-bit information of $x + y$: $\mathtt{ones}(x + y) = \mathtt{vz} \& \sim\mathtt{nc}$ and $\mathtt{zeros}(x + y) =$

vz | nc. Due to the use of the add operation, we handle carry bits correctly. For instance, 00?? 1110 + 10?? 1?10 results in 1??? 1?00.

A typical use case for constant-bit information is to determine the equivalence of multiple operations. If the operands of an addition have disjoint bits set, we can also use a | or $\oplus$ operation. Thus, the optimizer may apply local optimizations that are valid for the | operation but not in general for the addition.

4.2 Don't Care Analysis

The second insight to improve the optimization $(x + 2) \& 1 \rightarrow x \& 1$ is that due to the &, we only care for the least significant bit of the sum. The don't care analysis provides exactly this information: Its result is a bit vector that indicates relevant (1) and irrelevant (0) bits [11]. This allows to specify the more compact optimization rule care($x + 2$) == 1 $\Rightarrow$ $x + 2 \rightarrow x$, which also covers $(x + 2)$ | $\sim 1 \rightarrow x$ | ~ 1.

In contrast to the constant-bit analysis, the don't care analysis is a backward data-flow analysis. At the beginning of the analysis, all bits are set to irrelevant. Since the transfer functions of return or store operations always care for their operands, they create some initial relevant bits. These bits will then propagate through the program until the analysis reaches its fixpoint.

There are several expressions that can create more irrelevant bits for at least one of their operands: x | 1, x * 2, x & 2, and so on. In most cases, the don't care analysis uses known bits from one operand and derives irrelevant bits for the other one. Thus, we extend the don't care analysis to consider the constant-bit information. In consequence, if we use constant-bit information to gain precision, we must care for the bits that provided this constant-bit information.

4.3 Generalizing the Optimization Rules

Starting with the optimization rule $(x + 2) \& 1 \rightarrow x \& 1$, we manually derived the optimization ((zeros(y) | -zeros(y)) & care($x+y$)) == 0 $\Rightarrow x + y \rightarrow x$. The generalized rule encapsulates the essential optimization, while using the global analysis information to check whether the rule can be applied. This allows to perform the optimization even in complex scenarios.

The presented analyses allow an even more compact optimization: The creation of *occult constants* [11]. This optimization can be performed if all relevant bits are known to be constant: ((zeros(x) $\oplus$ ones(x)) & care(x)) == 0 $\Rightarrow$ x $\rightarrow$ eval(zeros(x) & care(x)). For instance, the constant 2 of the expression $(x + 2) \& 1$ is an occult constant that can be optimized to zero. However, in a larger program the constant 2 can have other users that render more bits relevant.

Currently, OPTGEN does not derive local optimization rules that use the presented analysis information. The constant-bit analysis would require another analysis that determines whether we need a conservative approximation of the set or cleared bits. For the don't care analysis, we would just need to perform the analysis for the expressions of the rule. Furthermore, we would need to adapt the generated formulas for the SMT solver. Similar to the generation of symbolic rules discussed in Section 3.2, superoptimization techniques could be helpful to find appropriate conditions for the derived rules.

5 Evaluation

In this section, we evaluate OPTGEN's runtime and compare its generated optimizations with state-of-the art compilers. All measurements are performed on an Intel Core i7-3770 3.40 GHz with 16 GB RAM. The machine runs a 64-bit Ubuntu 14.04 LTS distribution that uses the 3.13.0-37-generic version of the Linux kernel. For OPTGEN, we use Z3 4.3.1 as SMT solver [3].

5.1 OPTGEN Runtime

In order to evaluate the runtime of the generation of local optimizations, we run OPTGEN in multiple configurations. All runs include the unary operations $\sim$ and -, as well as the binary operations +, &, |, - and $\oplus$. Table 1 shows the different configurations as well as the resulting runtime and maximum memory usage for each configuration. The configurations differ in the used bit width for the rule generation, in the number of involved operations and in the usage of constants.

For a fixed number of operations, the results suggest two aspects that heavily influence the runtime: The use of constants and the bit width used during the rule generation. We already argued that the use of constants increases the number of generated rules and, thus, the runtime. However, the bit width only influences the SMT checks. Since the generation for two 8-bit operations is significantly faster than the generator for two 32-bit operations, the SMT solver does not scale very well with increasing bit width. Consequently, using different bit widths for generation and verification dramatically improves the runtime.

5.2 Testing State-of-the-Art Compilers

In order to give valuable feedback to compiler engineers, we let OPTGEN generate an optimization test suite. This test suite includes a test for each generated

Table 1. Runtime and maximum memory usage of OPTGEN for different configurations

Operations	Bit width		Constants	Runtime	Memory Usage
	Generation	Verification			
2	8	32	✓	6 h 7 min 0 s	1 046 568 kB
2	8	32	×	1 s	7456 kB
2	32	32	×	6 min 21 s	19 892 kB
3	8	32	×	36 s	17 900 kB
4	8	32	×	8 h 27 min 16 s	686 104 kB

optimization. Using these tests, it lets the compiler of interest generate x86-64 assembly and then counts the number of generated arithmetic instructions. If the compiler generates more instructions than expected, we found a missing optimization for the compiler.

We use the run of OPTGEN with two operations and constants to test state-of-the-art compilers. Table 2 shows the missing optimizations for GCC 4.9, LLVM 3.5, and ICC 15. In total, OPTGEN found 63 optimizations that are missing in at least one of the compilers. The optimizations include rules without constants (20.), rules with symbolic constants (54.), and rules with particular

Table 2. Missing local optimizations of state-of-the-art compilers. A ✓ indicates that the corresponding optimization is supported, whereas a × indicates a missing optimization.

	Optimization	Compiler		
		LLVM	GCC	ICC
1.	$-\sim$x $\rightarrow$ x + 1	✓	✓	×
2.	-(x & 0x80000000) $\rightarrow$ x & 0x80000000	×	✓	×
3.	$\sim$-x $\rightarrow$ x - 1	✓	✓	×
4.	x + $\sim$x $\rightarrow$ 0xFFFFFFFF	✓	✓	×
5.	x + (x & 0x80000000) $\rightarrow$ x & 0x7FFFFFFF	×	×	×
6.	(x | 0x80000000) + 0x80000000 $\rightarrow$ x & 0x7FFFFFFF	✓	×	×
7.	(x & 0x7FFFFFFF) + (x & 0x7FFFFFFF) $\rightarrow$ x + x	✓	✓	×
8.	(x & 0x80000000) + (x & 0x80000000) $\rightarrow$ 0	✓	✓	×
9.	(x | 0x7FFFFFFF) + (x | 0x7FFFFFFF) $\rightarrow$ 0xFFFFFFFE	✓	✓	×
10.	(x | 0x80000000) + (x | 0x80000000) $\rightarrow$ x + x	✓	✓	×
11.	x & (x + 0x80000000) $\rightarrow$ x & 0x7FFFFFFF	✓	×	×
12.	x & (x | y) $\rightarrow$ x	✓	✓	×
13.	x & (0x7FFFFFFF - x) $\rightarrow$ x & 0x80000000	×	×	×
14.	-x & 1 $\rightarrow$ x & 1	×	✓	×
15.	(x + x) & 1 $\rightarrow$ 0	✓	✓	×
16.	is_power_of_2(c1) && c0 & (2 * c1 - 1) == c1 - 1 $\Rightarrow$ (c0 - x) & c1 $\rightarrow$ x & c1	×	×	×
17.	x	(x + 0x80000000) $\rightarrow$ x	0x80000000	✓	×	×
18.	x	(x & y) $\rightarrow$ x	✓	✓	×
19.	x	(0x7FFFFFFF - x) $\rightarrow$ x	0x7FFFFFFF	×	×	×
20.	x	(x $\oplus$ y) $\rightarrow$ x	y	✓	×	×
21.	((c0 | -c0) & $\sim$c1) == 0 $\Rightarrow$ (x + c0)	c1 $\rightarrow$ x	c1	✓	×	✓
22.	is_power_of_2($\sim$c1) && c0 & (2 * $\sim$c1 - 1) == $\sim$c1 - 1 $\Rightarrow$ (c0 - x)	c1 $\rightarrow$ x	c1	×	×	×
23.	-x	0xFFFFFFFE $\rightarrow$ x	0xFFFFFFFE	×	×	×
24.	(x + x)	0xFFFFFFFE $\rightarrow$ 0xFFFFFFFE	✓	✓	×
25.	0 - (x & 0x80000000) $\rightarrow$ x & 0x80000000	×	✓	×
26.	0x7FFFFFFF - (x & 0x80000000) $\rightarrow$ x	0x7FFFFFFF	×	×	×
27.	0x7FFFFFFF - (x | 0x7FFFFFFF) $\rightarrow$ x & 0x80000000	×	×	×
28.	0xFFFFFFFE - (x	0x7FFFFFFF) $\rightarrow$ x	0x7FFFFFFF	×	×	×
29.	(x & 0x7FFFFFFF) - x $\rightarrow$ x & 0x80000000	×	×	×

Table 2. (*Continued*)

Optimization	LLVM	GCC	ICC
30. $x \oplus (x + \text{0x80000000}) \rightarrow \text{0x80000000}$	✓	×	×
31. $x \oplus (\text{0x7FFFFFFF} - x) \rightarrow \text{0x7FFFFFFF}$	×	×	×
32. $(x + \text{0x7FFFFFFF}) \oplus \text{0x7FFFFFFF} \rightarrow -x$	×	×	×
33. $(x + \text{0x80000000}) \oplus \text{0x7FFFFFFF} \rightarrow \sim x$	✓	✓	×
34. $-x \oplus \text{0x80000000} \rightarrow \text{0x80000000} - x$	×	×	×
35. $(\text{0x7FFFFFFF} - x) \oplus \text{0x80000000} \rightarrow \sim x$	×	✓	×
36. $(\text{0x80000000} - x) \oplus \text{0x80000000} \rightarrow -x$	×	✓	×
37. $(x + \text{0xFFFFFFFF}) \oplus \text{0xFFFFFFFF} \rightarrow -x$	✓	✓	×
38. $(x + \text{0x80000000}) \oplus \text{0x80000000} \rightarrow x$	✓	✓	×
39. $(\text{0x7FFFFFFF} - x) \oplus \text{0x7FFFFFFF} \rightarrow x$	×	×	×
40. $x - (x \,\&\, c) \rightarrow x \,\&\, \sim c$	✓	✓	×
41. $x \oplus (x \,\&\, c) \rightarrow x \,\&\, \sim c$	✓	✓	×
42. $\sim x + c \rightarrow (c - 1) - x$	✓	✓	×
43. $\sim(x + c) \rightarrow \sim c - x$	✓	×	×
44. $-(x + c) \rightarrow -c - x$	✓	✓	×
45. $c - \sim x \rightarrow x + (c + 1)$	✓	✓	×
46. $\sim x \oplus c \rightarrow x \oplus \sim c$	✓	✓	×
47. $\sim x - c \rightarrow \sim c - x$	✓	✓	×
48. $-x \oplus \text{0x7FFFFFFF} \rightarrow x + \text{0x7FFFFFFF}$	×	×	×
49. $-x \oplus \text{0xFFFFFFFF} \rightarrow x - 1$	✓	✓	×
50. $x \,\&\, (x \oplus c) \rightarrow x \,\&\, \sim c$	✓	✓	×
51. $-x - c \rightarrow -c - x$	✓	✓	×
52. $(x \mid c) - c \rightarrow x \,\&\, \sim c$	×	×	×
53. $(x \mid c) \oplus c \rightarrow x \,\&\, \sim c$	✓	✓	×
54. $\sim(c - x) \rightarrow x + \sim c$	✓	×	×
55. $\sim(x \oplus c) \rightarrow x \oplus \sim c$	✓	✓	×
56. $\sim c0 == c1 \Rightarrow (x \,\&\, c0) \oplus c1 \rightarrow x \mid c1$	✓	✓	×
57. $-c0 == c1 \Rightarrow (x \mid c0) + c1 \rightarrow x \,\&\, \sim c1$	×	×	×
58. $(x \oplus c) + \text{0x80000000} \rightarrow x \oplus (c + \text{0x80000000})$	✓	✓	×
59. $((c0 \mid -c0) \,\&\, c1) == 0 \Rightarrow (x \oplus c0) \,\&\, c1 \rightarrow x \,\&\, c1$	✓	✓	×
60. $(c0 \,\&\, \sim c1) == 0 \Rightarrow (x \oplus c0) \mid c1 \rightarrow x \mid c1$	✓	×	×
61. $(x \oplus c) - \text{0x80000000} \rightarrow x \oplus (c + \text{0x80000000})$	✓	✓	×
62. $\text{0x7FFFFFFF} - (x \oplus c) \rightarrow x \oplus (\text{0x7FFFFFFF} - c)$	×	×	×
63. $\text{0xFFFFFFFF} - (x \oplus c) \rightarrow x \oplus (\text{0xFFFFFFFF} - c)$	✓	✓	×
Sum	23	27	62

constants (26.). Since OPTGEN currently considers only generated expressions for conditional rules, the conditions of the rules 16, 21, 22, and 59 are created by hand.

As discussed in Section 4.3, we further tested whether the compilers prevent optimizations if all subexpressions are shared. Since such cases do not appear with two operations, we used the optimizations with three operations but without constants. Table 3 shows all cases, where at least one compiler increases the cost by applying the corresponding optimization. For instance, the first optimization $\sim(x \mid \sim y) \rightarrow \sim x \,\&\, y$ is supported by GCC and LLVM. However, only GCC prevents the application if the subexpression $(x \mid \sim y)$ is used by another operation.

5.3   Global Optimization Phase

In Section 4, we claimed that it is worthwhile to perform local optimizations until a fixpoint is reached. We used the LIBFIRM compiler [5] and the SPEC CINT2000 benchmark to prove our claim. Table 4 shows the number of executed instructions

Table 3. State-of-the-art compilers apply optimization rules even if the operands are shared. If the compiler supports the optimization ✓/✗ indicates whether the compiler prevents the optimization in case of shared operands. If the compiler does not support the optimization the item is left blank.

	Optimization	Compiler		
		LLVM	GCC	ICC
1.	$\sim(x \mid \sim y) \rightarrow \sim x \,\&\, y$	✗	✓	
2.	$\sim(x \,\&\, \sim y) \rightarrow \sim x \mid y$	✗	✓	
3.	$(x + x) \,\&\, (y + y) \rightarrow (x \,\&\, y) + (x \,\&\, y)$	✗		
4.	$(x + x) \mid (y + y) \rightarrow (x \mid y) + (x \mid y)$	✗		
5.	$(x \,\&\, y) \mid (z \,\&\, y) \rightarrow y \,\&\, (x \mid z)$	✓	✗	✓
6.	$x - ((x - y) + (x - y)) \rightarrow y + (y - x)$		✓	✗
7.	$(x - y) - (x + z) \rightarrow -(y + z)$	✓	✓	✗
8.	$((x - y) + (x - y)) - x \rightarrow x - (y + y)$	✓	✓	✗
9.	$(x + x) \oplus (y + y) \rightarrow (x \oplus y) + (x \oplus y)$	✗		
10.	$(x \,\&\, y) \oplus (z \,\&\, y) \rightarrow y \,\&\, (x \oplus z)$	✓	✗	✓

Table 4. Effect of local optimizations phase. The table compares the number of executed instructions of the generated code with and without an optimization phase that applies local optimizations until a fixpoint is reached.

Benchmark	Without Local Phase	With Local Phase	$\frac{\text{Without Local Phase}}{\text{With Local Phase}}$
164.gzip	306,800,522,532	290,253,056,191	105.70 %
175.vpr	215,443,006,054	203,496,140,283	105.87 %
176.gcc	150,470,998,502	149,081,148,091	100.93 %
181.mcf	48,034,571,679	48,924,041,098	98.18 %
186.crafty	192,013,840,675	184,861,683,227	103.87 %
197.parser	313,187,450,212	291,055,655,200	107.60 %
253.perlbmk	1,147,112,186	1,106,164,617	103.70 %
254.gap	220,455,529,344	216,480,669,077	101.84 %
255.vortex	329,083,783,116	311,764,008,973	105.56 %
256.bzip2	285,176,110,773	278,769,705,624	102.30 %
300.twolf	293,847,320,971	293,190,467,622	100.22 %
Average			103.22 %

Table 5. Effect of constant-bit and don't care analyses. The table compares the number of executed instructions of the generated code with and without the constant-bit and don't care analyses.

Benchmark	Without Analyses	With Analyses	$\frac{\text{Without Analyses}}{\text{With Analyses}}$
164.gzip	290,253,056,191	285,201,958,027	101.77 %
175.vpr	203,496,140,283	203,495,172,137	100.00 %
176.gcc	149,081,148,091	146,088,405,963	102.05 %
181.mcf	48,924,041,098	48,969,263,250	99.91 %
186.crafty	184,861,683,227	179,226,675,963	103.14 %
197.parser	291,055,655,200	291,053,327,116	100.00 %
253.perlbmk	1,106,164,617	1,106,163,127	100.00 %
254.gap	216,480,669,077	216,345,138,043	100.06 %
255.vortex	311,764,008,973	311,764,025,981	100.00 %
256.bzip2	278,769,705,624	278,229,736,806	100.19 %
300.twolf	293,190,467,622	293,190,431,795	100.00 %
Average			100.64 %

of the generated binaries. On average, the application of local optimizations until the fixpoints reduces the number of executed instructions by 3.22 %.

Furthermore, we evaluated the effect of the constant-bit and don't care analyses. Table 5 shows that using the analyses further improved the overall performance by 0.64 %. The enabled analyses achieve their best improvement for the 186.crafty benchmark that contains a lot of bit operations. Here, the analyses discover an occult constant that results in an improvement by 3.14 %.

6   Conclusion and Future Work

In this paper, we presented the local optimization generator OPTGEN. In contrast to generators for peephole optimizers, OPTGEN generates optimization rules that work on the IR level. This allows a more abstract view on the program behavior than working on assembly level.

A unique feature of OPTGEN is its full support of constants. This includes the generalization of syntactically equivalent rules to a rule with symbolic constants. Furthermore, we demonstrated that it is sufficient to generate rules for a small bit width and later extend them to a larger bit width. Together, these techniques allow the efficient generation of all rules that involve constants.

We further generalized the generated rules of OPTGEN by using the analysis information of the constant-bit and don't care analyses. This compacts the rule specification and allows to apply the local optimizations in more cases. Using the SPEC CINT2000 benchmark, we obtain an reduction of the executed instructions by up to 3.14 %, when using the analysis information.

We used OPTGEN to find unsupported optimizations in the state-of-the-art compilers GCC, ICC and LLVM. For these compilers, we identified more than 50 missing optimizations that involve at most two operations. Furthermore, we showed that compilers should prevent the application of some optimization rules due to shared subexpressions. For the state-of-the-art compilers, we identified ten optimizations that are applied in such scenarios.

During the development of OPTGEN, we identified three interesting research topics for future work. The first idea is the use of superoptimization techniques to derive appropriate conditions during the rule generalization as discussed at the end of Section 3.2. Furthermore, such techniques can be used to find optimal implementations for the transfer functions of the constant-bit analysis. The second idea is to extend OPTGEN to automatically derive condition expressions that are based on constant-bit and don't care information as discussed at the end of Section 4.3. The third research topic concerns the sharing of subexpressions. Here, algorithms that reassociate existing expression to allow the application of local optimizations or to improve the sharing with existing subexpressions would be worthwhile for state-of-the-art compilers.

Acknowledgments. We thank Christoph Mallon and Manuel Mohr for many fruitful discussions and valuable advices, and the anonymous reviewers for their helpful comments. This work was supported by the German Research Foundation (DFG) as part of the Transregional Collaborative Research Centre "Invasive Computing" (SFB/TR 89).

References

1. Bansal, S., Aiken, A.: Automatic generation of peephole superoptimizers. In: Proceedings of the 12th International Conference on Architectural Support for Programming Languages and Operating Systems, ASPLOS XII, pp. 394–403. ACM, New York (2006)
2. Braun, M., Buchwald, S., Hack, S., Leißa, R., Mallon, C., Zwinkau, A.: Simple and efficient construction of static single assignment form. In: Jhala, R., De Bosschere, K. (eds.) Compiler Construction. LNCS, vol. 7791, pp. 102–122. Springer, Heidelberg (2013)
3. De Moura, L., Bjørner, N.: Z3: An efficient smt solver. In: Ramakrishnan, C.R., Rehof, J. (eds.) TACAS 2008. LNCS, vol. 4963, pp. 337–340. Springer, Heidelberg (2008)
4. Joshi, R., Nelson, G., Randall, K.: Denali: A goal-directed superoptimizer. In: Proceedings of the ACM SIGPLAN 2002 Conference on Programming Language Design and Implementation, PLDI 2002, pp. 304–314. ACM, New York (2002)
5. libFirm – The FIRM intermediate representation library, http://libfirm.org
6. Lopes, N., Menendez, D., Nagarakatte, S., Regehr, J.: ALIVe: Automatic LLVM InstCombine Verifier, http://blog.regehr.org/archives/1170
7. Massalin, H.: Superoptimizer: A look at the smallest program. In: Proceedings of the Second International Conference on Architectual Support for Programming Languages and Operating Systems, ASPLOS II, pp. 122–126. IEEE Computer Society Press, Los Alamitos (1987)
8. Nelson, G., Oppen, D.C.: Fast decision procedures based on congruence closure. J. ACM 27(2), 356–364 (1980)

9. Schkufza, E., Sharma, R., Aiken, A.: Stochastic superoptimization. In: Proceedings of the Eighteenth International Conference on Architectural Support for Programming Languages and Operating Systems, ASPLOS 2013, pp. 305–316. ACM, New York (2013)

10. Schkufza, E., Sharma, R., Aiken, A.: Stochastic optimization of floating-point programs with tunable precision. In: Proceedings of the 35th ACM SIGPLAN Conference on Programming Language Design and Implementation, PLDI 2014, pp. 53–64. ACM, New York (2014)

11. Seltenreich, A.: Minimizing bit width using data flow analysis in libfirm (February 2013)

12. Tate, R., Stepp, M., Tatlock, Z., Lerner, S.: Equality saturation: A new approach to optimization. In: Proceedings of the 36th Annual ACM SIGPLAN-SIGACT Symposium on Principles of Programming Languages, POPL 2009, pp. 264–276. ACM, New York (2009)

13. Wegman, M.N., Zadeck, F.K.: Constant propagation with conditional branches. ACM Trans. Program. Lang. Syst. 13(2), 181–210 (1991)

Formal Techniques

Towards a Scalable Framework
for Context-Free Language Reachability

Nicholas Hollingum and Bernhard Scholz

The University of Sydney, NSW 2006, Australia
nhol8058@uni.sydney.edu.au, scholz@it.usyd.edu.au

Abstract. Context-Free Language Reachability (CFL-R) is a search problem to identify paths in an input labelled graph that form sentences in a given context-free language. CFL-R provides a fundamental formulation for many applications, including shape analysis, data and control flow analysis, program slicing, specification-inferencing and points-to analysis. Unfortunately, generic algorithms for CFL-R scale poorly with large instances, leading research to focus on ad-hoc optimisations for specific applications. Hence, there is the need for scalable algorithms which solve arbitrary CFL-R instances.

In this work, we present a generic algorithm for CFL-R with improved scalability, performance and/or generality over the state-of-the-art solvers. The algorithm adapts Datalog's semi-naïve evaluation strategy for eliminating redundant computations. Our solver uses the quadtree data-structure, which reduces memory overheads, speeds up runtime, and eliminates the restriction to normalised input grammars. The resulting solver has up to 3.5x speed-up and 60% memory reduction over a state-of-the-art CFL-R solver based on dynamic programming.

Keywords: program analysis, context-free language reachability, semi-naïve evaluation, quad-trees, matrix multiplication.

1 Introduction

The **Context-Free Language Reachability** (CFL-R) problem has been researched extensively since it was initially identified by Yannakakis [29]. In a pleasing symmetry to our own work, he viewed the problem as a means of solving a sub-class of Datalog queries via CFL-R. Not limited to logic programming though, CFL-R soon proved to be useful for diverse computational tasks, from formal security analysis [8] to a wide range of program analysis problems [22].

The importance of CFL-R as a program analysis framework cannot be understated. CFL-R encompasses shape analysis [22], data- [23] and control-flow [27], set-constraints [15] [18], specification-inferencing [3], object-flow [31], and a plethora of context, flow and field sensitive and insensitive alias [33] [17] [35] [25] [28] analyses, to name a few. We attribute this extensive utility to the fact that such analyses rely on dynamic reachability queries for program graphs, which is a common enough problem to deserve its own complexity class [11], and is expressed naturally

© Springer-Verlag Berlin Heidelberg 2015
B. Franke (Ed.): CC 2015, LNCS 9031, pp. 193–211, 2015.
DOI: 10.1007/978-3-662-46663-6_10

by CFL-R. The continuous stream of CFL-R research since the 90s indicates that it will remain an important problem into the future.

Unfortunately, the promise of CFL-R cannot be reached by the current state-of-the-art solvers. The original dynamic-programming algorithm, due to Melski and Reps [18], has cubic time-complexity. More recently, Chaudhuri [5] improved previous work slightly with an $\mathcal{O}(\frac{n^3}{\log n})$ algorithm utilising the Four Russians' Trick, which offers a relatively minor speedup at the cost of a significant memory increase. The complexity issue, coined the "cubic bottleneck" [11], spurs research in restricted sub-classes of CFL-R [31] [33] which have better time complexities, but limited applicability. To provide a general CFL-R framework for a large range of applications, our work restricts neither the graph nor the grammar classes.

It is unlikely [21] that algorithmic improvement will be made to the current $\mathcal{O}(\frac{n^3}{\log n})$ lower-bound. This work, therefore, focuses on improving performance in practice, by removing redundant computations and memory inefficiencies which occur for the current state-of-the-art solvers. The new approach has worse theoretical properties, but achieves better practical runtime performance by adapting efficient machinery from a similar problem-space. Thus, in a reversal of Yannakakis' formulation, we turn to Datalog as a scaffolding for the development of a new CFL-R algorithm. Redundant computations, which occur in the Melski-Reps algorithm, can be eliminated by an intelligent evaluation strategy. We specialise the machinery used in Datalog engines, called **semi-naïve evaluation**, to the CFL-R context. The adapted algorithm is implemented on top of an efficient **quadtree** binary-relation representation. Together, the quadtree-based semi-naïve algorithm achieves more efficient memory usage, improves the practical runtime performance, especially for sparse problems, and obviates the need for an expensive grammar-normalisation operation.

We outline our contributions as follows:

- We specialise the semi-naïve evaluation strategy from the Datalog context to CFL-R. This leads to a new algorithm with fewer redundant calculations, and performant behaviour for non-normalised input graphs.
- We present quadtrees as a vehicle for representing the input graph and evaluating the solution. Quadtrees provide further advantages to our approach, since they give new-information-tracking for free and have efficient memory utilisation for sparse problems.
- We experimentally verify the advantages of the new technique, showing up to 3.5x speedup and 60% memory reduction, on a Java points-to analysis problem.

Our paper is organised as follows: Section 2 provides background material about the CFL-R problem, and introduces the current state-of-the-art solvers. An explanation of our contributions is presented in Section 3, which includes our adaptation of the semi-naïve evaluation strategy, the explanation of quadtrees, and the reasons that normalisation is unnecessary. Section 4 presents our experimental findings, specifically on the superior memory and runtime performance of our approach. We survey the related literature in Section 5, and conclude our findings and plans for future work in Section 6.

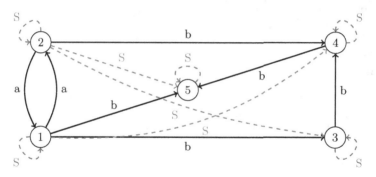

Fig. 1. Running CFL-R Example, its grammar is $\mathcal{P} = \{[S \to aSb], [S \to \epsilon]\}$. Dashed edges represent solutions to the CFL-R problem, lowercase letters are terminal symbols, and the non-terminal start-symbol is S.

2   Context-Free Language Reachability

We use the standard terminology to define the CFL-R problem as a 6-tuple $\mathcal{L} = (\Sigma, \mathcal{N}, \mathcal{P}, S, V, E)$, of terminals Σ, non-terminals $\mathcal{N}$, production rules $\mathcal{P}$, a start symbol S, vertices V, and edges E. For notational convenience we say $E \subseteq V \times V \times (\Sigma \cup \mathcal{N})$, such that an edge is a triple $(u, v, X) \in E$, denoting that vertex u is connected to v via an edge labelled with the terminal or non-terminal X. We will refer to the elements of an edge triple as its source, destination and label respectively. Henceforth, let n count the number of vertices in the input problem, and k the sum of the left and right-hand sides of all the production rules.

CFL-R is a generalisation of graph reachability and context-free recognition. Informally, we search a graph for those paths between vertices, whose labels concatenate to form a sentence in the context-free language. We use the standard notions [13] of production expansion and sentences here, so a sentence in the language must be reachable by finitely many production-rule expansions beginning with the start symbol. In this way the CFL-R problem can express both transitive reachability (according to a grammar $[S \to a^*]$) and context-free language recognition (reachability in a line graph). Figure 1 illustrates a CFL-R problem. Solutions to the problem are displayed with dashed lines, and summarise paths in the graph which traverse some (possibly zero) "a" labelled edges, followed by the same number of "b" edges.

We make use of two extensions to aid expressivity of the grammars. A non-terminal symbol may be parametric (written A_f), which is simply a stand-in for the distinct non-terminal A_f to make the grammar's presentation concise. Also, for notational convenience, symbols in the right-hand-side of the production may indicate the transposed relation, using $\overline{\text{overline}}$. In a CFL-R instance, this refers to reverse edges, which could be tracked by their own productions [22], but this would lengthen the grammar. The rule $[A \to B\overline{C}D]$ matches paths which travel backwards along the C edge.

Algorithm 1. Generalised worklist-based CFL-R algorithm

```
 1: procedure WORKLIST(L = (Σ, N, P, S, V, E))
 2:     for all v ∈ V, [X → ϵ] ∈ P do
 3:         add (v, v, X) to E
 4:     end for
 5:     W ← E
 6:     while W ≠ ∅ do
 7:         remove (u, v, Y) from W
 8:         for all [Z → X₀ ... Xₐ Y Xᵦ ... X_L] ∈ P do
 9:             B ← {u}
10:             for i = a  to  0 do
11:                 B ← {n : (n, u', Xᵢ) ∈ E, u' ∈ B}
12:             end for
13:             F ← {v}
14:             for j = b to L do
15:                 F ← {n : (v', n, Xⱼ) ∈ E, v' ∈ F}
16:             end for
17:             W ← W ∪ ({(u', v', Z) : u' ∈ B, v' ∈ F} \ E)
18:             E ← E ∪ W
19:         end for
20:     end while
21: end procedure
```

The state-of-the-art scalable algorithm for CFL-R is due to Melski and Reps [18]. The reader should note that Chaudhuri has introduced an improvement [5] using a fast-set representation. However, the fast-set representation requires at least $\Theta(kn^2)$ memory, such that even the smallest benchmark used in our experimental evaluation (cf. Section 4) would require over 138GB. The difficulty of using Chaudhuri's approach for Java benchmarks was similarly observed in [33]. A modified version of the Melski-Reps algorithm is shown in Algorithm 1. The $\mathcal{O}(kn^2)$-sized worklist must, for each edge, check $\mathcal{O}(k)$ production rules in an attempt to find L-length paths containing the dequeued edge. Extending the path in general requires finding $\mathcal{O}(kn^2)$ edges that join temporary B or F nodes to new nodes, resulting in a worst-case runtime complexity of $\mathcal{O}(Lk^3n^4)$. Typically, the worklist algorithm requires the production rules to be normalised to a **binary normal-form** [16], which creates new non-terminals that break up productions with more than two symbols on their right-hand-side. Our modification to the algorithm allows it to work (albeit inefficiently) with non-normalised grammars. Importantly, though, the complexity becomes the expected $\mathcal{O}(k^3n^3)$ [18] when the grammar is normalised, because the path is only expanded once, from a single node, requiring $\mathcal{O}(kn)$ work instead of $\mathcal{O}(Lkn^2)$. The cubic-time required by this algorithm is well understood in the literature to be the bottleneck for many program analyses [11].

3   Novel CFL-R Algorithm

3.1   Semi-naïve Evaluation

The CFL-R algorithm due to Melski and Reps [18], as shown in Algorithm 1, introduces inefficiencies. Consider Figure 1: the Melski-Reps algorithm would discover the $(2, 5, S)$ edge up to nine times, since there are three potential paths ($\langle 2, 1, 5 \rangle$, $\langle 2, 1, 2, 4, 5 \rangle$ and $\langle 2, 1, 2, 1, 3, 4, 5 \rangle$), and each one can be expanded from either the "a", "b" or "S" edge. The actual number of times it is discovered depends on which order edges are dequeued from the worklist, so the evaluation is also chaotic. This issue has been solved in the Datalog context before by a bottom-up strategy known as **semi-naïve evaluation** [2].

Datalog is a declarative programming model which derives information from base facts according to expansion rules. Facts are written $A(1, 5)$, meaning that the relation A contains a pairing between 1 and 5. A rule composes relations, so that $S(u, x)$:- $A(u, v), S(v, w), B(w, x)$ implies new S relations can be derived by stringing A, S, and B relations together. The example 1 could be translated to a Datalog program in this fashion.

When Datalog begins bottom-up evaluation, the relations are empty. Facts are inserted into the relations, and the bodies of the rules are evaluated to obtain new knowledge. Since Datalog relations are bounded, a fixed-point will be reached after a finite number of iterations, which constitutes the solution. A naïve implementation of the bottom-up strategy, would iterate over the bodies of clauses several times with the same knowledge over and over, rediscovering already-known relations many times. Yet worse, if a relation is already stable in an iteration (i.e. more iterations do not obtain more knowledge), the relation is re-computed in all subsequent iterations. To overcome the problem of re-computation, the semi-naïve evaluation was introduced.

The semi-naïve evaluation strategy is two-fold. Firstly, it uses the new information discovered in the previous iteration (or, initially, the base facts) to derive new information for the current iteration, called the Δ relation. Secondly, it only derives new information for relations whose dependant relations (those appearing in the rule body) have stabilised, or reflexive-transitively depend on it (such as recursive rules), until that relation stabilises. For a more in-depth presentation of semi-naïve evaluation, refer to [2].

Yannakakis, in his seminal work [29], introduced the fundamental relationship between Datalog and CFL-R, i.e., clauses in chain-rule format become productions:

$$[X \rightarrow Y_1 Y_2 ... Y_k] \Leftrightarrow X(a, c) \text{ :- } Y_1(a, b_1), Y_2(b_1, b_2), ..., Y_k(b_{k-1}, c)$$

and facts $X(u, v)$ become labelled edges $(u, v, X) \in E$ in the CFL-R input graph. In this way, labels in the CFL-R problem and binary relations in the Datalog formulation are conceptually identical. Yannakakis' original intention was to convert sub-classes of Datalog to CFL-R, obtaining an efficient solving vehicle. For our new algorithm, we use the semi-naïve evaluation as a scaffolding, and translate CFL-R instances to Datalog programs in the reverse direction of

Yannakakis' reduction. We specialise Datalog's semi-naïve evaluation to obtain a new algorithm for CFL-R, which is efficient by virtue of avoiding redundant computations.

Firstly, the evaluation strategy must only use recently discovered information to determine new information. We record a label's new information in a Δ relation, which is updated during the evaluation of production rules, and zeroed after it has been used, avoiding redundancy. The semi-naïve strategy also specifies that we should not compose label relations if the labels on which they depend have not stabilised. The correct order for these micro-fixed-point calculations is deduced from the **dependency graph** $G = ((\Sigma \cup \mathcal{N}), \{(X, Y) : [X \rightarrow ... Y ...] \in \mathcal{P}\})$, whose nodes are labels and whose edges express dependencies between two labels. The left-hand-side label in a production depends on all the labels on the right. In the case the dependency is cyclic, we simply iteratively evaluate the production rules until all inter-dependant relations reach a fixed-point.

The semi-naïve-based algorithm is presented in Algorithm 2. This algorithm assumes a binary-relation representation, where the label Y has a relational representation $\mathbf{Y} = \{(a, b) : (a, b, Y) \in E\}$. Instead of using relational algebra operations [2] for evaluating the body of a CFL-R clause, we observe that the CFL-R clauses resemble cascaded equi-joins, which are further reduced to relational compositions, i.e.,

$$\{(a, c) : (a, b_1) \in \mathbf{Y_1} \wedge (b_1, b_2) \in \mathbf{Y_2} \wedge \ldots \wedge (b_{k-1}, c) \in \mathbf{Y_k}\} \quad =$$
$$\{(a, c) : \mathbf{Y_1}(a, b_1) \bowtie \mathbf{Y_2}(b_1, b_2) \bowtie \ldots \bowtie \mathbf{Y_k}(b_{k-1}, c)\} \quad =$$
$$\mathbf{Y_1} \circ \mathbf{Y_2} \circ \ldots \circ \mathbf{Y_k}$$

where $\mathbf{P} \circ \mathbf{Q} = \{(r, t) : (r, s) \in \mathbf{P}, (s, t) \in \mathbf{Q}\}$.

3.2   Quadtrees

The Datalog formulation from Section 3.1 performs relational composition, set-difference and union operations (Algorithm 2, Line 14). We therefore require a data-structure with low space and runtime overheads for these operations. In this work the **quadtree** representation of Boolean matrices is chosen as a suitable data structure. Quadtrees have better time-complexity operations than, for example, adjacency lists [18], and smaller memory utilisation than a dense-matrix representation [5].

Initially, we examine Boolean matrices as a vehicle for relational composition. A binary relation A can be represented as a Boolean matrix $\hat{A}$ whose elements are defined by:

$$\hat{A}_{ij} = \begin{cases} 1, & \text{if } (i, j) \in \mathbf{A} \\ 0, & \text{otherwise} \end{cases}$$

Assuming a one-to-one mapping between the domains of the relation and the indices of the matrix, the well-known identity $\widehat{A \circ B} = \hat{A} \cdot \hat{B}$ can be established, permitting the computation of CFL-R using matrix calculus. Used in this way, Boolean-matrix relational-composition would increase the complexity

Algorithm 2. Semi-naïve CFL-R algorithm using quadtrees(c.f. Section 3.2)

```
1: procedure QUADTREE(L)
2:     ⟨C₁,...,C_q⟩ ← reverse_topological_strongly_connected_comps(P)
3:     for all [X → ε] ∈ P do
4:         X ← X ∪ {(v, v) : v ∈ V}
5:     end for
6:     for all X ∈ Σ ∪ N do
7:         ΔX ← X                          ▷ All Δs initialised to the problem state.
8:     end for
9:     for C_i = C₁ to C_q do
10:        while ∃Z ∈ C_i s.t. |ΔZ| > 0 do
11:            Temp ← ΔZ
12:            ΔZ ← 0
13:            for all [Y → X₀,...,Z,...,X_L] ∈ P do
14:                ΔY ← ΔY ∪ (X₀ ∘ ... ∘ Temp ∘ ... ∘ X_L) \ Y
15:                Y ← Y ∪ ΔY
16:            end for
17:        end while
18:    end for
19: end procedure
```

of the solver from $\mathcal{O}(k^3 n^3)$ to $\mathcal{O}(k^3 n^2 BMM(n))$, where the time complexity of Boolean-Matrix-Multiplication, $BMM(n)$, is roughly $\mathcal{O}(n^{2.3})$ [7]. This time bound is derived from Algorithm 2, which loops Line 10 at most kn^2 times, and propagates the chosen delta to at most k non-terminals each loop, requiring k matrix multiplications for each propagation.

To minimise the overhead imposed by the matrix-formulation we turn to a quadtree representation. Quadtrees are a well-known matrix representation in the field of computer graphics, and they have some useful theoretical properties. Figure 2 shows a quadtree and the Boolean matrix it represents. For the CFL-R application, we are interested in the time requirements for set-difference and multiplication operations, as well as the memory requirements of quadtrees. Our

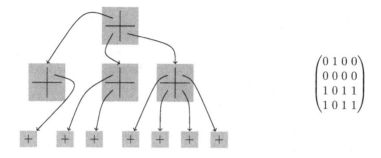

Fig. 2. Quadtree representation of a 4x4 Boolean matrix

intuition here relies on the fact that quadtrees perform very well for sparse matrices, let m be the number of set bits in the matrix, i.e. $m < n^2$.

Lemma 1. *The quadtree requires $\mathcal{O}(\min(n^2, m \log n))$ space to store.*

The absolute size of the quadtree is bounded above by $\mathcal{O}(n^2)$. Consider the 1-matrix with side-length n, it is clearly maximal, as all nodes have the maximum number of children. Its quadtree has n^2 leaves, each representing a single 1 element, with each layer having $\frac{1}{4}$ as many nodes as the layer below it. The total number of nodes is at most:

$$\sum_{f=0}^{\infty} n^2 \frac{1}{4^f} = \frac{n^2}{1 - \frac{1}{4}} = \frac{4n^2}{3}$$

For a more practical bound, we say that m bits are set. In this case, each set bit requires at most $\log n$ nodes joining it to the root of the tree, thus no more than $m \log n$ nodes are needed for m set bits. This count is bounded above by the known n^2 limit, requiring $\min(n^2, m \log n)$ nodes.

Corollary 1. *The time complexity of the elementary operations: union, intersection, set-difference and deep-copy, is also $\mathcal{O}(\min(n^2, m \log n))$.*

Multiplication of two Boolean matrices is defined intuitively for quadtrees:

$$\left(\begin{array}{c|c} A_0 & A_1 \\ \hline A_2 & A_3 \end{array}\right) \cdot \left(\begin{array}{c|c} B_0 & B_1 \\ \hline B_2 & B_3 \end{array}\right) = \left(\begin{array}{c|c} A_0 B_0 \cup A_1 B_2 & A_0 B_1 \cup A_1 B_3 \\ \hline A_2 B_0 \cup A_3 B_2 & A_2 B_1 \cup A_3 B_3 \end{array}\right) \tag{1}$$

Unfortunately, it is difficult to quantify the expected runtime of the recursive algorithm derived from that definition. In this paper we prove an upper-bound on the runtime, and provide an intuition as to the expected runtime for fixed m.

Lemma 2. *Multiplication of two quadtrees requires $\mathcal{O}(n^3)$ time.*

Via application of the master theorem for recurrence relations. The recursive algorithm for Equation 1 requires eight sub-multiplications and four sub-unions, and recurses to a depth of $\log_2 n$. We know the unions have $\mathcal{O}(n^2)$ complexity, from Corollary 1, hence the recurrence equation of this system is:

$$I_x = 8 I_{x-1} + 4x^2 + 1 \Rightarrow \mathcal{O}(8^{\log_2 n}) = \mathcal{O}(n^3)$$

Note that though this worst-case complexity does occur in practice (for two complete matrices), the time required can vary substantially. Furthermore, the computational load for matrices with m set-bits is difficult to reason about. Adverse arrangements of inputs with $m = \mathcal{O}(n)$ can incur output matrices with all or none of their bits set.

An intuition on the average-case complexity for fixed m arises by examining the case of balanced quadtrees. We call this a **J-tree** (jellyfish), because its nodes have maximal children towards the root (the bell) and at most one child below the bell (the tentacles).

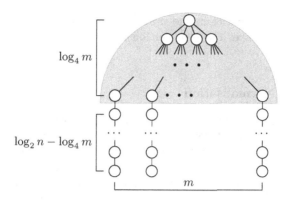

Fig. 3. A J-tree, showing the distinction between bell (upper semi-circle) and tentacles. Nodes in the bell have maximal branching factor, whilst tentacle nodes have at most one child. The height of a quadtree is always $\log_2 n$, so the height of the tentacle section is that height less the $\log_4 m$-high bell.

Lemma 3. *Multiplication of two J-trees requires $\mathcal{O}(m^{\frac{3}{2}} + m\log n)$ time.*

The structure of the J-tree allows us to break up the multiplication into the bell and tentacle components according to the depth of the recursion. We see that if the recursion depth is above $\log_4 m$ then the nodes of both trees typically have 4 children, which imposes the most computational work. Conversely, if we are below a recursion depth of $\log_4 m$ then the nodes have 1 child, and very little computational work is required. To reason about the necessary computations we will analyse work done above the $\log_4 m$ cutoff, the bell, separately from the tentacles below.

The bell's computation is slightly different to that from Lemma 2. Instead the recurrence is to a depth of $\log_4 m$, which yields $\mathcal{O}(8^{\log_2 m^{\frac{1}{2}}}) = \mathcal{O}(m^{\frac{3}{2}})$. This is a true upper bound for J-trees, as nodes with fewer than 4 children impose strictly less work.

The tentacle nodes all have 1 child, so at most one of the eight sub-multiplications are necessary and none of the unions. There are m tentacles on each J-tree, since there are m set bits, thus the recursion's breadth is also m. Unlike for the bell, the two single-child nodes of the input will incur at most one sub-multiplication and no sub-unions, because each node only has one child. Each tentacle is $log_2 n - log_4 m$ nodes long, with one subroutine-call per node, hence in total the m tentacles require $m\log n$ subroutine calls or fewer. Each call simply checks which of the sub-matrices it needs to recurse to and makes the call in constant time. Hence the total work required is the $\mathcal{O}(m^{3/2})$ work for the bell, and $\mathcal{O}(m)$ lots of $\mathcal{O}(\log n)$ work for each tentacle, totalling $\mathcal{O}(m^{3/2} + m\log n)$.

This section has shown the favourable properties of quadtrees, which makes them useful to our adapted semi-naïve Algorithm 2. Quadtree multiplication is a means of performing the relational composition operation ∘, and had a favourable $\mathcal{O}(\min(m\log n, n^2))$ memory footprint. The typical quadtree operations have favourable time-complexities in the worst and average case, and we intuit that multiplication itself takes $\mathcal{O}(m^{3/2} + m \log n)$ time, making it very efficient for sparse problems.

3.3   Notes on Normalisation

Conventional algorithms for CFL-R require the input grammar to be normalised, either to Chomsky normal-form, or the less restrictive binary normal-form. Normalisation increases the size of the grammar, typified by the Chomsky requirement that right-hand sides contain exactly two non-terminals, causing the number of non-terminals to double and the number of rules to expand quadratically.

From a complexity-theoretic standpoint, normalisation is acceptable, since it is computationally cheap, and the size of the grammar is often not a component of the algorithm's time complexity. In practice, liberal expansion of the grammar incurs large overhead in the memory requirements of the algorithm. Chaudhuri's sparse-set method [5] typifies this, as it requires $\Theta(kn^2)$ memory, requiring terabytes of RAM for typically sized problems.

In this work, we choose to remove the requirement that grammars be pre-normalised. As Section 2 showed, the time complexity of Algorithm 1 increases without normalisation. The Melski-Reps formulation's inner loop can no longer rely on the fixed-form of grammar rules. Searching the graph for paths whose labels exactly match the right-hand-side of a production can naïvely require $k(kn^2)$ steps, making the complexity $\mathcal{O}(k^4n^4)$, clearly worse than $\mathcal{O}(k^3n^3)$ when the grammar is normalised. The adapted semi-naïve method, Algorithm 2, composes binary relations via matrix multiplication. Its presentation already allows for arbitrarily long production rules, and therefore retains the $\mathcal{O}(k^3n^2BMM(n))$ running time.

From a theoretical standpoint, normalising the grammar makes no difference to our quadtree-based-semi-naïve formulation. Shortening the length of the matrix multiplication chains directly increases the number of such chains that must be evaluated. Indeed, normalisation may even be considered an unnecessary overhead, since despite having the same computational complexity, a normalised grammar imposes excess memory requirements by retaining the edge and Δ information for intermediate nonterminals.

4   Experimental Results

For the experimental evaluation of our new CFL-R algorithm we use a case study of Java based points-to analysis. We evaluate our algorithm in comparison to the Melski-Reps worklist algorithm [18]. Specifically we are interested in the execution time, memory utilisation, and sensitivity towards grammar normalisation for both approaches.

The competing implementations will be referred to as the worklist and quadtree methods, and refer to Algorithms 1 and 2 (using quadtrees) respectively. Both algorithms were implemented in C++ making partial use of the STL library. The source code of both algorithms is available online [12]. Our experimental evaluation is performed on a 32 core Intel Xeon E5-2450 at 2.1GHz, with 128GB ram.

Case Study. Our CFL-R case study is a points-to analysis expressed in CFL-R for Java. As a benchmark suite we choose the Dacapo benchmarks Version 2006-10. For extracting the labelled input graphs from the Java source code in the Dacapo benchmarks, we have used the DOOP extractor [4]. The extractor produces a set of relations representing input programs in relational format. The DOOP relations are sufficient to generate a labelled input graph for a context-insensitive, flow-insensitive, and field-sensitive points-to analysis, with minimal textual preprocessing. A vertex in the input problem is either a program variable or an object creation site (i.e. representing an object to the program analysis). The input edges are labelled with the following terminals:

- **New:** relating program variables to their object creation sites
- **Assign:** relating a source variable with a destination variable of an assignment statement
- **PutField$_f$, GetField$_f$:** for each field f, relating base variables of field loads/stores to the program variables that load/store information from/into the object of the base variable
- **GetInstanceField, PutInstanceField:** self-edges identifying base variables of field loads/stores
- **Cast$_t$:** relating program variables to the variables they are t-cast from
- **IsHeap$_t$:** self-edge identifying all polymorphic types t of an object

The Java points-to analysis uses the grammar shown in Figure 4. The result of the CFL-R algorithm produces output edges labelled with the following non-terminals:

- **VPT:** relating program variables to heap objects that they may point to
- **Alias:** relating two program variables if they may reference the same heap object
- **DAssign:** relating program variables which are assigned indirectly by field store and load
- **GetInstanceVPT, PutInstanceVPT:** relating the heap objects to the subset of variables which point to them that are derived by field load/stores

The CFL-R grammar is an extension of the grammar presented by Sridharan et al. in [25]. Field sensitivity is ensured by the $DAssign$ production, which is equivalent to

$$[flowsTo \rightarrow flowsTo \; putField_f \; alias \; getField_f]$$

from the Sridharan et al. formulation. We have extended the grammar to capture a type-safe casting with rule $[VPT \rightarrow Cast_t \; VPT \; IsHeap_t]$. Types are encoded in the input graph by a self edge $(h, h, IsHeap_t)$ for all types t which the h object can take. For performance reason, we compute $Alias$ relation only for base variables of field loads/stores.

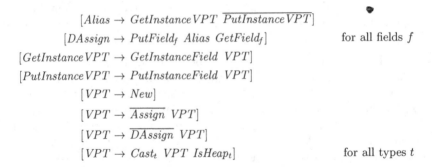

Fig. 4. The parameterised grammar for field-sensitive context-insensitive Java points-to analysis used in our experiments. We adapt the grammar by Sridharan et al. from [25]. The parameters f and t take arbitrary values depending on the fields and types in the input problem.

Problem Sizes. Table 1 shows the relationship between the problem size and the intermediate and output relation sizes. The n, m(avg) and m(max) columns respectively show: the number of vertices in the input graph, the number of edges (averaged across all relations) after running the CFL-R algorithm, and the maximum number of edges of all labels. Unparameterised nonterminals are counted as-is, but parameterised nonterminals are counted together, so that the $Load$ relation is the sum of the sizes of all $Load_{field}$ sub-relations. We also chart the associated sizes of the quadtrees (total number of nodes in the tree) in a similar fashion. As we have shown in Section 3.2, the quadtree's size is bounded by $\mathcal{O}(m \log n)$ nodes, yet the actual sizes are significantly better, the Norm. column shows the normalised fraction $QT_{max}/(m_{max} \log n)$, and improves our intuition on the quadtrees practical size.

The Labels and Labels-nf columns of Table 1 show the number (input and normalised, respectively) of labels in the problem. They show that normalisation imposes a 35%-43% increase in the number of labels. Here we acknowledge that this is an artefact of the grammar we are using. Nevertheless, the fact that our method obviates the need for normalisation still proves useful, as it will be no worse, and definitely can improve memory efficiency.

The sparse nature of the problem is difficult to see from the tables, and is better shown in Figure 5. Here we show the logarithmic index of m in terms of n, knowing that the theoretical maximum is two (i.e. an edge between every pair of nodes). In practice (at least for points-to) m is on average less than n^1, and even in the worst cases is only $n^{1.14}$ in the jython benchmark. This validates our intuition from Section 3.2, that CFL-R problems are highly sparse. We observe a pattern of increasing log-indices according to the size of the problem, which we attribute to over-approximation in the analysis as the potential for more edges increases.

Table 1. Statistical information for the Dacapo benchmarks (ordered by problem size n). Includes: the number of Labels ($|\Sigma \cup \mathcal{N}|$) for the input and normalised (-nf) grammar, the problem size (n) and the size of the average and maximum output set-bits (m) and quadtree node-count (QT). Norm shows the ratio between the expected quadtree size $\mathcal{O}(m \log n)$ and the maximum's actual size.

Benchmark	Labels	Labels-nf	n	m (avg)	m (max)	QT (avg)	QT (max)	Norm.
luindex	1653	2301	22699	3413.62	12993	16391	60986	0.32
pmd	1755	2399	32295	12833.23	54660	41645.92	143505	0.18
antlr	1095	1520	32927	5916.85	21891	25573.31	93252	0.28
eclipse	2257	3172	33912	4748.08	21313	23861.54	99813	0.31
bloat	1900	2650	40989	9068.77	57829	35733.54	177415	0.2
xalan	2449	3436	46780	8606.54	42461	38492.15	155194	0.24
chart	2914	4166	49893	8717.85	39753	40075.77	160375	0.26
fop	3495	4742	53851	8591.54	38802	41334.15	160827	0.26
hsqldb	2817	3974	63281	24412.38	200762	86334.77	592910	0.19
jython	3351	4588	78639	40349.77	383917	135013.23	1102813	0.18

Table 2. Absolute runtime (s) of points-to analysis for the Dacapo benchmarks by Worklist and Quadtree implementations of the solver with (-nf) and without grammar normalisation

Benchmark	Worklist	Worklist-nf	Quadtree	Quadtree-nf
luindex	2.518	2.05	0.726	0.862
pmd	25.348	18.462	8.806	8.436
antlr	3.218	2.614	0.968	1.038
eclipse	7.326	5	1.794	2.042
bloat	12.61	9.548	2.724	2.99
xalan	14.81	11.554	3.9	4.296
chart	17.392	13.782	4.266	4.602
fop	13.828	10.756	3.318	3.812
hsqldb	47.282	36.132	12.218	12.636
jython	96.688	73.264	24.72	24.208

Runtime. We first compare the execution time for the standard worklist algorithm. Table 2 records the absolute runtime (in seconds) of the Dacapo benchmarks for the Worklist and Quadtree implementations, with (-nf) and without grammar-normalisation.

Since we are interested in the performance and scaling behaviour of the quadtree implementation, Figure 6 plots the relative speedup of those implementations normalised to Worklist-nf. Observe that quadtrees universally outperform the worklist, with an average 2.93x speedup. The largest speedup occurs for the bloat benchmark, at 3.51x, and the smallest is pmd, with 2.10x. It is interesting that the extreme speedups/slowdowns do not occur with the largest and smallest benchmarks, jython and luindex respectively, which show 2.96x and 2.82x speedups. This is strong evidence that, although the worst-case complexity of CFL-R via

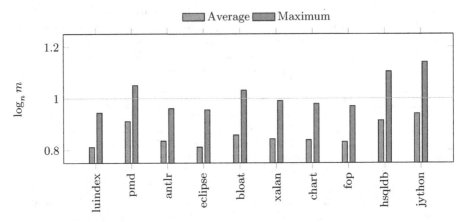

Fig. 5. Graphical plot for sparsity ($\log_n m$) from Table 1, showing that the average and maximum set-bits (m) range from $n^{0.8}$ to $n^{1.2}$ for all benchmarks

quadtrees is much worse, in practice it scales in the same manner as the worklist algorithm.

In support of our choice not to normalise the grammar, Figure 6 shows the effects of normalisation. We see the expected speed-increase for the worklist algorithm (which has historically been presented exclusively for normalised grammars). We also see virtually no change in execution times for the quadtree implementation, which intrinsically performs the work of the normalised grammar via intermediate matrices.

Memory Consumption. The peak memory consumption of the Worklist and Quadtree implementations in binary normal-form (-nf) and as-is, is recorded in Table 3. To assist understanding, relative memory usage against the normalised Worklist-nf implementation is plotted in Figure 7. We observe clear trends in the memory usage both between the implementations, and according to the normalisation of the grammar.

Firstly, the quadtree implementation clearly has a smaller memory footprint. Comparing the more favourable normalised worklist results against the non-normalised quadtree, we see universally less usage of memory, averaging to 0.39x. The greatest reduction occurs for `hsqldb`, one of the larger benchmarks, and the least for `antlr`, a smaller one. Furthermore, the smallest and largest benchmarks (`luindex` and `jython`) have 0.48x and 0.43x memory consumption respectively. Our results indicate that memory reduction does not seem to scale with problem size, but is more likely dependant on problem-specific information (such as the order of information).

We are also interested in how normalisation impacts memory usage. The worklist algorithm clearly benefits from normalisation in the expected manner, where

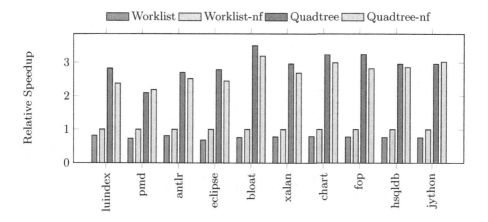

Fig. 6. Relative speedup of the Worklist, Quadtree and normalised Quadtree-nf against the normalised Worklist-nf implementation. Larger values show faster runtimes

Table 3. Absolute memory usage (MB) of points-to analysis for the Dacapo benchmarks by Worklist and Quadtree implementations of the solver with (-nf) and without grammar normalisation

Benchmark	Worklist	Worklist-nf	Quadtree	Quadtree-nf
luindex	149.86	72.5	34.87	35.13
pmd	347.88	163.29	53.73	89.31
antlr	149.43	80.07	51.46	51.71
eclipse	401.09	151.27	53.04	53.3
bloat	375.48	164.59	61.46	76.93
xalan	513.27	214.72	73.7	77.05
chart	568.72	239.61	79.84	81.65
fop	614.94	255.34	82.3	84.39
hsqldb	853.08	433.1	109.55	164.72
jython	868.43	415.32	177.75	277.91

memory consumption drops on average 0.46x. This result is not particularly interesting, since the worklist algorithm is not the focus of our research, however the reader should note that this memory drop must be attributed to the large intermediate-result set that is computed for longer rule chains. In comparison, we see a slight increase in memory consumption when normalising the grammar for the quadtree algorithm. Unlike other metrics, the experiments do show that the larger benchmarks `jython` and `hsqldb` show the largest increases, more than 1.5x. This result is to be expected, and motivates the ideas of Section 3.3, which is that maintaining intermediate results permanently becomes problematic for particularly large problems.

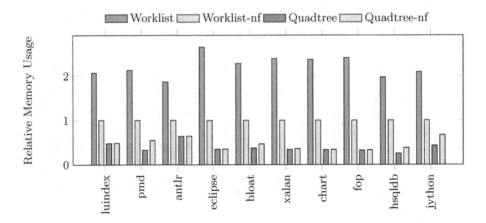

Fig. 7. Relative memory usage of the Worklist, Quadtree and normalised Quadtree-nf against the normalised Worklist-nf implementation. Smaller values show a reduced memory footprint

5   Related Work

Recognition of context free languages is one of the oldest formalisms in theoretical computer science. The first efficient algorithms for recognition were proposed independently by Cocke [6], Younger [30] and Kasami [14], and subsequently improved by Valiant [26] and generalised by Okhotin [20].

The reachability variant of CFL was formalised by Yannakakis [29] as a data-flow evaluation strategy. Our work relies on reversing this encoding, so that we can apply data-flow techniques to a new context. It was later, through Reps [22] [23] [18] [24] [21], that the problem was popularised as as a vehicle for solving a range of computational problems.

In particular, CFL-R has been identified as a viable solver for many analyses. Notable ones are: shape analysis [22], constant propagation [24], control-flow analysis [27], set-constraint solving [18] [15], but particularly points-to analysis. There is much demand in the literature for fast and scalable points-to analysis [10] [19]. CFL reachability is valuable in this context because it provides a queryable "as-needed" framework, useful in incremental [17] or demand-driven [35] [25] [28] contexts. For this reason, our work uses the points-to benchmarks as a case-study for viable CFL-R algorithms.

Another line of research focuses on improving CFL-R algorithms. Very fast algorithms have been developed for restricted cases, particularly Dyck-grammars and bi-directed graphs:

$$\mathcal{P} = \{[S \rightarrow \epsilon], [S \rightarrow SS], [S \rightarrow A_f S \hat{A}_f]\}$$

$$\forall u, v \in V \wedge A_f, \hat{A}_f \in \Sigma : (u, v, A_f) \in E \Leftrightarrow (v, u, \hat{A}_f) \in E$$

Here f is a parameter which can take any value according to the input being solved. Yuan and Eugster first formulated an efficient Dyck-reachability algorithm for bi-directed trees in [31]. Their work was later improved and extended by Zhang et al. in [33], which is able to solve bi-directed graphs in $\mathcal{O}(n + m \log m)$ and trees in $\mathcal{O}(n)$. In that work, the authors noticed that when a graph is bi-directed, Dyck-reachability forms an equivalence relation, whose equal members can be collapsed to representative nodes. Successively stratifying the intra-reachable sets in this way grants the significantly reduced time complexities which they reported. Unsurprisingly, there are few problem contexts in which the graph is naturally bi-directed. Introducing reverse edges for every parenthesis label leads the analysis to report an over-approximation of the actual reachable sets, which can still be useful depending on the problem context. The work in [33] is therefore of greatest use as a fast pre-processing step for a more precise and expensive analysis.

Unfortunately, results by Heintze and McAllester [11] and Reps [21] imply that the Dyck results are unlikely to generalise. Indeed, only Chaudhuri [5], using the Four Russians' Trick, has been able to improve on the long-standing cubic-time algorithm. As was stated in Section 2, we are unable to use Chaudhuri's advancement, since the memory required is excessive, though work by Zhang et al. has found a means of adapting it for C points-to analysis whilst retaining subcubic runtime [34].

Matrix multiplication has been used in the CFL context since Valiant [26]. Much of the theory surrounding matrices is concerned with efficient computations and representations of matrices in the natural domain, most famously the Coppersmith and Winograd algorithm for fast matrix-matrix multiplication [7]. For our CFL-R context, we are concerned with Boolean matrices, which are typically sparse. Long-standing algorithms for sparse matrix multiplication [9] have been improved recently by Yuster and Zwick [32]. This paper favours the quadtree representation, which was shown to be efficient both for memory and computations by Abdali and Wise in [1].

6   Conclusions

In this paper we present a radically different approach to the evaluation of CFL-R problems. Our work draws from well-researched ideas in the Datalog community, and applies them to a new context. We have successfully adapted the semi-naïve evaluation strategy of Datalog by using the memory-efficient quadtree representation both as a means of tracking Δ-information and as a relational-composition vehicle. The algorithm we develop has theoretical advantages over the traditional Melski-Reps approach [18], by eliminating many redundant calculations, and Chaudhuri's subcubic approach [5], by making efficient use of memory. Our advances have been implemented as a CFL-R solver, and compared experimentally with the current scalable state-of-the-art solver. The experimentation shows that our CFL-R algorithm brings up to 3.5x speedup and 60% memory reduction. Going forward, we intend to fully understand the average and worst-case runtime of quadtree-based semi-naive evaluation, to characterise the nature of real-world CFL-R problems, and to assess the viability of alternate data structures within the semi-naïve framework.

Acknowledgments. We would like to thank Andrew Santosa, Chenyi Zhang, Lian Li, Paul Subotic and Paddy Krishnan from Oracle Labs, Brisbane, Australia. This research is support by ARC Grant DP130101970.

References

1. Abdali, S.K., Wise, D.S.: Experiments with quadtree representation of matrices. In: Gianni, P. (ed.) ISSAC 1988. LNCS, vol. 358, pp. 96–108. Springer, Heidelberg (1989)
2. Abiteboul, S., Hull, R., Vianu, V. (eds.): Foundations of Databases: The Logical Level, 1st edn. Addison-Wesley Longman Publishing Co., Inc., MA (1995)
3. Bastani, O., Anand, S., Aiken, A.: Specification inference using context-free language reachability. In: Proceedings of the 42nd Annual ACM SIGPLAN-SIGACT Symposium on Principles of Programming Languages, pp. 553–566. ACM (2015)
4. Bravenboer, M., Smaragdakis, Y.: Strictly declarative specification of sophisticated points-to analyses. In: Proceedings of the 24th ACM SIGPLAN Conference on Object Oriented Programming Systems Languages and Applications, OOPSLA 2009, pp. 243–262. ACM, New York (2009)
5. Chaudhuri, S.: Subcubic algorithms for recursive state machines. In: Proceedings of the 35th Annual ACM SIGPLAN-SIGACT Symposium on Principles of Programming Languages, POPL 2008, pp. 159–169. ACM, New York (2008)
6. Cocke, J.: Programming languages and their compilers. Courant Institute Math. Sci., New York, USA (1970)
7. Coppersmith, D., Winograd, S.: Matrix multiplication via arithmetic progressions. Journal of Symbolic Computation 9(3), 251–280 (1990); Computational algebraic complexity editorial
8. Dolev, D., Even, S., Karp, R.M.: On the security of ping-pong protocols. Information and Control 55(1-3), 57–68 (1982)
9. Gustavson, F.G.: Two fast algorithms for sparse matrices: Multiplication and permuted transposition. ACM Trans. Math. Softw. 4(3), 250–269 (1978)
10. Hardekopf, B., Lin, C.: The ant and the grasshopper: Fast and accurate pointer analysis for millions of lines of code. SIGPLAN Not. 42(6), 290–299 (2007)
11. Heintze, N., McAllester, D.: On the cubic bottleneck in subtyping and flow analysis. In: Proceedings of the 12th Annual IEEE Symposium on Logic in Computer Science, LICS 1997, pp. 342–351. IEEE (1997)
12. Hollingum, N.: Source code for worklist and semi-naive cfl-r algorithms (October 2014), http://sydney.edu.au/engineering/it/~nhol8058/cfl/
13. Hopcroft, J.E., Motwani, R., Ullman, J.D.: Introduction to Automata Theory, Languages and Computation, International edn. Pearson Education International Inc., Upper Saddle River (2003)
14. Kasami, T.: An efficient recognition and syntax-analysis algorithm for context-free languages. Technical report, DTIC Document (1965)
15. Kodumal, J., Aiken, A.: The set constraint/cfl reachability connection in practice. In: Proceedings of the ACM SIGPLAN, Conference on Programming Language Design and Implementation, PLDI 2004, pp. 207–218. ACM, New York (2004)
16. Lange, M., Leiß, H.: To cnf or not to cnf? an efficient yet presentable version of the cyk algorithm. Informatica Didactica 8, 2008–2010 (2009)
17. Lu, Y., Shang, L., Xie, X., Xue, J.: An incremental points-to analysis with cfl-reachability. In: Jhala, R., De Bosschere, K. (eds.) Compiler Construction. LNCS, vol. 7791, pp. 61–81. Springer, Heidelberg (2013)
18. Melski, D., Reps, T.: Interconvertibility of a class of set constraints and context-free-language reachability. Theoretical Computer Science 248(1–2), 29–98 (2000)

19. Mendez-Lojo, M., Burtscher, M., Pingali, K.: A gpu implementation of inclusion-based points-to analysis. In: Proceedings of the 17th ACM SIGPLAN Symposium on Principles and Practice of Parallel Programming, PPoPP 2012, pp. 107–116. ACM, New York (2012)
20. Okhotin, A.: Fast parsing for boolean grammars: A generalization of valiants algorithm. In: Gao, Y., Lu, H., Seki, S., Yu, S. (eds.) DLT 2010. LNCS, vol. 6224, pp. 340–351. Springer, Heidelberg (2010)
21. Reps, T.: On the sequential nature of interprocedural program-analysis problems. Acta Informatica 33(5), 739–757 (1996)
22. Reps, T.: Program analysis via graph reachability. Information and Software Technology 40(11-12), 701–726 (1998)
23. Reps, T., Horwitz, S., Sagiv, M.: Precise interprocedural dataflow analysis via graph reachability. In: Proceedings of the 22nd ACM SIGPLAN-SIGACT Symposium on Principles of Programming Languages, POPL 1995, pp. 49–61. ACM, New York (1995)
24. Sagiv, M., Reps, T., Horwitz, S.: Precise interprocedural dataflow analysis with applications to constant propagation. In: Mosses, P.D., Nielsen, M., Schwartzbach, M. (eds.) TAPSOFT 1995. LNCS, vol. 915, pp. 651–665. Springer, Heidelberg (1995)
25. Sridharan, M., Gopan, D., Shan, L., Bodík, R.: Demand-driven points-to analysis for java. In: Proceedings of the 20th Annual ACM SIGPLAN Conference on Object-oriented Programming, Systems, Languages, and Applications, OOPSLA 2005, pp. 59–76. ACM, New York (2005)
26. Valiant, L.G.: General context-free recognition in less than cubic time. Journal of Computer and System Sciences 10(2), 308–315 (1975)
27. Vardoulakis, D., Shivers, O.: Cfa2: A context-free approach to control-flow analysis. In: Gordon, A.D. (ed.) ESOP 2010. LNCS, vol. 6012, pp. 570–589. Springer, Heidelberg (2010)
28. Yan, D., Xu, G., Rountev, A.: Demand-driven context-sensitive alias analysis for java. In: Proceedings of the 2011 International Symposium on Software Testing and Analysis, ISSTA 2011, pp. 155–165. ACM, New York (2011)
29. Yannakakis, M.: Graph-theoretic methods in database theory. In: Proceedings of the Ninth ACM SIGACT-SIGMOD-SIGART Symposium on Principles of Database Systems, PODS 1990, pp. 230–242. ACM, New York (1990)
30. Younger, D.H.: Recognition and parsing of context-free languages in time n^3. Information and control 10(2), 189–208 (1967)
31. Yuan, H., Eugster, P.: An efficient algorithm for solving the dyck-cfl reachability problem on trees. In: Castagna, G. (ed.) ESOP 2009. LNCS, vol. 5502, pp. 175–189. Springer, Heidelberg (2009)
32. Yuster, R., Zwick, U.: Fast sparse matrix multiplication. ACM Trans. Algorithms 1(1), 2–13 (2005)
33. Zhang, Q., Lyu, M.R., Yuan, H., Su, Z.: Fast algorithms for dyck-cfl-reachability with applications to alias analysis. In: Proceedings of the 34th ACM SIGPLAN Conference on Programming Language Design and Implementation, PLDI 2013, pp. 435–446. ACM, New York (2013)
34. Zhang, Q., Xiao, X., Zhang, C., Yuan, H., Su, Z.: Efficient subcubic alias analysis for c. In: Proceedings of the 2014 ACM International Conference on Object Oriented Programming Systems, Languages & Applications, OOPSLA 2014, pp. 829–845. ACM, New York (2014)
35. Zheng, X., Rugina, R.: Demand-driven alias analysis for c. SIGPLAN Not. 43(1), 197–208 (2008)

Protocols by Default
Safe MPI Code Generation Based on Session Types

Nicholas Ng, Jose Gabriel de Figueiredo Coutinho, and Nobuko Yoshida

Imperial College London

Abstract. This paper presents a code generation framework for type-safe and deadlock-free Message Passing Interface (MPI) programs. The code generation process starts with the definition of the global topology using a protocol specification language based on parameterised multi-party session types (MPST). An MPI parallel program backbone is automatically generated from the global specification. The backbone code can then be merged with the sequential code describing the application behaviour, resulting in a complete MPI program. This merging process is fully automated through the use of an aspect-oriented compilation approach. In this way, programmers only need to supply the intended communication protocol and provide sequential code to automatically obtain parallelised programs that are guaranteed free from communication mismatch, type errors or deadlocks. The code generation framework also integrates an optimisation method that overlaps communication and computation, and can derive not only representative parallel programs with common parallel patterns (such as ring and stencil), but also distributed applications from any MPST protocols. We show that our tool generates efficient and scalable MPI applications, and improves productivity of programmers. For instance, our benchmarks involving representative parallel and application-specific patterns speed up sequential execution by up to 31 times and reduce programming effort by an average of 39%.

1 Introduction

Message Passing Interface (MPI) [25] library is the most widely used API standard for programming high performance parallel applications using the message passing paradigm. MPI is a relatively low-level programming library, and according to a survey [12] the most common MPI programming error is the communication mismatch between senders and receivers. This type of error directly leads to lost messages, communication deadlocks and subtle calculation errors.

In this work, rather than directly verifying the correctness of a given piece of MPI code, we explore a compilation approach that automates the *generation* of a communication deadlock-free and type-safe MPI program, using as inputs the sequential code defining the algorithmic behaviour of the application and a language-independent interaction protocol. Code generation using abstractions of common parallel programming patterns (also known as *algorithmic skeletons*)

B. Franke (Ed.): CC 2015, LNCS 9031, pp. 212–232, 2015.
DOI: 10.1007/978-3-662-46663-6_11

is a well-developed field, and [15,31] survey a number of existing tools and frameworks supporting high-level structured parallel programming. More recently, this code generation technique has been used to teach undergraduate students parallel programming, and is reported to reduce programming errors [14,42], showing how accessible the technique is.

Our code generation framework is based on a novel approach which, in addition to common parallel programming patterns, supports general or application-specific communication patterns. The framework is driven by a theoretically-founded protocol language called Pabble [27]. Pabble is a protocol language based on the theory of multiparty session types (MPST) [19]. It is designed for expressing indexed and grouped processes interaction patterns in parallel algorithms based on the theories in [11], and distributed applications including web services [26].

Writing a program using the Pabble language starts with the specification of the *global* communication protocol, which is translated automatically to endpoint protocols. The endpoint protocols are localised projection versions of the global protocol. Our previous work type-checks C distributed parallel applications written with a customised API [28] or MPI [27] by a programmer against endpoint protocols. This paper presents the first session-based approach to automatically guarantee (by construction), type-safety, communication-safety (i.e. no communication mismatch) and deadlock-freedom for MPI applications.

Because of the expressiveness of parameterised MPST [10,11], our compilation framework can support parallel algorithms included in the Dwarf benchmarks [2] (i.e. algorithmic methods that capture common pattern of communication and computation). We can generate safe MPI programs using not only fixed topologies such as pipelines or stencils, but also any well-formed Pabble protocols. As a portable standard, MPI is being adapted as a common interface to different kinds of programming models, including FPGAs [32], stream programming [23] and fault tolerant [13]. General MPI applications exhibit more complex communication patterns than well-known, connected topologies found in scientific computing. The generality of MPST can provide a more flexible pattern programming approach based on code generation. In addition, structured session types can guide the optimisation process using MPI immediate operators, without compromising the safety properties of the original code. Through our Pabble-based workflow, snippets of sequential code are automatically combined to generate a distributed memory parallel application, exploiting the parallelism of multiple nodes and increasing programming productivity and reusability: the use of design patterns means that programmers do not need to write an application from scratch, and can reuse the same protocols and/or sequential code according to their needs.

Pabble Code Generation Workflow. Fig. 1 shows the overview of our approach. (a) Programmers decide which Pabble communication protocol to use for code generation: (a-1) If a standard protocol such as a ring, stencil or matrix is used, programmers can reuse a protocol from the Pabble repository so

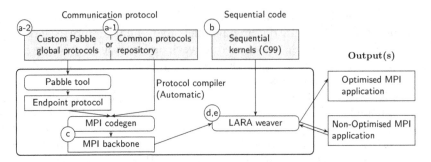

Fig. 1. Pabble-based code generation workflow. Shaded boxes indicate user inputs

that they do not have to write Pabble, or **(a-2)** If programmers wish to use a more specific protocol which is not provided in Pabble repository, they can write the intended protocol. In this case, the tool automatically checks whether the protocol is well-formed or not; **(b)** As the second step, the programmer needs to write sequential computation code (kernels) in C99 and annotate their code with pragmas to link the kernels with the protocol specification; **(c)** The tool generates an MPI backbone from the Pabble protocol in **(a)**; **(d)** The kernels are automatically injected into the MPI backbone using the LARA [6] weaver, an aspect-oriented compilation tool, resulting in a complete MPI application **(e)** As part of the merging project, the LARA weaver can optionally perform optimisations against previously generated source code, such as overlapping communication and computation, to improve the runtime performance.

Challenges. The technical challenges of this work include bridging the gap between the high-level Pabble specification describing the global communication protocol, and the low-level C kernels and MPI calls that realise computation and communication, requiring several implementation details to be automatically inferred. We are cautious to avoid unnecessary assumptions between the Pabble specification and the C code defining the behaviour of the application, by providing a simple and minimally intrusive interface for their interoperation. The use of session types to define communication patterns separately from computation means that data-dependent and non-deterministic protocols are not supported, but sufficient enough to generate safe representative algorithms (see Section 5).

Outline. Section 2 outlines the application development workflow through a running example; Section 3 explains the first of two stages of compilation, the generation of MPI backbone from protocol; Section 4 explains the second stage of compilation, merging the backbone with kernels and optimisation; Section 5 gives a number of case studies including scientific computations and flexible grid computations, and performance evaluation of our framework showing the flexibility and productivity. The Pabble homepage [30] includes the code generation framework information, including the Pabble library and benchmark results.

```
1    const N = 1..max;
2    global protocol Stencil(role P[1..N][1..N]) {
3      rec Steps {
4        LeftToRight(T) from P[r:1..N][c:1..N-1] to P[r][c+1];
5        RightToLeft(T) from P[r:1..N][c:2..N] to P[r][c-1];
6        UpToDown(T)    from P[r:1..N-1][c:1..N] to P[r+1][c];
7        DownToUp(T)    from P[r:2..N][c:1..N] to P[r-1][c];
8        continue Steps;
9      }
10   }
```

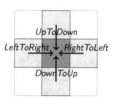

Listing 1. Pabble protocol for 5-point stencil

Fig. 2. Messages received by a process in a stencil protocol

2   Application Development Workflow

2.1   Interaction Protocols with the **Pabble** Protocol Language

Pabble [27], or Parameterised Scribble [33],represents interaction types as parametric protocols, such that the protocols are scalable over the number of participants (i.e. compute nodes) given as parameters.

Listing 1 presents an example of a Pabble protocol which defines a 5-point stencil design pattern, where $N \times N$ processes are arranged in a 2-dimensional grid, and each participant exchanges messages with its 4 neighbours (except for edge participants). A Pabble protocol consists of a preamble and a definition. Line 1 defines N to be in the range between 1 and max, where max corresponds to the maximum integer. The concrete value of N is known only at run time, and stays constant in the duration of the instantiated protocol. N can be used in the protocol body as indices for role definition, which is the mechanism used by Pabble to support parameterised protocols. The protocol definition starts from Line 2, with the keywords `global protocol` followed by the protocol name Stencil. The parameters to the protocols are the role declarations, `role P[1..N][1..N]`, which declares a 2-dimensional role P, with $N \times N$ participants. Individual participants can be addressed by integer indices, e.g. P[1][1], similar to an array access. A valid Pabble protocol ensures that all participants referenced in the protocol body are declared and within the index bounds ([27] provides a detailed list of well-formed conditions). For example, the following protocol is *not* well-formed because participants P[5] and P[i+1] are undefined when i is 3.

```
1    global protocol BadProtocol(role P[1..3]) {        Non well-formed protocol
2      Msg(T) from P[1] to P[5];
3      Msg(T) from P[i:1..3] to P[i+1]; }
```

Pabble protocols provide a guarantee of communication safety and deadlock freedom between participants in the protocol; this guarantee also extends to scalable protocols, where the number of participants are not known statically, and well-formed conditions ensure that the indexing of participants does not go beyond specified bounds. A Pabble protocol describes (1) the structured message interaction patterns of the application, and (2) the control-flow elements, excluding the logic related to actual computation, so that a Pabble protocol defining a parallel design pattern can be reused for different applications (see Section 5).

We provide a repository of common **Pabble** protocols describing common interaction patterns used by parallel applications. The `Stencil` protocol in Listing 1 is one example, and the other patterns in the repository include *ring pipeline, scatter-gather, master-worker* and *all-to-all.*

Our protocol body starts with a `rec` block, which stands for recursion, and is assigned with the label `Steps`. The recursion block does not specify the loop condition because a **Pabble** protocol only describes the interaction *structure* while implementation details are abstracted away. In the body of the recursion, we have 4 lines of interaction statements (Line 4-7), one for each direction. Interaction statements describe the sending of a message from one participant to another. For example, in Line 4 a message with label `LeftToRight` and with a generic payload type T is sent from `P[r:1..N][c:1..N-1]` to `P[r][c+1]`. The index expression `r:1..N` means that r is bound and iterated through the list of values in the range $1..N$, so the line encapsulates $N \times (N - 1)$ individual interaction statements. The other interaction statements in Listing 1 can be similarly interpreted. Fig. 2 shows the messages received from neighbours for participant `P[2][2]` in a 3×3 grid, which is defined in the protocol as `role P[1..3][1..3]`.

2.2   Computation Kernels

Computation kernels are C functions that describe the algorithmic behaviour of the application. Each message interaction defined in **Pabble** (e.g. `Label(T) from Sender to Receiver`) can be associated to a kernel by its label (e.g. `Label`).

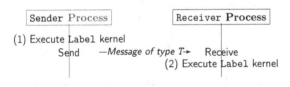

The figure on the left shows how kernels are invoked in a message-passing statement between two processes named **Sender** and **Receiver** respectively. Since a message interaction statement involves two participants (e.g. **Sender** and **Receiver**), the kernel serves two purposes: (1) produce a message for sending and (2) consume a message after it has been received. The two parts of the kernel are defined in the same function, but runs on the sending process and the receiving process respectively. The kernels are top-level functions and do not send or receive messages directly through MPI calls. Instead, messages are passed between kernels and the MPI backbone (derived from the **Pabble** protocol) via a queue API: in order to send a message, the producer kernel (e.g. (1)) of the sending process enqueues the message to its send queue; and a received message can be accessed by a consumer kernel (e.g. (2)), dequeuing from its receive queue. This allows the decoupling between computation (as defined by the kernels) and communication (as described in the MPI backbone).

Writing a kernel. We now explain how a user writes a kernel file, which contains the set of kernel functions related to a **Pabble** protocol for an application. A minimal kernel file must define a variable `meta` of `meta_t` type, which contains the process id (i.e. `meta.pid`), total number of spawned processes (i.e. `meta.nprocs`) and a callback function that takes one parameter (message label) and returns the send/receive size of message payload (i.e. `unsigned int meta.bufsize(int label)`). The `meta.buflen` function returns the buffer size for the MPI primitives based on the label given, as a lookup table to manage the buffer sizes centrally. Process id and total number of spawned processes will be populated automatically by the backbone code generated. The kernel file includes the definitions of the kernel functions, annotated with pragmas, associating the kernels with message labels. The kernels can use file (i.e. `static`) scope variables for local data storage. Our stencil kernel file starts with the following declarations for local data and `meta`:

```
1   typedef struct { double* values; int rows; int cols; } local_data_t;    Kernel header
2   static local_data_t *local;
3
4   unsigned int buflen(int label) { return local->rows - 2; } // local rows - halo rows/cols
5
6   meta_t meta = {/*pid*/0, /*nprocs*/1, MPI_COMM_NULL, &buflen};
```

Initialisation. Most parallel applications require explicit partitioning of input data. In these cases, the programmer writes a kernel function for partitioning, such that each participant has a subset of the input data. Input data are usually partitioned with a layout similar to the layout of the participants. In our stencil example where processes are organised in a 2D grid, we partition the input data in a 2D-grid of sub-matrices. The sub-matrices are calculated for each of the process using the `meta.pid` and `meta.nprocs` which are known at runtime when the kernel functions are called. Below is an example of the main part of the initialisation function.

```
6   #pragma pabble kernel Init                                     Kernel: Init
7   void init(int id, const char *filename)
8   { FILE *fp = fopen(filename, "r");
9     local = (local_data_t *)malloc(sizeof(local_data_t));
10    local->rows = 0; local->cols = 0; local->values = NULL;
11    ...
12    int proc_per_row = sqrt(meta.nprocs); // Participant per row
13    int proc_per_col = sqrt(meta.nprocs); // Participant per column
14    int row_offset = (meta.pid / proc_per_row) * row_size; // Start row of data
15    int col_offset = (meta.pid % proc_per_col) * col_size; // Start column of data
16    ...
17    if (within_range) { fscanf(fp, "%f", &local->values[i]); } // Copy data to local
18    ...
19    fclose(fp); }
```

Computation and Queues. The kernels are `void` functions with at least one parameter, which is the label of the kernel. Inside the kernel, no MPI primitive should be used to perform message passing. Data received from another participant or data that need to be sent to another participant can be accessed using a receive queue and send queue. Consider the following kernel for the label `LeftToRight` in the stencil example:

```
20  #pragma pabble kernel LeftToRight                        Kernel: LeftToRight
21  void accumulate_LeftToRight(int id)
22  { // Sender sends right col of submatrix and Recver receives left col.
23    if (!pabble_recvq_isempty() && pabble_recvq_top_id() == id) {
24      tmp[HALO_LEFT] = (double *)pabble_recvq_dequeue(); // Get received value.
25    } else { tmp[HALO_RIGHT] = (double *)calloc(meta.buflen(id), sizeof(double));
26      /* populate tmp[HALO_RIGHT] */
27      pabble_sendq_enqueue(id, tmp[HALO_RIGHT]); // Put buffer to be sent
28    }
29  }
```

Each kernel has access to a send and receive queue local to the whole process, which holds pointers to the buffer to be sent and the buffer containing the received messages, respectively. The queues are the only mechanism for kernels to interface the MPI backbone. The simplest kernel is one that forwards incoming messages from the receive queue directly to the send queue. In the above function, when the kernel function is called, it either consumes a message from the receive queue if it is not empty (i.e. after a receive), or produce a message for the send queue (i.e. before a send).

```
1   int main(int argc, char *argv[])                   Generated MPI Backbone
2   { MPI_Init(&argc, &argv);
3     MPI_Comm_rank(MPI_COMM_WORLD, &meta.pid);
4     MPI_Comm_size(MPI_COMM_WORLD, &meta.nprocs);
5   #pragma pabble type T
6     typedef void T; ⇒ typedef double T;
7     MPI_Datatype MPI_T; ⇒ MPI_Datatype MPI_T = MPI_DOUBLE;
8
9     T *bufLeftToRight_r, *bufLeftToRight_s;
10    /** Other buffer declarations **/
11    /** Definitions of cond0, cond1, ... **/
12  #pragma pabble predicate Steps
13    while (1) { ⇒ while (iter())
14      if (cond0) { /*if P[i:0..(N-1)][j:1..(N-1)]*/
15        bufLeftToRight_r = (T *)calloc(meta.buflen(LeftToRight), sizeof(T));
16        MPI_Irecv(bufLeftToRight_r, meta.buflen(LeftToRight), MPI_T, /*P[i][(j-1)]*/...);
17        MPI_Wait(&req[0], &stat[0]);
18        pabble_recvq_enqueue(LeftToRight, bufLeftToRight_r);
19  #pragma pabble kernel LeftToRight ⇒ accumulate_LeftToRight(LeftToRight);
20      }
21      if (cond1) { /*if P[i:0..(N-1)][j:0..(N-2)]*/
22  #pragma pabble kernel LeftToRight ⇒ accumulate_LeftToRight(LeftToRight);
23        bufLeftToRight = pabble_sendq_dequeue();
24        MPI_Isend(bufLeftToRight, meta.buflen(LeftToRight), MPI_T, /*P[i][(j+1)]*/...);
25        MPI_Wait(&req[1], &stat[1]);
26        free(bufLeftToRight);
27      }
28      /** similarly for RightToLeft, UpToDown and DownToUp **/
29      MPI_Finalize();
30    }
31    return EXIT_SUCCESS; }
```

Listing 2. Sequential stencil code using kernels

Kernels can have extra parameters. For example, in the `init` function above, `filename` is a parameter that is not specified by the protocol (i.e. `Init()`). When such functions are called, all extra parameters are supplied by command-line arguments in the final generated MPI application.

In the next two sections we describe: (1) the compilation process to generate the MPI backbone and (2) the merging process in which we combine the MPI backbone and the kernels.

3   Compilation Step 1: Protocol to MPI Backbone

This section describes the MPI backbone code generation from Pabble protocols. First the generated MPI backbone code of the running example is shown, then the translation rules from Pabble statements to MPI code are explained along with details of how to map Pabble participants into MPI processes.

3.1   MPI Backbone Generation from Stencil Protocol

Based on the Pabble protocol (e.g. Listing 1), our code generation framework generates an *MPI backbone* code (e.g. Listing 2). First it automatically generates *endpoint protocols* from a global protocol as an intermediate step to make MPI code generation more straightforward. For reference, the endpoint protocol of the Stencil protocol is listed in [22]

An MPI backbone is a C99 program with boilerplate code for initialising and finalising the MPI environment of a typical MPI application (Line 2-4 and 29 respectively), and MPI primitive calls for message passing (e.g. MPI_Isend /MPI_Irecv). Therefore the MPI backbone realises the interaction between participants as specified in the Pabble protocol, without supporting any specific application functionality. The backbone has three kinds of #pragma annotations as placeholders for kernel functions, types and program logic. The annotations are explained in Section 4. The boxed code in Listing 2 represents how the backbone are converted to code that calls the kernel functions in the MPI program.

In Lines 5 and 6, *generic type* T and MPI_T are defined datatypes for C and MPI respectively. T and MPI_T are refined later when an exact type (e.g. int or composite struct type) is known with the kernels.

Following the type declarations, are other variable declarations including the buffers (Line 9), and their allocation and deallocation are managed by the backbone. They are generated as guarded blocks of code, which come directly from the endpoint protocol. Line 14-20 shows a guarded receive that correspond to if P[i:0..(N-1)][j:1..(N-1)] LeftToRight(T)from P[i][j-1] in the protocol and Line 21-27 for if P[i:0..(N-1)][j:0..(N-2)] LeftToRight(T)to P[i][j+1].

3.2   MPI Backbone Generation from Pabble

Table 1 and 2 show how each Pabble construct is translated into MPI blocks for statements that involve P2P interactions and control-flow respectively. The online appendix [22] lists additional cases, the internal iteration and choice constructs).

1. Interaction. An interaction statement in a Pabble protocol is projected in the endpoint protocol as two parts: receive and send.

The first line of the endpoint protocol shows a receive statement, written in Pabble as if P[dstId] from P[srcId]. The statement is translated to a block of MPI code in 3 parts. First, memory is dynamically allocated for the receive buffer (Line 2), the buffer is of Type and its size fetched from the function meta.bufsize(Label). The function is defined in the kernels and returns the size of message for the given message label. Next, the program calls MPI_Recv to receive a message (Line 3) from participant P[srcRole] in Pabble. role_P(srcIdx) is a lookup macro from the generated backbone to return the process id of the sender. Finally, the received message, stored in the receive buffer buf, is enqueued into a global receive queue with pabble_recvq_enqueue() (Line 4), followed by the pragma indicating a kernel of label Label should be inserted. The block of receive code is guarded by an if-condition, which executes the above block of MPI code only if the current process id matches the receiver process id.

The next line in the endpoint protocol is a send statement, converse of the receive statement, written as if P[srcIdx] Label(Type) to P[dstIdx]. The MPI code begins with the pragma annotation, then dequeuing the global send queue with pabble_sendq_dequeue() and sends the dequeued buffer with MPI_Send. After this, the send buffer, which is no longer needed, is deallocated. The block of send

Table 1. Pabble interaction statements and their corresponding code

1. Interaction   Global Protocol   Projected Endpoint Protocol

Label(Type) from P[srcIdx] to P[dstIdx];

```
                                             if P[dstIdx] Label(Type) from P[srcIdx];
                                             if P[srcIdx] Label(Type) to P[dstIdx];
1  if (meta.pid == role_P(dstIdx)) {              Generated MPI Backbone
2     buf = (Type *)calloc(meta.bufsize(Label), sizeof(Type));
3     MPI_Recv(buf, meta.bufsize(Label), MPI_Type, role_P(srcIdx), Label, ...);
4     pabble_recvq_enqueue(Label, buf);
5     #pragma pabble kernel Label
6  }
7  if (meta.pid == role_P(srcIdx)) {
8     #pragma pabble kernel Label
9     buf = pabble_recvq_dequeue();
10    MPI_Send(buf, meta.bufsize(Label), MPI_Type, dstIdx, Label, ...); free(buf);
11 }
```

2. Parallel interaction   Projected Endpoint Protocol

Global Protocol

```
                                             if P[i:2..N] Label(Type) from P[i-1];
Label(Type) from P[i:1..N-1] to P[i+1];      if P[i:1..N-1] Label(Type) to P[i+1];
1  if (role_P(2)<=meta.pid&&meta.pid<=role_P(N)) {   Generated MPI Backbone
2     buf = (Type *)calloc(meta.bufsize(Label), sizeof(Type));
3     MPI_Recv(..., prevRank = meta.pid-1, Label, ...);
4     pabble_recvq_enqueue(Label, buf);
5  #pragma pabble kernel Label
6  }
7
8  if (role_P(1)<=meta.pid&&meta.pid<=role_P(N-1)) {
9  #pragma pabble kernel Label
10    buf = pabble_sendq_dequeue();
11    MPI_Send(..., nextRank = meta.pid+1, Label, ...); free(buf);
12 }
```

code is similarly guarded by an if-condition to ensure it is only executed by the sender. By allocating memory before receive and deallocating memory after send, the backbone manages memory for the user systematically.

2. Parallel interaction. A Pabble parallel interaction statement is written as `Label(Type)from P[i:1..N-1] to P[i+1]`, meaning all processes with indices from 1 to `N-1` send a message to its next neighbour. `P[1]` initiates sending to `P[2]`, and `P[2]` receives from `P[1]` then sends a message to `P[3]`, and so on. As shown in the endpoint protocol which encapsulates the behaviour of all `P[1.. N]` processes, the statement is realised in the endpoint as conditional receive followed by a conditional send, similar to ordinary interaction. The difference is the use of a range of process ids in the condition, and *relative* indices in the sender/receiver indices. The generated MPI code makes use of expression with `meta.pid` (current process id) to calculate the relative index.

3. Iteration and 4. For-loop. `rec` and `foreach` are iteration statements. Specifically `rec` is recursion, where the iteration conditions are not specified explicitly in the protocol, and translates to `while`-loops. The loop condition is the same in all processes. This may otherwise be known as *collective loops*. The loop generated by `rec` has a `#pragma pabble predicate` annotation, so that the loop condition can be later replaced by a kernel (see Section 4).

The `foreach` construct, on the other hand, specifies a counting loop, iterating over the integer values in the range specified in the protocol from the lower bound (e.g. 0) to the upper bound value (e.g. `N-1`). This construct can be naturally translated into a C `for`-loop.

5. Scatter, 6. Gather and 7. All-to-all. Collective operations are written in Pabble as multicast or multi-receive message interactions. While it is possible to convert these interactions into multiple blocks of MPI code following the rules in Table 2, we take advantage of the efficient and expressive collective primitives in MPI. Table 3 shows the conversion of Pabble statements into MPI collective operations. We describe only the most generic collective operations, i.e. `MPI_Scatter`, `MPI_Gather` and `MPI_Alltoall`.

Translating collective operations from Pabble to MPI considers both global Pabble protocol statements and endpoint protocol. If a statement involves the `__All` role as sender, receiver or both, it is a collective operation. Table 3 shows that translated blocks of MPI code do not use `if`-statements to distinguish between sending and receiving processes. This is because collective primitives

Table 2. Pabble statements and their corresponding code

3. Iteration	4. For-loop
Global/Endpoint Protocol	Global/Endpoint Protocol
`rec LoopName { ... continue LoopName; }`	`foreach (i:0..N-1) { ... }`
Generated MPI Backbone	Generated MPI Backbone

```
1
2   #pragma pabble predicate LoopName
3   while (1) {
4      ... }
```

```
1
2   for (int i=0; i<=N-1; i++) {
3      ...
4   }
```

Table 3. MPI collective operations and their corresponding Pabble statements

---

5. Scatter   Global Protocol

```
  Label(Type) from P[rootRole] to __All;
1 rbuf = (Type *)calloc(meta.buflen(Label), sizeof(Type)); Generated MPI Backbone
2 #pragma pabble kernel Label
3 sbuf = pabble_sendq_dequeue();
4 MPI_Scatter(sbuf, meta.buflen(Label), MPI_Type,
5              rbuf, meta.buflen(Label), MPI_Type, role_P(rootRole), ...);
6 pabble_recvq_enqueue(Label, rbuf);
7 #pragma pabble kernel Label
8 free(sbuf);
```

---

6. Gather   Global Protocol

```
  Label(Type) from __All to P[rootRole];
1 rbuf = (Type *)calloc(meta.buflen(Label)*meta.nprocs,    Generated MP Backbone
2              sizeof(Type));
3 #pragma pabble kernel Label
4 sbuf = pabble_sendq_dequeue();
5 MPI_Gather(sbuf, meta.buflen(Label), MPI_Type,
6             rbuf, meta.buflen(Label), MPI_Type, role_P(rootRole), ...);
7 pabble_recvq_enqueue(Label, rbuf);
8 #pragma pabble kernel Label
9 free(sbuf);
```

---

7. All-to-All   Global Protocol

```
  Label(Type) from __All to __All;
1 rbuf = (Type *)calloc(meta.buflen(Label)*meta.nprocs,    Generated MPI Backbone
2              sizeof(Type));
3 #pragma pabble kernel Label
4 sbuf = pabble_sendq_dequeue();
5 MPI_Alltoall(sbuf, meta.buflen(Label), MPI_Type,
6               rbuf, meta.buflen(Label), MPI_Type, ...);
7 pabble_recvq_enqueue(Label, rbuf);
8 #pragma pabble kernel Label
9 free(sbuf);
```

---

in MPI are executed by *both* the senders and the receivers, and the runtime
decides whether it is a sender or a receiver by inspecting the `rootRole` parameter
(which is a process rank) in the `MPI_Scatter` or `MPI_Gather` call. Otherwise the
conversion is similar to their point-to-point counterparts in Table 2.

Process scaling. In addition to the translation of Pabble statements into
MPI code, we also define the process mapping between a Pabble protocol and a
Pabble-generated MPI program. Typical usage of MPI programs can be parame-
terised on the number of spawned processes at runtime via program arguments.
Hence, given a Pabble protocol with *scalable* roles, we describe the rules below
to map (parameterised) roles into MPI processes.

A Pabble protocol for MPI code generation can contain any number of constant
values (e.g. `const M = 10`), which are converted in the backbone as C constants
(e.g. `#define M 10`), but it can use at most one *scalable constant* [27]. A scalable
constant is defined as:

```
const N = 1..max;
```

The constant can then be used for defining parameterised roles, and used in
indices of parameterised message interaction statements. For example, to declare
an $N \times N$ role P, we write in the protocol:

```
global protocol P (role P[1..N][1..N])
```

which results in a total of N^2 participants in the protocol, but N is not known until execution time. MPI backbone code generated based on this Pabble protocol uses N throughout. Since the only parameter in a scalable MPI program is its size (i.e. number of spawned processes), the following code is generated in the backbone to calculate, from size, the value of C local variable N:

```
MPI_Comm_size(MPI_COMM_WORLD, &meta.nprocs); // # of processes
int N = (int)pow(meta.nprocs, 1/2); // N = sqrt(meta.nprocs)
```

4 Compilation Step 2: Aspect-Oriented Design-Flow

This section focuses on the final stage of our code generation framework, which merges two input components to derive the complete MPI program: (1) the communication safe MPI backbone derived automatically from a Pabble protocol (Section 3.1), and (2) the user supplied kernels capturing application functionality.

The MPI backbone is automatically annotated with pragma statements referencing all the labels defined in the protocol; the programmer, on the other hand, must manually annotate each kernel with the corresponding label. This way, our code generation framework can automatically merge both components.

Our approach takes a similar path as OpenMP [8] and OpenACC [41], which parallelise sequential programs using non-invasive #pragma annotations. The difference is that while OpenMP operates on a shared memory architecture model and OpenACC operates via a host-directed execution (co-processor) model, our approach allows applications to target customised platform topologies defined by Pabble, since MPI works on both shared and distributed memory platforms.

LARA language. To support an automated merging process, our programming framework uses an aspect-oriented programming (AOP) language called LARA [6]. As far as we know, LARA is the only aspect-oriented approach that targets all stages of a development process allowing static code analysis and manipulation (e.g. source-level translation and code optimisation), toolchain execution (e.g. for design-space exploration) and application deployment (e.g. to extract dynamic behaviour). These various tasks, which are often performed manually and independently, can be described in a unified way as LARA aspects. These aspects can then drive LARA *weavers* to apply a particular strategy in a systematic and automated way. In our code generation framework, we use LARA's ability to analyse and manipulate C code to automate the merging process between the MPI backbone and the kernels sources (Section 4.1), and also to further optimise the MPI code by overlapping communication and computation (Section 4.2).

4.1 Merging Process

To combine the MPI backbone with the kernels, our aspect-oriented design-flow inserts kernel function calls into the MPI backbone code. The insertion points are realised as #pragmas in the MPI backbone code, generated from the input protocol as placeholders where functional code is inserted. There are multiple types of annotations whose syntax is given as:

```
#pragma pabble [<entry point type>] <entry point id> [(param0, ...)]
```

where *entry point type* is one of kernel, type or predicate, and *entry point id* is an alphanumeric identifier.

Kernel Function. #pragma pabble kernel Label defines the insertion point of kernel functions in the MPI backbone code. Label is the label of the inter-action statement, e.g. Label(T) from Sender to Receiver, and the annotation is replaced by the kernel function associated to the label Label. Programmers must use the same pragma to manually annotate the implementation of the kernel function. The first row in Table 4 shows an example.

Datatypes. #pragma pabble type TypeName annotates a generic type name in the backbone, and also annotates the concrete definition of the datatype in the kernels. In the second row of Table 4, the C datatype T is defined to be void since the protocol does not have any information to realise the type. The kernel defines T to be a concrete type of double, and hence our tool transforms the typedef in the backbone into double and infers the corresponding MPI_Datatype (MPI derived datatypes) to the built-in MPI integer primitive type, i.e. MPI_Datatype MPI_T = MPI_DOUBLE. Our tool also supports generating MPI datatypes for structures of primitive types, e.g. struct { int x, int y, double m } is transformed to its MPI-equivalent datatype.

Conditionals. #pragma pabble predicate Label is a pragma for annotating predicates, e.g. loop conditions or if-conditions, in the backbone. Since a Pabble communication protocol (and transitively, the MPI backbone) does not specify a loop condition, the default loop condition is 1, i.e. always true. This annotation introduces a way to insert a conditional expression defined as a kernel function. It precedes the while-loop, as shown in the third row of Table 4, to label the loop with the name Label. The kernel function that defines expressions must use the same annotation as the backbone, e.g. #pragma pabble predicate Label. After the merge, this kernel function is called when the loop condition is evaluated.

Table 4. Annotations in backbone and kernel

	Generated MPI backbone	User supplied kernel	Merged code
Kernel function	#pragma pabble kernel Label	#pragma pabble kernel Label void kernel_func(int label) { ... }	kernel_func(Label);
Datatypes	#pragma pabble type T typedef void T; MPI_Datatype MPI_T;	#pragma pabble type T typedef double T;	typedef double T; MPI_Datatype MPI_T = MPI_DOUBLE;
Conditionals	#pragma pabble predicate Cond while (1) { ... }	#pragma pabble predicate Cond int condition() { ... return bool; }	while (condition()) { ... }

4.2   Performance Optimisation for Overlapping Communication and Computation by MPI Immediate Operators

When designing a protocol with a session-based approach such as Pabble protocol, the resulting MPI backbone guarantees communication safety, i.e. the structures of interactions between the processes are compatible. However, that does not necessarily guarantee the most efficient communication pattern. For example the pipeline Pabble statement T() from P[i:0..N-1] to P[i+1] results in a communication safe pattern of Receive-Send for P[1] to P[N]. The protocol implies there is a dependency between the received message and the send message, hence each process in the pipeline must wait for the messages sent by processes up the pipeline, before they can start sending a message to processes down the pipeline. This is not optimal because the stall time between the beginning of the pipeline and when the first message is received is a waste of CPU resources. Often parallel applications can be modified such that the dependencies within the same iteration are removed, so the message passing can start sending straight away and overlap with receive using *asynchronous messaging mode*.

The use of asynchronous communication is dependent on the kernel functionality and how message dependencies must be handled. For this reason, programmers can use the **async** directive when annotating their kernels, e.g. **#pragma pabble async kernel LABEL**, in order to trigger this optimisation.

The LARA aspect-oriented weaver transforms the generated code without changing the ordering of the MPI message passing primitives, and hence preserves the communication safety guarantees of the MPI backbone.

This optimisation relies on the placement of MPI's immediate communication primitives, which is made up of two parts: (1) a primitive call (MPI_Isend or MPI_Irecv) to initiate the message transfer which returns immediately and after which the buffer should not be accessed, and a (2) second primitive call (MPI_Wait) to block and wait for the transfer to complete. Between the initial call and the wait, the application can perform computation in parallel with the message transfer to realise the communication-computation overlap.

The optimisation overlaps the computation which generates results to be sent in the following iteration and the communication of sending and receiving results of previous iteration to and from a neighbouring process. Since all computations are executed in parallel, and the communication overlaps with the computation, we achieve a speed-up for the parallel application over the sequential version of the same application.

Below we show an example before the optimisation (left) and after the optimisation (right) where the MPI_Wait is issued as late as possible:

```
1  if (cond) {                  Original   1  if (cond) {                      Optimised
2  #pragma pabble Label                    2    buffer = pabble_sendq_dequeue();
3    buffer = pabble_sendq_dequeue();      3    MPI_Isend(buffer, ..., request); }
4    MPI_Send(buffer, ...);                4    ...
5    free(buffer);                         5  if (cond) {
6  }                                       6  #pragma pabble Label
                                           7    MPI_Wait(request); free(buffer); }
```

Note that our transformation preserves the ordering of communication defined in the unoptimised backbone. The following presents an example that splits an ordinary MPI receive/send as in the `Stencil` example into a set of statements that interleave asynchronous receive/send.

```
1  MPI_Recv(...);          Original    1  MPI_Irecv(..., request1);          Optimised
2  MPI_Send(...);                      2  MPI_Isend(..., request2);
                                       3  /* Interleave with computation */
                                       4  MPI_Wait(request1, ...);
                                       5  MPI_Wait(request2, ...);
```

Since `MPI_Wait` is an operation that blocks until the send and receive buffers can be accessed, we can ensure that `MPI_Isend(..., request1)` is completed before `MPI_Irecv(..., request2)` even if the transmission of data for the latter primitive is finished before the former.

5 Evaluation

In this section, we first demonstrate that our protocols can automatically generate MPI programs using different parallel patterns, including application-specific patterns (flexibility); and save efforts in the development of MPI applications (productivity and reusability). Then we measure the performance and efficiency of the generated MPI programs.

5.1 Productivity and Reusability

The table below presents a comparison of different parallel algorithms developed using our approach. The second and third columns show the input `Pabble` protocol and whether it is available in our protocol repository. The Dwarf column denotes the categorisations of parallel computational and structural patterns defined in [2]; SG stands for 'Structured Grid', PM is 'Particle Methods'; DM is 'Dense Matrix'; and S is 'Spectral (FFT)'. The next three columns show lines of code in the input `Pabble` protocol, the generated backbone, and the input user kernel file. The final column shows the effort ratio of user written code against the total ($\frac{Kernels}{Backbone+Kernels}$ for protocols in repository or $\frac{Kernels+Pabble}{Backbone+Kernels}$). The higher the ratio, relatively more effort is needed to write an equivalent program from scratch.

	Protocol	Repo.	Dwarf	Pabble	Backbone	Kernels	Effort
heateq [3]	stencil	✓	SG	15	154	335	0.69
nbody	ring	✓	PM	15	93	228	0.71
wordcount	scatter-gather	✓		8	76	176	0.70
adpredictor [17]	scatter-gather	✓		8	76	182	0.71
montecarlo	scatter-gather	✓		8	76	70	0.48
montecarlo-mw	master-worker	✓	.	10	82	70	0.46
LEsovler [27]	wrapround mesh		SG	15	132	208	0.66
matvec	custom [29]		DM	15	130	117	0.41
fft64	6-step butterfly		S	11	64	134	0.68

heateq is an implementation of the heat equation based on [3], and uses the stencil protocol in our running example. nbody is a 2D N-body simulation implemented with a ring topology; it is optimised with the asynchronous messaging mode described in Section 4.2. wordcount is a simple application that counts the number of occurrences of each word in a given text, implemented using the scatter-gather pattern. adpredictor is an implementation of Microsoft's AdPredictor [17] algorithm for calculated click-through rate, also implemented in the same scatter-gather pattern, but with a different set of kernel functions. LEsolver is a linear equation solver parallelised with a custom wraparound mesh topology outlined in [27]. montecarlo is Monte-Carlo π simulation, implemented with two different patterns, scatter-gather and master-worker. A remarkable difference between the two patterns is that the former uses collective operations and all processes are involved in the main calculation, whereas with the master-worker pattern workers are coordinated by a central master process by P2P communication that does not perform the main calculation. Note that the kernels used for both implementations are the same (except with different kernel labels). matvec is matrix-vector multiplication parallelised using the MatVec protocol outlined in [29]. fft64 is an implementation of the Cooley-Tukey FFT between 64 processes using 6 steps of butterfly exchange between pairs of processes.

Reusability. Both our implementations of wordcount and adpredictor use the scatter-gather pattern. They exemplify the advantages of pattern programming – common parallel patterns are collected and stored in our protocol repository, and they are maintained separately from the user kernels so new parallel applications can be constructed by writing new kernels only. In addition to reusable protocols, some kernels can also be reused with different protocols. The scenarios for kernels to be reused are less common since partitioning of input data are usually dependent on the protocol, and the kernels are designed to be parallelised with a single protocol. For example, we show two montecarlo implementations, one with scatter-gather and another with master-worker pattern. Since the algorithm is embarrassingly parallel and does not depend on input data, both implementations can share the same kernel.

Our results show that our workflow saves development and debugging efforts for MPI parallel applications, especially for novice parallel programmers. The user can focus on developing and maintaining the functional behaviour of their application, knowing that the merging of updated kernels and the respective MPI backbones are correct.

5.2   Performance

We evaluate our approach with 4 parallel applications which uses 3 different Pabble protocols. All implementations are evaluated on cx1[1], a general purpose multi-core cluster, and compiled with icc with optimisation level -03, and tested using Intel's MPI library.

---

[1] http://www.imperial.ac.uk/ict/services/hpc/facilities

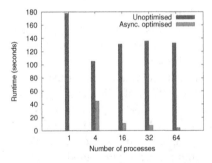

Fig. 3. N-body simulation (nbody)

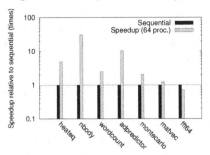

Fig. 4. Linear Equation Solver (LEsolver)

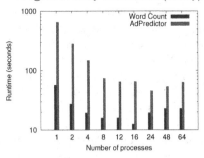

Fig. 5. Word Count (wordcount) and Ad-Predictor (adpredictor)

Fig. 6. Parallelisation speedup

In Fig. 3 we compare the performance of nbody with and without asynchronous optimisation described in Section 4.2. The optimisation overlaps the main calculation with the communication, and the results show significant improvements over the unoptimised version. Fig. 4 presents the runtime performance of LEsolver which uses a custom wraparound mesh protocol with asynchronous optimisation. In comparison with nbody, the optimisation effect on LEsolver has less impact. This is partly because the asynchronous kernel implemented by nbody is more complex than the kernel implemented by LEsolver, so the time spent on communication is dominant. The asynchronous kernel in LEsolver also represents a smaller proportion of the total computations, hence it has the less effect on the overall runtime.

Fig. 5 shows the results of two implementations, wordcount and adpredictor, both of which use the scatter-gather pattern and a different set of kernels. They follow a similar trend in scalability, which is dependent on the size of the input.

Fig. 6 compares implementations in our framework running in 64 processes against sequential C versions. Results show speedup for all algorithms except fft64 due to communication overhead of the more complex butterfly topology.

6   Conclusion and Related Work

This paper presents a session-based framework for generating safe and scalable parallel applications based on flexible protocols that capture parallel design patterns.

The framework consists of two parts: a compilation tool that derives a safe-by-construction parallel backbone from a Pabble protocol description, and an aspect-oriented compilation framework that mechanically inserts computation code into the backbone, and performs asynchronous optimisation. We demonstrate that our tool generates efficient and scalable MPI applications, and improves productivity of parallel application development with reusable patterns.

Pattern-Based Structured Parallel Programming. An algorithmic skeleton framework [15] is a high-level parallel programming approach which provides reusable parallel communication and interaction patterns programmers can parameterise to generate a specific parallel program. [15,31] describe a number of tools that were developed in the past decade, and most of the tools target a similar set of skeletons, including farm (master-slave), pipeline, iterations and map. Our approach uses Pabble language to define the patterns of the skeletons, and is able to represent all common patterns above. In addition, custom patterns can be defined as Pabble protocols, and the formal MPST basis of Pabble ensures that valid protocols are guaranteed to be communication-safe and deadlock-free, and these properties hold for our generated MPI backbones (i.e. skeletons) by construction. Sklml [37], an implementation of P^3L language in OCaml supports the common patterns above but without extensibility. Recently, pattern programming was employed as a parallel programming teaching tool for undergraduate students [42,14]. They used a pragma approach, and obtained positive feedback from the students. This motivated us to use the pragma annotation for sequential kernels for flexibility and preciseness. Other than teaching, most works in the field now target heterogeneous and embedded computing, for example, Fast Flow [20,4] for CPU/GPU code generation, which can take advantage of the high-level abstraction of skeletons to target and coordinate between different hardware, each with different programming style.

Verification of MPI. The state-of-the-art in MPI program verification has been surveyed in [16]. Verification approaches in [16] are diverse and we focus on works that verify and detect deadlocks in MPI. ISP [40] is a runtime model checker based on in-situ partial order as a heuristic to avoid state explosion. DAMPI [39] is a dynamic verifier for MPI based on ISP, but uses a distributed scheduling algorithm to allow scaling. Both of the tools suffer from interleaving explosion, where some execution schedule expands exponentially. MSPOE [34] improves on ISP's partial ordering algorithm to overcome the defect and detect orphaning deadlocks. All above tools are test-based and verify correctness with a fixed harness suite. MUST [18] is another scalable, MPI dynamic verification tool, which combines two MPI verification tools, Marmot [21] and Umpire [38], and overcomes scalability challenges in previous tools by comprehensive analysis of the semantics of the primitives. TASS [35] employs model checking and symbolic execution, but is also able to verify user-specified assertions for the interaction behaviour of the program and functional equivalence between MPI programs and sequential ones [36]. A user needs to specify the maximum number of processes (see [24] for further comparisons with protocol-based approaches). The concept of parallel control-flow graphs is proposed in [5] for static analysis of

MPI programs, e.g., as a means to verify sender-receiver matching in MPI source code. An extension to dynamic analysis is presented in [1]. As far as we know, no other work focuses on communication deadlock-free MPI code generation based on types or backbones.

Session-based Parallel Programming. Session C [28] is a programming framework designed for parallel programming with multiparty session types. Users implement endpoint programs using session-based APIs and type-check them against its endpoint protocols. The framework differs from this work that it does not use a parameterised type for type-checking and the approach presented here are top-down code generation as opposed to type checking. Similarly, the work [27] introduces Pabble and type-checking MPI by Pabble, but it does not consider code generation. [24] proposes another type-checking tool for MPI based on multiparty session types. It treats a fine-grained index analysis by using VCC [7] where a program requires annotations for loops, which can be semi-automatically generated by the program annotator. All of these session-based works study type-checking endpoint programs written by developers. As far as we know, this work is the first to automatically generate a complete, communication-safe MPI code specified by a protocol specification language.

Future Work. includes extending our approach to generate MPI one-sided communication from the current point-to-point messaging abstraction in Pabble, which is more efficient in some categories of communication patterns; and supporting recursive, divide-and-conquer parallel pattern, which is possible with recent advances in session types on *sub-protocols* [9].

Acknowledgement. We thank Raymond Hu, Dominic Orchard and the anonymous reviewers for comments and suggestions. The work is funded by EPSRC EP/K034413/1, EP/K011715/1 and EP/L00058X/1, EU project FP7-612985 (UpScale) 257906, 287804 and 318521.

References

1. Aananthakrishnan, S., Bronevetsky, G., Gopalakrishnan, G.: Hybrid approach for data-flow analysis of MPI programs. In: ICS 2013, pp. 455–456. ACM (2013)
2. Asanovic, K., Wawrzynek, J., Wessel, D., Yelick, K., Bodik, R., Demmel, J., Keaveny, T., Keutzer, K., Kubiatowicz, J., Morgan, N., Patterson, D., Sen, K.: A view of the parallel computing landscape. CACM 52(10), 56 (2009)
3. Balaji, P., Dinan, J., Hoefler, T., Thakur, R.: Advanced MPI Programming (Tutorial at SC 2013). http://www.mcs.anl.gov/~thakur/sc13-mpi-tutorial/
4. Boob, S., González-Vélez, H., Popescu, A.M.: Automated instantiation of heterogeneous fast flow CPU/GPU parallel pattern applications in clouds. In: PDP, pp. 162–169. IEEE (2014)
5. Bronevetsky, G.: Communication-Sensitive Static Dataflow for Parallel Message Passing Applications. In: CGO 2009, pp. 1–12. IEEE (2009)
6. Cardoso, J.: a.M., Carvalho, T., Coutinho, J.G., Luk, W., Nobre, R., Diniz, P., Petrov, Z.: LARA: an aspect-oriented programming language for embedded systems. In: AOSD 2012, pp. 179–190. ACM (2012)

7. Cohen, E., Dahlweid, M., Hillebrand, M., Leinenbach, D., Moskal, M., Santen, T., Schulte, W., Tobies, S.: VCC: A practical system for verifying concurrent C. In: Berghofer, S., Nipkow, T., Urban, C., Wenzel, M. (eds.) TPHOLs 2009. LNCS, vol. 5674, pp. 23–42. Springer, Heidelberg (2009)

8. Dagum, L., Menon, R.: OpenMP: an industry standard API for shared-memory programming. Computational Science and Engineering 5(1), 46–55 (1998)

9. Demangeon, R., Honda, K.: Nested protocols in session types. In: Koutny, M., Ulidowski, I. (eds.) CONCUR 2012. LNCS, vol. 7454, pp. 272–286. Springer, Heidelberg (2012)

10. Deniélou, P.M., Yoshida, N.: Dynamic multirole session types. In: POPL 2011, pp. 435–446. ACM (2011)

11. Denielou, P.M., Yoshida, N., Bejleri, A., Hu, R.: Parameterised Multiparty Session Types. Logical Methods in Computer Science 8(4), 1–46 (2012)

12. DeSouza, J., Kuhn, B., de Supinski, B.R., Samofalov, V., Zheltov, S., Bratanov, S.: Automated, scalable debugging of MPI programs with Intel Message Checker. In: SE-HPCS 2005, pp. 78–82. ACM (2005)

13. Fagg, G.E., Dongarra, J.J.: FT-MPI: Fault Tolerant MPI, Supporting Dynamic Applications in a Dynamic World. In: Dongarra, J., Kacsuk, P., Podhorszki, N. (eds.) PVM/MPI 2000. LNCS, vol. 1908, pp. 346–353. Springer, Heidelberg (2000)

14. Ferner, C., Wilkinson, B., Heath, B.: Toward using higher-level abstractions to teach parallel computing. In: IPDPSW, pp. 1291–1296. IEEE (2013)

15. González-Vélez, H., Leyton, M.: A Survey of Algorithmic Skeleton Frameworks: High-level Structured Parallel Programming Enablers. Softw. Pract. Exper. 40(12), 1135–1160 (2010)

16. Gopalakrishnan, G., Kirby, R.M., Siegel, S., Thakur, R., Gropp, W., Lusk, E., De Supinski, B.R., Schulz, M., Bronevetsky, G.: Formal analysis of MPI-based parallel programs. CACM 54(12), 82–91 (2011)

17. Graepel, T., Candela, J.Q., Borchert, T., Herbrich, R.: Web-Scale Bayesian Click-Through Rate Prediction for Sponsored Search Advertising in Microsofts Bing Search Engine. In: ICML 2010, pp. 13–20 (2010)

18. Hilbrich, T., Protze, J., Schulz, M., de Supinski, B.R., Müller, M.S.: MPI Runtime Error Detection with MUST: Advances in Deadlock Detection. In: SC 2012, pp. 1–11. IEEE (2012)

19. Honda, K., Yoshida, N., Carbone, M.: Multiparty asynchronous session types. In: POPL 2008, vol. 5201, pp. 273–284. ACM (2008)

20. Kolodziej, J., González-Vélez, H., Wang, L.: Advances in data-intensive modelling and simulation. Future Generation Comp. Syst. 37, 282–283 (2014)

21. Krammer, B., Bidmon, K., Müller, M.S., Resch, M.M.: MARMOT: an MPI analysis and checking tool. In: PARCO 2003, pp. 493–500 (2003)

22. Online Appendix., http://www.doc.ic.ac.uk/~cn06/codegen

23. Mancini, E.P., Marsh, G., Panda, D.K.: An MPI-stream hybrid programming model for computational clusters. In: CCGrid 2010, pp. 323–330. IEEE (2010)

24. Marques, E.R., Martins, F., Vasconcelos, V.T., Santos, C., Ng, N., Yoshida, N.: Protocol-based verification of C+MPI programs. DI-FCUL 13, U. of Lisbon (2014)

25. Message Passing Interface, http://www.mcs.anl.gov/research/projects/mpi/

26. Ng, N., Yoshida, N.: Pabble: Parameterised Scribble. SOCA, 1–16 (2014)

27. Ng, N., Yoshida, N.: Pabble: Parameterised Scribble for Parallel Programming. In: PDP, pp. 707–714. IEEE (2014)

28. Ng, N., Yoshida, N., Honda, K.: Multiparty Session C: Safe Parallel Programming with Message Optimisation. In: Furia, C.A., Nanz, S. (eds.) TOOLS 2012. LNCS, vol. 7304, pp. 202–218. Springer, Heidelberg (2012)

29. Ng, N., Yoshida, N., Luk, W.: Scalable Session Programming for Heterogeneous High-Performance Systems. In: Counsell, S., Núñez, M. (eds.) SEFM 2013. LNCS, vol. 8368, pp. 82–98. Springer, Heidelberg (2014)
30. Pabble project page, http://www.doc.ic.ac.uk/~cn06/pabble
31. Rabhi, F., Gorlatch, S. (eds.): Patterns and Skeletons for Parallel and Distributed Computing. Springer (2003)
32. Saldaña, M., Patel, A., Madill, C., Nunes, D., Wang, D., Chow, P., Wittig, R., Styles, H., Putnam, A.: MPI as a Programming Model for High-Performance Reconfigurable Computers. ACM TRETS 3(4), 1–29 (2010)
33. Scribble homepage, http://scribble.org/
34. Sharma, S., Gopalakrishnan, G., Bronevetsky, G.: A sound reduction of persistent-sets for deadlock detection in mpi applications. In: Gheyi, R., Naumann, D. (eds.) SBMF 2012. LNCS, vol. 7498, pp. 194–209. Springer, Heidelberg (2012)
35. Siegel, S.F., Zirkel, T.K.: Collective assertions. In: Jhala, R., Schmidt, D. (eds.) VMCAI 2011. LNCS, vol. 6538, pp. 387–402. Springer, Heidelberg (2011)
36. Siegel, S.F., Zirkel, T.K.: FEVS: A Functional Equivalence Verification Suite for High-Performance Scientific Computing. MSCS 5(4), 427–435 (2011)
37. Sklml webpage, http://sklml.inria.fr
38. Vetter, J.S., de Supinski, B.R.: Dynamic Software Testing of MPI Applications with Umpire. In: SC 2000, p. 51. IEEE (2000)
39. Vo, A., Aananthakrishnan, S., Gopalakrishnan, G., de Supinski, B., Schulz, M., Bronevetsky, G.: A scalable and distributed dynamic formal verifier for mpi programs. In: SC 2010, pp. 1–10. IEEE (2010)
40. Vo, A., Vakkalanka, S., DeLisi, M., Gopalakrishnan, G., et al.: Formal verification of practical MPI programs. In: PPoPP 2009, pp. 261–270. ACM (2008)
41. Wienke, S., Springer, P., Terboven, C., an Mey, D.: OpenACC – First Experiences with Real-World Applications. In: Kaklamanis, C., Papatheodorou, T., Spirakis, P.G. (eds.) Euro-Par 2012. LNCS, vol. 7484, pp. 859–870. Springer, Heidelberg (2012)
42. Wilkinson, B., Villalobos, J., Ferner, C.: Pattern programming approach for teaching parallel and distributed computing. In: SIGCSE 2013, pp. 409–414. ACM (2013)

Verifying Fast and Sparse SSA-Based Optimizations in Coq*

Delphine Demange[1], David Pichardie[2], and Léo Stefanesco[3]

[1] Université Rennes 1 – IRISA – Inria, France
[2] ENS Rennes – IRISA – Inria, France
[3] ENS Lyon, France

Abstract. The Static Single Assignment (SSA) form is a predominant technology in modern compilers, enabling powerful and fast program optimizations. Despite its great success in the implementation of production compilers, it is only very recently that this technique has been introduced in *verified* compilers. As of today, few evidence exist on that, in this context, it also allows faster and simpler optimizations. This work builds on the CompCertSSA verified compiler (an SSA branch of the verified CompCert C compiler). We implement and verify two prevailing SSA optimizations: Sparse Conditional Constant Propagation and Global Value Numbering. For both transformations, we mechanically prove their soundness in the Coq proof assistant. Both optimization proofs are embedded in a single sparse optimization framework, factoring out many of the dominance-based reasoning steps required in proofs of SSA-based optimizations. Our experimental evaluations indicate both a better precision, and a significant compilation time speedup.

1   Introduction

Single Static Assignment (SSA) is an intermediate representation of code in which variables are assigned at most once in the program text, and ϕ-functions are used to merge values at control-flow join points. Introduced in the late 1980's [1, 14], it has gained over the years a considerable interest in the compilation community. Indeed, although the static single assignment property looks simple, it entails fundamental structural properties in the program control-flow graph. These properties, materialized by e.g. the dominator-tree, or use-def chains, are in turn smartly exploited by program optimizations, whose implementations become simpler than on regular, non-SSA programs. In a way, converting a program into SSA can be seen as a pre-processing that embeds, explicitly in the program syntax, some rich semantic invariants of the program. By the same token, SSA-based optimizations can enjoy precision and efficiency improvement. It is hence not surprising that SSA has constituted, for over a decade now, the state-of-the-art technique in modern, production compilers, such as GCC

* This work was supported by Agence Nationale de la Recherche, grant number ANR-14-CE28-0004 DISCOVER.

B. Franke (Ed.): CC 2015, LNCS 9031, pp. 233–252, 2015.
DOI: 10.1007/978-3-662-46663-6_12

or LLVM. For instance, LLVM optimization middle-end includes numerous optimizations (25+ phases), including dead code elimination, loop invariant code motion, sparse conditional constant propagation, and aggressive common subexpression elimination based on global-value numbering, all of them working on SSA. Moreover, SSA is increasingly used in just-in-time (JIT) compilers, operating on high-level target-independent program representations (e.g. Java byte-code, .NET CLI byte-code, or LLVM bitcode), which gives even stronger evidence of the efficiency of SSA-based optimizations.

Undoubtedly, though these sophisticated optimizations are conceptually simpler, implementing them is far from trivial. Indeed, they exploit the subtle semantic invariants of the SSA form, and rely on highly efficient data structures for better performance. In the literature, it is well-known that the simplicity of SSA has sometimes been over-estimated, and designing bug-free (i.e. semantics-preserving) implementations is not so easy [4]. The recent work of Yang et al. [20] shows that bugs remain frequent in mainstream compilers. Compiler correctness aims to provide rigorous proofs that compilers preserve the behavior of programs they compile. After 40 years of rich history, the field is entering into a new era, with the advent of realistic and mechanically verified compilers. This new generation of compilers was initiated with CompCert [10], a compiler that is programmed and verified in the Coq proof assistant and generates compact and efficient assembly code for from C. The CompCert project has now reached the maturity to compete with non-verified compilers, such as GCC. However, it does not rely on an SSA-based middle-end.

Recently, the Vellvm [22, 21] and CompCertSSA [2] projects have been conducted, introducing SSA techniques in *verified* compilers. Despite the considerable progresses that these works made on the formalization of the semantics of SSA, and of several important of its properties, SSA-based verified compilers still suffer from two main bottlenecks, that clearly limit their application in real world scenarios. First, on the implementation side, verified compilers are usually restricted. Indeed, verified compilers must find a balance between efficiency and verifiability, and directly proving the correctness of the transformations they perform often requires to consider less optimized (i.e. less efficient, or precise) implementations. To by-pass this problem for the most efficiency-critical parts of the compiler, one can employ the technique of *translation validation*[12]. In this setting, an un-verified tool performs the required computations, and a verified checker ensures, *a posteriori*, the correctness of these results before they are put back in the verified tool chain, thus providing the same formal guaranties as a transformation that would be directly programmed and proved in Coq. This technique is increasingly favored in mechanically verified developments [18, 17]. We argue that this technique allows to achieve good performance in practice: the compilation overhead introduced by the checker does not exceed the performance loss induced by implementations that are easier to verify but less efficient. The second obstruction to the development of SSA-based verified compilers lies in the fact that, when it comes to proving, working on SSA can be quite constraining. In fact, the structural properties provably holding on the input program must be proved to be preserved by each transformation. In addition, compared to pen-and-paper proofs in which some technical arguments can be elided, mechanizing proofs requires making explicit every single reasoning steps. Previous proof efforts on SSA provide some general lemmas and proof architectures (e.g. the equation lemma of [2], or the scoping lemma about SSA strictness of [21]), but lack a systematic, formalized proof technique that would follow the usual dominance-based reasoning one uses when proving SSA-based optimizations[1].

This present work aims to make some progress in these two directions. More specifically, after recalling in Section 2 some background about the CompCert compiler, our on-going CompCertSSA project, and a brief overview of the two optimizations we consider in this paper, we present the following contributions in verified SSA-based optimizations. We provide realistic implementations, in a verified compiler chain, of leading SSA optimizations, namely Sparse Conditional Constant Propagation (SCCP) and Common Sub-Expression Elimination based on Global Value Numbering (GVN). Their implementations closely follow the choices made in production compilers, for techniques of intra-procedural and scalar optimizations. Hence, they are realistic in terms of efficiency (compilation time) and precision (number of instructions optimized). The GVN implementation is a major revision of the work presented in [2], and performs an order of magnitude faster. We resort on the use of efficient, verified, a-posteriori validators that do not practically penalize compilation time, even in regards of the efficient optimization implementations. On the proof side, we propose a generic proof framework (Section 3) that makes explicit the reasoning on dominated regions, an emblematic reasoning schema of paper-proofs of SSA optimizations. Factoring out many of domination-based reasoning makes the proof effort more lightweight. The proof framework also captures the SSA sparseness *adage* (it is enough to propagate dataflow information directly from definitions to uses, instead of along the control-flow graph). Indeed, our framework is parameterized by a generic, flow-insensitive, static analysis underlying the optimization. And we prove that, at each program point, it is sufficient to establish the correctness of the analysis for the variables that strictly dominate this program point. The correctness proofs of SCCP and GVN (Sections 4 and 5) are done by instantiating the framework on these two optimizations, and their underlying static analysis. Hence, compared to [2], the checker and soundness proof of GVN has been deeply revised. All our proofs are done within the Coq proof assistant, extending the CompCertSSA middle-end, an extension of the verified CompCert C compiler. Finally, we conduct an experimental validation of the Ocaml extracted compiler on a benchmark suite (Section 6), demonstrating that our middle-end is able to scale properly to large programs, with improved optimization opportunities. Our full development is available online at http://www.irisa.fr/celtique/ext/ssa_opt.

---

[1] Both works identified the need of such a framework, and the benefits it would permit.

2   Background

2.1   The Verified CompCert Compiler

CompCert is a realistic, formally verified compiler that generates PowerPC, ARM or x86 code from source programs written in a large subset of C. CompCert formalizes the operational semantics of a dozen intermediate languages, and proves a semantics preservation theorem for each phase.

Preservation theorems are expressed in terms of program behaviors, i.e. finite or infinite traces of external function calls (a.k.a. systems calls producing observable events), that are performed during the execution of the program, and claim that individual compilation phases preserve behaviors.

A consequence of the theorems is that for any C program p that does not go wrong (i.e. it does not reach a non-final state where no execution step is valid), and target program tp output by the successful compilation of p by the compiler compcert_compiler, the set of behaviors of p contains all behaviors of the target program tp. The formal theorem is:

```
Theorem compcert_compiler_correct: forall (p: C.program)(tp: Asm.program),
   (not_wrong_program p /\ compcert_compiler p = OK tp) ->
   (forall beh, exec_asm_program tp beh -> exec_C_program p beh).
```

Each phase of the compiler is formally proved relying on simulation techniques, and the formal development of CompCert provides the general correctness theorems of these simulation diagrams. We will build on these generic lemmas to prove the semantic preservation of GVN and SCCP (see Sections 4 and 5). The main lemmas to prove take the form of a forward lock-step simulation:

```
Variable prog:program. (* initial program *)
Variable tprog:program. (* target program *)
Hypothesis opt_ok: optimization prog = OK tprog. (* optim. succeeded *)

Lemma match_step : forall s1 t s2 s1',
    (step (genv prog) s1 t s2) /\ (match_states s1 s1') ->
    exists s2', step (genv tprog) s1' t s2' /\ match_states s2 s2'.
```

where binary relation match_states between semantic states (before and after optimization) carries the invariants needed for proving behavior preservation.

Some parts of the CompCert compiler are not directly proved in Coq. This is the case for register allocation, which is based on a graph coloring algorithm. The interference graph coloring algorithm is written in OCaml, and then validated a posteriori by a checker written in Coq [13]. The correctness proof of the checker (stating that if a coloring is accepted by the validator, then it is indeed a valid coloring) ensures this compilation phase provides the same guarantees as a transformation written and proved directly in Coq, with the additional benefit of abstracting away complex implementation details and heuristics.

```
Definition reg := ...                    (* type of variables *)
Inductive instr   :=                     (* instructions (excerpt) *)
| Inop (pc: node)
| Iop (op: operation) (args: list reg) (res: reg) (pc: node)
| Iload (chk:chunk) (addr:addressing) (args: list reg) (res: reg) (pc: node)
| Istore (chk:chunk) (addr:addressing) (args:list reg) (src: reg) (pc: node)
| Icall (sig: signature) (fn:ident) (args: list reg) (res: reg) (pc: node)
| Icond (cond: condition) (args: list reg) (ifso ifnot: node)
| Ireturn (src: option reg).

Definition code := PTree.t instr.        (* type of code graph *)
                                         (* partial map from nodes to instr *)
Inductive phiinstr := Iphi (args: list reg) (res: reg).  (* φ-functions *)
Definition phiblock:= list phiinstr.     (* type of φ-blocks *)
Definition phicode := PTree.t phiblock.  (* type of φ-blocks graph: partial
                                            map from nodes to phiblock *)

Record function := {
    fn_sig: signature;          (* function signature *)
    fn_params: list reg;        (* parameters *)
    fn_stacksize: Z;            (* activation record size *)
    fn_code: code;              (* code graph *)
    fn_phicode: phicode;        (* φ-blocks graph *)
    fn_entrypoint: node }.      (* entry node *)
```

Fig. 1. SSA abstract syntax

2.2   The Verified CompCertSSA Compiler

In a previous work [2], we developed CompCertSSA, that builds on top of
CompCert, by enriching it with an SSA-based middle-end. It is plugged in at the
level of RTL (a non-structured, CFG based, three-address like representation),
and generates from it a pruned SSA intermediate form. After optimizing on the
SSA form, the middle-end deconstructs it naively back to RTL, and then leaves
the remainder of CompCert's backend generating machine code. In this section,
we recall the required material and results achieved in this previous work. We
refer the reader to [2] for further details.

The SSA Language. The abstract syntax of the SSA form is given in Figure 1.
Functions (function records), are defined at the bottom of the figure. Their code
is organized into two distinct graphs: one for the regular instructions (of type
instr), and another one for φ-blocks (of type phiinstr). The idea is to attach
a φ-block at node pc whenever the φ-block must be executed before the regular
instruction at node pc. We will present in more detail the semantics of this
language in the next paragraph.

In addition, we equip the notion of SSA programs with a *well-formedness*
predicate capturing essential structural properties of SSA forms [2]. First, it
requires the single static assignment property of the function, i.e. the uniqueness
of variable definition points (we omit the formal definition). Next, it demands

```
Inductive state :=
 | State (stack: list stackframe)    (* call stack *)
        (f: function)                (* current function *)
        (sp: val)                    (* stack pointer *)
        (pc: node)                   (* current program point *)
        (rs: regset)                 (* register state *)
        (m: mem)                     (* memory state *)
 | Callstate (stack: list stackframe) (f: fundef) (args: list val) (m: mem)
 | Returnstate (stack: list stackframe) (v: val) (m: mem).

Inductive step: genv -> state -> trace -> state -> Prop :=
 | ex_Inop_njp: forall ge s f sp pc rs m pc',
   fn_code f pc = Some(Inop pc') ->
   ~ join_point pc' f ->
   step ge (State s f sp pc rs m) nil (State s f sp pc' rs m)

 | ex_Inop_jp: forall ge s f sp pc rs m pc' phi k,
   fn_code f pc = Some(Inop pc') ->
   join_point pc' f ->
   fn_phicode f pc' = Some phi ->
   index_pred f pc pc' = Some k ->
   step ge (State s f sp pc rs m) nil (State s f sp pc' (phistore k rs phi) m)

 | ex_Iop: forall ge s f sp pc rs m pc' op args res v,
   fn_code f pc = Some(Iop op args res pc') ->
   eval_operation sp op (rs##args) m = Some v ->
   step ge (State s f sp pc rs m) nil (State s f sp pc' (rs#res <- v) m)
```

Fig. 2. Semantics of SSA (excerpt)

that the function is in strict SSA form: each variable use must be dominated by its (unique) definition point. Formally:

```
Definition strict (f: function) : Prop :=
  forall (x:reg) (u d: node), (use f x u) /\ (def f x d) -> dom f d u.
```

Finally, it requires that the instruction code of the function is normalized, in the following sense: the only possible instruction that can lead to a junction point in the CFG of the function is an Inop. This design choice can look quite minor, but this greatly simplifies the definition of the semantics (ϕ-blocks can only be executed after an Inop), and subsequently the proofs about SSA optimizations, and the SSA destruction (as it entails an edge-split property). Note that these Inop will be easily removed by subsequent compilation phases.

SSA Semantics. The SSA language is provided with a small-step operational semantics, given in Figure 2. Here, we only describe the semantic states, and the main cases in the definition of the transition relation. We refer the reader to the full development for extra details. Depending on the execution phase of the program, there are three possible kinds of execution states: (i) regular, intermediate execution states (constructor State), (ii) call states (constructor Callstate), reached immediately after executing a function call, indicating the next function to execute and (iii) return states (Return), indicating, in addition to the current state of the stackframe and memory, the potential value to return.

Then, the small-step semantic transition relation, step, formalizes what it means for each instruction to be executed. For instance, in Figure 2, executing an Inop, when no ϕ-block is attached to the successor pc' of pc, just leaves the semantic state unchanged, except for the program pointer. If pc' is a junction point (rule ex_Inop_jp), then the ϕ-instructions in the ϕ-block phib will be executed on local registers rs, through the function phistore. This function basically performs the parallel copy of the k-th arguments of ϕ-functions to their respective destination registers. All other instructions have the expected, traditional operational semantics. For instance, executing an Iop instruction (rule ex_Iop) evaluates the operator op on the values of its arguments args in the current register state rs, and updates rs by setting the destination register res to the result value v. For the rules we selected, no observable event is produced, hence the empty trace nil is emitted.

Equation Lemma. The main result we previously achieved is the so-called equation lemma. This semantic lemma establishes a strong, global invariant, that allows to see SSA function as a set of equations relating variables and the right-hand side of their defining instructions. Its formal statement is indicated below. It considers well-formed SSA programs (all of its functions are well-formed), and states that in any reachable execution state, if a variable x is defined at point d in function f (condition (def f x d)), then the value of x in this state evaluates to (rhs f x i) (typically an arithmetic instruction Iop) in that exact same state, provided that execution state is in a region of the CFG that is strictly dominated by d (condition (sdom f d pc)).

```
Definition eq_lemma f sp rs pc := forall x d i,
    (def f x d) /\ (rhs f x i) /\ (sdom f d pc) ->
    [f, sp, rs]|= x == i.

Theorem reachable_eq_lemma : forall prog s f sp pc rs m,
    (wf_ssa_program prog) /\ (reachable prog (State s f sp pc rs m)) ->
    eq_lemma f sp rs pc.
```

This lemma makes it clear that syntactic information in SSA functions is rich, thanks to dominance-based structural properties of their CFG. This is what makes SSA so easy to manipulate in program optimizations. In our proof framework, we aim at exploiting the semantic counterparts of these constraints, to simplify our proofs. Indeed, we will make extensive use of the above invariant on SSA program in the proof of GVN (Section 5), and our framework helps to systematize the dominance-based reasoning steps.

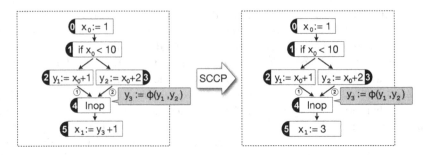

Fig. 3. Example of constant propagation (SCCP algorithm)

2.3   SSA-Based Optimizations

In SSA, flow-insensitive analyses are both simpler to implement and less memory expensive as their flow-sensitive counterparts, while giving rise to the same precision. SSA also provides a simplified notion of def-use chains that can be exploited to speedup fixpoint iteration. Below we briefly overview the two optimizations we consider in this paper.

Sparse Conditional Constant Propagation. Constant propagation (CP) is a key compiler optimization. It infers whether a variable will be assigned the same constant value on all feasible paths reaching that assignment. In that case, the assignment can be replaced by a simpler instruction, that just assigns that constant (instead of a more intricate expression) to the variable. Modern compilers like GCC and LVVM implement CP using the Wegman-Zadeck algorithm [19] called Sparse Conditional Constant Propagation (SCCP).

SCCP is a very fast constant propagation analysis that is able to perform a program transformation in almost linear time (size of the CFG, plus size of the SSA graph). It not only detects constants but also some unfeasible branches. Dead code and constant analysis are performed simultaneously, so that they benefit one from each-other.

Figure 3 illustrates this mutual benefit. In order to discover the constant 3 at node 5, it is necessary to prove that edge $(1, 3)$ is not feasible. This fact is discovered thanks to the propagation of the constant equality $x_0 = 1$ from node 0 to the conditional statement at node 1. While iterating traditional constant propagation and program simplification could achieve the same result, SCCP is able to generate it in one (fast) run.

SCCP is traditionally implemented with an *ad hoc* iterative workset algorithm. The computation maintains three worksets: $w_\top$ is a set of SSA variables that have been assigned a "I don't know" information ($\top$); w_{var} is a set of SSA variables whose constant information may depend on recently updated variables and must hence be reconsidered in a future iteration of the algorithm; w_{edges} is a workset of feasible edges. Initially, the entry edge is considered as feasible and every function parameter is assigned a $\top$ information. Elements in $w_\top$ are processed in priority during each round, as they may speedup fixpoint convergence. When the abstract information of a variable belonging to either $w_\top$ or w_{var} is updated, the algorithm exploits a SSA def-use chains data-structure to directly enable the recomputation of the abstract information associated to the variables which depend on that variable. When an edge in w_{edges} is considered, we only add to the workset the successor edges that are feasible according to the current abstract information given by each variable used in this node.

Global Value Numbering (GVN). Global Value Numbering [1, 5] is a common subexpression elimination optimization that discovers equivalence classes between program variables. Variables belonging to the same class evaluate to the same value. Each class is given a *number* that characterizes it.

Several implementation techniques has been proposed to perform fast numbering on SSA programs. The technique chosen by the current version of the LLVM compiler is the RPO algorithm [5]. It scans the CFG of the program in reverse-post-order and manages the numbering with a mutable hash-table assigning a number to each symbolic expression encountered in the program syntax. A complete explanation of the algorithm is out of the scope of this paper but two facts are worth mentioning. First, efficient implementations require mutable data-structures like hash-tables, which are not currently available when programming in Coq. The use of an external GVN solver, written in OCaml, is thus mandatory to achieve the efficiency of modern compilers. Second, the analysis does not fit the classical monotone framework generally considered in verified static analysis [10]: the computed fixpoint is wrong if not built using the RPO order, which makes a direct proof of this algorithm particularly difficult. Therefore, GVN is a perfect candidate for a posteriori validation.

CompCert includes a common subexpression elimination optimization based on Local Value Numbering (LVN). It does not work on SSA, applies on extended basic blocks only, and does not infer equalities across loop boundaries. Still, it handles intra-procedural redundant load elimination; GVN would require major adaptations. This extension is out of scope of this paper.

3   Generic Framework

We now present the general framework, in which we embed the formalization of SCCP and GVN. It is intended to capture a variety of SSA-based optimizations, and to provide the backbone of their correctness proof, by factoring out many of the required dominance-based reasoning steps.

It is made of three parts. The first part consists of the description of a generic optimization, satisfying some basic constraints ensuring the preservation of strict-SSA well-formedness. This optimization relies on the result of a static analysis, whose formalization, the second part of the framework, axiomatizes some of its properties and invariants. The last part of the framework is dedicated to the proof of a dominance-based invariant correctness result of the analysis, under the assumption that the analysis conforms to its specification.

The formalization of the analysis correctness invariant relies on a 3-place predicate (dsd f x n), that holds whenever in function f, the definition point of variable x strictly dominates the CFG node n. In our framework, we provide general lemmas about that predicate, and case-analysis proof schemes, that help structuring proofs. Intuitively, dominance-based reasoning is relatively easy for straight-line code, but conducting proofs in Coq can sometimes add a significant overhead. Reasoning about join points makes the reasoning even more intricate. In our development, we make use of the following two lemmas

```
Lemma dsd_not_joinpoint : forall f n1 n2 x,
   (is_edge f n1 n2) /\ (~join_point n2 f) /\ (dsd f x n2) ->
     (assigned_code f n1 x)
     \/ (ext_params f x /\ n1 = fn_entrypoint f)
     \/ (dsd f x n1 /\ ~ assigned_code f n1 x)

Lemma dsd_joinpoints : forall f n1 n2 x,
   (is_edge f n1 n2) /\ (join_point f n2) /\ (dsd f x n2) ->
     (assigned_phi f n2 x)
     \/ (ext_params f x /\ n1 = fn_entrypoint f)
     \/ (dsd f x n1 /\ ~ assigned_phi f n2 x).
```

which provide helpful case-analysis schemes. When proving lemmas taking the form of a subject-reduction property under the hypothesis that (dsd f x pc), each of the cases provides sufficient information for either knowing exactly the definition point of register x, or knowing that definition of x strictly dominates one of the predecessors of pc, allowing to use the dsd hypothesis to conclude.

Generic Optimization. The generic SSA-based optimization first assumes that the underlying static analysis has the following type:

```
Variable approx : Type.
Definition result := reg -> approx.
Variable analysis : function -> (result * m_exec).
```

It takes an SSA function as input, and returns (i) a flow-insensitive result (of type result), mapping to SSA variables an element of type approx (typically, an abstract domain formalized as a lattice) and (ii) a map (of type m_exec), from control-flow edges to execution flags (booleans) indicating feasibility of edges. In the most general case, the function analysis will compute simultaneously these two pieces of information so that the two corresponding static analyses can interact and benefit one from each other. On top of the analysis, we assume that the optimization relies on a per-instruction transformation function transf_intr, that is mapped on the whole SSA code. More specifically:

```
Variable transf_instr : result -> node -> instruction -> instruction.
Definition transf_function (f: function) : function :=
  let (res,exec) := analysis f in
  map_code (transf_instr res) f.
```

Note `exec` is not used by `transf_instr`, but improves precision of `res`, and is kept track of for proof purposes. On top of these basic assumptions, we require that for each instruction optimized by `transf_instr`, the changes of variable uses and definitions do not break the strictness of SSA:

```
Hypothesis new_code_same_or_Iop : forall f pc ins,
  (wf_ssa_function f) /\ ((fn_code f)!pc = Some ins) ->
    transf_instr (fst (analysis f)) pc ins = ins
    \/ transf_instr_preserves_strict f ins.
```

Here, predicate `transf_instr_preserves_strict` means that the optimization can change any local variable definition for a simpler statement of the form `Iop` (e.g. an arithmetic constant or a register move) assigning the same variable, so long as all newly introduced uses remain dominated by their definition. Other statements are not allowed to be optimized ((un)-conditional branches stay untouched, as we focus on optimizations that do not change functions CFG).

Under the hypothesis `new_code_same_or_Iop`, we can prove that the generic optimization (mapped to all functions of a given program) preserves the well-formedness of the initial SSA program:

```
Theorem transf_program_preserve_wf_ssa : forall prog,
  wf_ssa_program prog -> wf_ssa_program (transf_program prog).
```

This lemma is absolutely necessary to be able to compose several SSA optimizations passes. In addition, it has a high practical impact. Indeed, once the optimization has been defined with the help of this framework, proving `new_code_same_or_Iop` is the only thing we need to get the well-formedness preservation. Without this framework, the proof of this result would be duplicated for every optimization. It hence allows to focus the proof effort on more interesting aspects.

Analysis Specification. We turn now our attention to the axiomatic specification of the `analysis` function. In the sequel, to lighten the notations, we will assume to work only with well-formed SSA functions, and will write (`A_r f`) for the first component of (`analysis f`).

This specification is packed into the Coq record shown in Figure 4. First, we need to formulate the interpretation of the execution flags map returned by the analysis of a function. Hence, we assume a 2-place predicate (`exec f pc`), characterizing feasible CFG nodes. Essentially, it must be proved (by the developer of a specific analysis) coherent with the dynamic semantics of the function, i.e. the analysis must not infer a node as not non-executable if its predecessor in the CFG is analyzed as executable, and the function can make as step from the predecessor to that node.

The main part of the axiomatisation consists in specifying a concretisation relation between abstract values associated to SSA variables and concrete, runtime values they can take. This is done by predicate (`G rs a v`). It is intended

```
Record AnalysisProp := {
    exec      : function -> node -> Prop
  ; G         : regset -> approx -> val -> Prop
  ; is_at_Top: result -> reg -> Prop
  ; G_top : forall R r rs,
            is_at_Top R r -> G rs (R r) (rs# r)
  ; is_at_Top_eq : forall R r r',
            (is_at_Top R r) /\ (R r = R r') -> is_at_Top R r'
  ; A_intra : forall f pc r,
            (exec f pc) /\ (assigned_inter_mem_params f pc r) ->
            is_at_Top (A_r f) r }.
```

Fig. 4. Axiomatisation of the generic analysis

to hold whenever, in a context described by register state rs, the abstract value a is a correct approximation of the concrete value v.[2]

The third component we require is predicate (is_at_Top R r), whose intent is to characterize when, in a given result R, a register r is associated to the static information "I don't know". The type of this predicate alone is not sufficient to express this. We hence include in the specification record a proof obligation (field G_top) asking that a register whose analysis result is at $\top$ concretises to any possible value (rs# r, where register state rs is universally quantified).

Field is_at_Top_eq is required for more technical reasons than the others, but is quite natural to have, and can read as a sanity check on the definition of is_at_Top. This proof obligation asks that, whenever a register r is associated to $\top$ for a given result R, then any other register r' whose static information is equal to the one of r is also associated to $\top$ in R.

The last field of the specification record, A_intra, is a proof obligation saying that the analysis under consideration is intra-procedural, and deal with local variables of the function only. Indeed, it states that for any register r of the function, whenever, syntactically, it is a function parameter, or its value depends on the memory or function calls, then the analysis infers a $\top$ information for it. This is only required for registers defined at executable CFG nodes.

Generic Analysis Correctness Proof. Assuming that the generic analysis fits in AnalysisProp, proving the (instantiated) optimization requires to propagate the correctness of the analysis. We state this as an invariant of its result:

```
Definition gamma (f:function) (pc:node) (rs:regset) :=
  forall x, (dsd f x pc) /\ (exec f pc) ->  G rs (A_r f x) (rs# x).
```

where predicate (G rs (A_r f x) (rs# x)), reads as "the static information computed for register x correctly approximates the concrete run-time value of x in register state rs". We must stress the fact that, as can be seen in this

---

[2] Our development also keeps track of a global environment and stack pointer to, eventually, deal with symbolic information about read-only globals and offsets values.

definition, the correctness of the analysis needs only to hold on variables whose definitions dominate the current program point (dsd f x pc), and only when pc has been analysed as executable by the analysis (condition (exec f pc)).

The final invariance theorem we want to achieve in the framework is the correctness of the analysis (in the sense of gamma), for any state reachable during the execution of the program:

```
Theorem analysis_correct : forall prog s f sp pc rs m,
    reachable prog (State s f sp pc rs m) -> gamma f pc rs.
```

To do so, the analysis must satisfy two extra properties (giving rise to two other proof obligations). First, one must show that the analysis must compute a correct abstraction for Iop instructions:

```
Hypothesis iop_correct : forall f pc op args res pc' v rs ge sp m x,
    forall (SINV: eq_lemma f sp rs pc)
           (CODE: (fn_code f) ! pc = Some (Iop op args res pc'))
           (EVAL: eval_operation ge sp op (rs ## args) m = Some v)
    (gamma f pc rs) /\ (exec f pc) /\ (dsd f x pc') ->
    G (rs # res <- v) (A_r f x) ((rs # res <- v) # x).
```

which can read as follows: if gamma holds before executing the Iop instruction, it will hold after its execution, in the updated register state. In particular (when x and res are equal), the static information computed for res correctly approximates the concrete value v obtained by executing the instruction. Note the SINV hypothesis, which makes possible to exploit the equation lemma of the current function. The second proof obligation requires the gamma predicate to be preserved by ϕ-blocks execution:

```
Hypothesis gamma_step_phi: forall f pc pc' phib k rs,
    forall (REACHED: reached f pc) (EXE: exec f pc)
           (PC : (fn_code f) ! pc = Some (Inop pc'))
           (PC': (fn_phicode f) ! pc' = Some phib)
           (PRED: index_pred f pc pc' = Some k)
    gamma f pc rs -> gamma f pc' (phi_store k phib rs).
```

In the next two sections, we explain how to instantiate the framework on SCCP and GVN. Also, each of the section briefly comments on the correctness proof of the optimization itself (its semantics-preserving theorem). For both of them, we show a lock-step forward simulation lemma, where the matching relation between semantics states carries the invariants about (i) the well-formedness of SSA functions, (ii) the equational lemma and (iii) the correctness of the analysis through a gamma predicate on the current state.

4 Verifying SCCP in Coq

4.1 Overview of the Implementation

As explained in Section 2.3, SCCP simultaneously detects constants and infeasible paths in the control-flow graph of a function, and replaces arithmetic expressions detected to always evaluate to a constant by that constant. More precisely, our SCCP optimization is built from the following constituents.

The type `approx` of the underlying analysis is instantiated to the elements of the semi-lattice of constants. This lattice is rather standard and was already available in the CompCert compiler distribution. We just recall its definition for the sake of completeness[3]:

```
Inductive approx : Type :=
  | Novalue    (* No value possible, code unreachable. *)
  | Unknown    (* All values possible, no compile-time information *)
  | I (i:int)  (* A known integer value. *)
  | F (f:float) (* A known floating-point value. *)
```

We implement a data-flow solver on this constant lattice. The dataflow implementation is new. It iterates on both the CFG (for detecting dead branches) and the SSA graph (also called def-use chains) to propagate constant analysis information, following the algorithms described informally in Section 2.3.

The result of the dataflow solver is of the form `(const,exec)` where `const` maps variables to elements of type `approx`, and `exec` stores the execution flag of CFG edges, indicating whether or not an edge may be taken at run-time. We then send the result of the solver to a formally verified checker ensuring this result is a post-fixpoint of the usual equation system for dataflow constant analysis, augmented with extra equations on execution flags.

The optimization itself consists in propagating the constants detected by the analysis. Every (`Iop op args res _`) instruction, where `args` have been inferred to be constant are replaced by a (`Iop (opconst k) nil res _`) instruction. Note that it does not need to optimize instructions on paths inferred as infeasible.

4.2   Correctness Proof

The correctness of SCCP is relatively simple, once the post-fixpoint property is proved. Below, we explain how the analysis fits in our framework and give an intuition on how the proof obligations are discharged. The good news is that the instantiation is straightforward and intuitive for an optimization as simple as SCCP (the framework does not introduce extra overhead in the proof effort).

Analysis. To instantiate the specification of Section 3, the relation G between abstract and concrete values is standard. We reuse the definition from CompCert's Constant Propagation on RTL, and define predicate `is_at_Top` accordingly:

```
Definition G rs a v :=  match a with
                          | Unknown => True    | Novalue => False
                          | I p => v = Vint p  | F p => v = Vfloat p
                        end.
Definition is_at_Top (R: result) (r: reg) : Prop := (R r = Unknown).
```

---

[3] The type `approx` is also equipped with the expected partial order and *join* operator.

The interesting proof obligations of `AnalysisProp` are `iop_correct` and `gamma_step_phi`. The crux of the proof of `iop_correct` is that, as the SSA function is strict and well-formed, we know that all of the arguments `args` of the instruction (`Iop op args res pc'`) have a definition that strictly dominates the program point of the instruction. Hence, by hypothesis, we know that the analysis is correct for these, in the previous register state. In addition, the post-fixpoint checker ensures that the abstract value for `res`, (`A_r f res`) is greater (in the constants lattice) than the static evaluation of the operator `op` on arguments `args`. By correctness of the static evaluation, we get that it matches (in the sense of `G`) the concrete evaluation `v` of the instruction. Hence, (`A_r f res`) will, a fortiori, be a correct approximation of `v`. We show that for other registers, the correctness of the approximation is not altered, using the case-analysis `dsd_not_joinpoint`. The first case is a contradiction thanks to the SSA property, the second case is easily discharged by `G_top`, and in the third case, we use the hypothesis on `gamma` in the previous register state to conclude. The proof of `gamma_step_phi` is similar.

Optimization Correctness. The analysis and optimization described previously satisfy the various proof obligations of Section 3. First, we remark that it is simple to prove that the strictness condition is preserved, as SCCP only removes variable uses, and does not introduce any new definition. In proving the optimization correct, the main case is where an (`Iop op args r _`) instruction is optimized into a (`Iop (opconst k) nil r _`). But this is done only when (`A_r f r`) is a constant. Thanks to the post-fixpoint property, we hence know that its abstract value matches the concrete value `k` we assigned the register to in the optimized function.

5   Verifying GVN in Coq

5.1   Overview of the Implementation

Our implementation of GVN follows LLVM design choices. We rely on a reverse-post-order iteration and a mutable hash table that assigns numbers to symbolic expressions. Each number represents an equivalence class for program variables that hold the same runtime value. For each class we choose a representing variable whose definition must dominate all variables in the same class. Having an efficient dominance test is a keystone of the optimization efficiency. We rely on a fast immediate dominator tree [9] computation and a depth graph traversal numbering that allows constant time dominance test. Our GVN does not handle execution flags, we hence use a trivial map (all edges may be executable).

Then, we implement and prove correct in Coq a checker for that result. The checker is ensuring three properties. First, that the analysis puts in a singleton class any variable assigned through a memory load or function call. For variables defined by means of an `Iop` instruction, the checker ensures that either it is its own representative, or that the following condition is met: whenever at `pc`, we have the instruction (Iop op args r _), and the representative (A_r f r) of r is not r itself, then (A_r f r) is defined at a node pcr who strictly dominates pc, and (A_r f r) and r are congruent (i.e. the arguments used in their respective defining instruction have a common representative). A similar check is done by the checker on each ϕ-block of the function: a variable defined by a ϕ-instruction at node pc has either itself as a representative, or another ϕ-defined variable in the same block, and their respective ϕ-arguments have the same representative. Finally, the checker ensures that representatives are canonical for all classes.

The optimization itself consists in replacing all instructions of the form (Iop op args r pc') at a node pc, where the operator op does not depend on memory, by a simple register move (Iop OMove ((A_r f r)::nil) r pc'), under the assumption that r and (A_r f r) are distinct.

5.2   Proof of Correctness

Analysis. The case of GVN is a bit more intricate than SCCP. The first difficulty we must overcome is to deal with the intrinsic relational nature of GVN. Indeed, in essence, the GVN external tool computes equivalence classes among variables of a SSA function. Our framework as presented earlier strives for simplicity (so that we can factor out proofs as much as possible), and has a more non-relational flavor, as the analysis is supposed to associate an approximation to each variable.

By looking closer at how the optimization utilizes the result of the analysis, we observe that each time an instruction is optimized, an arithmetic operation is replaced by a variable which represents, symbolically, that arithmetic expression. This naturally leads us to formalizing the analysis as associating, to each variable, another variable (its representative), which concretizes to a single value, its value in the current context:

```
Definition approx : Type := reg.
Definition G rs a v : Prop := (rs# a = v).
```

Now, we must characterize the set of variables for which the analysis does not manage to infer any useful information (or "I don't know"). Following the same approach, the $\top$ information is associated to a variable if that variable is alone in its equivalence class. Therefore, we define predicate is_at_Top as follows:

```
Definition is_at_Top (R: result) (a: approx) : Prop :=
  (R a = a) /\ (forall a', R a' = a -> a' = a).
```

In this setup, we can prove that the analysis satisfies the first two conditions of AnalysisProp. For proving the last obligation, we resort on the specification provably established by our checker. The proof of iop_correct relies on the equation lemma of SSA: we need to prove that the value v of variable x assigned by an Iop instruction is correctly abstracted by (A_r f x). In the interesting case, x $\neq$ (A_r f x), and the equation lemma applies, since (A_r f x) strictly dominates x. Hence, we get that (A_r f x) equals the evaluation of its defining

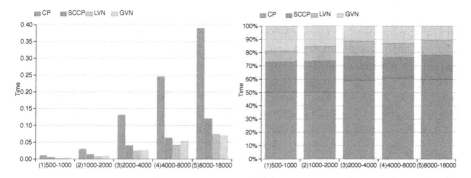

Fig. 5. Transformation times. Left: absolute time in seconds. Right: percentage.

right-hand side. By the correctness of the checker, (A_r f x) is congruent to x, and their respective Iop arguments have equal representatives. We conclude by using the **gamma** hypothesis and strictness of SSA. Here again, other cases are tackled using **dsd_not_joinpoint** (which applies by the normalization of SSA code). The preservation proof of **gamma** by the execution of ϕ-blocks follows the same idea, using the representatives specification of ϕ-defined variables, and the case-analysis scheme provided by **dsd_joinpoint**.

Correctness of the Optimization. Here again, the specification enforced by the checker helps us discharge the obligation **transf_instr_preserves_strict**. The proof of semantic preservation of the optimization goes smoothly with the choice of definition for predicate G. Indeed, when an Iop instruction is optimized, then the variable x that it defines will be, after the optimization, defined by variable move from (A_r f x) to x. By correctness of the analysis, and the definition of G, the arguments of the Iop defining (A_r f x) evaluate to the same values as their representatives. But, by the congruence specification, they also evaluate to the same values as the arguments of the Iop defining x.

6   Experiments

We evaluate the performances of the verified SSA middle-end by extracting its Coq implementation into OCaml code, and running it on some realistic C program benchmarks. These include around 130.000 lines of C code, and fall into the following categories of programs: compression algorithms, a raytracer, the Spass theorem prover, the **hmmer** and **mcf** from the SPEC2006 benchmarks and **nsichneu** and **papabench** coming from WCET-related reference benchmarks. These programs range from hundreds of lines of C code, to several thousands.

Below, we evaluate the middle-end according to the following criteria: (i) compilation time of SCCP and GVN, compared to the CompCert's corresponding optimizations on the RTL non-SSA form (Constant Propagation and a Common Subexpression Elimination based on a Local Value Numbering), (ii) the efficiency of the SCCP and GVN checkers, relatively to the time required for analysing the code, and optimizing it and (iii) the gain in precision for SCCP and GVN, compared to CompCert's corresponding optimizations.

To evaluate the middle-end scalability in extreme conditions, we force the compiler to always inline functions below 1000 nodes. We classify our results by categories of function size (number of CFG nodes): $[500; 1000[$ (196 functions), $[1000; 2000[$ (98 functions), $[2000; 4000[$ (89 functions), $[4000; 8000[$ (38 functions), $[8000; 18000]$ (23 functions). Experiments are run on a MacBook OSX 10.8.5, 2.9GHz Intel Core i7, 8GB 1600MHz DDR3.

Optimization times. Figure 5 shows the average time, in seconds and by category, required to compile the functions in this category. The left graph measures the absolute time, while the right graph shows the timing distribution among the various optimizations. As expected, the results show that SCCP, compared to a flow-sensitive analysis like Constant Propagation (CP), scales very well on huge CFG graphs. As for GVN, its computation time is of course higher than the Local Value Numbering of CompCert, but the latter is only block-local, and GVN's computation time keeps reasonable.

Checkers efficiency. On our benchmarks, the SCCP checker represents between 17% and 23% of the whole SCCP optimization, and is amortized as the function CFG grows. The GVN checker represents between 8% and 12% of the whole GVN-based CSE optimization, uniformly on all five categories of function sizes.

Precision. For measuring the precision gain brought by SCCP compared to Constant Propagation, we measure, for both optimizations, the number of non-constant Iop instructions that are optimized to a numeric, constant Iop instruction in the optimized program (and this only for feasible paths, as detected by SCCP, which, on average, detects around 14% of dead-branches). For measuring the precision of GVN compared to LVN, we count how many arithmetic Iop instructions were optimized into register moves. The numbers are given below.

	arcode	hmmer	lzss	lzw	mcf	nsichneu	papabench	raytracer	spass
SCCP	90	587	80	51	9	0	40	0	472
GVN	66	235	102	152	40	0	700	0	5900

7 Related Work

Most well known achievements in the area of mechanized proof of compilers are the CompCert C compiler [10], Chlipalas's compiler for an impure functional langage [6] and the CakeML compiler [8] that is able to bootstrap itself. All these works are major achievements in verification of semantics preserving transformations but few of them provides advanced program optimizations.

Tristan and Leroy [18, 17] have applied the verified validation approach to instruction scheduling and lazy code motion but their optimizations are more local than GVN, able to infer global loop invariant to perform common subexpression elimination. Leroy has also performed a direct verification of a Local

Value Numbering (LVN) optimization [10] without requiring an SSA form but it is limited to extended basic blocks.

The first attempt to formalize SSA semantics was done by Blech et al.[3], using the Isabelle/HOL proof assistant. They verified the generation of machine code from a representation of SSA programs that relies on term graphs. Mansky and Gunter [11] uses Isabelle/HOL to formalize and verify the conversion of CFG programs into SSA. None of these works consider program optimizations.

Zhao et al. [22, 21] formalize the LLVM SSA intermediate form and its generation algorithm in Coq. Their work follow closely the LLVM design and their verified transformation can be run inside the LLVM platform itself. However, their work doesn't provide leading optimizations such as SCCP or GVN, and doesn't consider compilation time.

Unverified translation validators have been designed to validate some LLVM optimizations. Stepp et al. [15] uses a technique named Equality Saturation to infer symbolic equalities between source and target. Tristan et al. [16] independently report on a translation validator for LLVM's inter-procedural optimizations, based on Gated-SSA.

8   Conclusion and Perspectives

Our work provides two major verified SSA optimizations. Their implementation closely follows the design choices of realistic compilers (LLVM). We extend the CompCertSSA verified compiler with a new proof framework able to capture the soundness proof of these two optimizations. We also demonstrate the scalability of our optimizations in terms of compiler efficiency and precision.

We foresee two ambitious extensions to this work. First, we would like to extend our optimizations to memory accesses. Modern compilers perform these kinds of memory optimizations but they differ in the way they incorporate alias analysis inside their SSA form. GCC provides a specific program representation with explicit definitions and uses of memory locations. Such a design suffers from compiler memory consumption issues. LLVM proposes a more lightweigth approach with well-chosen queries to alias information. Understanding which approach fits best a verified compiler requires a specific study, taking into account proof engineering and efficiency concerns. A second extension should consider code motion and partial redundancy elimination [7]. GVN provides an important pre-processing for these optimizations.

References

[1] Alpern, B., Wegman, M.N., Zadeck, F.K.: Detecting Equality of Variables in Programs. In: Proc. of POPL 1988, pp. 1–11. ACM, San Diego (1988) ISBN: 0-89791-252-7

[2] Barthe, G., Demange, D., Pichardie, D.: Formal Verification of an SSA- Based Middle-End for CompCert. ACM TOPLAS 36(1), 4:1–4:35 (2014) ISSN: 0164-0925

[3] Blech, J., et al.: Optimizing Code Generation from SSA Form: A Comparison Between Two Formal Correctness Proofs in Isabelle/HOL. In: COCV 2005. ENTCS, pp. 33–51. Elsevier, Amsterdam (2005)

[4] Boissinot, B., et al.: Revisiting Out-of-SSA Translation for Correctness, Code Quality and Efficiency. In: Proc. of the 7th annual IEEE/ACM International Symposium on Code Generation and Optimization, CGO 2009, pp. 114–125. IEEE Computer Society, Washington, DC (2009) ISBN : 978-0-7695-3576-0

[5] Briggs, P., Cooper, K.D., Simpson, L.T.: Value Numbering. Software, Practice and Experience 27(6), 701–724 (1997)

[6] Chlipala, A.: A verified compiler for an impure functional language. In: POPL 2010, pp. 93–106. ACM, New York (2010)

[7] Chow, F., et al.: A New Algorithm for Partial Redundancy Elimination Based on SSA Form. In: Proc. of PLDI 1997, pp. 273–286. ACM, New York (1997)

[8] Kumar, R., et al.: CakeML: A verified implementation of ML. In: Proc. of POPL 2014, pp. 179–192 (2014)

[9] Lengauer, T., Tarjan, R.: A fast algorithm for finding dominators in a flowgraph. ACM TOPLAS 1(1), 121–141 (1979)

[10] Leroy, X.: A Formally Verified Compiler Back-end. JAR 43(4), 363–446 (2009)

[11] Mansky, W., Gunter, E.: A Framework for Formal Verification of Compiler Optimizations. In: Kaufmann, M., Paulson, L.C. (eds.) ITP 2010. LNCS, vol. 6172, pp. 371–386. Springer, Heidelberg (2010)

[12] Pnueli, A., Siegel, M.D., Singerman, E.: Translation validation. In: Steffen, B. (ed.) TACAS 1998. LNCS, vol. 1384, pp. 151–166. Springer, Heidelberg (1998)

[13] Rideau, S., Leroy, X.: Validating Register Allocation and Spilling. In: Gupta, R. (ed.) CC 2010. LNCS, vol. 6011, pp. 224–243. Springer, Heidelberg (2010)

[14] Rosen, B.K., Wegman, M.N., Zadeck, F.K.: Global Value Numbers and Redundant Computations. In: Proceedings of the 15th ACM SIGPLAN-SIGACT Symposium on Principles of Programming Languages. POPL 1988, pp. 12–27. ACM, San Diego (1988) ISBN:0- 89791-252-7

[15] Stepp, M., Tate, R., Lerner, S.: Equality-Based Translation Validator for LLVM. In: Gopalakrishnan, G., Qadeer, S. (eds.) CAV 2011. LNCS, vol. 6806, pp. 737–742. Springer, Heidelberg (2011)

[16] Tristan, J., Govereau, P., Morrisett, G.: Evaluating value-graph translation validation for LLVM. In: PLDI 2011, pp. 295–305. ACM, New York (2011)

[17] Tristan, J., Leroy, X.: A simple, verified validator for software pipelining. In: POPL 2010, pp. 83–92. ACM, New York (2010)

[18] Tristan, J., Leroy, X.: Verified validation of lazy code motion. In: PLDI 2009, pp. 316–326. ACM, New York (2009)

[19] Wegman, M.N., Zadeck, F.K.: Constant Propagation with Conditional Branches. ACM Trans. Program. Lang. Syst. 13(2), 181–210 (1991)

[20] Yang, X., et al.: Finding and Understanding Bugs in C Compilers. In: Proc. of PLDI 2011, pp. 978–971. ACM, New York (2011) ISBN:978-1-4503-0663-8

[21] Zhao, J., et al.: Formal verification of SSA-based optimizations for LLVM. In: PLDI 2013, pp. 175–186. ACM, New York (2013)

[22] Zhao, J., et al.: Formalizing the LLVM Intermediate Representation for Verified Program Transformation. In: POPL 2012, pp. 427–440. ACM, New York (2012)

Author Index

Printed in the United States
By Bookmasters